The Struggle for Justice, Equity, and Peace in the Global Classroom

Marva McClean
Editor, USA

A volume in the Advances
in Educational Marketing,
Administration, and Leadership
(AEMAL) Book Series

Published in the United States of America by
    IGI Global
    Information Science Reference (an imprint of IGI Global)
    701 E. Chocolate Avenue
    Hershey PA, USA 17033
    Tel: 717-533-8845
    Fax: 717-533-8661
    E-mail: cust@igi-global.com
    Web site: http://www.igi-global.com

Library of Congress Cataloging-in-Publication Data

Names: McClean, Marva, DATE- editor.
Title: The struggle for justice, equity, and peace in the global classroom
  / edited by: Marva McClean.
Description: Hershey, PA : Information Science Reference, [2023] | Includes
  bibliographical references and index.
Identifiers: LCCN 2023010044 (print) | LCCN 2023010045 (ebook) | ISBN
  9781668473795 (hardcover) | ISBN 9781668473832 (paperback) | ISBN
  9781668473801 (ebook)
Subjects: LCSH: Multicultural education--Case studies. | Culturally
  relevant pedagogy--Case studies. | Education--Aims and objectives--Case
  studies.
Classification: LCC LC1099 .S84 2023 (print) | LCC LC1099 (ebook) | DDC
  370.117--dc23/eng/20230322
LC record available at https://lccn.loc.gov/2023010044
LC ebook record available at https://lccn.loc.gov/2023010045

This book is published in the IGI Global book series Advances in Educational Marketing, Administration, and Leadership (AEMAL) (ISSN: 2326-9022; eISSN: 2326-9030)

British Cataloguing in Publication Data
A Cataloguing in Publication record for this book is available from the British Library.

All work contributed to this book is new, previously-unpublished material.
The views expressed in this book are those of the authors, but not necessarily of the publisher.

For electronic access to this publication, please contact: eresources@igi-global.com.

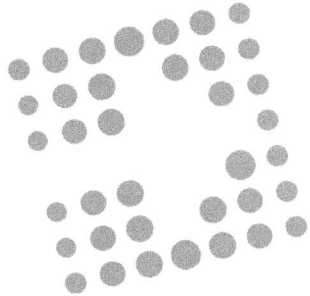

Advances in Educational Marketing, Administration, and Leadership (AEMAL) Book Series

ISSN:2326-9022
EISSN:2326-9030

Editor-in-Chief: Siran Mukerji, IGNOU, India, Purnendu Tripathi, IGNOU, India

MISSION

With more educational institutions entering into public, higher, and professional education, the educational environment has grown increasingly competitive. With this increase in competitiveness has come the need for a greater focus on leadership within the institutions, on administrative handling of educational matters, and on the marketing of the services offered.

The **Advances in Educational Marketing, Administration, & Leadership (AEMAL) Book Series** strives to provide publications that address all these areas and present trending, current research to assist professionals, administrators, and others involved in the education sector in making their decisions.

COVERAGE

- Faculty Administration and Management
- Educational Management
- Educational Leadership
- Academic Administration
- Technologies and Educational Marketing
- Academic Pricing
- Students as Consumers
- Enrollment Management
- Direct marketing of educational programs
- Educational Finance

IGI Global is currently accepting manuscripts for publication within this series. To submit a proposal for a volume in this series, please contact our Acquisition Editors at Acquisitions@igi-global.com or visit: http://www.igi-global.com/publish/.

Titles in this Series

For a list of additional titles in this series, please visit:
http://www.igi-global.com/book-series/advances-educational-marketing-administration-leadership/73677

For an entire list of titles in this series, please visit:
http://www.igi-global.com/book-series/advances-educational-marketing-administration-leadership/73677

701 East Chocolate Avenue, Hershey, PA 17033, USA
Tel: 717-533-8845 x100 • Fax: 717-533-8661
E-Mail: cust@igi-global.com • www.igi-global.com

Table of Contents

Detailed Table of Contents

Chapter 1
Who Shall Teach Our Children? 1
  Marva Sylvana McClean, Independent Researcher, USA

This chapter presents decolonized research methodologies that interrogate the profile of a conscientized teacher, qualified and prepared to teach Black and Brown children within the African Diaspora. Based on research spanning more than twenty years at three school sites, this chapter identifies five specific qualities that characterize a teacher who is conscientized into a historical consciousness that goes beyond narrow margins of the socially constructed race and geographic borders to embrace the humanity of the children within classrooms across the globe. Methodologies and theories including reflexivity, auto-ethnography, life stories, student narratives and social media inquiries are central to the research design that enabled this interrogation of education beyond borders. This international inquiry led to the uncovering of a worldview of what constitutes effective education and who qualifies as an effective teacher. Social media facilitated the crossing of borders and allowed space for collaborative inquiry that touched upon the anxiety and tensions educators face in their practice. It also highlighted the potential international collaborative inquiry holds as a site for creativity which speaks to what is possible in global education that promotes conscientization of the curriculum. In this examination of transnational approaches to educational equity this research has revealed the significance of knowledges beyond the textbook, including stories, spiritual knowledge, and ceremonial practices. Of special importance are transgenerational stories of strength, endurance, and survival transmitted by the students in global classrooms. This research has demonstrated It is impossible to create a model of the good teacher without taking issues of culture and community context into account. The result is a set of strategies that provides insights into how educators may re-conceptualize and reconstruct the classroom as a borderland, a site for both critical analysis and as a potential source of experimentalism that engages the student as central to classroom pedagogy.

Anne Bouie, Independent Researcher, USA

Enslavement is indelibly etched in the historiography of the United States of America. In fact, it extends across the entire globe. This chapter asserts that it is the original content and continued context of the Black experience in America. In interrogating the dogma of racism and the extent to which it defined and has continued to define the characteristics distinguishing the free and the oppressed, this researcher acknowledges that race is not merely a social construct, it is the foundation for all of the political and economic systems on which this country is constructed. As the USA continues with the struggle to attain educational reform with the emphasis on the achievement gap that exists between white and Black students, this researcher interrogates the educational development and attainment of the enslaved Black population who were the ancestors of the Black and Brown children that the USA identifies as lagging behind the performance of white students. What are the historical factors that have led to this? Did the ancestors have access to education? What were the enslavers' response to the education of the enslaved? If education was denied all Black people, how did they navigate this particular form of oppression? What are the outcomes of this resistance against the denial of literacy? Did the ancestors create an alternative system of literacy? What were/are the outcomes of this alternative system and to what extent has this shaped and continues to shape the lives of Black/Brown school children today? Is there education beyond/outside of literacy? This chapter interrogates the journey of Africans and their descendants in their bid to attain literacy in a state antagonistic to this purpose.

Zuleka R. Woods, Virginia Tech, USA
Isil Anakok, Virginia Tech, USA
Shania Clinedinst, Virginia Tech, USA
Shernita Lee, Virginia Tech, USA

In order for educational institutions to attain social justice and equity, we must challenge persistent and normative whiteness in higher education curriculum to include the voice of students of color. The dominant Eurocentric narrative present in higher education curriculum demands inclusive pedagogy in classrooms that create space for students to share their funds of knowledge and experience inclusion within an atmosphere of belonging. This chapter utilizes qualitative methodologies to decolonize the curriculum and craft such an inclusive space. It argues for ways to reshape knowledge production by encouraging diverse forms of learning and critical pedagogy that rest on a foundation of a multicultural curriculum. This decolonizing process must become an essential part of critical pedagogies within higher education curriculum that includes all cultures and knowledge systems in ways that recognize and frame students' funds of knowledge within the inclusive space of the classroom.

Chapter 4

Higher education presents students with many opportunities for educational advancement, but not all encounter these opportunities equally. Academic organizations, rooted in structural racism, perpetuate cycles of perceived failure that can prevent students from receiving the encouragement they need, which can result in inadequate career and societal preparation. Not all students benefit from traditional education in the same ways, and when they must all meet the same criteria, then, it is difficult for some to meet their own learning needs and goals based on their own definitions of success. Innovation spaces, such as makerspaces, within academic libraries, have a particular ability to help level the playing field and add equity value to both the classroom and lifelong learning. This chapter delineates current equity issues and provides managers of innovation spaces, especially those in academic libraries, with methods for recognizing opportunities for developing and marketing spaces and services to promote success for every student, both within the classroom and outside of it.

Chapter 5

The civil unrest following the murder of George Floyd exerted a tremendous burden on educational institutions across the USA during the critical era of the global pandemic. Educational leaders including district leaders and principals were taxed with the responsibility of effectively communicating with their stakeholders and bringing a sense of peace and calm to the school environment. This study engaged in a critical discourse analysis of the methods these leaders used to communicate with their constituents in order to determine the extent to which they effectively utilized antiracist strategies to lead, support and build bridges during this turbulent time. Primary source documents created by these leaders were scrutinized in order to determine how they used language to challenge policies and practices within a school district to ensure a safe and supportive environment for all members of the school community. The authors suggest that additional training and resources are necessary for educational leaders to enhance effective crisis response from an anti-racist stance especially in response to issues of social justice. This chapter highlights the challenges for educational leaders in creating culturally responsive, appropriate, and timely communication with recommendations on how to connect across borders.

Chapter 6

This chapter utilises an autobiographical and creative approach that links cultural history to the education children receive in the classroom. I present a narrative account of my personal story as a child of mixed racial identity as well as mixed cultural identity to explicate the range of emotions, the expanse of experiences evoked by racial hostility and the child's response as he navigates this landscape and journey towards making sense of these experiences in the shaping of his identity. This chapter is grounded in funds of knowledge theory, identity theory and culturally relevant theory. The process of the building and resulting production of my own funds of knowledge challenge the validity of the traditional Eurocentric Western epistemologies that shaped the education I received in the British classrooms of my youth. From this investigation, I have come to the conclusion that bi-racial children have the benefit of a rich, three-dimensional, dual heritage which provides a much-needed emotional foundation that allows them to thrive even within hostile settings. Teachers face the challenge of recognising, acknowledging and tapping into this gourd of cultural capital and effectively using it to heighten students' performance and guide them on the path to academic achievement.

Chapter 7

Countries, including the USA, are examining ways in which they can bring a high-quality program of Science, Technology, Engineering, and Math (STEM)to their youth in preparation for the role they must play in economic development.

Black and Brown students are traditionally reported as lagging behind in academic performance, and there is concern that this status may lead to their exclusion from STEM programs and thus limit their ability to participate in a program that leads them to higher academic achievement with an inroad to higher education and higher financial rewards in a profession that is high yielding, not only in the USA, but the across the globe. The chapter highlights how three mentoring programs support Black high school students to do STEM, including collaborations between STEM professionals and students, a summer camp, and an after-school program. It includes curricula to influence students' interest in STEM. Recommendations for program revisions include e-mentoring, hosting workshops in central locations, and incorporating reflections after workshops to improve session quality.

Foreword

The internecine cultural warfare in the United States of America has played a paramount role in these authors' heightened interest in how the children of African descendants are educated within the interdependent global polity. They write with a clear focus on the importance of understanding how life in school is shaped by the forces of history rooted in colonization, imperialism and globalism. They seek to find ways in which these children may gain a sense of worth and equality with their peers elsewhere. These scholars have been deeply influenced by Pablo Freire's Pedagogy of the Oppressed. They are concerned about how these children break the shackles of Eurocentric education which since the earlier days of Trans- Atlantic chattel slavery, and concomitantly, its off-springs, imperialism, colonialism and neocolonialism within their borders have imposed on them an external doctrine of education that is deleterious to their cultural heritage and identity.

These scholars are shaped not only by the theory of conscientization of Paulo Freire, the globally recognized Brazilian educational theorist, but also by the revolutionary ideology of Marcus Garvey, Franz Fanon and the Reggae Super Star Bob Marley, who pointed out the negative impact of European education and cultures on the performance of students of colour within the classroom.

These scholars are united in their belief that there has to be a decolonization of the curriculum on the African continent and throughout her Diasporas. There is an urgency or persistency by these scholars in this volume to provide the information and the strategies to break the hegemonic, Eurocentric domination within the classroom. It is critical that a similar paradigm shift as Pablo Freire advocated in his 1968 magisterial work takes place throughout this race, class, gender and religious globally stratified polity. While these authors focus on dismantling the Eurocentric paradigm, there does not appear to be an adequate balance in the interrogation of the students' responsibility and accountability in shaping their education journey. How are educators working to guide students into becoming change agents and how are these students taking on the responsibility of shaping the future of the countries in which they attend school? Are they armed with enough knowledge and agency to dismantle the old guard and establish new paradigms which reflect the independence and sovereignty of their countries, pushing for an educational system that befits the culture of the people and the specific needs of the population beyond external influences of the superpowers that once colonized them or the newly emerged leaders who may be focused on their own aggrandizement and upward mobility? These are urgent questions to be examined.

The brutal death of George Floyd and the pivotal role that the global Information Superhighway played in bringing this tragedy to millions of people has provided these dedicated de-colonialists with the platform to gain supporters throughout the corridors of power. These advocates of the Decolonization of the Curriculum are fully aware that it is not an easy fight to achieve their goal.

Through this volume, they are involved in organizing supporters into a collaborative of community politics and parent - teacher meeting. This asserts their beliefs that they have a primary responsibility to link theory with practice. It is not only through their writings that they see they can contribute to fundamental change, but also in their collaboration to strengthen and support each other; a necessary strategy in building the bridge for change across the globe. To succeed in the struggle for justice, peace and equity in the global classroom, there must be unity amongst the warriors for change.

Rovan Locke
Independent Researcher, Jamaica

Preface

PROBLEMATIZING EDUCATION INJUSTICE

In the current state of global upheaval with the rallying call for human rights and justice for people who have been historically marginalized, the curriculum must be decolonized to ensure that children identified as marginalized and at risk are receiving an equitable education that is based on respect and acceptance of their cultural heritage as well as their human rights. This collection of chapters asserts this perspective in the interrogation of the historical continuities of educational injustices across the USA and the world and offers methods of disrupting and dismantling barriers that alienate Black and Brown school children and position them as at risk for failure. The authors' research findings and recommendations converge in the assertion that educators, regardless of their geographic location, must look to peripheral sites that are other locations for learning which may serve to engage students in co-constructing a curriculum of empowerment. This is an alternative approach to the current system and one that focuses on developing a critical consciousness of the curriculum as a living cultural, political and historical document which corrects the marginalization of the history of Black, Brown and Indigenous people in the literature and school texts.

This book asks the essential question, *What are the characteristics, educational credentials, and worldview of the educator leading for transformation?* The scholars present a combination of chapters that addresses this pressing question with an offering of strategies to ensure the acknowledgement of student voices within the curriculum and an assertion of respect for their cultural heritage and the funds of knowledge that they bring with them into the teaching and learning space.

As people across the globe seek to rise from the quagmire of the pandemic and the USA faces the continuing trauma of gun violence in schools, educators are pressed to find strategies to educate all of the world's children, bearing in mind that 787m are not provided access into these rooms. How then can we effectively educate those within our rooms? These chapters investigate this challenge and invite an examination of racial discord, poverty, and disenfranchisement as central to this process. At the same time, the researchers share findings and recommendations which offer strategies for creating global classrooms grounded in justice, peace and equity.

RESPONDING TO THE CALL FOR JUSTICE, PEACE, AND EQUITY

Despite its organizational management and transactional governance, the school site is a place that is rooted in emotionalism and the subjectivities of all participants. The authors of these chapters assert that this cannot be ignored. They call on district leaders, state departments of education and school site administrators and teachers to recognize and acknowledge the way history has shaped educational systems across the globe and to respond to the specifics of each context. In that response, they must seek innovative ways to creatively handle this without losing sight of teaching and learning goals. A shared perspective of the scholars is that educators must be schooled in the knowledge of the global history of slavery, colonization, and imperialism. This must then be extended to the investigation of the central role heritage plays in the life of school children, ensuring the inclusion of this consideration within classroom pedagogy.

COLLABORATING FOR SOLUTIONS

This book engages in a rigorous interrogation of the global classroom as a site of transformation for educators who dare to take action to replace oppressive and repressive practices with emancipatory strategies grounded in critical consciousness. This gathering of researchers presents the pluralism that defines the field of education across the globe, noting that the pedagogy used at school sites must be grounded in context as there is no generic student or generic classroom. To arrive at solutions for the troubling crisis of education injustice, the researchers all affirm that educators must re-envision the future through an engagement with the past and an understanding of how the historical continuities of racial intolerance and social injustice continue to impact classroom teaching and the outcome of children whose lives are shaped by the afterlife of slavery and oppression. Through a combination of research strategies rooted in decolonized research methodology, these investigators problematize the existing inequities of the K-university classroom and juxtapose them with slavery, colonization, imperialism, and the contemporary era of Black Lives Matter in conceptualization of education as a constant and fluid construction rather than a fixed tool of pedagogical administration that centers on current developments.

There is a persistent call to extend the discourse of educational transformation across the globe to examine transnational approaches to educational equity including spiritual knowledge and ceremonial practices. Collectively, the chapters enquire into the global classroom as a borderland, a site for both critical analysis and as a potential source of experimentalism, creativity, and transformation with educators, parents and the community engaged as social justice agents and advocates. In other words, all participants must be engaged as change agents within the village that is education.

ORGANIZATION OF THE BOOK

The book is organized into seven chapters, each examining a particular aspect of education which demands our attention and bears heavily on the researchers' praxis and advocacy for change.

Chapter 1: Who Shall Teach Our Children?

The researcher examines the state of education across the globe and calls into question the pervasive failure of Black and Brown children, noting that the residual effects of slavery and colonization continue to shape the way children are taught, the physical space in which they are taught, which often, is quite deficit. The chapter strongly asserts that for education justice to be achieved, all children must be embraced into a cultural space that honors their funds of knowledge and acknowledges their capacity to be collaborators in the construction of classroom pedagogy. The chapter offers specific strategies to prepare teachers to effectively teach the world's children.

Chapter 2: The Politics of Literacy and Spirituality: Crafting a Culture of Resistance to Enslavement

The writer explores the ideological premises that inspired enslaved Black people to attain literacy and the oppositional culture that nurtured this. Black institution and community building, autonomy, leadership development, creating an economic base, and control over the kind and quality of education were undergirding principles that countered assertions of racial and cultural inferiority. According to the researcher, a knowledgeable, unbiased analysis of the purposes, goals, beliefs, expectations, pedagogy, curriculum, leadership building, and outcomes that emerged from enslavement and repression may conclude that there is much to be mined from this legacy. The chapter places the historic Brown vs Board of Education within the mix of this process and vigorously asserts that the landmark case only served to infringe upon the centuries of community building and the identity of the Black student that had been crafted during and after enslavement. According to the researcher, to educate for justice and equity, schools must follow the guidelines established by Black educators during and after enslavement.

Chapter 3: Decolonizing the Curriculum in Higher Education: Reconceptualizing Multicultural Pedagogy at Predominantly White Institutions

This chapter reflects on the alienation that many students of color experience at white institutions where they are often made to feel as outsiders. In an examination of what constitutes multicultural education, the researchers call for these institutions to examine specific strategies to become more inclusive including pedagogy that incorporates the history and legacy of Black and Brown people with a focus on their historical empowerment.

Chapter 4: Empowering Underrepresented Students: Designing Innovator Spaces as Sites of Justice, Peace, and Equity Within University Library Ecosystems

In this chapter which asserts the university library as a space for engendering community and creating spaces of innovation and sanctuaries for reflexivity, the researcher notes that utilizing maker spaces is an apt strategic move towards creating a site of diversity and inclusion. This chapter focuses especially on innovation spaces within the academic library, highlighting makerspaces most prominently, as well as spaces for digital creation and spaces for gaming, showing how these spaces can be transformed to promote practices surrounding Diversity, Equity, Inclusion, and Accessibility. The chapter asserts that this is necessary in order to dismantle structural racism in the institution by both supporting students outside of the classroom and partnering with instructors to begin that same process within the classroom.

Chapter 5: Language and Leadership in the Midst of Social Unrest: A Critical Analysis of Educational Leaders' Responses to Racial Violence in the Era of the Pandemic

These researchers cite the language of communication as an essential strategy in attaining education justice. In an examination of the strategies district and school site leaders utilized in the aftermath of the murder of George Floyd within one school district, the researchers note that language must be at the heart of the mission to create a community of practice that is inclusive of all its constituents. They present case studies that reveal the deficiencies and lack of preparation to handle the social crisis that evolved during the pandemic with an emphasis of the necessity to use language that is inclusive and inspirational, especially in times of crisis.

Chapter 6: The Triumph of Bi-Racial Identity: Funds of Knowledge as Student Agency

In this chapter grounded in a mix of qualitative methodologies, the researcher engages in an autobiographical investigation of how the foundation of his bi-racial and bi-cultural identity served as a buffer against the racism he experienced in the classroom and wider society in 1980's Britain. Based on this experience, he offers strategies educators may use to incorporate students' funds of knowledge, the history of slavery and colonization and the historical empowerment of Black people into classroom pedagogy in creative ways that subvert the traditional Eurocentric perspective and raise the historical consciousness of all participants.

Chapter 7: Everyone Wins: Mentoring BIPOC Students Into STEM Programs

This chapter states that after centuries of educational reform, the education of Black and Brown children remains marginalized. The researcher comments on the USA's bid to remain at the center of global economic development and growth by tapping into the rewards of STEM education. To achieve this, all of America's children must be effectively prepared. The review of literature reveals that children of color are not adequately prepared for participation in the field. To counteract this malady, the researcher suggests that educators investigate unusual sites, spaces and opportunities to create programs that meet the students where they are, including the location of their communities. Data derived from an after-school program, summer camp and e-mentoring crafted by the researcher present creative strategies for educators to use as a blue-print to effectively incorporate Black children in STEM and STEAM programs. The researcher asserts that when parents, educators and the community invest in the crafting of programs that encourage and support secondary students' participation in these programs, everyone wins.

Marva McClean
Independent Researcher, USA

Acknowledgment

To acknowledge is to express gratitude for the goodness others have bestowed on you. Indeed, I am deeply grateful for the words of wisdom, the guidance and the support that others have extended in the journey towards the completion of this volume. Special thanks to the contributing writers for sharing the conceptualization of their chapters and working with me through the process of crafting drafts, enduring reviews and responding to recommendations for revisions. Your commitment to social justice and equity propelled your participation right through to the final submission of the manuscript. Thank you. I am especially grateful to my colleague, Dr. Rovan Locke whose sharp mind and critical eye helped to keep me on course and keep my mind alert to the poetics of education. My children Ronald and Nicole, offered me wise counsel during times of stress and helped to sustain me especially during the loss of my mother and their grandmother. As I grieved the loss of my mother, Desrene Elizabeth Wade during the near final stages of the organization and publication of the book, it is my remembrance of the purpose driven life that she led, her commitment in guiding me to hold fast to my dreams that provided the energy that anchored me in completing the work that I had set out to do. To IGI Senior Development Editor, Jocelyn Hessler, I extend a special thank you for your positive spirit and support during this challenging period.

To all of you, your grace is much appreciated.

With respect and gratitude, I say thank you.

Introduction

For decades, social justice activists in the USA and the world have been calling for an equitable system of education, where all children across the globe have access to this right. At the heart of this discourse, an essential question must be asked: How are the children doing? This ancient African proverb begs yet another question: Who shall teach our children? The focus of this volume is the presentation of content that interrogates possible answers to these urgent questions. In responding to the first question, the scholars reveal in their chapters, the complex interaction between history, schooling and culture. In responding to the second question, what surfaces is the intersection of culture, community and accountability. Both questions lead to the search for education justice and strategies to disrupt and dismantle racism in global education.

The call for chapter submissions to this book rested on the knowledge of the disruption slavery and colonization wreaked on the lives of Black, Indigenous and people of color across the globe. In response, the contributors write to disrupt age old educational patterns and offer strategies to teach for social justice and equity within the specific context of the classroom. As they do so, there is a strong assertion of the right to conduct research in a manner that acknowledges the efficacy of cultural mores and the truth of the history and the creativity of Black people.

This book comes at an exciting time in our history, where worldwide people are united in the call for human rights and justice. The recording and global exposure of George Floyd's death became a visual metaphor for the brutality that engulfs the life of people who have been disenfranchised by the oppression that emanates from marginalization and the residual effects of slavery and colonization. It also points to the complexity and interconnection of the citizens of this globe. All across the continents, children have become producers of knowledge which they share through technology. They hold control over the telling and sharing of data, using apps to be producers of knowledge and establish relations with new allies. They are no longer mere consumers of knowledge. This untapped civic global movement taking place via the internet demands the attention of the educator who shall teach our children.

The call for education justice recognizes the central role school plays in the child's socio-economic future. In tandem with this call is the assertion that in order to right the status quo and treatment of people who have been historically marginalized, the curriculum must be decolonized to ensure that children identified as marginalized and at risk are receiving an equitable education that is foregrounded on context and based on respect and acceptance of their cultural heritage as well as their human rights. The scholars of this text seek to mobilize this vision by moving beyond conversation into a discourse based on research that points the way forward into specific pathways to decolonize education. They directly confront the vexing issue of reported school failure of Black and Brown children and highlight the influence of history, geography, race and ethnicity on their academic identities.

This volume is intended to deepen educators' understanding of what it means to be students of color within the Americas. Across the Americas, descendants of the legacy of colonization continue to face monumental problems including the lack of education. UNESCO (2022) reports that 285 million children, adolescent and youth across the globe do not have access to an education. How are formerly colonized countries dealing with the challenges of educating their children? Do they have the resources to educate all eligible youth? Can struggling countries provide adequate education for Science, Engineering, Technology and Mathematics (STEM) programs? This field is regarded as the most rapidly developing one with the potential to yield the highest incomes for graduates.

There are no set answers to these questions. However, these scholars' shared philosophy and themes reveal a common concern regarding the need to right the wrongs of an educational system based on the scrouges of racism and poverty. Despite Brown vs Board of Education; despite the election of the first Black US president and the first Black-Asian female vice president, stark racial divides remain in the USA. Scholars examine education within their own context, only to reveal that globally, they are all confronted with the same issue of creating a cultural space in schools where students are embraced as active participants poised to collaborate with teachers in the construction of the pedagogy which shapes their education. These scholars highlight the fact that history is central to any consideration of educational reform. All chapters explore qualitative research methodologies that embody and reflect the cultures of children whose ancestors were victims of colonization.

The utilization of decolonized research methodologies to question and challenge the accuracy and validity of traditional Eurocentric research, signals the paradigm shift that is being demanded. Findings from the research presented assert that money, as we tend to focus on in the USA, is not the primary factor for school failure or the achievement gap. It is that sense of belonging that schools create for students that has the most significant impact on teaching and learning. Decolonized research methodology unearths alternative data that tells a fuller more expansive story about who our children are and how they are doing.

This then, is the message of this volume: We must embrace our children in from the cold of alienation and marginalization. For as the ancient proverb states, We must embrace the children from the cold so they don't burn the village to feel the heat. The curriculum must fill cultural gaps within the classroom. Classroom pedagogy must allow for students to be innovative and creative so they can demonstrate their ability to engage in knowledge production.

These chapters acknowledge how a market driven school system has damaged all students. The research offers the possibility of the restructuring of education by using multi-modal strategies to script with our students, narratives of identity and belonging. It is a way to heal and transform racial tensions and multicultural discords. We must confront the legacies of slavery and colonization. Interrogate Racism. Demand an end to school violence. Disrupt defacto segregation in schools. Put an end to cultural silencing if we are to understand the dynamics in the classrooms where we teach.

To achieve these desired changes in education, school leaders must be held accountable for creating an atmosphere of inclusion at the school, one that addresses children's funds of knowledge and effective discipline so all children have the space to learn without being bullied or alienated. It is that place where diversity and bold creativity meet. This is the space where students and teachers and administrators meet and connect. Each school site must take the responsibility of creating this space that reflects the specific needs of that particular community; a place where cultural rituals are acknowledged and celebrated. Having a sacred space within school does not come easy. It is a luxury-but an ESSENTIAL ONE. It is that place where educational leaders and teachers can meet with students and connect in an understanding of their common humanity. Something special happens when we own that part of ourselves that feels important and true. This volume offers strategies to accomplish this on behalf of students across the globe.

Chapter 1
Who Shall Teach Our Children?

Marva Sylvana McClean
Independent Researcher, USA

ABSTRACT

This chapter presents decolonized research methodologies that interrogate the profile of a conscientized teacher, qualified and prepared to teach Black and Brown children within the African Diaspora. Based on research spanning more than twenty years at three school sites, this chapter identifies five specific qualities that characterize a teacher who is conscientized into a historical consciousness that goes beyond narrow margins of the socially constructed race and geographic borders to embrace the humanity of the children within classrooms across the globe. Methodologies and theories including reflexivity, auto-ethnography, life stories, student narratives and social media inquiries are central to the research design that enabled this interrogation of education beyond borders. This international inquiry led to the uncovering of a worldview of what constitutes effective education and who qualifies as an effective teacher. Social media facilitated the crossing of borders and allowed space for collaborative inquiry that touched upon the anxiety and tensions educators face in their practice. It also highlighted the potential international collaborative inquiry holds as a site for creativity which speaks to what is possible in global education that promotes conscientization of the curriculum. In this examination of transnational approaches to educational equity this research has revealed the significance of knowledges beyond the textbook, including stories, spiritual knowledge, and ceremonial practices. Of special importance are transgenerational stories of strength, endurance, and survival transmitted by the students in global classrooms. This research has demonstrated it is impossible to create a model of the good teacher without taking issues of culture and community context into account. The result is a set of strategies that provides insights into how educators may re-conceptualize and reconstruct the classroom as a borderland, a site for both critical analysis and as a potential source of experimentalism that engages the student as central to classroom pedagogy.

DOI: 10.4018/978-1-6684-7379-5.ch001

It is important for our diverse student body to be engaged in pedagogy that acknowledges and integrates into the curriculum the actual historical, social, and cultural conditions that contribute to the forms of knowledge and meaning that they bring to school.

IN SEARCH OF TRUTH AND JUSTICE IN THE GLOBAL CLASSROOM

The enslaved engaged their minds as a powerful weapon against chattel slavery mastering acts of resistance that befuddled their oppressors and weakened the institution of slavery.

Teaching is a political act which demands a balance between the emotional and the practical; the transformative and the transactional; the personal and the public. The pervasive statistics about the failure of Black and Brown children in school is disturbing. Knowing as I do, that these children possess critical thinking skills which have allowed them to successfully navigate themselves within a world that constantly seeks to constrain and cast them out, I am preoccupied with my responsibility to find answers. How can we harness their insight and skills in the classroom to prevent their disengagement? What drastic actions can we take to disrupt the movement of our children into gang membership and embrace them instead into a place of inclusion? Why aren't more teachers working to place our Black and Brown children into universities instead of prisons? For decades, the USA has reported that Black/Brown students lag behind their Anglo counterparts and now, their Asian peers as well.

"In school year 2018–19, the national adjusted cohort graduation rate (ACGR) for public high school students was 86 percent, the highest it has been since the rate was first measured in 2010–11. Asian/Pacific Islander students had the highest ACGR (93 percent), followed by White (89 percent), Hispanic (82 percent), Black (80 percent), and American Indian/Alaska Native (74 percent) students" (NCES, 2022).

While I acknowledge that discipline is a major concern at schools worldwide and I agree that students must be held accountable for their behavior in school, this chapter does not address that issue. In keeping with Freire (2005), the lenses of this research initiative are focused directly on the skills, creativity and responsibility of educators to take all relevant issues into account and teach the children in their schools for success.

This chapter poses an invitation to educators worldwide, to engage in a reflexive practice that includes and interrogates ways in which new narratives of belonging and achievement can be constructed at the school site to disrupt normalized recounts of history and empower the educational community with a truthful narrative that acknowledges both student's and teacher's vulnerabilities while at the same time celebrates their strengths as contributors to global educational culture (Freire, 1993). This self -study (Boylorn & Orbe, 2014; Schon, 1983) draws parallels between the author and the Black and Brown children in 21st century classrooms, asserting that in much the same ways ancestral stories shaped my subjectivities and nurtured my identity, contemporary students will also benefit from tapping into this reservoir of their cultural retentions and history. This investigation honors the survival stories that have sustained the people of the African Diaspora through the trauma of oppression, slavery, and colonization that continue to wreak an influence on their lives. Stevenson (2015, p. 5) affirms, "Still the records of natural increase, long-term marital relations, vibrant cultural expression, unrelenting and diverse challenges to white authority, and creative and courageous acts that led to self and sometimes group emancipation document the slaves' determination to assert their agency against tremendous odds in order to control important aspects of their private lives, working conditions, and human expression."

Unfortunately, too many of our children are not embraced into an understanding of their historical and cultural background. It is cast aside, excluded. African American children in particular, have been systematically deprived of a rich cultural legacy of rites of passage, rituals and ceremonies which are useful to root them in their heritage and provide guidance on how to be in this world. Their rich history has been ignored and undermined. If we do not help our students to understand, respect and admire their place in history, what can we expect?

We have the responsibility to share with youth how the society has been built by slave labor of people from a continent rich in gold, art, culture, music; stripped of their citizenship and human rights in the USA (Stevenson, 2015). A people who bore within them the memories of their past, their land, their culture and the raging desire to be free. These descendants of the formerly enslaved continue to bear the after- life of this enslavement with disenfranchisement that has stalled their ability to grow and thrive and accumulate generational wealth. The lack of effective education looms large within this circle.

For centuries, Black people have been denied an education in the USA. During slavery it was illegal for Black people to be taught to read and write, and if caught, they would receive harsh punishment sometimes including dismemberment or death. The oppression during Jim Crow and beyond, saw African descendants subjected to an education deficit in both content and resources. Despite this, Black people persevered and engaged in extensive and creative methods to gain literacy and subvert attempts to undermine and oppress them. The enslaved engaged their minds as a powerful weapon against chattel slavery mastering acts of resistance that befuddled their oppressors and weakened the institution of slavery. Across the Americas, history abounds with the stories of resistance asserted by the enslaved,

3

yet these stories are not included in the curriculum. It is important for teachers to examine these historical truths and put them in perspective when designing programs to teach Black/Brown children so the classroom may become a cultural space, a site of empowerment and not one where the Black/Brown child is made to feel deficit. As described by McClean and Waters (2020), cultural spaces are created where people grow and thrive; ideas flourish and adult and children unite to transform society. It is here where we must maintain sustained dialogue in a climate of peace.

Evidence from my longitudinal study supports the assertion that children must be engaged as co-constructors of the curriculum in order to experience academic achievement in schools across the globe. The findings speak directly to the empowerment of students utilizing culturally relevant pedagogy and racial literacy that validate their background and honor the gifts they bring with them. This qualitative inquiry embraces decolonized research methodologies (McClean & Waters, 2020; Tuhiwai-Smith, 2012) and culturally responsive theory (Gay, 2000) as a platform to investigate education that honors the concept of social justice. My journey as a social justice and equity advocate is positioned as a roadmap to investigate how best to prepare the educator to teach for social justice, equity and peace. The development and use of these research methodologies are in response to the need to question and challenge the accuracy and validity of Eurocentric and Western approaches traditionally employed to study adults and children within particular contexts of the diasporas of African descendants.

Who am I? What is my purpose?

These questions have pushed me inward into the liminal space of my heritage, empowering me with tools to disrupt, challenge and renegotiate the hegemonic construction of classroom pedagogy with the legitimacy to create a borderless world that is inclusive and healing and enhanced by the collegiate model of intellectual exchange. Integral to this study has been the recognition of the value of forging a relationship with international scholars as it is important for us to to have informed allies outside of our local communities (Semali and Kincheloe, 2002, p. 19). From this realization, the value of storytelling in education has emerged as a significant tool to navigate the journey to become a historically conscious teacher.

Decolonized research methodology heightened the significance of respecting those you research beyond subjects and grant them equity within the research process. Throughout this journey, I have deconstructed my engaged research process as experiential pedagogy necessary to decolonize Western methodology and honor the cultural capital of my heritage as well as that of the students in the classroom. Honoring the students' cultural background and the funds of knowledge that they bring with them has been central to my continued evolution as an effective educator.

I have worked to integrate both Eurocentric knowledge (acknowledging that it prevails in education) and Afro-centric, Indigenous and New World sensibilities of the Americas as a central act of advocacy on behalf of the peoples' children that I teach (Delpit, 2006). In much the same way my teachers did when I was a student in Jamaica, I pay respect to the knowledge and set of skills that children bring to the classroom in full awareness that they bring experiences, their grandparents' stories, their parents' cultural norms and their community values that are of high importance to them and so should be to me as well.

DECOLONIZING THE RESEARCH PROCESS

When students are allowed cultural space their agency and a new paradigm will emerge: teacher as student; student as teacher.

This chapter utilizes research data collected over a span of twenty plus years, 1995-2018, within the school districts of Miami Dade and Broward counties. Miami Dade is the third largest school district in the country with students from 160 countries and has a graduation rate of 94%. In 2022, M-DCPS' graduation rate of 88.2 percent showed that Hispanic students increased by 2.2 percentage points compared to 2018-19 rising from 86.7 percent to 88.9 percent, surpassing the current state rate of 85.9 percent. White students increased by 2.7 percentage points compared to 2018-19 rising from 91.8 percent to 94.5 percent, surpassing the current state rate of 90.6 percent. Black students increased by 2.9 percentage points compared to 2018-19 rising from 79.5 percent to 82.4 percent, surpassing the current state rate of 82 percent (Miami Dade County Public Schools).

Broward County Public Schools (BCPS) is the sixth largest school district in the nation and the second largest in the state of Florida. BCPS is Florida's first fully accredited school system since 1962, serving more than 256,000 students and approximately 110,000 adult learners in 240 schools, centers and technical colleges, and 90 charter schools. BCPS supports a diverse student population representing 170 different countries and speaking 147 languages.

These two districts offered up diverse demographics of race and ethnicity. I engaged in a holistic interpretation of the qualitative data collected including students' interaction through questioning, body language, responses to guided questions, verbal comments and their written pre and post session reflections. I also noted their performance on the mandated state tests after the application of the strategies I initiated. This subjective data was scrutinized for interpretation of human experiences/interaction in relation to the implementation of critical pedagogy rooted in a culturally relevant platform.

Subjective and analytical data points to the efficacy of decolonized teaching practices based on the context of the school. This leads to the recognition that when the curriculum is alive, immediate and there is a constant stream of interaction between student and teacher, the environment and the community; the past and the present, students become attuned to their location within this process. This is pedagogy that garners alternative data that disrupts the standardized data of student deficiency. In this focus on human experience, the researcher observed students navigating their school context and acquiring agency. Inequity affects different aspects of schooling including the expectations educators have of children, the design and implementation of curriculum and allocation of resources. Further, it reveals ways in which the lives of teacher and students intersect as active participants in the classroom story and demonstrates that when students are allowed cultural space their agency and a new paradigm will emerge: teacher as student; student as teacher (Freire, 1990).

This study contributes to the discourse on contemporary literacy that addresses global educational injustices. It points to ways educators may engage students by incorporating a critical layer of complexity through social justice based on culturally relevant pedagogy. It reaffirms that collaborative inquiry opens up a wide- angle lens on the world as one seeks to eschew rigid definitions of what constitutes meaningful and useful research in the process of the conscientization (Freire, 1970) of the curriculum.

The data from three school sites revealed that educational inequity is not only about race or ethnicity. It is also about socio-economic status; it is about history and it is about culture. It is about the lack of creativity. It is about teachers' inability to connect with students and meet them where they are. As I worked to better understand the demands of this work, decolonized research methodology allowed me to pursue an interrogation of the context in which I live and work and connect that with an interpretation of how the past history of slavery-colonization-imperialism continues to shape the present (Kelly, 2023). The big question arose, how can this educator navigate the journey and find a niche to be creative and productive? I present below, narratives from three school sites (All names are pseudonyms) which suggest answers to these questions.

NARRATIVES FROM THE SCHOOL SITES

Cool Shade Middle School: Miami Dade County_

The journey of a thousand miles begins with the first step.

EAST SIDE-WEST SIDE! This was the chorus I heard coming from the hallway while I rushed to ensure my classroom door was locked during my first teaching experience at a low socio-economic school in Miami Dade County, Florida, USA during the 1990's.

In this school identified as failing by the state, students were organized in classes based on test scores and, I suspected, other categories as well that were not stated on paper. The use of hegemonic language to identify students as high performing, average and at risk was part of the status quo at the school. From the start, I felt this narrow definition of success was one that had been encouraged by the school's instructional agenda and bore witness to Kincheloe & Steinberg (1997) declaration that "As the politicians mandate test-driven curricula, they create new forms of educational pathology and social injustice that once again marginalize those outside the mainstream (p.39)." All Florida students are required to sit a standardized state test to determine their academic level, and each school is given a summary aggregate of the students' performance which assigns their level of performance as high, passing or failing. At the time the state assessment was named the Florida Comprehensive Assessment Test (FCAT). Currently, it is called the Florida State Assessment (FSA). The FCAT scores were used to organize students into categories of high performing, average and low performing. They were then sorted into classes determined as best suited to their abilities and the school's chances for moving upward on the grading scale.

Students carried around a consciousness of the academic identity imposed on them and often responded in a variety of ways including indiscipline, silence and indifference. Routed into my classroom as remedial students, many of them entered with an attitude. Scholars have documented the adverse impact this can have on students where many become preoccupied with the pressure to conform to the rules of success, while others resist or even alienate themselves (Flores-Gonzales, 2003) and drop out. This paper confronts the low expectations many teachers have of children of color in schools and the low performance outcome of children as a result.

There were constant fights in the hallways-based on membership in street gangs called Eastside and Westside. When fights broke out, you could hear the children shouting like the refrain from a song-*Eastside-Westside*. In my language arts and creative writing classrooms, I faced my own challenges. I am not sure what side Shaneka (pseudonym) belonged to, but she soon became my biggest challenge, questioning the relevance of language arts instruction, speaking out of turn, and often refusing to work.

We not interested in dis English junk, she once told me.

I soon realized that I was not adequately prepared to handle this environment and so engaged in informal research, including reaching out to teachers at the school, local community centers and even my family at home. My then fourteen -year old's response gave me pause to reflect and encouraged me be more opened-minded and reflective.

"Mom, stop being so hypocritical. You are forcing English on your students, insisting that they speak what you term as *proper* English when you encourage us at home to speak and celebrate our language."

The reprimand stung; however, it pushed me into a critical stance of reflecting on my double standards and the fact that I had bought into the mind-set that some languages were better than others.

A turning point came one morning when Shaneka got out of her seat and admonished a male student:

Bwoy, if you bodder me again, a gwine knock the taste outta yo mout.

I was struck by the poetry in those words. (I was also relieved that she returned to her seat when I requested that she did so).

I seized the opportunity and moved quickly to capture the essence of the moment. (After reprimanding both students) I remarked on the figurative language Shaneka had used in her outburst and shifted the lesson from grammar to the use of metaphors and similes in the way we speak. This centered Shaneka as an expert and she seemed pleased with the attention.

As the months rolled on, I was able to continue to draw parallels between what we were studying and the students' use of language and their lives in the community. I took special care to establish connections between the vernacular of their homes and community and the language Arts curriculum of the classroom. This incident and my response became the first step that began the journey of a thousand miles into the realm of social justice and equity.

In this environment, I struggled to discern ways to root myself and engage in work that lifted my spirit and pushed me forward. I questioned myself and engaged in a personal/professional audit. This reflection initiated a deep immersion into journal writing and poetry. Writing became a sanctuary of self- expression and validation of identity and storytelling and poetry became central to the border crossing and disrupting of racial barriers so inherent in the society. We launched into a study of poetry and prose from a textbook that was in the language arts department storeroom but not being used: African American Literature -Holt Rhinehart and Winston (1992). This text provided us with an extensive array of Black authors representing the Diaspora. We examined the connections between Black and Brown people across the globe and texts such as Claude McKay's We Wear the Mask, Maya Angelou's I

Know Why the Caged Bird Sings along with Merle Hodge's Crick Crack Monkey helped in expanding their understanding of the people of the African Diaspora. We pulled away the borders that separated Black people from different geographic regions and I believe, the essence of our common humanity became clearer and clearer to the students as the year rolled along. Their engagement reassured me that the changes I had made were resulting in creating a climate of collaboration that highlighted the authenticity of the human experience.

Over time, as my techniques evolved, I observed my students becoming more engaged, sharing their stories, writing for the school newspaper that I had launched and in general, classroom discipline improved and we openly worked towards establishing and maintaining tolerance and mutual respect. The students thrilled to the use of figurative language, oftentimes working in small groups to decipher the meaning of phrases, then working to use similar phrases in their own writing. It was clear that they were tapping into the conceptual underpinnings `of figurative language to voice their expression of their identity. As they delved into their cultural background, making connections with their classroom experiences, they grew into awareness that they had something to say and a rich reservoir from which to pull.

Shaneka's resistance was the turning point that shaped me into becoming a social justice educator. She made clear her resistance from the very start. She demanded to be seen and recognized, bringing her classmates along with her into this broad worldview of the class and she was their leader.

Together, students and I, had begun to craft a narrative of developing critical consciousness from which evolved new questions for me as a teacher and writer. I recognized the need to reframe how I thought about language within school as well as out of school environments. This, I discerned would help me to bridge social skills with education. Our lives in the classroom were characterized by the ideals we crafted together of what a shared humanity meant to us and what it looked like. I felt a profound obligation to these children for pushing me into boundary crossing and intercultural exchange leading to an expansion of my worldview of what it means to be Black in the Americas. This experience pushed me into research that related specifically to the context of the school and my classroom. As I was working on my doctorate at the time, I included this experience as part of my research on the education of African American students. I arranged for, and completed an internship in the department of curriculum and testing at the Florida Department of Education which expanded my understanding of standardized testing and gave me insights on strategies I could use to prepare the students for these tests without undermining their home life and cultural background. The work of Freire (1970; 1990, 1993) became crucial to my program of study and I questioned the process, my background and teaching style. To bolster my development, I participated in a series of seminars that were part of a partnership between the school district and Florida International

University. This international program extended the discourse to include international scholars and practitioners whose multiple perspectives extended my vision. Many of the same issues educators in developing countries faced were evident at my school site and others in large urban centers like Chicago, New Orleans and Miami Dade.

One participant shared best practice of using proverbs and idioms, and wise sayings from the community to teach children about figurative language. Another shared how she used rap music in a Chicago school to teach poetry, form and self- expression. That led us into a discussion about the African spiritual and cultural art forms that were the precursor to rap in this hemisphere, carried over by the African ancestors via the Middle Passage. Yet another presenter emphasized the value of sharing with students that they are writers too with skills and something important to say.

I reflected on my experience as a student in Jamaica and recalled how my teachers incorporated our culture and historical background into the classroom pedagogy, bolstering our identity and giving room to express our funds of knowledge. I worked to become **that** teacher who acknowledged the historical background of the students, investigated the community concerns and values and sought to utilize strategies that addressed the particularities of the context in which she taught. Over time, I grew in my understanding of the importance of creating a village in my classrooms; a cultural space where the students felt validated and important (Johnson, 2019; Kanu, 2006). This was the only way they were going to give me the grace to teach them. I know now that the students we teach are not generic children. They are human-beings with the capacity to contribute and make a difference (Gonzalez, Moll, & Amanti, 2005). They know so much more than we realize. They have so much more to teach us than we acknowledge.

Instead, they are not seen. They are regarded as data to be regulated, manipulated and then used to create strategies for improvement based on external imposition. Simply stated; they are not embraced as part of that village. The African proverb, *If you don't embrace the children out of the cold, they will burn the village to feel the heat,* became a guiding force in my work. As I worked with my students, researching the quality of education at the state, district and school site levels, I grew in awareness of my complicity in the state of education and committed to take steps to become an effective teacher. In addition to work on the doctoral program, I attended district workshops, nationwide conferences, community work and secured guidance from a veteran teacher experienced in innovative strategies to teach for inclusion and diversity.

I was reminded by bell hooks (1994) of my responsibility to analyze myself as a teacher-researcher within this particular context and to assess the efficacy of the strategies I considered essential to teach in conscientization (Freire, 1970). It was my intention that my classroom would become a site where each child would be actively involved as both teacher and learner in an instructional practice based on critical literacy. I also yearned to create a community of practice with the teachers at the school so we could share our strategies, support each other and raise our voices in response to district impositions on our curriculum at the school.

I had reached the conclusion that as long as the resources of schooling are so vastly different for diverse groups of children standardized tests can be far more a reflector of the results of inequity than that of the real potential and actual gains of many children (McClean & Waters, 2020).

Walker Middle School: Miami-Dade County

We are the world

My tenure at Walker Middle School provided me with a different set of lenses through which to view the world of school. This school was situated in a suburban community with a high population of Hispanic students (approximately 79%) and small percentages of Black and white children.

A forthright, committed and creative principal, also of Hispanic heritage, affirmed that the school belonged to the community and success would be achieved only to the extent that schooling became a community project. She stated emphatically that everything at the school was part of the curriculum. When I interviewed her as part of the data collection for my doctoral studies, she emphasized, "Children are surprisingly perceptive, and they have a lot to say. I think we should listen to them. I want to hear their voices." She also spoke with confidence of the teachers' integrity, admitting that she recognized them as professionals in charge of the classroom pedagogy and that she was there to support them and provide material and content they needed to be effective teachers. One language arts teacher noted that the interdisciplinary organization of the Language Arts curriculum which was linked to social studies as a vehicle for multicultural education allowed the students to take their work home and out into the community. This open, democratic way of schooling, centered heavily on students' funds of knowledge, communal living and the involvement of parents and the community. I realized that within this setting the students felt seen, respected and validated. The school was a high performing one with an A Plus rating based on state standards. As I worked in continuing my research studies, I began to discern that measures of preventing the children from burning the village were in place. They were part of the village with a strong unshakeable sense of belonging. In this open-atmosphere, deeply rooted in cultural exploration, this made all the difference.

My challenge here was to work with these students to move beyond the confines of their world to understand other cultures and other students who did not have access to the vast resources that they did. I worked with intention to extend their global awareness and build historical consciousness. I hoped that from our exploration of literature and writing about that literature, students would be able to understand and empathize with others. I intentionally expanded the definition of literature as I had utilized it before and exposed students to worlds outside of their small, close knit suburban community and beyond their heavily resourced school site.

I wanted them to interrogate the United States' relationships with other nations as well as their common humanity with other children across the globe. Especially because there were a few students of Haitian heritage in the school and knowing how easy it may become for them to experience marginalization in a setting such as this, I set out to bring alive Haitian culture and history in the classroom and address the stigma and stereotype that I knew was part of the culture within the Miami Dade School system, where Haitian students were often teased and called Boat People. I have witnessed first -hand the lingering feelings of vulnerability that enshrouds the lives of many Haitian-American students within the public -school system and so, I wanted to further investigate this phenomenon and make a contribution to the educational discourse in this under-investigated area. Students pursued research that unearthed information on education in Haiti-including a review of that educational system since Haiti became the first Black Republic, having won its independence in 1803. Thinking of these students as youth leaders with agency, I felt it of value to infuse this content into the curriculum to present an accurate portrayal of the Haitian people beyond the common pejorative descriptors of the Boat people.

I stirred up a conversation on the history of Haiti and directed the student to work in teams of two to research and present their findings in different formats. A summary discussion, using the Socratic method followed what turned out to be an interesting and passionate display of the students' understanding of how Haiti came to be poor, going all the way back to slavery and colonization and the Haitian Revolution (Kaisary, 2023). Students critiqued the sanctions placed against Haiti by France and the role of the USA in undermining the autonomy of the *new* nation and the ongoing atrocities against the nation. "It is estimated that the fine imposed against Haiti would be equivalent to $21.7 billion today. Haiti was forced to shut down its schools in order to funnel these funds towards payment of this crushing debt. A consequence of this arrangement is the underdevelopment of the school system" (McClean, 2019, p. 80). This prelude led us to a study of the prose of Edwidge Danticat's Kric Krac and poetry centered on the Haitian Revolution and culture. The students' interest level raised when I shared that I knew Danticat and had presented with her at the Miami International Bookfair.

This study of world literature which included movies such as Freedom Writers, The Diary of Anne Frank, James Berry's prose, The Banana Tree and the video/documentary, We Are the World, helped to -provide context for our study. These texts became a touchstone to create dialogue and engage students in inquiry about issues of power, discrimination and inequities. Their views of social issues in their worlds were expanded through dialogue and their journey into in-depth investigation of a world beyond borders. In writing about the literature, they studied, students recognized the rich diversity of the United States. They also acknowledged the structural racism on which it is grounded and how the voices of certain groups of people have been kept out. This critical assignment was intended to address the missing narratives from the discourse on children of color and their place within the public education system; and most important, elevate the voice of the Haitian child within that discourse. This raised further questions: What is the perspective of the Haitian American student? How does he/she utilize the literature, including folklore, stories, proverbs and wise sayings to inform school life and navigate the challenges that are a product of a history of discrimination? The important aim of this investigation was to write truth into history in such a manner that it raised the historical consciousness of the students. Below is a sample of other questions we explored using Socratic seminars.

Critical Questions Designed to Raise Historical Consciousness

1. How can we eradicate extreme hunger and poverty?
2. Why is it important to show respect and tolerance for others?
3. What can we do to stop global warming?
4. How can we use literature to improve our lives?
5. Why does our educational system focus on standardized testing?
6. To what extent is the media center essential to our school?
7. Are children the product of our environment, or do children produce the environment?
8. Has technology improved our lives, or has it weakened the fabric of our society?
9. To what extent are we what we eat?
10. How can we work to connect our minds, hearts, bodies and souls? Or, what can young people do to bring balance to their lives? Or, To what extent is it necessary that schools maintain art and music as an essential part of the curriculum?
11. How are our lives influenced by weather?
12. What are the functions of the writer in society?
13. What is a community? What are the factors that shape your community? What are the issues that are important to your community? To you as a member of that community?

These questions informed the critical pedagogy and culturally relevant curriculum we embarked on with the objective of raising the critical consciousness and the historical awareness of the students. It was crucial for students to understand the social culture of other communities and countries as well. Below is one student's writing sample that illustrates how they were expanding their global footprint through research and classroom discourse.

Journal Reflection 2013

We should celebrate women and their achievements and history to remember all the important actions and ideas they contributed to the world with their determination. For example, Malala Yousafzai stood up nonviolently for her educational rights and other girls' educational rights. With her action, she has influenced many other people to stand up for their rights and she has changed the future for many girls. Additionally, female writers including Edwidge Danticat and Maya Angelo share important information about the lives of Black people across the world, through the stories and poetry they write. By celebrating Women's History Month, you can remember the important ideas and helpful actions women have contributed to the world with determination.

    Anjali

Dressekie Middle School: Broward County

How are the children doing?

The opportunity to direct the curriculum at this site was an exciting one as it provided the opportunity for me to further delve into a program of critical pedagogy rooted in culturally relevant teaching and learning. At this site I worked first with the teachers, creating curriculum, designing training programs, monitoring and supporting their practice. Later on, I went into the classroom and experienced first hand the effects of the strategies I had identified as effective ones to embrace students as collaborators and active participants in the teaching and learning process

In taking up this third experience, having garnered transformative experiences at the previous two schools, I took seriously bell hooks' (1994) comment that educators must let students see their vulnerabilities and their humanity and connect with them in meaningful ways. I regarded this as part of the poetics of education and so I sought to capture the students' interests and humanize the teaching and learning process.

The school is heavily resourced, located in a suburban community largely populated by students from the surrounding middle class community. Students have access to the latest in technologies and local, national and in some cases, international fieldtrips/experiences. Students go on to college with a ninety eight percent graduation rate. The curriculum is strongly supported by parents who involve themselves in every aspect of the school program. The students tend to be engaged with the capacity to advocate for themselves. This school setting, with the normalized status of student engagement and support and the open acknowledgment of their funds of knowledge was a direct contrast to Cool Shade Middle. It was clear that different systems exist for different students depending on their socio-economic status and the geography of the school site. While I undertook an analysis of the three schools investigating issues of race and location, this is not the focus of this chapter and I am not able to engage in that analysis here.

With all the resources available to this student body, self- advocacy and agency was apparent. A primary thrust of my work thus became the objective to heighten their historical awareness and extend their understanding of the global educational landscape and the inequities that exist. I engaged them in research that highlighted the conditions of schooling and community life for children who were not as privileged as they were. I shared with them that millions of school age children do not have access to an education. UNESCO (2020) reports that currently 258 m worldwide do not have access to an education. We investigated questions such as, *Why is Haiti poor? What are the barriers to education across the globe? Why are there homeless children in Florida? How do you explain the high rate of starving children in the USA?*

If these students were to be change agents of the future, it was extremely important that they became conscientized into the disparities that exist so they could take this awareness into their professional pursuits into the future.

The students understood the reflective process I was engaged in and were enthusiastic in sharing their perspective on the methods I used with them in the classroom. They wanted to participate in the data collection for my first academic book and offered samples of their writing. I shared with them my reason for selecting a decolonized research methodology process. One important unit I initiated was global literature which incorporated a study of authors from the different continents. This was useful in examining how colonization shaped the Americas and other continents resulting in disparities and inequities (Kelly, 2023). I soon realized that connecting with international authors and students should be the next step in this inquiry and so we utilized the technology available and connected with scholars and students in distant countries. For example, the students studied the work of an Aboriginal (Australia) scholar and wrote their reflections as well as created questions in response to their study of his rites of passage for Aboriginal youth. They met with the scholar via Skype and engaged in a two- hour discussion, questioning and sharing ideas. Their reflections indicated how the session had served to help shatter stereotypes they had held prior to this unit of study and expanded their understanding of the common bonds of humanity regardless of one's location. The following student's reflection presents an example of their analysis of this experience:

Rhonda

At first, I was amazed to see that Dr. Wade appeared to be white, even though he stated that he was Black. It made sense when he shared that his mother was a Black Aboriginal woman and his father was Irish. I had no idea that there were Black people in Australia. Dr. Wade also said that teens like us listened to rap and hip hop and they loved reggae music too. It was interesting to hear him say that his race was irrelevant as that has no determination about your humanity. He said that race was made up by people who wanted to oppress others and to keep people contained and really was not real. While I get it somewhat, I do need to learn more so I can understand it better.

Taking Steps to Learn Together: Family Stories as Classroom Pedagogy

From my own childhood experiences, I understood that families from all cultures have unique literacy knowledge and practices that elders convey directly and indirectly to subsequent generations. I knew how valuable a resource the family/home connection could be and I wanted to capitalize on this with this group of youth. So, I instructed them to gather stories from their culture to share with classmates. They worked in small groups of four to identify an ethnic folktale from the different cultures of continental regions and compare to their own. In each case, these conversations provided rich data that helped to shape the intellectual framework of the classes. This led to deeper questions about work in school and what they were capable of doing. The students contributed topics for research, authors, locations for field trips and methods of instruction. Such conversations embraced the students' funds of knowledge and encouraged me to break free of routinized pedagogies to co-construct curriculum with them, enriched by the subtle prodding and nuances of their culture.

This is well supported by Delpit (2006) who stresses the urgency for teachers to work with students to build their literacy skills within the context of critical and creative thinking. She reminds us that these skills are best taught through meaningful communication and best learned in meaningful contexts that draw on the students' knowledge and the critical literacies that they bring with them from their cultural heritage. Delpit (2006) argues that "students need technical skills to open doors, but they need to be able to think critically and creatively to participate in meaningful and potentially liberating work inside those doors" (p. 19). The students were very instrumental in guiding me in the use of technological tools used in the classroom and the world around them. For the end of year project, I directed them to create a virtual memoir, using digital tools to chronicle the years' experience in language arts, highlighting their favorite pieces of writing from their portfolios. The response was immediate, infused with excitement. They readily responded to this opportunity to fuse technology with their writing and critical analysis skills to design a document that reflected their growth and position in the 21ˢᵗ century community. The presentation was titled, *The Me You See* and incorporated selections from their journals, pictures, photographs, inserted interviews, clips about their homeland and other countries and places they had studied during the year. The production was a splendid autobiographical digital presentation asserting their identity and confirming the space they occupied in the school.

As I charted and analyzed my development, I recognized that I was immersing myself in the poetics of education. I have coined this phrase to mean the areas of educational development where teacher and student engage in mutual dialogue; understanding their common humanity. I began to understand the poetry inherent in this proverb, *When the student is ready-the teacher appears.* I was understanding my role as an educator and I knew the students were always ready, but the teacher must first prepare him or herself to meet them right where they are.

From this contemplation, I crafted the poem below in testimony to this conceptual underpinning of social justice and equity within the classroom.

When The Student Is Ready; The Teacher Appears
The first day of middle school.
Students file in,
Some look at me with curiosity
Others pretend I don't exist;
Others glare with dark animosity.

I brace myself, for I have seen this before
they enter with memories of disappointment
rooted in their hearts,
Defiance, their tool of resistance.

You don't know me.
What the hell, do you care?
I won't ever use this.
Why should I be here?

I don't have to listen to you.
What can you tell me that I need to hear?

Their bodies speak their resistance.

I want to say,
I see you
I know you are more than the test scores
that shuffled you into my remedial reading class.
I want to say
Come join me & let's find a way
To write a new curriculum together
One that sings with the biography
of your ancestors' empowerment
Your stories and celebrations
Let's analyze the verse and the poetry of your playlist
Let's carve space for your cultural rhythms
Come, share your grandparents' stories that inspire and enchant.

And so,
under the required Learning Goal on the white board,
I write (for the eyes of the administrator who might come in)
Students will express themselves
and write in response to the questions
WHO ARE YOU?

What is it you would like me to know about you?
I smile as they put their pencils to
the colored paper I have placed on their desk
and begin to write themselves into the curriculum.

Writing like this became an essential part of my teaching practice, a ritual firmly grounded in the practice that tells the students I am ready to be their teacher. I leaned into the patterns and rhythms that are the rituals that governed the life of the school. I learned that children rely on this and expect it and respond to it. This process and experience have helped me to more clearly define and understand my research methodology which is a direct response to the African proverb:

How are the children doing?

The more deeply I engage in self-analysis, the more I realize, I am part of the despair within our educational system. I have witnessed the failure of school children, with the realization that we are not just failing Black and Brown children, we are failing white children as well. We are failing them when we do not expose them to the history of Black people in the USA. When we do not expose them to the historical development of this country (Kaisary, 2023) and allow them to engage in the discourse of how to repair the damage that has been done and identify and assert how we may heal and move forward.

Below, I present a summary of the valuable lessons I discerned from working in these locations and the extent to which these experiences shaped me into becoming an educator teaching for justice, equity and peace.

LESSONS LEARNED

Cool Shade Middle

This redesigning of the process of teaching and learning placed the children as a central force in the development of the class, shifting the perspective of learning as static and focused entirely on the state's standardized tests to that of a fluid process, incorporating reflections, revisions and action.

Working at Cool Shade Middle school taught me the value of teaching in context and subverting a standardized curriculum in order to meet student needs. I altered my approach to the routinized language arts curriculum I was assigned to one which met the standards but moved beyond to embrace student voices with space for them to use their journals as a safe place to write and share their stories. Students researched and wrote about topics of interest to them, and engaged their home life as a crucial part of their identity as writers. These pedagogical activities worked to affirm that schooling is much more than achievement on tests. In this process we validated family and community practices alongside classroom instruction. This approach gave value to the children's identity as leaners and fostered their potential for growth. This redesigning of the process of teaching and learning placed the children as a central force in the development of the class, shifting the perspective of learning as static and focused entirely on the state's standardized tests to that of a fluid process, incorporating reflections, revisions and action. From the research I learned that students with non-standard speech are often regarded as less competent and socially different from students with a more standard dialect (Delpit and Dowdy, 2008). This perspective often leads to assumptions about the child's proficiency and the decision to place her in a particular group. Shaneka and her peers taught me a valuable lesson of listening intently to the student's expressions, the way they told their stories and the fire they brought to the analysis of literature. As I developed my understanding of teaching in context, I focused less on grammar, sentence structure and my erroneous assumption of the correctness of speech. My classroom pedagogy shifted from an unrewarding curriculum and embraced divergent thinking, communication skills and the vitality of the students' expressions.

In order to tackle the many tensions and emotions wrought by the situation, I turned to a group of colleagues in Canada, Jamaica, and the USA to seek their advice. They shared ideas on how to shape conversations with my students, handle confrontations, and strategically tackle the scrutiny of the administration to handle power plays. A most crucial piece of advice I received was the importance of documenting my work with the students and provide evidence of proven research to support my pedagogy. I was reminded of Kincheloe' s and Steinberg's (1997) affirmation that critical educators must give thoughtful consideration to the methods by which individuals assert their agency and self-direction in relation to power plays. I learned a valuable lesson from Shaneka that the children in the classroom are not generic people. They are unique with important stories to share and much to teach me. I worked to implement strategies that would create the space for my students to reposition themselves as achievers, resistant to the school's and district's narrow definition of success. Plagued by a strong sense of complicity, I needed room as well to settle into the rhythm of schooling and build relations of trust and respect with my students.

When the state's results were published that year, Shaneka received a Level 5 for the Writing test, one level shy of a perfect 6. Her performance dismantled long-standing pattern of underachievement at the school. All but one student in that class passed the test at different levels. I would like to say that the school climate changed and there was upward mobility at Cool Shade Middle, but unfortunately that was not the case. For years after, the school struggled with academics and discipline remained low. Eventually the school was closed some years after I had left for Walker Middle.

Walker Middle School

This exploration of personal and global culture led to writing about literature and its place in their lives.

In this school community led by a principal highly focused on the value of the cultural landscape, at school and at home, cultural heritage and students' funds of knowledge were given high priority. As a student who had been educated on the value of storytelling and the linguistic legacy of one's vernacular, I was very interested in working with my students to see and value the symbolic content of the literature of their heritage and its connections to the literature of the classroom and generalize this to global literature of cultures they had not explored before. We explored a variety of folktales, fables, legends and other forms of rich storytelling from the Americas, including Haiti, Jamaica and Cuba. I felt that this form of literacy would support my students as they journeyed throughout the school year. They would develop and foster their intellectual identity and express this in a variety of ways. Inspired by the ideology of critical literacy (Kincheloe & McLaren, 1999) and culturally relevant pedagogy (Gay, 2002), I saw this as an opportunity to raise the students' voices in an investigation of cultures beyond their door-steps and for them to understand the extent to which heritage and cultural background shape our academic and social lives. This exploration of personal and global culture led to writing about literature and its place in their lives. They utilized a variety of expressive modalities, including the production of a newspaper, cultural fairs and research papers.

Dressekie Middle School

These diverse forms of investigating the world beyond their school and community revealed students who were steadily becoming agents of change, eager to interrogate the world's complexity.

This school site fostered students' funds of knowledge and created open spaces for cultural expressions. The curriculum was embedded with a variety of extra-curricular activities, including field trips and out of state travel to venues like the Smithsonian African American Heritage Museum. As I aimed to raise their critical consciousness about the role of writing in their lives, I asked my students to think about ways in which they could use writing as a strategy to change their world. This would remain an essential question that informed everything we did in the class. In carrying forward my agenda, I was determined to become an activist and reflective practitioner, who would ultimately prepare critical thinkers who were so uneasy by the disparities they had unearthed, they would be moved with a sense of urgency to make changes. I envisioned the classroom setting as a site of critical theory in action, positioning myself and students as both teacher and learner.

A major turning point was our implementation of a program of cultural diversity which included an annual Native American heritage presentation, an African American heritage assembly and a National Women's History Month Panel Discussion with female leaders from the different sections of the state. In each presentation, interactive with song, dance and music, blooming cultural activists presented diverse perspectives about being in the world and in particular, the diaspora. They demonstrated that there are multiple pathways to learning and reaffirmed the multiple ways of knowing. In each case, my students acted as hosts, welcoming the guests, introducing them and with my help, coordinating the moderation of the presentations. All of these activities evoked the attention of the entire school community and engaged discussion and reflection. These diverse forms of investigating the world beyond their school and community revealed students who were steadily becoming agents of change, eager to interrogate the world's complexity.

While the students welcomed and seemed to enjoy these strategies, the administration was not entirely supportive of these changes I made to the pedagogy of the school site which it felt met the school's vision and mission adequately.

This was an A Plus school with Blue Ribbon status and the administration felt the changes I was making were not necessary and were disrupting the status quo, which was exactly my intention. During that first year back in the classroom, I was observed without warning seven times between August and October. I ensured that I was prepared with both validity of lesson plans and teaching strategies as well as classroom/discipline control. The students' engagement and enthusiasm spoke volumes of the validity of my approach. Nonetheless, I was summoned to meetings many times and had to defend my approach. Each time I did so with synthesis of research regarding pedagogy and student engagement, referencing the students' involvement in the class. The experience I had gathered over time, the students' engagement and the continued collaboration with international scholars served to bolster my position and provided the insight and energy to stand up to this white-washed form of oppression.

Classroom Discourse Equals Counter Discourse

I faced the challenge of critiquing my praxis and setting forth a profile of the teacher qualified to teach school children across the globe, leading to the attainment of justice, equity and peace in the global classroom.

These three experiences opened my eyes to the possibilities of radicalized action needed to disrupt the social injustice and inequities that persist in our (educational) communities across the globe. The teachers who shall teach our students must work with all children to create historical consciousness. Whether it be science, history, language arts, physical education reading, or mathematics, there are opportunities in daily teaching to connect historical content and truth into your subject area. Any form of storytelling will work to open up the world to our common humanity. I have used stories consistently to emphasize the funds of knowledge both teacher and student bring to the class, regardless of the subject area. These stories have the capacity to foster a positive classroom environment and build cultural competence and belonging. As I grew in critical consciousness and historical awareness, I faced the challenge of critiquing my praxis and setting forth a profile of the teacher qualified to teach school children across the globe, leading to the attainment of justice, equity and peace in the global classroom. I share these teaching and learning experiences as a pathway to answering the question: *Who shall teach our children?*

Who Shall Teach Our Children?

1. The Dream Keeper

Dreaming and the mythologies and memories of our archetypes can contribute to healing our wounded soul.

"Bring me all of your dreams, you dreamers,
Bring me all of your heart melodies
That I may wrap them in blue cloud cloth
Away from the rough fingers of the world"
—Langston Hughes

Hughes' poem speaks to the central position of dreaming in the cosmology of people of color. The ability to dream and intuit a world beyond the physical reality of oppression, has kept people of the African Diaspora and their culture alive. This teacher understands the value of narrative as an affirming tradition of intellectual development beyond that which is connected to an act of colonization. This teacher is a dreamer whose idealism pushes her to yearn for and obtain peace and justice in the classroom. So, she takes action to cut across cultures and geographies, determined to transform teaching and learning into a third space that fosters the intellectual and socio-cultural development of students in the community.

This teacher pushes the concept of dreaming as central to the identity of Black and Brown children, using it as a metaphor of the hope and possibilities that lie ahead. It is a state, a world, we want to open up to our children and imbue them with the desire to aspire and thrive even under the harshest of circumstances enwrapped within "the rough fingers of the world" (Hughes, 1932/1994, p. 2). For too long our children have been located in classrooms which excluded them as those whose history and cultural practices are not relevant to the curriculum. Based on my understanding and relationship to my heritage I know that *dreaming* and the memories of our archetypes and mythologies can contribute to healing our wounded soul. I believe that sharing our stories and bringing them within the classroom for teacher and student is an important step to internationalize the curriculum, investigate the world, and recognize and honor the perspectives of others. This, I believe, will improve the education of children of African descent across the globe.

2. The Historically Conscious Teacher

Slavery was used to build the economic wellbeing of the USA.

Perhaps the most important question anyone undertaking research should ask is: Who am I? What is my purpose? These questions lead one to look inward and examine the factors that have shaped her. This consciousness directly influences the way one conducts research and teaches children. A teacher who has faced the history of the on-going oppression that resulted in the failure of Black/Brown children in schools across the globe and recognized her complicity in this, is one who is prepared for the journey in becoming the teacher who will teach our children in this 21st century and prepare them to journey into the future. She immerses herself in understanding history and breaking the chains of academic oppression.

It is our duty to fight for our freedom. It is our duty to win. We have nothing to lose but our chains.

—Sarah O'Neil

One of five winners in the Raise up Project 2015 contest, seventeen-year-old Sarah eloquently and emotionally addresses the failure of children of color in schools in the United States. Her poetry asserts the role educators must play in addressing the needs of children and positioning them within a pedagogy of hope in the classroom. Her militant call to fight against academic oppression invokes a history of colonization and the fact that "we have nothing to lose but our chains." It is the voice of youth such as Sarah's that keeps me alert to the value of exploring the history of the Americas and bringing that to life in the classroom regardless of the content area, for it is of great value to teach the history of the Americas and how we all came to be here.

This should lead to an examination of the meaning of racism and how and why it was socially constructed.

I am reminded that the teacher who shall teach our children must confront the negative learning environment prevalent in the school system where students like Sarah and Shaneka who openly resist the official curriculum in which they do not see themselves or their history are often identified and rejected as failures. The students of the Raise Up Poetry project remind us that we are responsible to free our chains and "emancipate ourselves from mental slavery" (Bob Marley, 1980).

When the classroom conversation is extended to include themes of historical empowerment from their cultural inheritance, this offers a confirmation of the history and dignity of children. Stevenson (2015) reminds us of the resiliency of the enslaved and their courageous moves in resisting oppression to maintain their dignity and persevere. Information like this must be included in the curriculum in acknowledgment that the children of African ancestry have a historical and cultural background that is valid, substantial and of great merit.

Stevenson notes that the USA became the largest slave holding society during the nineteenth century, with more than four million enslaved. She describes the system of managing the enslaved as a brutal and dehumanizing process: "Slavery meant physical and psychological abuse. For slave women, and to a lesser extent, men and children, it meant sexual abuse. This humanity shadowed every aspect of a slave's life; marital status, working conditions, intellectual/cultural expressions, punishment and representation in law. It was a crime if slaves were caught learning to read and write. The enslaved received the menial and minimum material, medical, social and psychological rewards for their labor even though that labor was used to build the economic wellbeing of the country. Regardless of their brutal economic exploitation and denunciation as racial inferiors, enslaved Africans and their descendants managed to survive their enslavement physically, psychologically, culturally, spiritually, and intellectually (Stevenson, 2015, p.5).

Writing about the enslaved in Cuba, Barcia (2006) notes, that "the enslaved never stopped trying to test the Spanish colonial (p.1) system to its limits, and on some occasions, they succeeded in improving their condition."

These stories of the complicated experiences of the enslaved who were imbued with courage, wit and resiliency are not included in classroom texts. I myself, just learned recently of the famed musician Joseph Bologne, Chevalier of France. After seeing the film, Chevalier, I thought to myself, what a wonderful story of empowerment and one that should be taught to our youth! In addition to movies and documentaries, social media platform including Instagram sites such #blackhistoryuk and #blackcurriculum serve to highlight interesting facts about the achievements of Black people during enslavement and beyond. These sites present history and storytelling with the power to bring the wisdom traditions of Black, Indigenous and Brown people into the classroom. This form of oral and performance pedagogy allows the presenter to share with the rest of the world that which is sacred to us, that which reflects our truth and humanity (McClean & Waters 2020)) in such a manner that it serves to connect student to teacher and each to the broader global community. As schools address the rising drop-out rates and persistent achievement gaps between school children, it is important that the silenced history of Black and Brown people be awakened and incorporated into 21st century pedagogy.

3. The Storyteller

The teacher must create spaces for school children to tell their stories. Tapping into the symbolic power of cultural stories direct students to see the world through the eyes of warriors of resistance, rather than the victimized and oppressed.

When the teacher enacts her role as storyteller, she expands her capacity to travel across borders, to travel into history and locate and share stories that not only invigorate the classroom but also bring the children, their stories and their histories alive in a setting of vibrancy and inclusion. Students awaken to the diversity of the classroom and the world and grow in respect and tolerance of others. Yet, the stories of Black/Brown people are consistently left out of the narratives of classrooms. This, of course, reflects the complexities and contradictions of life lived in a post/neo colonial society where we are still regarded as the *other*. One of the greatest fears of children is that they will be deemed inadequate as indeed the education system has been informing them. To counteract this, the teacher must share stories of her culture and create spaces for school children to do the same.

Stories of Nanny of the Maroons, a warrior who fought against the British and shattered the chains of oppression have been central to my journey as an educator. These stories have worked to give substance to the shaping of my identity as a student in Jamaica and now as an adult, veteran educator and social justice advocate in the USA. These stories not only shaped my identity but also gave me the strength to maintain belonging when I felt alienated. Tapping into the symbolic power of cultural stories such as these, I point out the value of seeing the world through the eyes of warriors of resistance, rather than the victimized and oppressed. I shift the research process into the realm of students' subjectivities and strategies to embrace their funds of knowledge into classroom pedagogy, acknowledging them as knowledge creators, who today are experts within the global village of social media.

Young people across the globe are accessing a broad range of media and technology strategies to connect with others and to elevate their voices. Across all continents. Technology plays an important role in assisting our students to become producers of knowledge shared across the globe. They hold control over the telling and sharing data, using apps to be producers of knowledge and establish relations with new allies. They are no longer just consumers of knowledge. They are using technology in a more critical and deliberate way. The effective teacher is prepared to access this technology as an empowering tool in teaching for social justice, equity and peace.

4. Global Collaborator

It is essential for the teacher to seek out cross- cultural experiences that are globally inclusive, generating empowerment.

This researcher's collaborative inquiry, utilizing digital technology across continents bears implication for cross cultural and international discourse at a time when the world is facing challenges that are interconnected, including widespread illiteracy investigated as education injustice by this study. It is essential for the teacher to seek out cross- cultural experiences that are globally inclusive, generating empowerment. This includes examination of the need to extend the conversation beyond popular conceptions of Black/White race relations and the history of racism across the Americas, acknowledging issues of survival, wellbeing, and negotiations of identity that characterize the lives of Back/Brown people and their children. In 2014, after meeting a group of social justice scholars at a Maroon conference in Jamaica, I committed to engage with them in an ongoing exploration of education across the globe and the decolonizing strategies we could employ in this process. We have agreed that this relationship works to address the isolation and despair we often experience in our places of work. From my collaboration with these international scholars, I have learned that stories, poetry, and reflections are essential to teaching and learning.

This international collaboration has led me to field work in countries across the globe where I have been awakened to the reasons for the ongoing failure of Black and Brown children in schools in the USA. In Cuba, I visited schools where students shared pencils; where you had to go to the office to get toilet paper. Often, students sat on the floor in classes. Yet, in these heavily under-resourced settings, the children appeared happy, well -adjusted and were respectful and tolerant. Research revealed that the literacy rate in Cuba is 97-99% (The Castro Reader). In New Zealand, I visited maraes where the Māori elders teach children about their great ancestry, their ceremonies and rituals. In Australia, where there are Elder-in Residence programs in schools and museums, Aboriginal elders practice ceremony with children and take them through rites of passage experiences which confirm their identity and elevate their historical consciousness (McClean & Waters, 2020). In Jamaica, I observed Maroon children in elementary school interpret centuries of their ancient history through dances such as Kumina, Pocomania and Dinki Mini.

When you are an *Other*-entering a world every day where you do not feel that you truly belong, this creates a sense of divergence where there is often an overwhelming sense of being in two worlds and disparate spaces. Issues of race, ethnicity, skin shade, poverty/classism, ethnicity are some of the factors that interfere with children's access to education and their academic outcome in countries all over the globe. The school teacher must work to create a space where all children feel accepted. What

I have witnessed in the USA is the continuous division and organization of youth based on race-gender-financial status-food availability-parental status-indiscipline-violence -failure-achievement. This results in the nonstop and destructive labeling of children as if they are commodities. This commodification of children is the antagonist to acceptance and inclusion. It keeps school children excluded, left out in the cold. At a time when Black/Brown youth are under siege the world over, when police brutality continues to cut them down in the middle of their lives, they need to be embraced into the village.

It is necessary to push conceptual thinking from our heritage into the reality of classrooms across the globe and push for pedagogy to help to restore the dreams of our youth. Such pedagogy can raise the quality of teaching by creating a third space, a cultural space that reflects Freire's notion of Conscientization, upholding the opportunity to raise up the silenced voices of our children as viable curriculum production. Teaching within the crucible of historical consciousness across the globe should spark a revolution, emphasizing that the curriculum must be altered to incorporate an imaginative discourse that addresses issues of globalization and the pluralism that is an inherent part of educational systems worldwide. It is one based on justice, equity and peace.

5. The Subversive Warrior of Resistance

When teachers share their lives with students, they personalize the curriculum and invite students' collaboration.

The teacher who shall teach our children must guide them in analyzing their experiences and applying the tools of social justice to question dominant discourses and then respond through social action. hooks (1994) argues that when teachers share their lives with students, they personalize the curriculum and invite students' collaboration. This teacher envisions a classroom environment where the teacher subverts the scripted curriculum typically in place and incorporates stories of resistance and empowerment of historically disenfranchised people. These must become narratives of historical empowerment which cast the spotlight on the agency of the ancestors of the children in the classrooms. All content area teachers must take on the responsibility of disrupting the normalized representations of the colonized and the colonizer in the historiography of slavery and emancipation. The truthful and accurate history of the USA and the founding of the Americas must be told. Stories from my culture echo Nanny's valiant fight against oppression, her ability to harness both the human resources and that of the physical landscape to forge a warfare so aggressive that the British recognized her as a thorn in their side. Forced to negotiate with the Maroons, the British offered peace treaties in 1739 resulting in sovereign ownership of land which upholds to this day.

Stories expressing the cultural landscape of peoples all over the Americas must be included in the curriculum to point to the possibilities that can emerge from courageous action. Using any methods possible, depending on the teacher's geographic location, these stories must be told, for children must be allowed to identify with their ancestral heroes and experience the empowerment that comes with that action.

Under the teacher's watchful eye, social media provides countless opportunities for students to experience global culture and engender relationships with other students across the globe. For instance, my knowledge of educational concerns across the globe has certainly been expanded through my inquiry on the Instagram platform. Instagram handles including #blackhistoryuk, #black curriculum and #ancestral voices have presented information on the historical movement of Black people across the globe that I was not privy to before. In addition, I have been able to establish relationships with writers, teachers and researchers with similar concerns as I have. The work that they have embarked on has emphasized the various approaches that social justice educators may undertake in pursuit of their journey. The work is accessible, the relationship empowering and rooted in the determination to break the silence and raise up our voices in stories to the world. Educators can appropriate lessons in heroism, techniques in figurative language, and strategies to uplift the heritage of people of color into the school system. Through the stories shared on social media, I am strengthened in my understanding of the substance of the heroism of our elders, the history of our ancestors and the route forward. For this cadre of social justice warriors are standing firm in their commitment to bring the truth of our empowerment, the achievement of our ancestors and the creativity of our people in full light to the world.

UNRAVELING THE TRUTH: FIVE STRATEGIES TO DECOLONIZE THE GLOBAL CLASSROOM

From my journey into decolonized research methodologies, I have arrived at the conclusion that student failure in school is not due to lack of resources, but lack of belonging.

I therefore recommend the following approaches:

1. **Create Cultural Spaces in The Classroom:** Educators must create cultural spaces within classrooms that embrace and validate all children. This is central to the social and political work that educators must undertake.
2. **Teach In Context:** Academic programs must interrogate the complications of city life/rural life as this will determine the pedagogy, texts, and extra-curricular activities that will be used in the classrooms.

3. **Embrace Students' Identity:** The curriculum must create space for students to enquire into their subjectivities, understand who they are and the place they hold in their community and in school.

4. **Teach Students How to Navigate the Society:** Children must be taught the gate-keeping points of the society so they can successfully get through the gate (Lisa Delpit, 2006).

5. **Collaborate With Students:** Teachers must embrace Freire's admonition that the journey must center on the foundation that students are not empty vessels; they must be regarded as collaborators who are equipped to exchange roles with the teacher in an environment where the teacher becomes the student and the student, the teacher.

CONCLUSION

Acknowledging Complicity: Pursuing Action for Change

It is important for our diverse student body to be engaged in pedagogy that acknowledges and integrates into the curriculum the actual historical, social, and cultural conditions that contribute to the forms of knowledge and meaning that they bring to school.

The educator who will lead classroom change must address her complicity in the failure of children in classrooms across the globe. This acknowledgement leads to the essential descent into one's inner realm needed as a precursor to the arduous journey into the struggle for social justice and the movement towards equity on behalf of children worldwide. I continue to aspire to uphold the challenge posed by my primary school teachers years ago as I search for methods of renewing myself and sustaining my practice with imaginative strategies. I especially enjoy the rich choreography of conversations about the transformative power of education with international scholars.

My work with youth from nondominant communities has emphasized the development of literacies in which every day and institutional literacies are reframed into powerful literacies oriented towards cultural heritage and intergenerational teaching; allowing students to look more critically at who they are and what they may become outside of the stereotypes crafted by society and face up to the inequities that push children into that fragile existence that would keep them vulnerable and hesitant to move forward.

A requirement of educational reform is the development of a critical consciousness. Without such a consciousness, educational leaders cannot begin the journey towards magnificence. The performance of our children continues to remind us of our failure. Successful educators recognize and acknowledge students' problems in schools, family, and the community. They acknowledge the value of implementing a curriculum based on culturally relevant pedagogy and inclusion.

Despite the questions that linger, I feel that together, the students at the three school sites and I were able to alter the official curriculum to create an alternative curriculum that opened up spaces for us to resist those mechanisms of social control and domination asserted by the administration and district. The socio-cultural and situated learning that evolved from our efforts in co-constructing the curriculum strengthened their capacity as learners to push beyond those borders into more meaningful learning where they acquired skills that would stay with them for a lifetime. As I reflect on my own experience as a young student, I truly believe that the classroom presents critical educators with an opportunity to assist children, who are by nature, unique and creative, to soar and attain great heights.

It is important for our diverse student body to be engaged in pedagogy that acknowledges and integrates into the curriculum the actual historical, social, and cultural conditions that contribute to the forms of knowledge and meaning that they bring to school. A positive classroom environment can help to orient children to the circumstances of their world and provide them with the space to develop and strengthen their identity. An educator concerned with closing the achievement gap can actively work on embracing all students into the classroom by incorporating strategies that will engage and empower them, particularly those who have been disempowered by the system. In this complex thing called schooling, the teacher must embrace the children into the village.

REFERENCES

Barcia, M. (2006, October). The usage of the colonial legal framework by 19th century Cuban slaves. [Taylor & Francis, Routledge.]. *Atlantic Studies*, *3*(2). doi:10.1080/14788810600875307

Boylorn, R. M., & Orbe, M. (2014). *Critical Auto-ethnography: Intersecting cultural identities in everyday lives*. Left Coast Press.

Broward County Schools. (n.d.). *Home*. Broward County Schools. https://www.browardschools.com/site/default.aspx?PageType=3&DomainID=14019&ModuleInstanceID=60855&ViewID=6446EE88-D30C-497E-9316-3F8874B3E108&RenderLoc=0&FlexDataID=292587&PageID=39081

Delpit, L. (2006). *Other people's children: Cultural conflict in the classroom*. New Press.

Delpit, L., & Dowdy, K. J. (2008). *The skin that we speak: Thoughts on language and culture in the classroom*. New Press.

Flores-Gonzales, N. (2003). *School kids/street kids: Identity development in Latino students*. Teachers College Press.

Freire, P. (1970). *Pedagogy of the oppressed*. Seabury Press.

Freire, P. (1993). *Pedagogy of the City*. Continuum.

Freire, P. (2005). *Teachers as cultural workers: Letters to those who dare to teach*. Westview Press.

Gay, G. (2000). *Culturally responsive teaching: Theory, research and practice*. Teachers College Press.

Gonzalez, N. Moll, L. & Amanti, C. (Eds.). (2005). Funds of knowledge: Theorizing practices in households, communities, and classrooms. Mahwah, NJ: Lawrence Erlbaum.

hooks, b. (1994). *Teaching to transgress: Education as the practice of freedom*. New York: Routledge.

Hughes, L. (1994). *The Dream keeper and other poems*. Alfred A. Knopf.

Johnson, A. M. (2019). *A walk in their kicks: Literacy, identity & the schooling of young Black males*. Teachers College Press.

Kaisary, P. (2023). *The Haitian revolution in literary imagination: Radical horizons Conservative constraints*. University of Virginia Press.

Kanu, Y. (2006). *Curriculum as cultural practice*. University of Toronto Press. doi:10.3138/9781442686267

Kelly, S. (2023). *Slavers: Merchants, mariners and the Transatlantic commerce in captives 1644-1865*. Yale University Press.

Kincheloe & Steinberg. (1997). *Changing multiculturalism*. Open University Press.

Ladson-Billings, G. (2009). *The dream- keepers: Successful teachers of African American children*. Jossey Bass.

McClean, M. (2019). *From the middle passage to Black lives matter: Ancestral writing as a pedagogy of hope*. New York: Peter lang.

McClean, M., & Waters, M. (2020). *Indigenous Epistemology: Descent into the womb of decolonized research methodologies*. Peter Lang.

Miami Dade Public Schools. (n.d.). https://www3.dadeschools.net/news/33613/details

National Center for Education Statistics. (NCES). (2022). *Public High School Graduation Rates*. https://nces.ed.gov/programs/coe/indicator/coi/high-school-graduation-rates

O'Neil, S. (2015). *Young People on the Drop Out Crisis*. Raise Up Project. www.raiseupproject.org.

Schon, D. (1983). *The reflective practitioner*. Basic Books.

Semali, L. M., & Kincheloe, J. (Eds.). (2002). *What is Indigenous Knowledge? Voices from the Academy*. Routledge. doi:10.4324/9780203906804

Stevenson, B. (2015). *What is slavery?* Polity Press.

Tuhiwai-Smith, L. (2012). *Decolonizing methodologies: Research and Indigenous peoples*. London & New York: Zed Books.

UNESCO. (2018). *Out of school Children & Youth*. https://uis.unesco.org/en/topic/out-school-children-and-youth

Chapter 2
The Politics of Literacy and Spirituality:
Crafting a Culture of Resistance to Enslavement

Anne Bouie
Independent Researcher, USA

ABSTRACT

Enslavement is indelibly etched in the historiography of the United States of America. In fact, it extends across the entire globe. This chapter asserts that it is the original content and continued context of the Black experience in America. In interrogating the dogma of racism and the extent to which it defined and has continued to define the characteristics distinguishing the free and the oppressed, this researcher acknowledges that race is not merely a social construct, it is the foundation for all of the political and economic systems on which this country is constructed. As the USA continues with the struggle to attain educational reform with the emphasis on the achievement gap that exists between white and Black students, this researcher interrogates the educational development and attainment of the enslaved Black population who were the ancestors of the Black and Brown children that the USA identifies as lagging behind the performance of white students. What are the historical factors that have led to this? Did the ancestors have access to education? What were the enslavers' response to the education of the enslaved? If education was denied all Black people, how did they navigate this particular form of oppression? What are the outcomes of this resistance against the denial of literacy? Did the ancestors create an alternative system of literacy? What were/are the outcomes of this alternative system and to what extent has this shaped and continues to shape the lives of Black/Brown school children today? Is there education beyond/outside of literacy? This chapter interrogates the journey of Africans and their descendants in their bid to attain literacy in a state antagonistic to this purpose.

DOI: 10.4018/978-1-6684-7379-5.ch002

THE HISTORICAL FLOW OF THE BLACK EXPERIENCE IN THE USA

Resistance was endemic and relentless at each phase of the process of enslavement.

This chapter places the state and outcomes of contemporary education as the historical flow of the Back experience. It considers the educational process and the outcomes during enslavement and creation of the Underground Literacy Movement. It examines the ideology and intentions of enslaved and free Africans and their descendants to attain literacy during and after enslavement. The findings reveal that the social, religious, spiritual, political and cultural constructs of enslaved people were not merely retentions, inadvertently remembered and incorporated from Africa, but components of a fully formed culture of opposition and resistance to enslavement that was not only defensive in nature, but proactive in outreach. The enslaved engaged in intentional action, both overt and covert, that engendered and sustained pre-emptive assaults that characterized enslavement as war.

Attaining the ability to read and write may be understood as an integral component of an ideology consisting of a multi-pronged repudiation and condemnation of the oppressive system enslavers established and maintained. Using the foundation of grounded theory as an analytical process, I identify the habits of mind and key content variables encompassed by the ideology of resistance to enslavement as reflected in the quest for and attainment of literacy.

An analysis of the characteristics of contemporary public and community-based schools and programs, this research reveals that ideals and strategies the enslaved used to combat oppression and attain literacy have journeyed throughout the centuries into the current struggle of Black and Brown children to attain education. In questioning whether or not there is any continuity in the ideology, methods, and premises of those who employed literacy as a weapon against enslavement and oppression, it was revealed that restructured forms of these methods are in place today, offering Black people, then and now, innovative methods of education that consolidates identity within an oppositional culture.

Through a repudiation of the conventional histography of enslavement derived primarily from plantation records, contemporary observations and accounts, slave autobiographies, and the Works Progress Administration (WPA) slave narratives, this researcher calls out the inaccuracy of the information presented and asserts the agency of the enslaved as is characterized by the ingenious ways they sought and attained literacy based on the resolve that it was a tool essential to one's navigation in a society that sought to keep them contained.

This body of primary sources, despite its appeal, is inadequate and does not tell the complete story. The narrative that characterizes enslavement as a hermetically sealed, all-encompassing, systematic oppression, with the enslaved having no control over their lives or their destinies, is a false one. Enslavers and the society they established was intended to be rigid, proscribed, and closed with absolute dominion over every sphere of the enslaved lives, accompanied with draconian prohibitions upon failure to generate wealth and profits from the forced labor wrested from captive bondspeople. In the attempt to degrade, debilitate and create a workforce with no sense of self, beaten down, and completely stripped of their humanity the enslavers depicted the enslaved as a docile, traumatized, and ignorant people who were engaged with, and in a benevolent system, which actually provided instruction and guidance. The conventional interpretation often preempts, denigrates, or ignores effective countermeasures, considered responses, intentional strategies and tactics, all grounded in a transcendent spirituality of the enslaved of this nation. Over the past decades, a revised characterization of enslaved Africans and their descendants has emerged to challenge the orthodoxy found in theory and practice. This has brought to the public attention, what was already known but not publicly stated: The existence of a counter Black culture, an intangible dynamic which challenged resisted white dominance every step of the way.

Research into every sphere of Black life and culture has challenged myths that are embedded into contemporary society. The material culture of enslaved folk and archeology have contributed new learning and findings that unequivocally dismiss assertions of inferiority, docility, and disregard of themselves as a people who needed to be told what to do and how to function. In particular, the desire for literacy, and the risks taken to achieve it give lie to any who would assert innate inferiority and lack of *high order thinking skills*.

Whether bursting open with individual and collective acts of public defiance, or silent subterfuge, resistance was endemic and relentless at each phase of the process of enslavement. It began with capture, festered along the trek by land or river to the coast, percolated during internment in the castles, erupted during the Middle Passage, and finally, embarked and established itself on new, foreign soil (Taylor, 2006). Contrary to the narrative of lost culture and psychic destruction, Blasingame (1972) and Young (2007) document that the culture and sensibilities of enslaved Africans were not lost during enslavement. It gives the lie to suggesting that such avatars as Harriet Tubman, Frederick Douglass, Ida. B. Wells, Sojourner Truth and others were the exception to the rule and were different from other enslaved people, as if they popped up from nowhere like mushrooms from the earth.

History supports the fact that all of these individuals were taught, nurtured, encouraged, and fostered. They emerged from an oppositional culture created by enslaved people. Indeed, without the quarters and the fields, hideaway churches, a grapevine that rivaled Western Union, whose foundation were rooted in Africa, it is safe to say that they were molded and nurtured into a culture of empowerment that posed a monumental resistance and subterfuge in response to enslavement.

The enslaved asserted a culture of empowerment that posed a monumental resistance and subterfuge in response to enslavement.

He maintained a set of hidden transcripts which facilitated communication, were proactive, offensive actions, and courage that took place outside, and frequently within the public purview. Scott (1992) notes that the enslaved engaged in a complex range of practices, perceptions, and modes of walking through the world as to constitute an alternate, oppositional culture that existed side-by-side with the public, allegedly dominant transcript, and, finally, the extreme importance of the invisible, yet permeable divide between public and hidden transcript was a multifaceted, intricate web of indefatigable, implacable, and under constant negotiation.

The time-honored public narrative that justified enslavement does not allow it to address or include the existence of the multilayered, multifaceted, hidden transcript that generated its own narrative, fostering cultural, spiritual, religious, poetical establishment of individual and collective autonomy. Young, (2007) observed that, over forty years ago, Sterling Stuckey demanded that sources from the lived experiences of the enslaved, including the aesthetics of visual art, song, dance, material culture, artifacts, and vernacular traditions be brought to public attention. This subaltern world of political and cultural conflict often left almost no trace in the public record.

Scott (1985) offers a way to examine the dynamics and operation of the subaltern culture-including its ideology and politics. He notes that this genre of politics represented the day-to-day counter attacks for most of the world's disenfranchised who lived in autocratic settings and oppressive systems of chattel enslavement. This was an oblique, carefully evasive politics that typically avoided obvious, overt risks; it was a method quite in keeping with the reputation of the peasantry and enslaved people whose actions were rooted in *cunning*.

Such politics, though made up of thousands of small acts, were of enormous aggregate consequence. These thousand acts of political resistance were typically disguised or covert, actions that were affirming, and typically a means of supplementing various aspects of their lives. Collectively, they became the soil and water from which an oppositional cultural expression, and spiritual autonomy were rooted in an African ethos transported to the New World. Scott (1985) observes that while all proactive agency, be it individual or collective, hidden insurgency, proactive agency and public defiance and challenges may not have directly challenged the institution of enslavement, they all nurtured solidarity among the enslaved and weakened the institution itself. More important, like rich humus and earth, they created an environment that nourished and encouraged resistance. They served as an invisible nest that incubated, nurtured and cultivated what became an oppositional culture lived under the very noises of attempted wholesale domination. Indeed, there may not have been a Harriet, Frédéric or Anderson, had they not been nurtured and fertilized by the rich loamy soil of *the thousand acts* which, served to thwart, and often neutralize the enslaver's definition of their personalities and character, and established the moral autonomy of the enslaved (Anderson, 1988).

STEAL AWAY, STEAL AWAY

Little did they know the song was used as an oral cue to meet at a selected sacred site for their secret brush arbor meetings.

The spiritual, Steal Away, Steal Away, encouraged the faithful to find quiet time to commune with their Creator. Enslavers loved the singing of the enslaved, taking it as an indicator of cheerfulness and contented satisfactions with being enslaved. Little did they know the song was used as an oral cue to meet at a selected sacred site for their secret brush arbor meetings. While everyone may have heard the song, only a select few knew where to go and how to get there. Legend has it that Harriet Tubman would sing it as she surreptitiously entered the area of a planned abduction of prepared freedom seekers ready to run. Christianity was subverted and reinterpreted to become a source of perseverance, affirmation of the justness of their case, vison and political strategy. The quest for literacy became a keystone in the arch of freedom. Among all Black people, but particularly among the enslaved, reading and writing were among the quintessential tools of resistance. In fact, literacy represented, and was experienced as not only functional, but self-affirming as well. Literacy was at the very heart of a frequently indiscernible oppositional culture nurtured in the quarters, a rich multifaceted oral, and vocal culture, and a spiritual life where, unbeknown to those who took piety and the *sorrow songs* literally.

The determination and fortitude of enslaved African Americans to educate themselves provided the most profound examples of the value antebellum Blacks placed on literacy. Despite the slave codes and harsh repercussions associated with a slave acquiring some degree of literacy, countless enslaved Blacks were willing to endure severe punishments, maiming, and even the possibility of losing their lives, to acquire even a rudimentary education. Laws, custom, and terror aside, enslaved people did indeed attain varying degrees of literacy during the years before the Civil War. Literacy revealed worlds beyond the proscribed walls of tyranny, and enabled even more proactive tactics for the enslaved. In addition to a profound oral traditional of folk literature, proverbs, and teaching stories, literacy was yet another means of resistance, giving them the ability to oppose oppression in ways that complemented and affirmed their strategies of resistance. Literacy afforded the means to write passes to freedom, to complement the underground grapevine and learn of abolitionist activities-as well as dangers and plan to thwart them.

As it was not wise to let enslavers know that one was literate, it is not far-fetched to speculate that the acknowledged ten percent of enslaved persons who were indeed literate could be easily doubled, it is not unreasonable to suggest that there was probably at least one literate enslaved person on every plantation in the South, or close enough to be accessed by the enslaved community. The values and ideology that undergirded the enslaved's determination were covert assaults, autonomy, defiance, and self-direction. Over time, these individual, yet wide-spread defiance and intentions evolved into an ideology that challenged and refuted the ideas of white supremacy.

Enslaved Blacks were willing to endure severe punishments, maiming, and even the possibility of losing their lives, to acquire even a rudimentary education

The necessity to *steal away* and learn in the secret places fostered not only literacy, but solidarity and the makings of trust networks that could be used for other purposes. The very act of learning in secret undermined the enslaver-enslaved relationship, puncturing enslavers' efforts to establish tentacles of invasion and control in the lives of the enslaved. Another aspect of the hidden, private life among the enslaved proved to serve not only the literate, but their community as well. Once literate, many used this hard-won skill *to trouble the waters* as the desire for literacy fused with, and nurtured the desire for freedom. Black people saw it as a duty to teach other enslaved people. Parents instilled in the offspring that, although learning to read and write required great risk, courage and stealth, that freedom would be their just reward. Interestingly, fewer owner-taught slaves assumed leadership careers after slavery. *Stealing* their own learning and obtaining subsequent leadership positions suggests that certain talented slaves acted effectively upon their belief in the liberating quality of learning to read (Cornelius, 1983, Givens, 2021).

FUGITVE PEDAGOGY: NARRATIVES OF SUBVERSION

dem who had some learning would teach the others

This secrecy meant that essential aspects of Black education have always occurred underground; Tessie McGee hid her textbook by Carter G. Wooden under a desk. Richard Parker of Virginia, hid his copy of Websters Blueback Speller under his hat. Mandy Jones recollected books being hidden in pits under the earth, far out in the woods surrounding the Mississippi plantation where she labored. This is what Givens characterizes as fugitive pedagogy; a veiled educational world of substance and form, nurtured minds and souls (Givens, 2021).

In Georgia, Susie King Taylor accessed an intricate web of clandestine schooling where, after moving to Savannah, she learned in secret with a fluid group of teachers in assorted locations, times and days. The state of Georgia and Savannah itself made teaching enslaved and free people to read and write punishable by whips, jail and even death. Each afternoon, Susie and twenty-five other children would carry schoolbooks disguised as paper, and slip, one at a time into the home of a Ms. Susan Woodhouse, a free black woman. After two years she then went to Ms. Mary Beasley's home; subsequently she learned from a white playmate and the son of her white landlord

Williams (2005), reveals the ingenuity of the enslaved in securing the tools of literacy. Rural bondswoman Mandy Jones knew of a young man who stole away to a cave to learn to read and write. Others would dig pits in the ground, covered with vines and bushes; fugitives sometimes inhabited those same pits, but they also served as schools. As the numbers of literate members increased in the quarters, folks would slip out of the quarters at night to engage in teaching and learning. Ann Stokes' cousin taught her the alphabet "in the middle of a field underneath a 'simmon tree." Edmond Carlisle A literate man in South Carolina, would cut blocks from pine bark and worked them until he had himself a slate; he used oak, soaked it in water, frequently used for dye, to make ink, and used a thin stick for a pencil (Williams, 2005).

Fathers also figured as teachers, even when they did not live with their families. Anderson Whitted's father, for example, lived fourteen miles away from him, but was allowed to use a horse to visit him. He taught Anderson to read on his biweekly visits. "The children in Henry Bruce's family shared the knowledge learned from their white playmates. The older one would teach the younger, and while mother had no education at all, she used to make the younger study the lessons given by the older sister or brother, and in that way we all learned to read and some to write" (Willems, 2005, p. 23).

Following Emancipation, formerly enslaved people recalled the roles played by literate slaves in the spread of the news of the war and the coming of freedom. Literate enslaved folk made it a prime responsibility to help other slaves. Milla Granson, who learned to read and write in Kentucky, was relocated to Natchez where she established a midnight school and taught hundreds of fellow slaves to read. In Georgia, for example, Minnie Davis' mother stole newspapers during the war and kept the other slaves posted as to the war's progress. Cora Gillam's uncle was jailed until the Union soldiers came because he had a newspaper with the latest war news and gathered a crowd of fellow Mississippi slaves to read them when peace was coming (Cornelius, 1983). Enslaved people who could not read often furnished newspapers, pamphlets, and broadsides stolen or purchased by other slaves to distribute to those who could read.

Those who could read maps could also include the locations of caves, groves of wild fruit and berries, hiding pits, and trails invisible to the ordinary eye.

It is not implausible that literate enslaved teachers did more than simply teach their students, more than simply read; what was the good of the skill if it were not used to foster not only self-respect and independence, but as a functional tool to escape bondage? Those who could read maps could also include the locations of caves, groves of wild fruit and berries, hiding pits, and trails invisible to the ordinary eye. They also most certainly would have had knowledge of the location of safe houses, signs and symbols communicating relevant messages in plain sight. (Bouie, 2021). Among other selected endurance practices on the farm or planation were absconding with livestock, appropriating all manner of food stored in pantries and barns, and often selling these or vegetables they raised to people on the underground economy.

Reading the bible for personal salvation and liberation was a significant motivation for the formerly enslaved o gain literacy (Span, 2005). The bible became a political tool that nourished the soul and the mind. It must have been lost on enslavers that, so like many others who used the Bible for their own ends, citing such passages as "slaves obey your masters" and " thou shall not steal," were contained in the same book, in the same language of Moses successfully challenging Pharoah, and set his people free, or of Daniel emerging from the fiery furnace with nary a hair even shingled, and of David's five smooth stones which took down Goliath himself, the most feared warrior in the known world, and poignantly, "those who survived the sword found grace in the wilderness" (King James Bible, Jeremiah 31:2) because they knew that enslavers would never believe that they actually followed these secret teachings.

The acquisition of literacy played a crucial role in the revolt led by Nat Turner. Turner was, an enslaved man who, from early childhood was told by his mother that he was born to do "great things." His development of his spiritual and psychic powers, were fueled by his knowledge and re-interpretation of the King James Bible. Turner used the Bible as recruiting tool, showing the converted actual passages affirming freedom, using these passages as text for hidden sermons. In planning the rebellion, he and other literate Blacks also recruited conspirators. Indeed, the knowledge that literate Blacks were deeply involved in the revolt prompted legislation forbidding free and enslaved Blacks to be taught to read and write.

ARCHEOLOGICAL EVIDENCE SUPPORTS SUBVERSION

These artifacts bear witness to literacy among the enslaved

Archaeological findings also reveal evidence of the enslaved mastering letters. Pencil leads, pencil slates, writing slates, and, to a lesser extent, unidentified slates have been found at several sites excavated in the Tidewater and Piedmont regions of the Chesapeake (Fountain, 1995). In the Richneck Quarter in York County, for example, three writing slates and three unidentified slates were uncovered. Similarly, in the Palace Lands Quarter in York County, one writing slate and eight unidentified slates were excavated. One might surmise that the eight slates belonged to eight different people, and suggest the notions of secrecy, solidarity and study by a small cell operating under a public cover of masquerade, accommodation and compliance while maneuvering covertly with stealth, dissemblance and deception. Archaeologists have also unearthed one unidentified slate at the slave site at the Governor's Land estate in James City County. Identical artifacts were found at George Washington's Tidewater plantation. At his estate in Mount Vernon, one unidentified slate was discovered in the first president's slave quarters.

Particularly compelling are the artifacts unearthed at the slave quarter sites at Thomas Jefferson's estate at Monticello. There 237 unidentified slates, 27 pencil leads, 2 pencil slates, and 18 writing slates were uncovered in houses once occupied by Jefferson's Black bond servants. In **Free Some Day**, Lucia Stanton (2001) took these writing slates in slave quarters as evidence of enslaved Virginians' reading and writing. In her view, evidence "unearthed in archaeological excavations below Mulberry Row attests to the hunger for education at Monticello. The writers probably had only the hours of darkness to practice [their] letters and found a piece of locally available stone that saved the purchase of pen and paper (p. 33).

Much like runaway notices that appeared in the Virginia Gazette and in other colonial newspapers, these artifacts bear witness to literacy among the enslaved. Indeed, as this archaeological evidence shows, the ideology, even at basic levels, emphasizes nurture, trust, interdependence, care, autonomy and assuming responsibility for furthering the learning of not just the individual, but the community as a whole. Whether the enslaved chose to study as a gathering, or steal away into the wilderness, the enslaved engaged in literacy, learning and practicing letters, passing it on to others as an essential part of the underground system they had so connivingly created to mask their subterfuge from the enslavers.

CIRCLE OF SUPPORT

Trust was formed, souls were affirmed, minds were fed

While held in physical bondage, the collective served to create a womb of spiritual and psychological freedom that affirmed the humanity and value of the individual and the collective. Enslaved people were ensconced in the womb of the quarters where they were molded from birth in an educational process articulated and managed by the quarters. Like other elements of the oppositional culture that evolved from African roots, this was functional to the enslaved in ways that differed from enslavers and even free Blacks. It was a tool of forming an identity that belied public posturing. It was a tool that insulated them and enabled them to not merely survive, but prevail over conscious, deliberate attempts to render them soulless, helpless and hopeless. Literacy, particularly under the circumstances, created bonds of community that would not be broken. Trust was formed, souls were elevated. Anderson, (1988) astutely observed that, though enslaved people were physically constrained, their minds and souls were not. Anderson asserts the same when he cogently observes that there was no way enslavement did not affect, and often inflected life-long physical and spiritual scars, this did not affect their humanity and the reality that enslavers could not control Black minds.

The battle for literacy, education and freedom by African-Americans, reminds one of Malcom X who said, "The battle is fought on many fronts " (Goodman, 2015). The campaign for literacy and self-definition went from study under persimmon trees, and stealth in the dark of night to the establishment of literacy to institutions where Blacks studied the classics. Over time, their efforts reflected the true substance of the contribution of African-Americans, not merely to their own country, but the world.

A NATION AGAINST BLACK LITERACY

Black people took it upon themselves to progress. A top priority was their children's educational needs.

The South was not alone in restricting access to education. Nearly every Northern state that provided free common schooling established a two-track system: one for its white students and one for its Negroes. In the early nineteenth century, local school committees throughout New England frequently assigned Black children to separate institutions, no matter where they might live. Despite the attempts to constrain the educational journey of Black people, throughout the nation, Black people took it upon themselves to progress. A top priority was their children's educational needs.

Reflecting a concern about the steady stream of fugitives arriving in the state, Connecticut forbade establishing any educational facility for nonresident African Americans. Colonial and antebellum New York authorized the segregation of white and Black students, in response to which, African Americans established a small number of private schools known as African Free Schools. The state offered no support for these schools until 1824 (Litwack,1961; Span, 2005). Michigan and Wisconsin, assigned students to African American institutions, regardless of the district where they lived. Black people in the North experienced more autonomy and openness in the quest for literacy. In 1831, delegates at The Convention of Colored Men, supported by white abolitionists William Lloyd Garrison, Artur Tappen and others, proposed establishing a college on the manual labor system in New Haven. The white citizenry was fervently opposed to providing higher education for African Americans, with the notion of post-secondary education being particularly upsetting. The city's political leaders went as far as to assert that a college to educate Black people would be incompatible with the prosperity, if not the very existence, of Yale College and other institutions, and vowed to use every lawful means possible to halt the establishment of a Black institution (Williams, 2005). Efforts by a white Quaker school teacher to establish a boarding school for Black girls were halted after angry white residents set the occupied school on fire, while vandalizing it with clubs and iron bars.

Pennsylvania and Ohio provided segregated schooling for African American children. Blacks in Michigan and Wisconsin waited until after the Civil War to gain access to state-sponsored schooling. Indiana, Illinois and Kansas passed legislation barring or circumscribing free Blacks access to formal educational. Pennsylvania like Massachusetts, provided for all children, Yet, even these pro-abolitionists established unwritten rules of requiring district school directors, if possible, to provide separate educational facilities for African-Americans (Span, 2005).

Similarly, antebellum free Blacks in the cities of Buffalo and Troy, New York, and Boston, Massachusetts, achieved comparable educational successes. In 1837, the five hundred Black residents in Buffalo had two churches and two private schools to accommodate their educational needs. They too had a literary and debating society, and collectively these Black residents had a net worth of approximately $100,000 in property and other assets. Also in this year, Troy's 990 free Black residents independently maintained three churches, two private schools, two Sabbath schools, one literary society, one debating society, four moral-reform societies, and two temperance societies (Porter, 1995).

Establishing and running schools was often fraught with danger in the North. Many served fugitives who, in addition to the need for food, shelter, and safe passage, also sought to read and write. In several large cities, Vigilant Committees, often secret, were established to serve and protect. While establishing public meetings, writing pamphlets and serving those in need, many had secret factions who brought surveillance, subterfuge and weapons to the struggle. They were instrumental in establishing safety under duress (Olsavsky, 2019; 2022).

CRAFTING THE FRAMEWORK: THE IDEOLOGY OF ENSLAVEMENT IN LAW, IN ACADEMIA, THE MEDIA AND THE STREETS

Formerly enslaved people shook off the shackles of bondage with a near sacred belief in the necessity to learn to read and write.

Antiliteracy laws targeting Black people predated the formation of the United States. For approximately the first 250 years of the African American experience (1619-1865), every American colony and later state, prohibited or stridently restricted teaching free and enslaved African Americans even the rudiments of literacy. Williams (2005), noted there was no coherent platform articulating the pro-slavery position. Likewise, before the American Revolution, anti-slavery societies began to emerge in the Northern states. Pennsylvania's Abolition Society was established in 1775. In the early 1800s, the Protestant religious movement known as the Second Great Awakening added religious zeal to abolitionist advocacy and helped fuel the rise of numerous anti-slavery organizations.

States and legislators set against the abolition of slavery and the freedom of Black people, held rigidly to the perspective that Black people should not be allowed to learn to read and write.

The colonial legislature outlawing the teaching of writing (Span, 2005), South Carolina had already acknowledged that earlier laws had been insufficient to keep Blacks in their subordinate state. The legislature broadened the scope of unlawful activity and the categories of people included. Any assembly of slaves, free negroes, mulattoes and mestizos among themselves or with white people for the purposes of "mental instruction" constituted an unlawful meeting and would be treated as such. In addition to defining writing as mental instruction, memorization, arithmetic, reading and writing were also prohibited. While the earlier laws had included teaching only the enslaved, the new law outlawed free Black people as well. Lawmakers instructed all officials to enter at will, and destroy property in the capture of rebels, and each person of color was to receive up to twenty lashes as corporal punishment.

Close study suggests that while the South may have lost the war; it won the battle for a conceptual framework and sociopolitical systems and institutions intent on continuing the oppression of the formerly enslaved. The ideology and accompanying propaganda it created not only withstood the Civil War and Reconstruction, it served as the basis for structured, institutionalized policy, programs practice and practice based on one characteristic: The color of one's skin.

In spite of this, Reconstruction brought initiative and opportunity to African-Americans, who made significant advances establishing schools, building and maintaining, paying teachers, establishing boards to oversee schools and hiring principals and teachers to staff them.

The intangible aspects of Black education, its conceived purpose, transmission, curriculum, beliefs and values are the essential elements that led to its effectiveness and engagement. This educational movement began before northern benevolent societies entered the South in 1862, the Emancipation Proclamation of 1863, and the establishment of the Freedmen's Bureau in 1865. Formerly enslaved and freepersons, pooling money, materials and labor, had already begun teaching their own, and making plans for systematic instruction. Early *native* schools in rural areas and cities were largely supported and established through African Americans' own initiative (Bush, 2004).

In 1865, John Alvord was appointed inspector of schools for the Freedmen's Bureau (Anderson, 1988). Alvord traveled through-out the Southern states and found what he called native schools; common schools formed and maintained exclusively by African Americans. Many of these schools were in the interior of Southern states and had never been seen by whites before Alvord. Alvord estimated in his report to the Freedmen's Bureau in 1866 that more than 500 native schools were operating in the South (Anderson, 1988).

The Sabbath school system was largely Black dominated, relied on local Black communities for support, and generally had all Black faculties and administrators. In some instances, they were the only viable system of free instruction available to Black people. He reported that Sabbath schools "have opened throughout the entire South, providing basic instruction and reaching literally thousands of anxious learners who could not attend during the week. Large schools gathered on Sunday, sometimes with hundreds of people, dressed in newly shined shoes, go-to-meeting-dresses and hats, newly braided hair, sitting in rows, eager for instruction (p.53). Alvord reported that the management of the schools was impressive, with faithful teachers, the majority of whom were from the communities where they served.

Ex-slave Charlotte Stephens began teaching as a substitute teacher in Little Rock when she was fifteen. She was hired permanently when a teacher from the North failed to return for the new school year. She recalled problems in obtaining books in those early years. Aspiring Black people responded with creativity. Stephens reported that, "Pupils came desiring to learn and they brought whatever books they could find: almanacs, paper back novels, ancient dictionaries missing half their pages" (p. 3).

Formerly enslaved people shook off the shackles of bondage with a near sacred belief in the necessity to learn to read and write. Just as they had been proud of those who pulled one over, appropriated food,, hid some runaways, look one of them dead in the eye, while lying through his teeth, and those who followed that North star on to freedom, they were proud of their kinspeople when they spoke of those who had become literate and the great esteem in which they held literate free and former bondsmen (Givens, 2021).

Though not included in formal reports sent to governmental agencies, Alvord requested estimates of enrollment and faculty. The reports would obviously be conservative; many schools, particularly in rural areas would be unknown and uncounted. Even so, the reports found 1,552 Sabbath schools across the South, with 6,146 teachers and an enrollment of 107,109 students. In 1868, the AME church reported an additional 40,000 students in Sabbath schools; by 1885, enrollment was reported at 200,000 students. Though held on Sundays, Booker T. Washington himself recollected that the principal book studied in the Sabbath schools was the spelling book. Clearly these schools were yet another means of a free people seeking to institute, establish and sustain their own schools (Anderson, 1988).

In the years following 1869, African Americans stood virtually alone in the fight for universal public education. During this time in the South, public education for African Americans and whites was basically nonexistent. Formerly enslaved activists, along with their free brothers and sisters, struggled for schooling for over two decades before the Populist campaigns of the late 1880s and 1890s. The ex-slaves' campaign also predated the organized movement for free schooling by southern middle-class progressives. The South's white middle classes, unorganized and sub- servient to planter interests throughout the 19th century, did not begin their campaign for universal education until the dawn of the twentieth century (Anderson 1988). The establishment of the public school system representing one of the lasting benefits and positive accomplishments of governments organized under the Congressional plan of Re- construction has been attested to by a number of reputable scholars of the period. Thomas Miller, one of the six Negro delegates to the South Carolina constitutional convention of 1895, listed as one benefit derived by the state from Reconstruction government the building and maintaining of school houses (Anderson, 1988).

According to Dorothy Porter (1936), northern and southern free Black leaders recognized the necessity and expediency of education given the group's limited and insecure existence in the American social order. Throughout the nation, various welfare, temperance, Bible, moral reform, and educational societies, established by and for free Blacks, catered to the group's educational expectations at a time when the nation was withdrawing or restricting its efforts regarding African American education. For more than employment purposes, education was to render free Blacks "useful to society and acceptable to God," eradicate the notion of them as "indolent and shiftless" people, and "replace idleness and intemperance" with "good taste and manners" (Porter, 1995, p.79-80). In 1834, the Reverend Joseph M. Corr of Philadelphia affirmed this sentiment in his Fourth of July oration before the Humane Mechanic's Society of Philadelphia. Corr regarded education as the "means whereby the shackles of ignorance may be unriveted, and man be qualified for usefulness in all the pursuits of life; for knowledge is light - knowledge is power" (Span, 2005, p. 35).

Though the chains which controlled Black bodies were very real, try as they might, whites could not control Black minds.

Home- grown leadership was a core value, and essential in the counterattack inherent in Black educational ideology. The underground literacy network needed and begat leadership that often transitioned after enslavement into those who would guide and direct newly created schools, both public and private. The values of self-help and self-determination underscored the desire for autonomy. Self-reliance was accompanied by a profound desire to control and sustain schools for their children and the larger community. Newly unbound and free Black people acknowledged the need for assistance and support from missionaries and philanthropists, but insisted on no interference and control from outsiders. Though the chains which controlled Black bodies were very real, try as they might, whites could not control Black minds. These were molded from birth in an educational program managed by the quarter community. While still legally slaves, women, and children of the quarter community successfully accessed psychological freedom and celebrated their human dignity (Cornelius, 1978). The struggle for education was an expression of freedom. Free schools and churches were the guardians of civic and religious freedom, and the prerogative to worship, learn and organize as one saw fit and appropriate.

From the Native schools, free schools, homeschooling, and subterfuge, bush arbor schools, Sabbath schools, and school houses were established and sustained with Black people, many formerly enslaved, at the helm. Schools and the ministry were at the forefront, and served as the training grounds to produce a generation of competent, savvy leaders who negotiated hostile, obstructing territory where Black people had suffered for centuries with inadequate funding, a lack of books and supplies along with intrusive and often patronizing interference by white leadership who wanted to lead and shape Black schools.

Many enslaved persons took the initiative to learn any way they could. Some paid teachers to teach them; one former bondsman said he never went to school; white people taught him to read and write. The ex-slave obtained schooling from a variety of sources other than those offered by the Freedmen's Bureau. Schools for freed bondspeople, especially children, were established in towns and on plantations. A former Confederate general hired a teacher from Iowa, and he provided education for hundreds of freedmen from two plantations. The Pioneer School of Freedom opened in 1860 in New Orleans; Mary Peak opened her school in Fortress Monroe, Virginia in 1861; a Black school in Savanah had been operating clandestinely since 1833; its founder, commenced to expand during and after the war (Anderson, 1988). As early as 1863, around 400 children were attending schools in Alexandria, Virginia; in 1867, Camden, Arkansas, the Black community had established twenty-two schools with an enrollment of more than 4,000 students. Responsible committees were organized to personnel, secure supplies and run the schools (Span, 2005).

For a people who generally were not allowed to read or write or attend school, formerly enslaved citizens made significant advances during Reconstruction.

The Freedmen's Schools gave Black children a significant start. Several slave narratives indicate that the ex-slaves attended these first schools. Apparently by far the majority of those who attended school with some degree of regularity completed only a few terms. Evidence suggests that the ex-slave was probably a victim of economic necessity and the rural character of the state. The closing of the school system that occurred under the post-Reconstruction regime affected primarily those few ex-slaves who could afford the time to attend. For a people who generally were not allowed to read or write or attend school, formerly enslaved citizens made significant advances during Reconstruction. By 1890 the literacy rate among ten years old or older was 46 percent. Only three states had a higher percentage of newly literate citizens. Oklahoma reported 61per cent, Florida, 49.5 percent, and Texas at 47.5 per cent (Nash1989). Regretfully, these percentages are higher than today's African-American students are achieving. According to the National Assessment of Educational Progress (NAEP), a sector of the U.S. Department of Education, 84 percent of Black students lack proficiency in mathematics and 85 percent of Black students lack proficiency in reading skills (Education Trust, 2015).

By 1866, just a year after the Civil War ended, various aid societies under Freedmen's Bureau were providing schools. The Society of Friends (Quakers) was one of those societies that established schools in Arkansas (Bush, 2004). The signing of the Emancipation Proclamation by President Abraham Lincoln brought wave after wave of Northern white missionaries to the South with the intent of setting up schools for African Americans. However, to their astonishment (Anderson, 1988), they found formerly enslaved Africans who had already established schools that were staffed, financed, and controlled entirely by African Americans. And where there were no schools, these white missionaries were further surprised by the will of the formerly enslaved Africans to educate themselves. Books or fragments of books were seen in the hands of African American men, women, and children everywhere they traveled in the South (Anderson, 1988; Bush, 2004).

After the Freedmen's Bureau withdrew its support, freed people took control of the schools and transformed federal schools into local free schools. The Louisiana Educational Relief Association believed it to be their responsibility to provide education for its children.

They were thrilled with the opportunity to imprint their image upon the nearly four million souls unyoked from enslavement. "We can make them all that we desire them to be" (Litwack, 1980, p.179) which translated into assuming ta dominant role in leadership, and inserting themselves into the most intimate spheres of life: family relations, moral responsibility, self-reliance, frugality, and sobriety, along with the virtues of self-reliance (Litwack, 1980).

The reaction of the white missionaries to the thrust for African American independence went from being one of surprise to outright indignation and resentment. White missionaries experienced cognitive dissonance, because they expected to find tractable and helpless formerly enslaved Africans in desperate need of their aid and full of gratitude. Instead, they found African Americans who preferred sending their children to schools established and maintained in and by their own community rather than the less expensive white schools. The steadfast plans to establish and maintain control over schools and other institutions brought them into conflict with their white benefactors. Black demands for control and autonomy were usually muted or veiled by aid societies, who preferred to picture their charges as docile. Nonetheless, evidence exists suggesting that the freedmen intended to extend their independence from whites.

Missionaries confronted the reality that self-teaching and what John Alvord called "native schools" were to be found throughout the entire South, and that many of these efforts were in locations where no missionary-Black or white, or the Freedman's Bureau, and northern benevolent societies had ever set foot. The schools were found in all the middling to large local communities and way into the rural interior as well. Alvord's field agents reported that, in 1866, there were at least 500 schools of this sort already in operation throughout the region (Williams, 2005).

Enthusiastic northern teachers were taken aback to discover that some Blacks preferred to teach in, and operate their own schools without the benefit of northern largess. Formerly enslaved people, as a rule, initiated and supported education for their communities and its children and stridently repelled external control of home-grown established and nurtured educational institution. An edition of the 1867 Freedman's Record lamented that unshackled African-Americans preferred sending their children to Black-controlled private schools rather than supporting the less expensive northern white dominated free schools (Litwak,1979).

African-Americans were intent on their role and adequacy in providing for their own. In 1866, the official newspaper of the African-American Georgia Educational Association, The Loyal Georgian, felt it necessary to clarify the work being done to educate formerly enslaved bondspeople. While it did defend Northern teachers, some of whom were guarded by cadres of armed Black men against southern criticism, it chided missionary teachers lest they come to the South "in any vein reliance on their superior gifts, either of benevolence or intelligence, or any foolish self-confidence that they have a special call to this office, or special endowments to meet its demands" (Anderson, 1988, p. 11).

Self-help and racial solidarity became increasingly popular among Blacks as discrimination and the failure to obtain basic human and civil rights by agitation and protest became apparent. In all phases of life, behind the bulwark of segregation, the majority of Blacks had come to believe in the necessity of binding together and building counter- parts to white institutions-whether cultural, welfare, religious, political, economic or educational. By the last decade of the 1800s, the main theme of Black thought in Louisiana on the race question was that for the most part Blacks must work out their own salvation in a hostile environment. Black educators and parents saw a tremendous gap to be bridged if they were ever going to step into or challenge the social, political, or educational structure of the state. Many recognized that there were significant problems which the state educational leaders were ignoring.

For contemporary educators, the educational history of antebellum African Americans represents an alternative ontology to consider when discussing American slavery, the African American response to this "peculiar institution," and the unrelenting reverence African Americans - enslaved or free - maintained toward literacy and schools. Despite the societal conditions or restrictions imposed upon them, free and enslaved African Americans' sheer determination in acquiring an education illustrated the group's historic fortitude, ability, and appreciation of learning, freedom, and universal self-improvement (Span,2005).

THE TRIUMPH OF BLACK FOLK

The fugitive slave was the bedrock theme of Black classroom content.

In addition to autonomy, self-help, homegrown leadership and service, freed people wanted control over the content, instructional materials and strategies used in their schools. These people saw themselves not as missionaries, but as people on a mission that would be accomplished in the face of inequity, neglect, doubt and disdain. The themes of the curriculum developed by Black folk began during enslavement reflected the ideology of self-determination and resistance and continued in the post slavery environment. The fugitive slave was the bedrock theme of Black classroom content. Given the backlash and push back from the powers that be during and after enslavement, we can assume they hit a nerve and were recognized as a threat to the existing order. After enslavement, Reconstruction, the terror of post Reconstruction, and the establishment of Black schools to teach agriculture and domestic skill based on the Hampton and Tuskegee models of vocational education designed to educate a workforce for northern and southern industrialists, the dual system of separate but equal was entrenched in not only the South, but the North as well.

Laws, the threat of dismemberment and death, or the efforts to prove their inferiority did not . deter them. The formerly enslaved focused on their faith based upon the re-interpretation of scriptures, oral traditions, and community developed in the quarters. This was manifested in the establishment and maintaining of the schools they built, the principals and teachers they hired and the curriculum they taught. In choosing their own teachers, they patently refused efforts to usurp control, leadership, and what was taught. Litwack (1979, p. 460) refers to Thomas Wentworth Higgins, a missionary who had commanded a Black regiment during the Civil War who observed that, "the enslaved worship." He concluded, "in retrospect, we abolitionists had underrated the suffering produced by slavery, but had overrated their demoralization."

Formerly enslaved and freepersons, pooling money, materials and labor had already begun teaching their own, and making plans for systematic instruction. Early native schools in rural areas and cities were largely established staffed and supported through African Americans' own initiative.

The first textbooks written by Black Americans were written by fugitives successfully escaping enslavement. James W. C. Pennington, a blacksmith, authored, *A Text Book on the Origins and History of the Colored People* in 1841. Pennington produced a Black counternarrative asserted against mainstream historians, such as Noah Webster, who, in 1843, wrote the first dictionary for the nation, asserted that Black people had no history.

In contrast, Pennington began a new tradition that challenged the existing order. He was concerned that his people suffered from the lack of a collection of facts so focused on bringing the true history of the Black experience in the USA to light. Later, he was joined by Frederick Douglas, Harriet Jacobs, and others. (Givens, 2021, p. 127). Enslaved men and women who absconded from enslavement were among the first in the Black intellectual tradition which countered the tradition of focusing upon Black enslavement and suffering the response. Instead, they focused on the oppositional culture whose ideology was founded on resistance, assertion of selfhood, competence and serving the collective. There is a reverberation through time and space connecting Pennington's text book and the narratives proclaiming freedom. This exploration of key themes in textbooks was published and grounded in the understanding that they were part of the cornerstone in the pedagogy of Black teachers and their curriculum (Givens, 2021). After the Civil War, Black teachers and schools continued the tradition of honoring those who had defied and testified of their escape. The textbooks they wrote celebrated the lives of formerly enslaved escapees, Black insurrectionists such as Nat Turner, the Louisiana revolt of 1811, and others.

Like John Henry, Brer rabbit, and the spider, the fugitive became a powerful symbol beating the odds with their trickery. Slyness, e.g., hiding reading books under a hat, rotating homes as sites for teaching, preaching one thing here and another there. Like Moses leading the people of Israel through the wilderness, they faced many trials on their journey, while keeping their eyes on the goal. Archetypes were celebrated including John Henry whose strength and determination was celebrated as legendary. John Henry evolved into an archetype of strength, pride and the man whose work determined whether any railroad would be built. Like John Henry, the Fugitives, like Douglass, Tubman, Jacob, Pennington and others became avatars of symbols of the quest for freedom and autonomy; for self-determination and autonomy (Givens, 2021).

Texts written by Black school teacher between the late nineteenth century and early twentieth century, actually preceded Carter G. Woodson's first textbook, which included extensive material on formerly enslaved fugitives, including the Maroons of Dismal Swamp, and insurrections -large and small by enslaved persons (Apthacker, 1983).

African-American authors observed that while white history and texts omitted not only the mere existence, but the acts of Nat Turner, Denmark Vesey, and others, their stories persisted. Though silenced by mainstream history, the 1811 revolt in Louisiana brought over 500 people, with over 50 languages among them, was inspired by the victory of Africans in gaining their freedom in Haiti had a powerful and stimulating effect on Africans held in bondage all over the world, especially in the Western Hemisphere. It gave enormous encouragement to the Africans on plantations in Louisiana. Some of the leaders were captured, placed on trial and later executed. Their heads were cut off and placed on poles along the river in order to frighten and intimidate the other slaves. This display of heads placed on spikes stretched over 60 miles. Their protractive resistance over many years and lifetimes (Givens, 2021).

THE EARLY ORIGINS OF EDUCATIONAL JUSTICE ACTIVISM

In traditional Black education, teachers strategically select or develop instructional approaches that facilitate student learning.

From the Native schools, free schools, homeschooling, and subterfuge, bush arbor schools, Sabbath schools, and school houses were established and sustained with

Black people, many formerly enslaved, at the helm. Schools and the ministry were at the forefront, and served as the training grounds to produce a generation of competent, savvy leaders who negotiated hostile, obstructing territory where Black people had suffered for with inadequate funding, a lack books and supplies along with intrusive and often patronizing allows who attached strings to the largess; often at the expense of Black Educational Councils and site level leadership deemed "not the kind of Negro" wanted to lead and shape black schools.

In North Carolina and Virginia, teachers were developing supplementary materials for students in Chicago, Houston, New York and New Orleans during the 1930's and 40's that elevated The Fugitive, Overture and others.-On the Sea Islands of Georgia, Charlotte Grimke (1983) insisted that newly freed children "should know what one of their own color had done for his race" (p. 11). She declared that Black people were historical and political actors, and as such, she supplemented the curriculum with material that included such figures as Toussaint L'Overture and the revolution in Haiti (Givens 2021).

Education was perceived as the primary tool for free humanity, merit, and capabilities in an American society as slaves or inferior people (Williams, 1985). In traditional Black education, teachers strategically select or develop instructional approaches that facilitate student learning. Such approaches acknowledge, respect, and build upon student learning propensities, cognitive schema, experiential backgrounds and perceptions in order to provide equitable access to learning. Schools were intended to be institutions that informed African American youth of their precarious societal statuses; they were to assist freeborn African American children in learning the literacy skills necessary for combating discrimination, segregation, and slavery in adulthood; and they were expected to aid African Americans in acquiring equality, or at least some degree of social mobility.

RESEARCH & REFLEXIVITY

Is education the vehicle to combat racism and second-class citizenship?

As I looked back and wondered, I tried to get at the essence of just what was going on in those schools. Especially what with the present-day state of Black education becoming a historical reversal that is not even a shadow of the long-established legacy of educational and cultural and spiritual excellence that generations of African-Americans established. This was a legacy forged in oppression, nurtured and sustained against efforts to dehumanize, and bore fruit in the oppositional culture to challenge and resistance. In reality, enslavement was a ceaseless, protracted, all-encompassing war on every front of the human experience. For African-Americans, education was a spiritual salve as well as a political and economic tool.

Despite the societal conditions or restrictions imposed upon them, free and enslaved African Americans' sheer determination in acquiring an education illustrated the group's historical fortitude, ability, and appreciation of learning, freedom, and universal self-improvement. For contemporary educators, the educational history of antebellum African Americans represents an alternative ontology to consider when discussing American slavery, the African American response to this "peculiar institution," and the unrelenting reverence African Americans - enslaved or free - maintained toward literacy and schools (Span, 2005).

Among free Blacks, in particular, education was perceived as a primary vehicle to combat racism and second-class citizenship (Williams, 1985, p. 3). According to Dorothy Porter (1995), northern and southern free Black leaders recognized the necessity and expediency of education given the group's limited and insecure existence in the American social order. Throughout the nation, various welfare, temperance, Bible, moral reform, and educational societies - established by and for free Blacks - catered to the group's educational expectations at a time when the nation was withdrawing or restricting its efforts regarding African American education.

Black people expected their antebellum educational opportunities to serve as the foundation for the race's societal advancement. Schools were intended to be institutions that informed African American youth of their precarious societal statuses; they were to assist freeborn African American children in learning the literacy skills necessary for combating discrimination, segregation, and slavery in adulthood; and they were expected to aid African Americans in acquiring equality, or at least some degree of social mobility. Education was perceived as the primary tool for humanity, merit, and capabilities in an American society which attempted to define them as slaves or inferior people.

This ideology began with individuals stealing away to read and write, and then teaching others what they had learned. It spawned individuals who used subterfuge, guile, trickery and determination to obtain literacy, or run hidden enclaves where small groups of children learned to navigate public spaces, making themselves unseen and unnoticed as they attended schoolrooms in ladies' kitchens and living rooms. Laws, the threat of dismemberment and death, or the efforts to prove their inferiority did not deter them. This ideology manifested itself in the establishment and maintenance of the schools they built, the principals and teachers they hired and the curriculum they taught. They rigidly refused efforts to usurp their leadership, control their operation, and what was taught.

Brown vs Board of Education

Integration: Hope for a Future or a Dream Deferred?

Present educational policy and ideology bears an uncanny and unsettling resemblance to the rationalizations and justification for enslavement (Bell, 1975), emerged to explain and justify the reasons Black students fared so poorly attending integrated schools. Initially labeled as "culturally deprived," this less offensive label came into use, along with the conclusion of a "lack of cultural capital." Irrespective of the label, the ideology replicates that of reasons purported to justify enslavement. The failure of Black students to achieve even an "within range" level of achievement could be laid at their feet because they had been given the opportunity to attend white schools. It was their fault; the assumptions of inadequate parenting, a lack of exposure to the larger world, a disinclination toward education, and reading in particular, rendered their failure.

The land mark Brown v. Topeka decision was handed down by the Supreme Court in 1954. This decision was initially believed to be the solution to unequal schooling, and nearly dealt a death blow to the ideology and principles of education as a tool of resistance to enslavement and second-class citizenship. This was to lead to autonomy, control of the curriculum and teachers and reinforcement of self-confidence and achievement on the part of Black students. Instead, it resulted in the dismantling of a pillar the Black community: its schools. After, 1954, the goals and tenets of a Black ideology of schooling were relegated to private community and boarding schools and historically black colleges and universities.

Today, most Black children attend public schools that are both racially isolated, often underfunded, and frequent turnover of staff and administrators, most of whom are young, white and female who have not been trained and coached to be effective teachers in an urban setting. It has been likened to sending people on an important, life-saving mission with no map, no compass, inadequate supplies and threadbare clothing. Demographic patterns, white flight, and the inability of the courts to affect the necessary degree of social reform render further progress in implementing Brown almost impossible (Bell, 2004). The traditional measures of academic achievement between Blacks and whites, has been debated and analyzed among scholars, legislators, and practitioners for decades. The federal Elementary and Secondary Education Act (ESEA) of 1965 was authorized to address the achievement gap. However, since its passage, the achievement gap has changed relatively little. The Education Trust found that the White-Black gaps are approximately 10 points wider, about a year's worth of learning, than they were a decade ago.

Nationally, too few African Americans read or do math at proficient levels. In reading, for instance, a mere 12% of African American 4th graders reach proficient or advanced levels, while a heartbreaking 61% have not been taught to attain even the basic level. And, the story is worse in math. The same proportion of African American 8th graders fall below the basic achievement level compared to only 7% who reach the proficient level or above on the National Assessment of Educational Progress, the gold standard of student achievement examinations. By the end of high school, African American students have math and reading skills that are virtually the same as those of 8th grade White students. In the last 20 years, the college enrollment rates of African Americans have steadily increased to the point that they now go to college at about the same rates as White students. However, African American college completion rates have not increased at the same pace, and a gap in college attainment remains where less than half, 41 per cent of African American, graduate from college; 61 per cent of white students do so (Education Trust, 2023).

The writing assessment of the National Assessment of Educational Progress (NAEP, 2022) measures narrative, informative and persuasive writing, the three purposes of writing identified in the NAEP framework; it has a writing scale score range from 0 to 300. The District of Columbia's score for 8th grade students was 128; the nation's was 152. When the nation's capital is compared to national level public school students, the results are equally disheartening. For eighth graders, over a third, 34 per cent of District of Columbia students scored at the below basic level; 56 percent were at the basic level; a mere ten per cent were proficient; none were at the advanced level. In contrast, just 16 percent of the country's students were at below basic; 54 per cent were at basic level; 28 per cent were proficient and two percent were at the advanced level (The National Center for Educational Statistics, 2023)).

With the exception of physical education, Black and white students are receiving separate and unequal educations-even though they are physically under the same roof.

Most Black students were, and are, deemed unable, and often, incapable, to perform in higher tracks, and are given work thought to be suitable, for them. The assumption that alienation from, resentment toward, and lack of engagement with educators and schools accompany these outcomes is not at all farfetched (McClean, 2019). Essentially, in spite of the huge investment in material and finances in contemporary schooling, dismal outcomes of urban schools still exist. Most schools have installed and maintain "tracks" into which students are consciously and deliberately sorted. Most of the students of color are in the "lower track, while other students, mostly white, attend classes in the upper tracks. With the exception of physical education, Black and white students are receiving separate and unequal educations-even though they are physically under the same roof. The traditional function of the tracking system sorts students into different segments with the appropriate attitudes and capacities needed for different levels of the occupational hierarchy (Dreeben, 2002; Oakes, 1986,).

Contemporary schools are burdened with a model that suggests children do not come to school 'prepared' and that parents are not involved, or caring about their children's education. Thus, like the well-meaning missionaries of the past, the schools are often more concerned with, and prioritize addressing poverty, culture, and living in poor neighbors often beset by crime, unemployment, lack of services, including hospitals, shopping, drug abuse, and grocery stores. These barriers to learning must be remedied before the children can be taught. These circumstances are blamed as the chief, and foremost causes of low student achievement. These circumstances, though daunting, are incomparable to teaching children and adults who were formerly enslaved, whose families had and began with nothing but grit and hope, endured and persisted. The horrors of enslavement are well documented to the exclusion of examining the oppositional culture and world view the enslaved developed to maintain their humanity and wage protracted warfare to thwart efforts to establish absolute control over their minds and spirits. Thus, contemporary schools have invested large sums of funding and human resource to address the culture of poverty, cultural deprivation, a lack of cultural capital that place Black students at risk of failure. The circumstances are challenging, but they are not the principal cause of the graphic differences in educational outcomes between Black and white students.

Academia, assuming the same supportive role as their counterparts in the antebellum south produced reams of books, research and opinion paper justifying and revealing why Blacks were particularly suited for enslavement, and indeed, why it was necessary for their civilization and salvation. Presently, as in the past, contemporary academic, researchers and other members of the media, along with social and cultural intelligentsia produce thousands of pages of research, books, and documents that explain the consistent failing and disruptive behavior of Black students in schools. There are programs that, purport to teach Black students higher order thinking skills, because the thinking kills that they have may be useful for the streets, but are not suitable or sufficient for schools.

While supporters of racially integrated schools ground their advocacy in empirical research that credits desegregation and race-conscious education policies for improved achievement among students of color, the increases they reported did little, if anything, to significantly lessen the gap between Black and other students. Today, most Black children attend public schools that are both racially isolated, suffer from high teacher and administrative turnover, with younger, less experienced teachers whose education may or may not correlate with the subject matter being taught. Often, there is also and strained relations with the immediate community. Demographic patterns, white flight, and the inability of the courts to affect the necessary degree of social reform render further progress implementing Brown almost impossible (Bell, 1980). The focus needs to be placed on protecting Black children against discriminatory policies, including re- segregation within desegregated schools, the loss of Black faculty and administrators, suspensions and expulsions at much higher rates than white students, and varying forms of racial harassment ranging from exclusion from extracurricular activities to physical violence. Indeed, children as young as six years old have been handcuffed and put in police cars. Such remedies, then, while effective in forcing alterations in school system structure, often encourage and seldom shield Black children from discriminatory retaliation (Bell,2004).

A DESIGN FOR THE ATTAINMENT OF HIGH ACADEMIC ACHIEVEMENT FOR INNER-CITY STUDENTS

Superintendents credited the high expectations of their supportive communities, persistent parents, and demanding teachers as critical to children forming their self-concept as Black students.

A growing body of research conducted by and from the perspectives of African American students, parents, and educators tells a more complicated story concerning the inferiority of these all-Black segregated schools. Their leadership staff and effectiveness are being challenged and found wanting. Black researchers, joined by many non-Black academicians and community leadership, have challenged this, and other allegations about the desire for literacy, the price paid for it, and the quest for control of their own education (McClean, 2019).

The traditional notions of learning as a function of teaching offer a narrow vision of what happens in the schooling process. Conventionally, schooling is to be an addition to students' psychological and attitudinal knowledge base; it is not intended to undo or replace in any fundamental way, the prior learning in the family and community (Ladson-Billings, 2009; McClean, 2019). The quality of the buildings, books, facilities while pleasing, and often imposing, is deemed just one aspect of the schooling process. There is equal emphasis placed on the "invisible aspect of any educative enterprise (Dreeben, 2002). Indeed, schooling, as with other spheres of Black life and culture: family, spirituality, religion, and a relationship with the Earth, was a cornerstone of oppositional reality that countered systemic tyranny and oppression.

Despite the painful memories of overt racism, government-sanctioned segregation, and limited economic and educational resources in the pre-Brown era, participating superintendents credited the high expectations of their supportive communities, persistent parents, and demanding teachers as critical to forming their self-concept as Black students. Collectively, their stories painted a picture of how school, home, and community connections served as a source of strength for Black students in "separate and unequal" schooling contexts and enabled them to succeed despite dire forces designed for their failure. As counternarratives to the commonly held assumptions that all Black schools were inherently inferior beyond their lack of adequate funding, facilities, and resources, the perspectives of the educators asserted otherwise.

Ideology of Contemporary Effective Schools for African-American Children

The most striking feature of the model was its failure to acknowledge the validity of any culture other than the dominant culture.

Throughout history, mainstream American society has exhibited low expectations and negative beliefs about Black students (Ladson-Billings, 2009). Previous attempts to provide education for children of color were based on the idea of acculturation which involved compensatory education. The compensatory model of urban and rural education rested on the premise that minority group children needed more of what white children had. The model, then, perceived the minority group child as deficient in comparison to the mythical norm. The most striking feature of the model was its failure to acknowledge the validity of any culture other than the dominant culture. The very language used denoted a negative conception of the students that these programs were initiated to benefit. These children were labeled underprivileged, culturally deprived, culturally dis- advantaged, and culturally handicapped. In the middle sixties, revisionist educators began to point out the pejorative message conveyed by such labels-that those who were different were inferior. The notion of cultural inferiority was extended to children's speech patterns, to their vocabulary, and to the ways in which they adjusted to school. A whole way of life stood condemned as inadequate. Compensatory programs rested implicitly on the premise that the melting pot approach was the only approach. Pluralism was assumed to be neither possible nor desirable.

Kenneth Clark, the renown Black scholar whose research contributed to the Brown v Board of Education litigation, came to the conclusion that belief that one cannot expect much from children whose families don't have books in the home rationalized the failure of children from poor families. He challenged the use of IQ tests to predict a child's ability to learn, saying they should be used instead to determine what a child needs to learn. Clark derided what he called "the cult of 'cultural deprivation'" among educators and social scientists. Those who attributed the academic failure of Black children to the environmental disadvantages of their family or neighborhood, he said, were merely finding a polite way of saying that those children could not be expected to learn to read or do arithmetic in the elementary grades. He considered such determinism to be indistinguishable from earlier, discredited notions about the biological bases of academic failure. This determinism also echoes a pillar of the rhetoric of pro-slavery advocates insisting that enslaved people where inferior intellectually, and hence could not be expected to learn (Ratvich, 2000).

The facts remain, that in spite of efforts to desegrigate or integrate public schools (Bell, 1975), the quality of education in most schools for poorer children, often range from inadequate to appalling. Since most Black and Latino teachers have been trained in the very institutions that produce teachers who are-ill-equipped for the future posts, they are not necessarily more talented or dedicated than other teachers. While some may have a better sense and knowledge of the pedagogy and content most likely to engage and motivate Black and Latino_students, and have an affinity with their communities, all teachers need preservice and in-service professional development to teach in context. Without this, and having been thrown directly from the fire and into the frying pan, many reluctantly walk away. Site administrators often cannot focus on their schools due to the steady flow of paperwork from assorted central office staff, where turf wars render them at-site central office administrators (Bell, 2004).

There are literally hundreds of after-school programs where dedicated staff with high expectations literally turn the tables on the trope that poor Black children cannot excel in school.

Disenchantment has led to the search for alternate, or supplementary means of achieving effective schooling for the many Black students not able to flee to the suburbs or costly private schools. Black people search for new and more realistic schooling to provide equal educational outcomes for their children is based more on what we can do to gain for ourselves rather than accept or depend what we can obtain from the educational system. The principle of gaining equal educational outcomes for Black children is of course, right and just. Black people have worked across the country to provide effective education based on the needs of the children's present, turning negatives influences into positives for learning. There are literally hundreds of after-school programs where dedicated staff with high expectations literally turn the tables on the trope that poor Black children cannot excel in school (Bell, 2004; Bouie, 2007; Collins 1990; Delpit, 1995; Edmunds,1981; Hollins, 1996; Marshall, 1995).

The Education Trust (1989) documented and listed an array of integrated and predominately minority children which have surpassed all expectations. The Ford Foundation (1989), produced a document detailing the exemplary academic achievement among formerly under- achieving students. In addition, there are popular films and documentaries that document the effectiveness of principles that undergird the practices found in traditional Black schooling.

A synthesis of the characteristics of effective schools serving African-American students shows that belief in the ability of students to meet high expectations for student achievement and deportment included expanded learning time and opportunities; family and community engagement and collaborative leadership and practice. These factors combined led to achievement gains.

Cohodes (2018) surmised that these practice inputs followed no excuses tenets: intensive teacher observation and training, data-driven instruction, increased instructional time, intensive tutoring, and a culture of high expectations. Levin, et al (1990) cited five characteristics of unusual effectiveness, originally identified by Edmonds (1982), included high expectations for students, strong administrative leadership, emphasis on student learning of basic skills, frequent monitoring of student progress, and orderly climate conducive to learning (Levine, Daniel, Cooper & Hilliard, 2000).

The independent schools and successful, effective after school programs which operate on several of these common principles, achieve academic success for Black students. They address community and personal problems indirectly. They have teachers who know how to light the spark, fan it and get a good blaze going that challenges their honor, recognizes and rewards the effort needed to change, grow and achieve. Motivation to learn is also engendered by challenging, rigorous curriculum presented in a manner which connects learning and their interests; and knows and incorporates topics of concern to them. Effective public schools such as the Duke Ellington School of Performing Arts in Washington, and Harlem Academy in New York place 100% of its middle school graduates. Black students enter with median standardized test scores in the 74th percentile and graduate at the 90th percentile; 98% of whom gradate to attend colleges across the country. The case studies support the conclusion that effective principals of Black urban schools:

1. believe that Black children can learn and master designated instructional objectives that enhance conditions that facilitate learning and eliminating those that do not;
2. recognize and reward teachers;
3. establish procedures to monitor students' progress;
4. take risks and disagree with their superiors;
5. know instruction and supervise and coach their teachers by visiting classrooms every day;
6. encourage and train parents to be partners in their child's education
7. set goals and execute well-conceived plans to achieve them;
8. recruit competent teachers and involve them in decision making and planning;
9. provide meaningful staff development sessions for their staffs;
10. seek outside funding from local businesses and national foundations (Jordan-Irvine, 1998).

Black students who attend independent Black schools consistently perform at higher levels on standardized tests, than Black students who attend traditional public schools (Ratteray, 1992). For example, Boston charter schools outperformed Boston traditional public schools from the 2001-2002 academic year through the 2006-2007 academic year. Across grade levels, elementary charter school students, on average, perform better than elementary traditional public school students. Charter middle school students, far outperform their traditional public school peers, and charter high school students substantially outperform their counterparts traditional public schools.

Other practices associated with Black charter schools exist, such as student advisory teams, uniforms and dress codes, family and student contracts, behavioral systems (demerits/merits, small rewards/small penalties), a direct instructional style of teaching, use of the Blackboard and a greater amount of instructional time devoted to English Language Arts, and other foundational subjects (Hoxby,2013; Merseth, 2009). These practices distinguish many predominantly Black charter schools from their traditional public schools. There is something more enticing about these schools than their racial and ethnic make-up. Instead, they appear to be, as researchers have been articulating for years, implementing culturally relevant learning that is specifically catered to the needs, desires, and assets of Black children (Ladson-Billings, 2009).

After school programs that are successful have ignited a spark and engaged students, and families along with the immediate and larger communities.

A case study on effective afterschool programs revealed that directors were strong instructional leaders; each school had its own unique culture processes and structures that were in concert with the needs of the students and local community. The schools had differing instructional modes, history of staff recruitment and training and community politics were all relevant factors which varied from school to school. Modes of leadership ran the gamut from autocratic to democratic and schools grew and functioned in specific contexts (Ford Foundation, 1989). The common characteristics Jordan-Irvine, (1988) observed, were visionary leadership, with clear stated goals that are understood and accepted by all stakeholders. Although the schools were unique ad reflected the communities they served, they had principals who had a vision for the school, and kept their eyes on the prize. They were instructional leaders who practiced student monitoring and regular professional development. These principals fostered relationships with caregiver, the immediate and larger communities.

Supplementary and after school students academic pipeline programs that enroll and persist in the goal of student achievement come in different forms, including in-school programs, after-school programs, out-of-school enrichment programs, summer camps, and residential bridge programs. Successful precollegiate pipeline programs are measured by their ability to (1) engage young people intellectually, socially, and emotionally; (2) respond to young people's interests, experiences, and cultural practices; and (3) connect discipline-specific learning within school, home, and other out-of-school settings (National Research Council, 2018).

Precollegiate programs prepare students to enter community colleges or four-year colleges and universities. The services and environments created by precollegiate academic pipeline programs have been demonstrated to increase pass rates in gate-keeper courses and increase collegiate grade-point averages and graduation rates (Lauer, at al, 2006), increase self- efficacy (Strayhorn, 2010) and foster the pursuit and attainment of STEM and non- STEM careers (Bell, 2004; Lauer, et al, 2006; Strayhorn, 2010).

After school programs that are successful have ignited a spark and engaged students, and families along with the immediate and larger communities. The content of the programs does not seem to matter. The Harlem Boys Choir uses music to engage and channel student energy and connects them with the world outside, as do schools focusing on strictly academic concerns. As with independent schools, supplementary programs use an array of strategies, typically subtle and indirect to address poverty, lack of exposure to the larger community and opportunities to be found, the provision of positive role models, and the assurance of success are among them (Bell, 2004).

At one program, the director stated that there are some words that are never used such as tutors and individual learning contracts. Students are not labeled as culturally disadvantaged and labeling their parents and families as uncaring never takes place. Tutors and one-on-on tutoring are loaded terms, and the one-on-one approach contradicts the collective nature of many Black families where most things are done in groups. They play in groups. A trip to the barber or getting one's hair done is a communal activity. When students are placed in heterogeneous Study Groups, where they work with their Study Group Leader and with one another complements learning styles and build engagement around academics. Student behaviors such as stretching, making rubbing their hand together and such, are seen for what they are: prepping behaviors to begin work.

Teachers skilled in pedagogy that acknowledges an array of learning styles, cultural differences and the ability to engage students will find that their students perform for success. To be effective in the affective domain, a teacher must be willing to teach social and psychological skills in the classroom (based on the child's own cultural milieu) that will allow him to compete on his own terms with the vast majority of Americans (White, 1973). Of all the affective attributes necessary to the inner-city teacher, this is perhaps the most essential, and yet the most difficult to implement in terms of specific programs or techniques. Additionally, teacher attitude is an important variable because it affects the student's performance, and perhaps more important, the student's self-concept. An appropriate teacher attitude can help engender self-confidence in the child. The challenge for the teacher, then, is to help the student gain positive attitudes regarding his own abilities without imposing a false set of values or alienating him from his own cultural background.

CONCLUSION

Teachers skilled in pedagogy that acknowledges an array of learning styles, cultural differences and the ability to engage students will find that their students perform for success.

Based on my investigations, I can assert that with highly competent teachers who believe in the children's capacity to learn and pursue the relevant methods to achieve that, Black students will attain academic success. A major part of the problem is the double set of standards that are often found within the school system. Black children as well as Black teachers must be held to the same high standards of academic performance as their white counterparts. Black students cannot be excused for shoddy performance simply because they are Black, or poor. To do so, would simply highlight the injustices of racism.

To educate for justice and equity, schools must follow the guidelines established by Black educators during and after enslavement. Black people were taught within context and all aspects of their lives bore upon this education. Contemporary schools must intentionally and consciously respond to the social ills that systemically discriminate against poor Black people and their children (Frye, 1989). These include crime, poverty and lack of neighborhood social services. Site administrators must be held accountable for nurturing a sense of cultural pride, providing students with constructive and affirming Black role models. Teachers must be held accountable for teaching the skills that their students need to survive and flourish.

To educate for justice and equity, schools must follow the guidelines established by Black educators during and after enslavement.

Throughout the centuries of slavery and right through its abolition and the aftermath of Emancipation, Black people maintained a focus on attaining literacy that was deeply rooted in their spiritual and political ideology. They saw literacy as an essential tool to navigate their way through the cruelty of oppression and to liberate themselves from the confines within which the planter class sought to constrain them. Contemporary education must have at its center, similar objectives of liberating Black students from the yolk of oppression passed down through the ages. The school must embark on the essential role of building community in such a way that all aspects of the student's life is taken into consideration though pedagogy that is inclusive and life affirming.

REFERENCES

Almond, M. R. (2012). The Black charter school effect: Black students in American charter schools. *The Journal of Negro Education, 81*(4), 354–365. doi:10.7709/jnegroeducation.81.4.0354

Anderson, J. (1988). *The education of Blacks in the South: 1860-1935*. University of North Carolina. doi:10.5149/uncp/9780807842218

Aptheker, H. (1983). *American Negro slave revolts*. International Publishers.

Bell, D. A. (1975). Waiting on the promise of "Brown.". *Law and Contemporary Problems, 39*(2), 341–373. doi:10.2307/1191105

Bell, D.A. (2004). *Silent covenants: Brown v Board of Education: And the unfulfilled hopes of racial reform*. New York, Oxford University Press.

Blassingame, J. (1972). *The slave community*. Oxford University Press.

Bly, A. T. (2008). "Pretends he can read": Runaways and literacy in colonial America, 1730—1776. *Early American Studies, 6*(2), 261–294.

Bouie, A. (2007). *Afterschool success: Enrichment strategies for urban youth*. Teachers College Press.

Bouie, A. (2021). *Material Culture and Visual Art: Tools in Resistance to Enslavement: Of Course, He Had Help: Bluford's Journey*, Academia https://www.academia.edu/50550269

Bush, L. (2004). Access, school choice, and independent Black institutions: A historical perspective. *Journal of Black Studies, 34*(3), 386–401. doi:10.1177/0021934703258761

Byrd, C. D., & Mason, R. S. (2021). *Precollegiate ptograms in academic pipeline programs: diversifying pathways from the bachelor's to the professoriate*. Lever Press.

Cohodes, S. (2018). Policy Issue: Charter schools and the achievement gap. *The Future of Children, 1000*(1), 1–16. doi:10.1353/foc.2018.0008

Collins, M. (1990). *Ordinary Children, Extraordinary Teachers*. Torcher Perigold.

Cornelius, J. (1983). "We slipped and learned to read:" Slave accounts of the literacy process, 1830-1865. *Phylon (1960-), 44*(3), 171–186

Delpit, L. (1995). *Other Peoples' Children: Cultural Conflict in the Classroom*. New Press.

Dreeben, R. (2002). *On what is learned in school*. University of Illinois Press.

Edmonds, R. R. (1981). A report on the research project "Search for effective schools …" and certain of the designs for school improvement that are associated with the project. [Unpublished report prepared for NIE, Institute for Research on Teaching, Michigan State University].

Elementary & Secondary Education Act. (1965). *American Youth in California* (Vol. 1). Education for Children of the Poor.

Fountain, D. L. (1995). Historians and historical archaeology: Slave sites. *The Journal of Interdisciplinary History*, *26*(1), 67–77. doi:10.2307/205550

Givens, J. (2021). *Fugitive pedagogy: Carter G. Woodson and the art of Black teaching*. Harvard University Press.

Goodman, A. (Ed.). (2015). *Remembering Malcolm X on his 90th Birthday: By Any Means Necessary, speech delivered June 28, 1964*. Audubon Ballroom., https://www. democracynow.org/2015/5/19/by_any_means_necessary_remembering_malcolm

Grimke-Forten, C. (1983). *The Journals of Charlotte Forten Grimke. Schomburg Library of Nineteenth-Century Black Women Writers*. Oxford University Press.

Harrison, L. (1949). Thomas Roderick Dew: Philosopher of the Old South. *The Virginia Magazine of History and Biography*, *57*(4), 390–404.

Hollins, E. R., & Spencer, K. (1990). Restructuring schools for cultural inclusion: Changing the schooling process for African-American children. *Journal of Education*, *172*(2), 89–100. doi:10.1177/002205749017200208

Horsford, S. D. (2009). From Negro student to Black superintendent: Counternarratives on segregation and desegregation. *The Journal of Negro Education*, *78*(2), 172–187.

Hoxby, C., & Avery, C. (2013). The missing "One-Offs": The hidden supply of high-achieving, low-income students. *Brookings Papers on Economic Activity*, 1–50.

Irvine, J. J. (1988). Urban schools that work: A summary of relevant factors. [JSTOR]. *The Journal of Negro Education*, *57*(3), 236–242. doi:10.2307/2295422

Ladson-Billings, G. (2009). *The dreamkeepers: Successful teachers of African American children*. Jossey Bass.

Lauer, P., Akiba, M., Wilkerson, S. B., Apthorp, H. S., Snow, D., & Martin-Glenn, M. L. (2006). Out-of-School-Time Programs: A meta-analysis of effects for t-risk students. *Review of Educational Research*, *76*(2), 275–313. doi:10.3102/00346543076002275

Levine, D. U. (1990). Update on effective schools: Findings and implications from research and practice. *The Journal of Negro Education*, *59*(4), 577–584. doi:10.2307/2295314

Levine, D. U., Cooper, E. J., & Hilliard, A. (2000). National Urban Alliance Professional Development Model for improving achievement in the context of effective schools research. *The Journal of Negro Education, 69*(4), 305–322. doi:10.2307/2696247

Litwack, L. L. (1979). *Been in the storm so long: The aftermath of slavery, The.* Athlone Press.

Marshall, J. E. Jr. (1995). Street soldiers: Violence prevention over the airwaves, a phenomenon. *Journal of Health Care for the Poor and Underserved, 6*(2), 246–251.

Mays, B. (1974), Comment: Atlanta-Living With Brown Twenty Years Later. 3 *BLACK L. J., 184*, 191-92.

McClean, M. (2019). *From the Middle Passage to Black lives matter: Ancestral writing as a pedagogy of hope.* Peter Lang.

Merseth, K. K., Sommer, J., & Dickstein, S. (2008). Bridging worlds: Changes in personal and professional identities of pre-service urban teachers. *Teacher Education Quarterly, 35*(3), 89–108.

Nash, H. D. (1989). Blacks in Arkansas during Reconstruction: The x-slave Narratives. *The Arkansas Historical Quarterly, 48*(3), 243–259.

Oakes, J. (1986). Keeping Track, Part 2: Curriculum Inequality and School Reform. *Phi Delta Kappan, 68*(2), 148–154.

Olsavsky, J. (2019). Runaway slaves, Vigilance Committees, and the pedagogy of revolutionary abolitionism, 1835–1863. In M. Rediker, T. Chakraborty, & M. van Rossum (Eds.), *A Global History of Runaways: Workers, Mobility, and Capitalism, 1600–1850* (1st ed., pp. 216–234). University of California Press.

Olsavsky, J. (2022). *The most absolute abolition: runaways, Vigilance Committees, and the rise of revolutionary abolitionism, 1835-1861.* Louisiana State University Press.

Porter, D. B. (1936). The organized educational activities of Negro literary societies, 1828-1846. *The Journal of Negro Education, 5*(4), 555–576. doi:10.2307/2292029

Porter, D. B. (1960). The anti-slavery movement in North Hampton. *Negro History Bulletin, 24*(2), 33–41.

Porter-Uzelac, C. (1995). *Dorothy Porter Wesley (1905-1995): Afro-American Librarian and Bibliophile: an Exhibition.* February 1-March 16, 2001

Ratteray, J. D. (1992). Independent neighborhood schools: A Framework for the education of African Americans. *The Journal of Negro Education, 61*(2), 138–147. doi:10.2307/2295411

Ravitch, D. (2000). A different kind of education for Black children. *The Journal Of Blacks In Higher Education, 30*, 98–106.

Scott, J. C. (1985). *The Weapons of the Weak. Everyday Forms of Peasant Resistance.* Yale University Press.

Scott, J. C. (1992). *Domination and the arts of resistance: hidden transcripts.* Yale University Press.

Span, C. M. (2005). Learning in spite of opposition: African Americans and their history of educational exclusion in antebellum America. Counterpoints, 2005. Peter Lang, New York

Stampp, K. M. (1942). An analysis of T. R. Dew's review of the debates in the Virginia Legislature. *The Journal of Negro History, 27*(4), 380–387. doi:10.2307/2715183

Stanton, S. (2001). *The Virginia Magazine of History and Biography, 109*(3), 331–332.

Strayhorn, T. L. (2010). The role of schools, families, and psychological variables on math achievement of Black high school students. *High School Journal, 93*(4), 177–194. doi:10.1353/hsj.2010.0003

Stringfield, S., Teddlie, C., & Suarez, S. (2017). Classroom interaction in effective and ineffective schools: Preliminary results from Phase III of the Louisiana School Effectiveness Study. *Journal of Classroom Interaction, 52*(1), 4–14.

Stuckey, P. S. (2013). *Slave culture: nationalist theory and the foundations of Black America.* Oxford Press. doi:10.1093/acprof:oso/9780199931675.001.0001

Taylor, E. R. (2006). *If We Must Die: Shipboard Insurrections in the Era of the Atlantic Slave Trade (Antislavery, Abolition, and the Atlantic World).* Louisiana State University Press.

The National Center for Educational Statistics. (2023). *District of College Grade 8 NEP Writing assessment, Washington DC*, https://nces.ed.gov/nationsreportcard/pdf/stt2002/writing/2003532DC8.PDF

White, L. R. (1973). Effective teachers for inner city schools. *The Journal of Negro Education, 42*(3), 308–314. doi:10.2307/2966666

Williams, H. A. (2005). *Self-taught: African-American education in slavery and freedom.* University of North Carolina.

Young, J. R. (2007). *Rituals of resistance: African Atlantic religion in Kongo and the Lowcountry South in the era of slavery.* Louisiana State University Press.

Chapter 3

Decolonizing the Curriculum in Higher Education:
Reconceptualizing Multicultural Pedagogy at Predominantly White Institutions

Zuleka R. Woods
Virginia Tech, USA

Shania Clinedinst
Virginia Tech, USA

Isil Anakok
Virginia Tech, USA

Shernita Lee
Virginia Tech, USA

ABSTRACT

In order for educational institutions to attain social justice and equity, we must challenge persistent and normative whiteness in higher education curriculum to include the voice of students of color. The dominant Eurocentric narrative present in higher education curriculum demands inclusive pedagogy in classrooms that create space for students to share their funds of knowledge and experience inclusion within an atmosphere of belonging. This chapter utilizes qualitative methodologies to decolonize the curriculum and craft such an inclusive space. It argues for ways to reshape knowledge production by encouraging diverse forms of learning and critical pedagogy that rest on a foundation of a multicultural curriculum. This decolonizing process must become an essential part of critical pedagogies within higher education curriculum that includes all cultures and knowledge systems in ways that recognize and frame students' funds of knowledge within the inclusive space of the classroom.

DOI: 10.4018/978-1-6684-7379-5.ch003

INTRODUCTION

The persistent and normative whiteness of college curriculum may hinder the growth of a globally competent student. The average student's overall abilities and experiences (funds of knowledge) are often shaped by the dominant narrative of a Eurocentric curriculum and the lack of inclusive pedagogy in classrooms (Ndofirepi et al., 2022). For example, the norm for most classroom examples and studies derives from a Eurocentric curriculum that portrays a White, male and heterosexual view as the dominant and acceptable view. This not only excludes the voices of people of color, women, and other often historically oppressed groups from the learning space, but it also shapes students' consciousness. It promotes the white, male, and heterosexual voice as the bar for learning. This chapter uses inclusive pedagogies to share strategies for decolonizing the curriculum of predominantly white institutions (PWI). Based on this approach, we will discuss ways to *reshape knowledge production,* using *critical pedagogies and inclusive practices* as intentional methods to create space for dialogue through a *multicultural curriculum.* This chapter envisions classroom settings where all cultures and knowledge systems are recognized and students' funds of knowledge are embraced for a more inclusive classroom. It gives practical examples of how to include often excluded voices in the classroom by sharing inclusive practices as alternatives to the dominant Eurocentric narrative. Drawing from scholarship on Diversity, Equity, and Inclusion (DEI), and experiences teaching a Diversity in a Global Society course taught at a PWI, the chapter contributes to the discourse on decolonizing the curriculum as an essential route to achieving justice, peace and equity in global classrooms. In the constant struggle for justice and equity, building an inclusive classroom is vital and concepts of diversity, equity and inclusion must be practically incorporated based on the context. This chapter presents concrete examples and steps to building a global classroom for colleges, universities, and other educational institutions.

Asserting Inclusive Pedagogies

Inclusive pedagogy draws from a large body of scholars on teaching and learning and is said to improve learning outcomes by making all students feel seen and included in the classroom (Spratt & Florian, 2015). To alert the consciousness of students and promote other voices often ignored, inclusive pedagogy involves decolonizing the curriculum. This perspective works to disrupt and dismantle the pervasive view of a Eurocentric curriculum and the lack of inclusive pedagogy in classrooms (Ndofirepi et al., 2022). The persistent and normative whiteness of the curriculum may hinder the growth of globally competent students. For example, the norm for most classroom examples and studies in the USA is from a Eurocentric curriculum that portrays a White, male, and heterosexual view as the dominant and acceptable view. In this study, we argue for a decolonized curriculum that recognizes and values the funds of knowledge students of color bring with them to the classroom for we know that this essential component will extend the curriculum into a space that is productive and inclusive where all members, regardless of race, ethnicity or gender, stand to benefit.

The social, cultural, political, and economic conditions of the U.S.A is one that is situated on the domination of non-European people and cultures. The colonial makings of subordinating cultures of non-white peoples continue to serve as the foundation of many institutions, including colleges and universities. Although many strides have been made toward equality in the United States, schools and many communities remain divided (Goldstein & Selby, 2000). As such, the need to decolonize educational curricula is essential to understanding and challenging the ways in which the world is shaped by normative whiteness, biases, and racism. The U.S.A educational system was not legally integrated until 1954 with the landmark case of Brown v. Board of Education. However, in practice, many school systems continue to support the separation of people based on race, which affects the quality of education many Black students receive. As a result, students of color continue to be disadvantaged in the education system. Key to this disadvantage is the lack of representation and inclusive space for each student. Education that lacks representation cannot better inform students of the diversity of cultures outside of their own. Higher education institutions are vital in grounding systems of knowledge production and can perpetuate coloniality (Alvares & Faruqi, 2014; Mignolo, 2003; Smith, 2001). It is therefore important to examine how such institutions are educating for social justice and equity and present strategies that these institutions may utilize strategically to improve the content and methods of teaching and thus shaping the lives of their graduates.

Higher education institutions in the U.S. have not always been inclusive spaces for non-white students. Champions of education for African-Americans like W.E.B. Du Bois and Booker T. Washington fought for education as a tool of liberation for Blacks in America (Morgan, 1995). The majority of institutions were not very supportive of integrated education, and in some cases, learning spaces were violent for Black students (see Ruby Bridges – Meadows, 2011). With the racial climate a threat to the effective participation of Black students, Historically Black Colleges and Universities (HBCUs) were established in the 19th century to provide higher education opportunities for Black students. As a result, Black students moved towards HBCUs that were built to ensure their participation in a positive environment. While many students at PWIs may relate to the dominant narrative of whiteness, for Black, Brown, and other non-white students, colleges and universities are often, a reminder of their exclusion. The discourse of power and privilege cannot be ignored in the struggle to belong, as the intersection of identities for many nonwhite students places them at a disadvantage. For example, a Black woman, or Queer student might complete their entire college career without reading a single author who reflects their experiences regarding race, gender, or sexuality. These types of markings beg for action for working toward a more inclusive space within higher education institutions.

Working towards a more inclusive space means practicing ways to decolonize classrooms to enable educators to go beyond raising the bar and in addition, aim to change the bar. In practice, this looks like evaluating the curriculum to re-establish how learning takes place, deepening our understanding of who defines what we know to be successful, and encouraging other types of learning. Normative whiteness often ignores storytelling, oral history, and lived experiences, deeming them as less than formal learning. This harmful act of exclusion sidelines the voices of excluded groups. For example, when teaching about people and cultures in countries outside of the West, academics in those countries have called for using their own works with non-Eurocentric or western paradigms (Alveres & Faruqi, 2014). This is important because it focuses on the narratives of people who are often ignored. By doing this, educators can create a new standard that elevates new voices and disrupts the dominant narratives of Eurocentric views in the classroom.

Decolonization presents an alternative method relative to the dominant white curriculum by creating a space for dialogue through a multicultural curriculum. Mignolo's (2011) work on the geopolitics of knowledge shows that the very concept of knowledge is politically and socially created, and consideration of power relations must always be given. Creating an inclusive space that acknowledges the power relations in how knowledge is created also entails questioning history as it has always been told. Of course, there are complexities and nuances surrounding how history gets told in curriculum development, but it is essential to emphasize a multifaceted account inclusive of often ignored voices in acknowledgement that Black, Brown, and Indigenous voices are often ignored or left out, or rendered invisible (Margolis, 2001). Pedagogy, as we will discuss in detail later, must be a multifaceted practice. In order to have inclusive pedagogies as part of learning strategies, learning must entail extracting from the dominant accounts that often exclude languages and stories of Black and Indigenous people to include diverse voices. These stories are what will formulate multicultural education.

Predominantly White Institutions

In the U.S., higher education institutions with more than half or greater of the student population identifying as white are considered predominantly white institutions (PWIs). These types of institutions are often progenitors of the dominant white narratives that ignore historically marginalized groups. Although some PWIs are aiming for more diversity, there is still a strong line of difference at those institutions and the atmosphere is generally not intercultural (Tanaka, 2003). In the *Miseducation of the Negro,* Woodson (1933) argues the education of Blacks at PWIs supports an explicitly white supremacist/nationalist curriculum. Woodson encourages Blacks to remain vigilant and engaged in critical reflective work. In doing critical reflection, learning spaces like higher education classrooms must be open to criticism of the exclusionary practices of higher education institutions, particularly, PWIs. For students from historically marginalized backgrounds, PWIs as learning spaces can be very isolating and challenging (Jiles, 2020). Jiles (2021) studying Black student adjustments at a PWI, demonstrated a different comfort level and perception of difference for Black students compared to white students. Also, according to Waldoff et al. (2011), students reported the lack of inclusivity negatively affected their learning.

The deficiency of PWIs often extends beyond the classroom. Besides a threat to student learning, there is also a lack of community for students of color. For example, the cultural values of community and collectivism that are part of many Black college student experiences are often lacking in the PWI environment for Black students. Colleges and universities have begun to center recruitment models on practices that support students of color and address their issues of adjustment and isolation (Eakins & Eakins, 2017). Institutions are now asking how they can move towards creating a more equitable learning space. It is important in the discourse of equity and justice to include decolonizing education. It is already part of many disciplines (e.g. political science, philosophy, women's studies, sociology and anthropology), although this effort is mostly focused on research methods and theoretical frameworks. Recently, the need to shift the conversation toward interrogating the curricular and pedagogical practices beyond just discussion of racialized structures and power in the academy has become much more apparent (Sanchez, 2018). Critical scholars have long been discussing power structures in the academy and moving away from a colonial perspective, but the recent push is a combination of scholarship and activism.

Defining Decolonization in Higher Education

When defining decolonization, it has to be done in ways that show a continuous action. Decolonization goes beyond the colonial era when colonial powers violently took land and territories to exercise control over Indigenous people. Decolonization, according to the Oxford dictionary, refers to the dismantlement of colonies or the process of colonies becoming independent. It is also pertaining to the violence of slavery as an institution and the use of stolen land to enslave Black people . Decolonization efforts in education reference rebuilding school systems built on years of colonial practices, like forces of assimilation, language, and thinking. As a field, decolonial scholarship focuses on deconstructing systems of western hegemony. In discussing the politics of representation, Fanon and Philcox, (2008) contended that the European governments sought to legitimize colonization by asserting that their nations' cultures were superior to those they held in bondage. He criticized the way westerners treated other cultures as "backward" and the assumption that European cultural values and practices should serve as benchmarks for all others. Fanon (1963) suggested in *The Wretched of the Earth* that the colonized world is divided into geographical configurations that often center on Eurocentric values. Fanon's (1963) work also addresses the broader argument of the politics and poetics of how Black and Brown bodies are presented in a compartmentalized world of "us" and "them," or "black" and "white."

In the discourse of decolonizing education, the presumption is that if the curricula are built on colonial foundations, students are influenced by that perspective. Discussing representation, Hall et al. (2013) argued that people socially construct values and assign meaning to them. Vital to this discourse of being influenced and assigning meaning is the dance of interpretation and intentions. Often, interpretation and intention become how we see others or even ourselves. If students at PWIs are taught Eurocentric configurations of the world, their interpretations could ignore and furthermore discount the history of the enslavement of Blacks and the lasting impression within Black history as well as discount the success and other positive achievements of Black people across the globe. By empowering Black students to explore the history and recognize the power of the Black narrative they will be encouraged to see themselves within the Black heroic stories.

Decolonization of the curriculum is part of the larger concept of confronting power relations within learning institutions. Decolonizing the curriculum stems from educators' quest to break away from a Eurocentric paradigm (Alvares & Faruqi, 2014) and question what voices dominate and which ones are excluded (Hussain & Jones, 2021). Decolonizing the curriculum forces educators to reflect on the role of the classroom in shaping knowledge production. It asks questions about who produces knowledge and who consumes it. It also examines how we define and contextualize knowledge. Eurocentric knowledge production threatens representation and multicultural learning. Learning centered on Eurocentric views homogenizes history and knowledge systems (Ermine, 1995). By decentering knowledge production away from a Eurocentric curriculum, educators can expand the curriculum to highlight Black history and celebrate the contributions that were omitted (Ng-A-Fook, 2013; Battiste, 2012).

To decolonize the curriculum also means dismantling the years of colonial Eurocentric views and acknowledging the history of the classrooms and the academy as violent and excluded spaces for people of color. Critical Race Theory (Crenshaw, 1988) argues that race as a social construct is embedded in systems and policies, including educational institutions. How can we break away from these systems and work to construct policies that are inclusive of people of color in educational settings? Can we change the curriculum to include diverse voices that not only counter normative whiteness but co-exist with this ugly past? Decolonization of classroom spaces criticizes the subjugated presentation of the racialized other and exploitation of colonized people as a lens to diversify learning spaces. This kind of work moves towards cultivating inclusive classroom practices (Salend, 2015).

In postcolonial research, decolonization goes beyond the independence of previous colonial territories or economic and political control. It is inclusive of also decolonizing the mind, which can be a difficult process. Decolonizing the mind calls for reflection to deconstruct assumptions previously held (Merryfield, 2000) and recognize our own epistemological foundations and biases that shape our worldviews. Decolonization of the mind also entails an understanding of language as a tool that carries tradition and history (Thiong'O, 1986). When language, history, and culture shape our view, Andreotti (2007) argues, transformational learning occurs. Language and culture can help us unlearn while learning by replacing the old narratives with new ones. Therefore, decolonizing the mind must be facilitated by intentionally re-evaluating our own views, biases, and assumptions. Research shows when we are re-evaluating our assumptions, both facilitators and those they are facilitating should be open to a reflexive process (Brock et al., 2006). In one of the activities offered in this chapter, teachers are encouraged to reflect with students about which viewpoints are present in the curriculum, and which may not be included. By performing such activities, it teaches the teacher new knowledge and application to help them become a better and more effective educator.

Colonial education ultimately stripped Black, Brown and Indigenous people of their learning structures and ways and replaced them forcibly with the knowledge and structure of the colonized (Fanon, 1963). In Black Skin, White Mask, Fanon argues that language as a tool of colonization makes the colonized subjects assume the culture of the colonized. In learning, the language we use and the attributes we assign to people and places ultimately become important to our identity. To justify colonization, colonial education convinced Indigenous people to abandon their ways and be forced into assimilation (Battiste, 2019). To decolonize education is to undo the colonial teachings and reintroduce new kinds of learning, knowledge production, and multicultural curricula. Before we begin to expand on knowledge production and other inclusive practices, the graph below lists concrete ways to reshape and decolonize the classroom or learning spaces.

Decolonizing Academia and Curriculum

There are several dimensions to colonial power and its depiction within the United States. One example is cultural appropriation, which is typically associated with Indigenous groups and negates the experience of those who were forced to be in this country. This may be extended further by mocking Indigenous people using mascots (Steinman, 2016). History cannot be excluded or glamorized. Instead, the narratives of those whose families were impacted for generations should be shared. There is power in knowledge, even if it infringes on academic freedom or controversy (Dei, 2016). The colonization of higher education reaches all disciplines, and its approach is oppressive. Exploration of visible and hidden curriculums suggests that decolonization does not have to be equivalent to disruption (Shahjahan et al., 2022). Rather, the opportunity is explored to find gaps and discover academic needs in order to promote change. The histories are uncovered and the (re)discovery of lost voices and perspectives strengthens communities through its truths (Shirley, 2017). Irrespective of discipline preferences or limitations, examination of literature from other geographical areas removes barriers to students' learning experience (Skopec et al., 2021). Assigned reading lists or allowing students to generate their own reading lists should encourage them to experience the empowerment of choice and to utilize library resources to expand their knowledge.

Decolonizing academia takes time and is an iterative process to be approached with positivity and open-mindedness, with the goal constantly in mind (Dei, 2016). However, the responsibility of decolonizing the curriculum does not fall on the shoulders of persons of color, whether they are students or faculty (Jivraj, 2020). It should not be a burden on particular groups. Decolonization of the curriculum throughout the academic journey has the power to expand student viewpoints through exposure to truths, whether they are political, scientific, emotional, or other aspects of being. The activities below are reflective tools to help decolonize by incorporating diversity into the classroom. Table 1 and the next section will expand on more concrete ways to decolonize classroom spaces.

Activity 1: At the beginning of each semester, ask each student to reflect on diversity and what it means to them. How do they define it? What does it mean to be diverse? For some students, diversity (and other jargon like minority, marginalized, or People of Color-POC) is a new term. Educators must make time to see where everyone is and listen to how their worldview shapes their understanding of diversity.

Activity 2: **Reflecting on the current curriculum-**Take a look at your syllabus. How many Black, Brown, or nonwhite people are integrated there? How many whites? Both the teacher and students are encouraged to use this activity as a reflective process.

Table 1. Concrete ways to decolonizing classroom spaces

Diverse Language Usage	Re-design Assessment
Re-shape Knowledge Production	Funds-of-Knowledge
Technology Innovation	Embrace Community Resources

Embracing Diverse Language Usage

In the Miseducation of the Negro, Carter G. Woodson (1933) shares that it is terrible to think that a child with five different present tenses comes to school to be faced with books that are not in his native language only to be told things about his language, which are sometimes permanently damaging. Embracing diverse languages in the classroom is a way to reshape the curriculum as it recognizes that students communicate differently and recognizes the history and experiences within language usage. The language used in the classroom or academic language, which describes the lexical, grammatical, and interpersonal skills specific to classroom settings (Gottlieb & Ernst-Slavit, 2014) can sometimes be biased toward certain groups of students. For example, African-American vernacular language can sometimes be considered less than or unacceptable in academic spaces.

Many Black students in predominantly white learning spaces tend to code-switch as learning space reinforces white professional and learning standards as the norm (McCluney et al., 2021). In the history of colonial violence in the classrooms and learning spaces, academic language is used to disguise the racist practice of maintaining linguistic hierarchy in schools (Alim & Smitherman, 2012). When students from historically marginalized communities are told their language is not "academic'' enough or does not fit the standards of learning, it reinforces colonial attitudes of hierarchy among people and cultures. American colleges and universities in the early 1970s were forced to address bringing diverse languages into schools that supported a variety of social, economic, and cultural backgrounds (CCCC, 1974). It is vital to acknowledge the role that language plays in social movements' struggles to include excluded voices in learning spaces.

A lack of consideration for the multiple diverse languages represented in a learning environment is unfortunate since this recognition improves the student's experience and learning outcomes. While English is the dominant language within the United States, learners enter classrooms with other language backgrounds. Even in the English language, there is observable diversity in geographical history and even generational phrases. Creating linguistically diverse spaces within the classroom increased cross-language friendships (Johnson et al., 2020). This is advantageous irrespective of the class size. Often in larger classrooms, there is a fear that students will not be able to get to know each other and/or the professor. Through the use of inclusive learning activities, the odds are improved to help support the student's sense of belonging while teaching them transferable skills.

An instructor's goal to help students feel welcomed in the space requires intentional efforts and activities to promote that environment. Sometimes, students feel supported, but they can also feel anxious from that same support. The perceived support that a student feels within the classroom in a higher education setting is often coupled with anxiety (Jin & Dewaele, 2018). If a student is positive in their perception of emotional support from their teacher and/or peers, then the student's anxiety is reduced. For intentional college courses focused on contemporary pedagogy, inclusive strategies provide support for students who are not comfortable with their use of the English language and can use the classroom space to improve their skills, learn the "unofficial" nuances of the English language, and practice in a safe environment.

RE-DESIGNING ASSESSMENT

While educators make sure students feel welcomed in their learning spaces, they also need to re-design the assessment tools to ensure students succeed and learn regardless of their differences (Montenegro & Jankowski, 2017). Assessing learning is a vital contribution to building an inclusive classroom and education.

Schilling and Schilling (1998) defined assessment as "a range of methods for investigating the phenomenon and outcomes of student's learning" (Schilling & Schilling, 1998; p.12). In essence, assessment is how educators measure what they teach and how it is learned. When designing assessments within higher education, the needs of all students should always be considered. Educators should take into consideration cultural differences, backgrounds, and lived experiences of students that would affect how students learn, participate, and demonstrate their knowledge (Nortvedt et al., 2020). For example, some students might not respond positively to assessments that relied heavily on grading systems. Higher education teachers have been engaged in conversations about upgrading. Upgrading according to the Chronicles of Higher Education (2022) is going beyond letter grades for individual assignments (Miller, 2022). These educators shared their experiences in using reflections for finals instead of letter grading. In some instances, teachers reported little changes like dropping penalties for late work to emphasize the best version of their work over last-minute-rushed-work or being available for questions and concerns from students as they complete assignments. All of these examples showed learning is not linear and therefore requires flexibility. This positively impacts all students, especially those with Black identities. It encourages students to seek knowledge irrespective of personal and academic challenges. As educators continue to improve on innovative ways of assessing student learning, it is important to note the role of assessment in building an inclusive space. Montenegro and Jankowski (2017) state that

"Assessment, if not done with equity in mind, privileges and validates certain types of learning and evidence of learning over others, can hinder the validation of multiple means of demonstration, and can reinforce within students the false notion that they do not belong in higher education." (p. 5)

Acknowledging assessment is as crucial as teaching pedagogies for student learning, educators should make efforts to diversify their assessment tools. For example, active learning practices such as activities that do not simply provide answers to the student, but make room for discoveries and grappling with real-world scenarios is useful in promoting deep learning and desirable student outcomes (Hundley et al., 2019). An assessment like this includes essays instead of multiple choice or assignments that have multiple options for students to complete. An educator can ask for a demonstration of the subject in a variety of ways to ensure students with different learning styles are considered and all students benefit.

Considering the cultural differences and backgrounds of students in a diverse classroom setting, educators must ensure assessment tools are accommodating to the demography of the classrooms. For example, consideration must be given to students for whom English is not their first language. English language learners might demonstrate their learning differently. While higher education imposes an expectation that students pass a standardized test to demonstrate English proficiency, for the content of many lessons, these students still experience challenges in translating the information and instructions. It is helpful when assessing learning to identify whether students need additional time to prepare, how they adjust to oral presentations, or what challenges they face with written documents. McNair (2012) reinforced the need for educators to think about diverse

Figure 1. Assessment cycle from northwestern searle center for advancing learning and teaching (2022)
https://www.northwestern.edu/searle/assessment-of-student-le
arning/assessment-process/index.html.

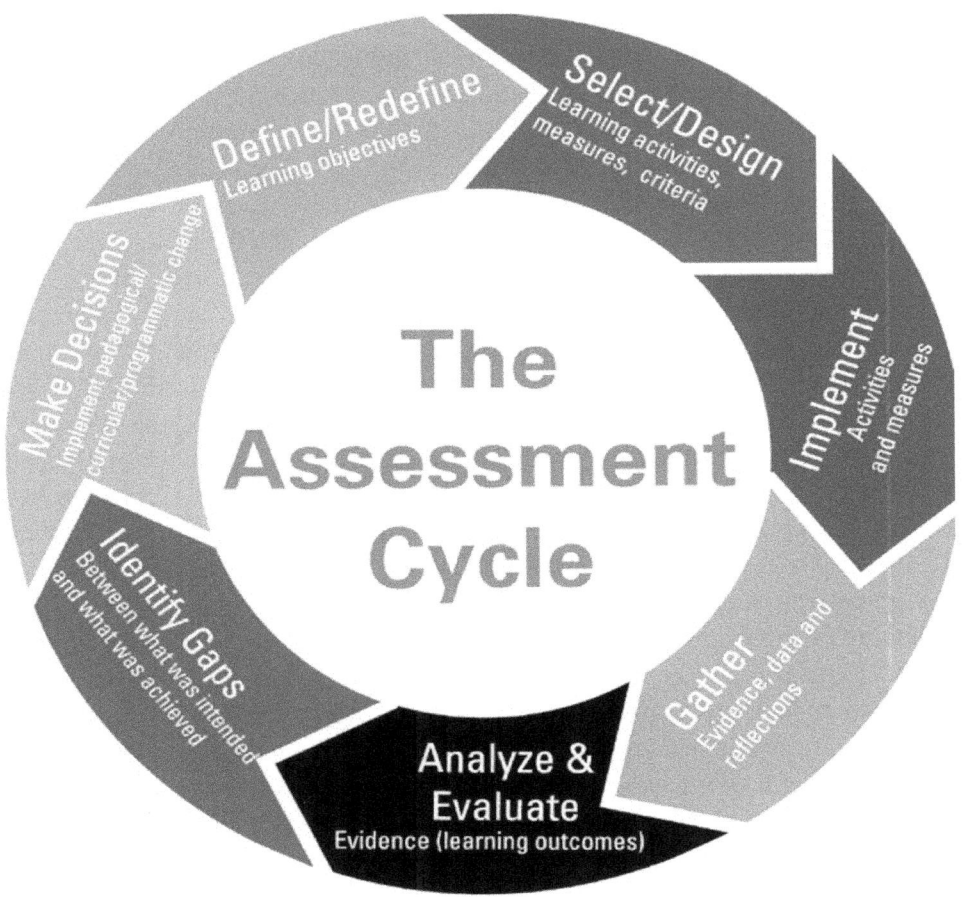

students in ways that equip-them and meet their needs. For example, instead of thinking about what students are lacking, educators can identify barriers to minoritized students and offer ways to address them. Last, another example to help re-design assessment for inclusive learning environments is reviewing the rubric or assessment tool with students and asking their reflection on how to adjust it to reflect their learning styles. Learning should be constantly assessed, re-evaluated, analyzed, and re-assessed. Figure 1 shows a learning assessment cycle that can be incorporated into the classroom as educators make selections on assessment tools.

RESHAPING KNOWLEDGE PRODUCTION

How do we come to acquire knowledge and how do we share that knowledge? Knowledge production refers to the self-interactive construction of how we come to obtain information. While obtained knowledge must be derived from a reliable source, it must also provide transferable skills of social and cultural dynamics to the learner. Higher education institutions such as PWIs should include the diverse perspectives of their scholars within the curriculum to shape how students come to know things. The way knowledge is produced can help bridge the gap between learning and the environment. As the world moves towards a more inclusive and globalized community, higher education institutions will need to evaluate the scope of their classroom to include the instructor, texts and reading materials, technology, student participants, and others. This holistic cycle of learning, inclusive of the materials, teacher, technology and etc., produces the best results for knowledge aggregation which effectively transfers obtained knowledge applicable outside the classroom (Kallio & Houtbeckers, 2020).

The challenge with current modalities of classroom knowledge production within PWIs is the heavy Western focus on social identity (race, class, and gender). This is often placed above the lived experiences of students of color (Elabor-Idemudia, 2012). Marginalization of knowledge threatens values and norms that disrupt corresponding engagement between the student and the instructor. The standards of representation in the classroom must include stakeholder groups to better disseminate knowledge and define structural measures to cultivate diverse thought or produce different ways of thinking. As knowledge is produced, standardized, and influenced by dominant cultures, knowledge will lean in favor of its producers. Unfortunately, within the classroom, students receive biased knowledge that is modeled, refined, and interpreted within the dominant culture (Akena, 2012). For example, students are taught about Africa and other non-western countries as lacking resources or underdeveloped. In reality, so many of these places are lacking due to the extraction of native resources being given to countries now considered developed. It also goes beyond resources. Western scholars and thinkers are credited for knowledge and scholarly contributions that are often criticized by other scholars as knowledge extracted from elsewhere.

Producing inclusive knowledge is critical to the success of classroom instruction. Various approaches to teaching must meet the needs of the diverse student population and educators must provide a safe environment for experiences and perspectives to be discussed. Texts utilized in the classroom must also highlight multicultural backgrounds, ethnicities, races, and genders to bring attention to diverse talents and perceptions of learning. The traditional "one size fits all" modality of instruction ignores diverse students and their funds of knowledge. How can teachers make use of the knowledge and skills of students from diverse backgrounds in ways that maximize their efforts and highlight inclusive practice? First, teachers need to strive to serve all students, regardless of their background or identity. This means not only making accommodations for students who need them but also being accepting of the diverse perspectives and creating the space for these to enrich the classroom. Next, taking into consideration student success and learning achievement, teachers must allow students to draw on relevant experiences and connections from their lives, which increases motivation (Ambrose et al., 2010). Last, teachers must be willing and open to knowledge co-production in the classroom in ways that will be highlighted in the next section.

Funds of Knowledge and Knowledge Production

Funds of knowledge is the accumulation of observed and lived experiences, generational stories, and cultural practices that become a resource to be used in the classroom setting (Molt et al., 1990). This simple premise that competency is based on their lived experiences counters the Eurocentric view that only formal classroom education is valued intellectually, while working-class families are often grouped with the majority view (Taylor & Dorsey-Gaines, 1988). This devalues the expertise and knowledge that each student possesses when entering a classroom. Research shows family beliefs about education as it relates to opportunities have a big impact on students (Ogbu, 2003). How and what students learn at home can enhance the classroom environment. Figure 2 gives examples of added values that comprise funds of knowledge. In reshaping knowledge production, educators must bring in funds for knowledge as a form of pedagogy.

Funds of knowledge allow teachers to celebrate differences in the classroom. The key to using funds of knowledge to reshape knowledge production is to first recognize the difference in the classroom. One of the most effective ways to

Figure 2. Understanding funds of knowledge

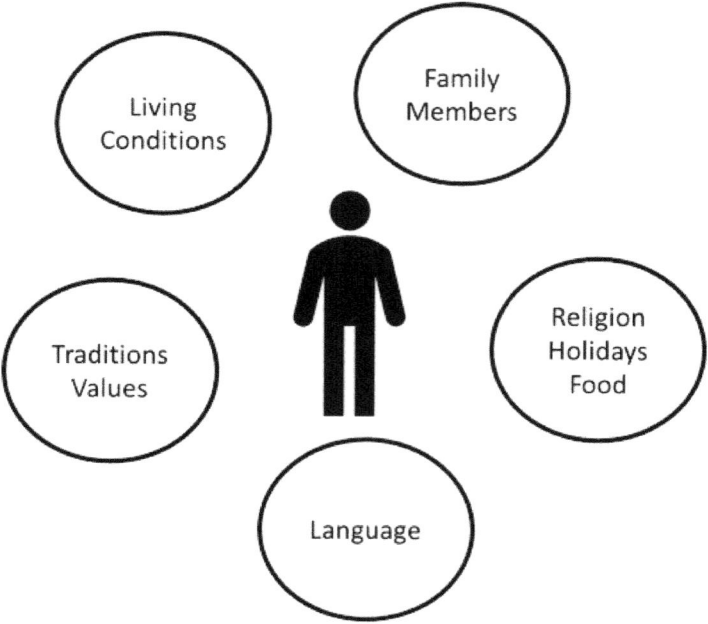

recognize these differences is to get to know your students right from the beginning of the semester. In a Diversity course, in the first week of class, students are asked to share their names, background, and something interesting about themselves. Students are also encouraged to use a name tag inclusive of their preferred name and pronoun. This not only helps teachers remember their students, but it sends a message to the students that the teachers acknowledge their preferences and value their individuality. Teachers also have to try to understand the cultural background of students and leverage it to enrich classroom learning. For example, a lecture on higher education exploring its similarities and differences among different parts of the world is a great way to showcase diversity. In a critical pedagogy course, a classroom mixed with international students and students from the U.S., students were asked to use their own experiences having learned at other institutions outside of the U.S. to speak about higher education in a global context. This is a sign of adjusting the curriculum to include the student's experience. Culturally diverse students should feel included by highlighting their sociocultural strength and building it into learning.

Connecting positionality within the classroom delegates the learner and their individual expertise on the subject (Takacs, 2002). By exploring modes of multiculturalism in higher education serving PWI, we will teach students to better understand their unique positionality in relation to others and how their positionality will ultimately shape their view of the world. Using authentic practices of introspection and organic group dialogue, classrooms may eliminate the accuracy of opinion or judgment and highlight their positionality based on the broad experiences of their student population. Utilizing resources outside of the classroom, such as cultural and community centers, may also serve to develop funds knowledge to strengthen the curriculum for teaching communities of color. Maintaining partnerships with these valuable stakeholders may build diverse interests and help create a diverse classroom curriculum that emphasizes multiple identities. Knowledge and skill obtained by both the student and faculty will extend beyond the classroom experience. In addition to utilizing cultural and community resources in the classroom, there are several ways PWI faculty may assess their classrooms for diverse knowledge production.

1. *Focus on course delivery:* The strategies that implement instruction and facilitate learning must be diverse and build on existing knowledge to construct meaningful educational experiences that allow students to solve real-world problems. Course design and delivery should consider the ethnic, racial, language, and gender issues that potentially exclude under-represented groups or subgroups of people (Baylor University, 2020). Faculty and instructors must remember the learner is unique. The course should motivate learners beyond the successful completion of tasks. Technology can be an innovative way to facilitate learning. Table 2 shows ways in which technology can help students and educators co-produce knowledge.

2. *Embrace unique perspectives*: Faculty/instructors and the students should share the dynamic in facilitating unique interpretations of the content. Collaboration should be viewed as an active social process. By embracing unique perspectives, students may encounter new philosophies, outcomes, and behaviors that will lead to creative and strategic ideas to dispel past ideas or attitudes within a particular curriculum.

3. *Regularly assess the curriculum:* Curriculum taught in the classroom should model real-life experiences with application to current events. With the evolving political and social events at the local, state, national, and global levels, these topics are integral to the students' learning experience. Taking time to acknowledge the events as well as create space to discuss them proves valuable for educators. It is important to be mindful of educator bias, or the unconscious stereotypes and attitudes of racial or socioeconomic bias towards the learner (Staats et al., 2017) which may affect the classroom experience. The curriculum should have diverse authorship, and the materials used should provide open access opportunities for equitable learning regardless of socioeconomic status.

Table 2. Technology as an innovative way to co-produce inclusive knowledge within the classroom

Technology	Integration	Concept/Benefit	Potential Challenges
TikTok, Snapchat, Vimeo	Social Media	Increased interest/ build virtual portfolio (video)	Video/audio quality (poor/dated equipment)
Wix, WordPress, Squarespace	Scholarly Websites (blogs, about me, research, etc.)	Build a professional/Scholarly portfolio. May continuously update throughout career	Digital Literacy (lack of motivation/skill)
Blackboard, Canvas, Tumblr	Discussion boards, communication prompts	Facilitate collaboration and encourage communication	Internet connection / Network instability (potential for issues)
Bubblr, Storybird	Digital storytelling	Promote unique perspectives and emotional intelligence	Continuity amongst other institutions/ classrooms

INCLUSIVE PRACTICES AND CRITICAL PEDAGOGIES

Inclusive practices are necessary to train the next generation of students to be prepared to tackle diversity issues. It is imperative for instructors to reflect deeply on the ways in which they desire their students to learn, which will likely contrast with their own educational experiences (Dewsbury & Brame, 2019). This can be achieved through the development of self-awareness and empathy for students and their evolving needs within the classroom. Several techniques can be employed to create inclusive spaces and/or utilize inclusive practices inside and outside of the classroom to enhance student learning.

The adaptation of the use of the term integration versus inclusion avoids calling the practice what it truly is (Thomazet, 2009). Reflection upon the integration of schools in the 1950s within the United States, particularly in the deep South, revealed levels of anger, the hesitancy of acceptance, and blatant racist acts that were spewed toward students of color from K-12 levels to university levels to maintain "white-only" learning institutions. The use of the word integration to make some comfortable negates any progress in higher education and therefore this chapter encourages the intentional use of the word inclusion. The multiple definitions of inclusion determine its value and execution of it (Nilholm, 2021).

Implementation of inclusive practices requires understanding and knowledge among instructors and needs to account for the multiple disciplines and settings in which they teach. While comfortability levels vary among educators, for reasons such as unfamiliarity with the techniques, fear of misuse of the techniques, and worry of causing more harm than good, even the attempt to implement

Table 3. List of inclusive teaching methods

Method	Description	Reference
Class wide Peer Tutoring	Students teach one another and demonstrate a high percentage of accuracy for all types of learners, including those with varied abilities.	(King-Sears & Cummings, 1996)
Evidence-Based Teaching	This method aims to help students generate meaningful networks to increase access to resources and community.	(Dewsbury & Brame, 2019)
Research in Action	Use community issues to develop real-life examples to expand learning objectives	(Ballard,1995)
Self-Management	After first establishing guidelines for the class, students remain on task, monitor their progress, and aim for attentiveness	(King-Sears & Cummings, 1996)
Research as Stories	Incorporate narratives from real-life persons to generate the struggles and wins	(Ballard,1995)
Flipped Classroom	Students learn material prior to the class and the instructor reiterates the content to build upon the base knowledge	O'Flaherty & Phillips, 2015)
Case Studies	Use theoretical examples to implore critical thinking skills to determine the multiple perspectives and potential outcomes and solutions.	(Nilholm, 2021)

inclusive methods is progress. Comfortability will increase with practice and by learning from mistakes. When the classroom is inclusive, students can learn in environment that is empowering with lasting impact beyond duration of the learning experience...

Many recommendations address inclusion in higher education reference diversifying literature and the curriculum. However, strategies to implement diversity in the curriculum are rarely employed and or incorporated into practice. In practice, this would be multiple groups participating and engaging in the learning materials. This further affirm intersectionality, the interconnectedness of social identities and individuality (Ballard, 1995). That process of engaging with diversity through the learning process creates a space for collaboration with a colleague in a different department, or another institution, or using external resources to find appropriate representation.

To be effective, educators must be willing to adapt and shift their practices to benefit their students. Inclusive practices are not one size fits all. Determination of the best method is dependent on the course, the student composition and profile, class size, and even the time dedicated to lesson planning and implementation. However, Table 3 serves as a foundation for instructors by highlighting methods used by others in hopes that they will determine the best method(s) for their teaching style as well as new methods they can incorporate in the classroom.

Classroom climate sets the tone of respect and collegiality and is helpful when instilled through the syllabus and within the first few weeks of the course (Dewsbury & Brame, 2019). The attitude of teachers, students, and all others involved influences the success of inclusive practices but the type of, availability of, and consistency of resources complement the attitude (Paseka & Schwab, 2020). It is difficult to maintain motivation to incorporate inclusive practices if the infrastructure is not in place to equip instructors with the tools that they need to be successful with their students. For example, a large desk, audio/visual learning equipment or an adaptive keyboard supports inclusive practices. Many institutions utilize evaluation surveys at the completion of a term to evaluate the effectiveness of an instructor's teaching methods. These evaluations must take into consideration inclusive languages that address issues related to marginalized populations, nonsexist language, both online and offline options, color contrast, and other accessibility needs.

Many concepts from the art discipline are applicable to other fields within higher education such as the creation of *undisciplined spaces* (Anila, 2017). The spaces, whether abstract or physical, exceed boundaries or restrictions created and even reinforced by institutions. This allows new thoughts to emerge and in ways that builds on existing knowledge. Reflecting on the concept of time, research shows students' knowledge should increase in time and explore their presence within spaces (Shahjahan, 2015). There needs to be organization and structure to prepare instructors for a continuation of methods learned as well as consistency despite challenges that may arise (Burstein et al., 2004). A model for change suggests introspection and reflection are integral for the commitment, planning, preparation, and support for change. This model should be adopted by the institutional leadership to demonstrate that commitment to inclusive practices leads to sustainability (Burnstein et al., 2004).

Syllabus Presentation and Implementation

Despite the various disciplines represented in the classroom, the syllabus is a universal guiding document. It shares the expectations of the instructor, pertinent deadlines, assessment methods, and opportunities for continued dialogue with the instructor. Best practices that have been implemented and work well to promote inclusive learning spaces are as follows:

1. Improve the syllabus' content by having a student-focused syllabus that is more representative of the diverse student body and incorporates cultural representation (Zidani, 2021). Integration of the voices and contributions of non-Western individuals advances the curriculum (Arday et. al., 2021).
2. Distribute the syllabus prior to the first day of class. This allows all students the opportunity to review it in advance and to prepare any questions or comments for the instructor to address.
3. Review the syllabus on the first day of class. It may seem time-consuming, but the review process allows the instructor to expand on statements that may be unclear or ambiguous to provide clarification. While it is likely that questions will arise throughout the course, setting aside this time demonstrates a commitment to inclusion.
4. Include affirmations in the syllabus. Consider important institutional principles around diversity, equity, and inclusion and affirm that the classroom is a space where all students are welcomed and respected.

Towards a Critical Pedagogy

To move towards a more critical pedagogy, institutions must be willing to examine the demographics of the schools served, faculty population, and surrounding areas. This is beneficial as it connects the institution to the students and their surrounding community and not only the student on the personal level, (Han et al., 2015). Critical pedagogy increases civic engagement opportunities to transform oppressive forces, especially towards those from underrepresented groups and backgrounds and better equip them to tackle any future causes (de los Ríos et al., 2015). Limiting critical pedagogy to only race and the need to dismantle whiteness within the curriculum oversimplifies critical pedagogy and ignores the shared responsibility of educators to practice it for the greater good of their students (Berchini, 2017). Examples of activities to adopt in educational settings are listed in Table 4.

The future of critical pedagogy is supported since, while the classroom and places of learning are independent, the city, state, national, and political issues permeate those boundaries (Mclaren, 2020). Critical pedagogy empowers students to challenge and tackle societal or community oppression (Zion et al., 2015). Mapping of space through a participatory process allows students to generate deeper knowledge through cultural immersion (Palipane et al., 2020). A common criticism is a lack of tools available to truly promote change, but solutions may be presented through the exploration process for students (Foley et al., 2015). Table 4 gives examples of some activities that could be used as critical pedagogy efforts.

Table 4. Examples of activities to increase critical pedagogy efforts

Activity Type	Reference
Family Literacy Night	(Han et al., 2015)
Movie Viewings	(Han et al., 2015)
Literature Circles	(Han et al., 2015)
Placemaking Sandbox	(Palipane et al., 2020)
Social Justice Clubs	(de los Ríos et al., 2015)
Video Observations	(Zion et al., 2015)
Examine Achievement Gaps	(Zion et al., 2015)
Explore Traditional and Nontraditional Holidays	(Zion et al., 2015)

Towards a Multicultural Curriculum

In this chapter, we define the term multiculturalism within the context of curricula and teaching practices as the inclusivity of all underrepresented cultures and their uniqueness. Multiculturalism as defined by Brown and Ratcliff (1998) includes all persons, many alienated and oppressed groups to create visions of their culture in which they are included within the dominant culture. Multiculturalism functions as part of a broader political movement advocating for the inclusion of marginalized groups (Glazer 1997; Hollinger, 2006; Taylor et. al., 1988). We acknowledge the differences in language in literature as the terms have been changing over time. Brown and Ratcliff (1998) refer to this as the multiple contexts of multiculturalism within curriculum development and teaching. In U.S. higher education, we have started to see the efforts to make the transition from the dominant Eurocentric curricula to a culturally responsive, multicultural curriculum. Building a multicultural curriculum is a continuous learning process for educators due to the variety of students and contexts (Sleeter, 2000).

Freire (2014) argued that the silenced voices have to emerge with reflection and action on how to transform the world. Only when we address the needs of the silenced voices can we bring them forward. As such, the U.S. classroom can sometimes be multicultural, but it is still unevenly distributed by race, gender, and socio-economic class. The multicultural curriculum brings into conversation the dominant white narrative and the cultural other, but instead of domination and subordination, the relationship is one that coexists with respect to the often-silenced voices

In this section, we will provide examples of how we could include all cultures and backgrounds in PWIs to sustain a multicultural curriculum and teaching practices. The overall suggested practices are shown in Figure 3. We note here that

Figure 3. Examples of the multicultural curriculum elements

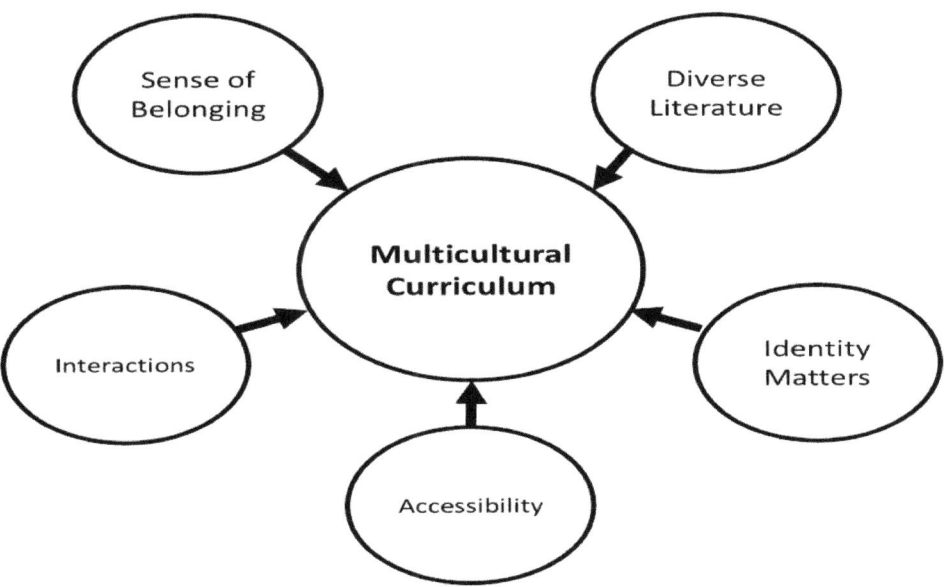

Table 5. Incorporating culture into the curriculum using instructional design (see Appendix for detailed template)

Action	Objective	Presentation Strategy	Generative Strategy	Assessment
Define Multiculturalism	The learner shall be able to define the word Multiculturalism.	State the definition of Culture.	Have the learner list synonyms or describing phrases for the culture	*Given a list of synonyms and descriptive phrases,* the learner shall be able to match the keywords of each statement to the corresponding synonyms and descriptive phrases with *100% accuracy.*
Identify Stereotypes	The learner shall be able to identify stereotypes associated with members of higher education	Identify stereotypes of higher education classrooms.	Have the learner list the stereotypes associated with members of higher education based on role.	*Presented with a list of generational stereotypes and each generation,* match the stereotypes to the correct generation with *100% accuracy.*
Define DEI	The learner shall be able to define the words diversity, equity & inclusion	State the definition of Diversity, Equity & Inclusion (DEI)	Within groups, the learner will define and list synonyms for each word	*Given a list of synonyms and definitions,* match the keywords of each statement to its corresponding synonyms and definitions with *100% accuracy.*

the suggested practices are based on the authors' backgrounds and experiences, and they may vary during the practice. Table 5 expands on ways to incorporate culture into the curriculum using instructional design.

Building an Inclusive Classroom

Diverse literature: Course materials should be chosen from diverse literature and textbooks. Students should be able to make connections with selected resources. Research shows that selecting course materials that are diverse allows for open discussions and engagement with diverse perspectives including a consideration of global issues (Adam & Harper, 2016). Similarly, a review of course materials for First-Generation college students found that students are able to improve their academic learning and advance in their discipline when they are able to connect their lived experiences to the academic content of the lesson (Ives & Castillo-Montoya, 2020). Diverse literature helps students make meaning during their learning process. One way to connect literature to students' backgrounds is to ask for continuous feedback from students about their experiences with the course materials. A simple survey or class Dropbox to generate topics or a list of authors can help to create an inclusive learning environment. Higher education teachers and practitioners have a responsibility to not only understand how their students learn but support them in what they learn. For students of color, it is important that they see themselves in some of the classroom materials by including Black and Brown authors as part of the reading materials.

Accessibility: While providing diverse literature, educators should also consider that materials need to be accessible. Accessibility in the classroom, according to the Oxford dictionary, is the quality of being easily used by people who have a disability. This is vital to an inclusive classroom space as it ensures that all students are able to participate fully in the learning process. The definition of disability varies, and it is important to note that the way people define or think about disability impacts their expectations and how they interact with people who have disabilities (Haegele & Hodge, 2016). Educators should be knowledgeable of their students and their needs. Research on introductory college courses during the beginning of the Pandemic showed that while technology forced classroom learning to be more interactive, it did not account for accessibility. Students from under-sourced background, unfortunately, experienced barriers to learning and other social class issues, like lack of internet or working space, which were also a challenge (Gillis & Krull, 2020). While it is challenging to meet every single need of each student, educators should try to make their learning spaces meet the universal design for learning (UDL) framework. UDL provides adequate suggestions and examples for a learning environment that best meets the needs of differently-abled students, first generation students as well as those from under-sourced background.

Besides using the UDL framework in the classroom to ensure it is accessible for all students, educators should also implement other strategies that can be effective. For example, educators should try to provide open-access resources and free or discounted textbooks and materials. etc. There should always be options for students to choose from, which shows that the educator is in fact sensible to the needs of a diverse student population. Students should have a choice of whether they prefer to make a purchase of course materials or use free resources (Baylor University, 2020). If there is no open-access option, efforts should be made to find other ways to get the materials or alternative open-access materials. Educators should always pay attention to their student's abilities and be able to identify methods to assist them and make learning accessible for them. Classroom teachers are encouraged to collaborate with school administrators and student service units to prepare and edit the course materials before the beginning of classes.

Identity matters: Understanding student identity supports academic learning (Ives & Castillo-Montoya, 2020). On the first day of class or as soon as possible within a new classroom setting, educators should practice asking students for their names not as it is written on the school's roster, but as the students prefer to be called. Students can create name tags and/or desk plates. The instructor can use this activity to not only learn about their student's preferred name but also about pronunciation. Focus group data on undocumented students at a Hispanic-Serving Institution showed that students were more willing to participate when they felt their identity was recognized in the class and emphasized with a simple highlight of their names (Valdez & Golash-Boza, 2020). Another small activity that allows educators to support student preference is to make room for them to share their preferred pronouns. This is usually a repetitive activity at the beginning of each class. For example, *Hi, my name is Luisa, and my pronouns are she/her/hers.* Educators are encouraged to have students use name tags with their pronouns so that other students can get familiar with the preferences of one another. It is important to acknowledge each other's identities to show value for their preferences in public or in classrooms (Wentling, 2015). As educators, the broader message to the students should be *I see you, I respect how you identify, and the classroom space supports you.* All efforts must be made to not only recognize preferred pronouns and names but also to use inclusive language and avoid saying things like "ladies and gentlemen" or "Mr. and Mrs." A classroom where identity matters should strive to use language such as "folks", y'all" or just say the names of students.

Interactions: The size of the classroom affects students' interactions with their peers and their lecturers. Beattie and Thiele (2016) found that the more interaction students have in the classroom, the more learning outcomes are improved. In big-size classrooms with more than 30 students, educators must still try to recognize individuality by having intentional talking points with students, perhaps at the beginning or after delivering the class materials. Dr. Homero Murzi, a culturally responsive educator at the Department of Engineering Education at Virginia Tech, shares that what works for encouraging interaction is simply asking, "Tell me something I do not know about you" (Murzi, 2022). He poses this question to his students when he encounters them before or after class. Starting a conversation with students by getting to know them creates a welcoming environment for students and educators. He also mentions that he asks students their favorite songs and creates a playlist, and plays these songs before the class begins. These activities help to create a friendly environment.

Another example for encouraging interaction in the classroom is using activities or exercises to get students to explore common interests and experiences. These questions are usually chosen related to students' character and social lives. Questions useful for such interactions are "If you became famous, what would you be famous for?" and "Name three things you enjoy doing in your free time." These activities can be executed by having students use journals and combine reflection techniques.

Research shows that ice-breaker activities can be used to build relationships in groups. Beyond that, ice-breaker activities can be used to help students practice speaking and listening and create a social culture in the classroom (Almethhib, 2009). Educators should give students multiple opportunities to talk in small groups, which aids community building. By engaging with other students, educators can help create an environment where students can share their values and interests, discover their commonalities and differences and appreciate the diverse dynamics within their classrooms. So, the next time an educator begins a course, instead of reading the syllabus or asking for students' names, maybe begin with Bingo about things they enjoy or your favorite icebreaker to initiate community (Holbert, 2015).

Sense of Belonging: Students' sense of belongingness plays a critical role in college success and retention (O'Keeffe, 2013). Sense of belonging is defined as the psychological feeling of belonging to a social, cultural, spatial, or professional community (Hurtado & Carter, 1997). This is developed through shared beliefs being recognized, a supportive environment, or opportunities for interaction (Ma, 2003). Humans and the need to belong and affiliate and be accepted by members of a group fits into what social psychologists call intrinsic motivation to affiliate with others (Schneider & Kwan, 2013). Research shows college students who have a greater sense of belonging, have higher motivation, self-confidence, and higher levels of academic achievement (Pedler et. al., 2021). Belongingness is also associated with basic social needs as in Maslow's Hierarchy of needs (Addison and Brundrett, 2008), and students can develop their sense of belonging within the classroom just by having a supportive and welcoming environment (O'Keeffe, 2013). Glass and Westmont (2014) found that cultural events, leadership programs, and community services tend to increase college students' sense of belonging. In practice, this looks like celebrating heritage months, getting students involved in community services, and taking an active role in planning and implementing those services. These activities not only enrich students' belongingness but can be added to the curriculum to enrich student learning. A multicultural curriculum disrupts the normative curriculum that does not recognize innovation with co-curricular activities. Another example that fosters a sense of belonging is having students share important dates from their religious, ethnic, or cultural background that should be observed or celebrated. For example, a school calendar that only has Christian holidays ignores other important holidays and ignores the diversity of the classroom. Educators are encouraged to ask students for important dates to be a part of the classroom calendar. This inclusive practice again sends a message that all are welcome.

Educators may also connect diverse community leaders to students in order to demonstrate diversity in leadership positions. Glass and Westmont (2014) found that leadership programs' interaction with college students increases belongingness. This also creates opportunities for collaboration, which is needed for developing career skills, fostering collaborative-learning strategies, and student learning (Premo et al., 2018). College educators can invite guest lecturers from within the community to share both professional and lived experiences and provide students the opportunity to interact with others engaging in philanthropy and stay motivated. Last, by organizing community services for people from diverse backgrounds, educators can invite diverse voices into the classroom space. A great way to welcome diversity through community service is to search for nearby community organizations that are working on issues affecting historically marginalized communities or issues related to the demography of the classrooms. Encouraging students to be a part of the decision-making, planning, and implementation of community service projects nurtures a sense of belonging.

Activity: If you really knew me

Many students are familiar with activities that encourage others to learn something about them that otherwise may be unknown. In a classroom setting, this activity can be implemented by presenting the class with the prompt "If you really knew me, you would know that. . ." The students in the class are encouraged to complete the phrase by adding something they want others to know about them. This declaration may be something related to their hobbies, family, friends, education, and more. The advantage of such an activity is that it is open-ended and allows students to utilize creativity in their responses. When reflecting on the core principles of diversity and inclusion, this activity allows students to observe what they have in common or dissimilar to others in the class. This promotes a sense of belonging and community.

CONCLUSION

The history of the USA situates unfavorable social, political, and economic conditions for non-European people and cultures. The colonial makings of subordinating non-European cultures continue to serve as the foundation of many institutions, including colleges and universities. Although many strides have been made towards equality, there is still some division in schools that calls for a need to decolonize and build a more inclusive society. Starting with the classroom, this chapter calls for decolonizing the curriculum of higher education institutions to create a more inclusive space. Using examples, educators are given tools to effectively convert learning spaces. For example, reflections on class syllabi are used to demonstrate how both teachers and students are a part of inclusive practices. From asserting diverse language re-designing assessment tools and capitalizing on funds of knowledge, this chapter is a practical guide towards decolonizing the classroom in a global society.

The classroom is a political space, as it is situated within institutions and states where power is exerted, resisted, or negotiated. The activity, designs, and practices in this chapter present ways to negotiate the power structures in the classroom and disrupt systemic oppression and normative whiteness. We shared examples and resources that envision all cultures and knowledge systems in a way that recognizes and celebrates diversity. By using critical pedagogy and inclusive practices, college educators can create their own multicultural learning environment equipped with a curriculum that reflects the students and a more inclusive classroom. Educators at predominately White institutions are given an opportunity to learn, reflect and re-design their classroom into a space that celebrates and reflects. This chapter challenge biases and racism embedded in our teaching and learning.

REFERENCES

Adam, H., & Harper, L. (2016). Assessing and selecting culturally diverse literature for the classroom. *Practical Literacy: The Early and Primary Years*, *21*(2), 10–13. doi:10.3316/aeipt.212531

Addison, R., & Brundrett, M. (2008). Motivation and demotivation of teachers in primary schools: The challenge of change. *Education 3-13, 36*(1), 79–94. https://doi.org/ doi:10.1080/03004270701733254

Akena, F. A. (2012). Critical Analysis of the Production of Western Knowledge and Its Implications for Indigenous Knowledge and Decolonization. *Journal of Black Studies*, *43*(6), 599–619. doi:10.1177/0021934712440448

Alim, H. S., & Smitherman, G. (2012). *Articulate while Black: Barack Obama, language, and race in the US*. Oxford University Press.

Almethhib, M. (2009). The Impact of Ice Breaking Exercises on Trainees' Interactions and Skill Acquisition: An Experimental Study. *Journal of King Abdulaziz University-Economics and Administration*, *23*(1), 3–20. doi:10.4197/Eco.23-1.1

Alvares, C., & Faruqi, S. S. (2014). *Decolonising the University: The Emerging Quest for Non-Eurocentric Paradigms (Penerbit USM)*. Penerbit USM.

Ambrose, S. A., Bridges, M. W., DiPietro, M., Lovett, M. C., & Norman, M. K. (2010). *How learning works: Seven research-based principles for smart teaching*. John Wiley & Sons.

Andreotti, V. (2007). An ethical engagement with the other: Spivak's ideas on education. *Critical Literacy: Theories and Practices*, *1*(1), 69–79.

Anila, S. (2017). Inclusion Requires Fracturing. *Journal of Museum Education*, *42*(2), 108–119. doi:10.1080/10598650.2017.1306996

Arday, J., Zoe Belluigi, D., & Thomas, D. (2021). Attempting to break the chain: Reimaging inclusive pedagogy and decolonising the curriculum within the academy. *Educational Philosophy and Theory*, *53*(3), 298–313. doi:10.1080/00131857.2020.1773257

Ballard, K. (1995). Inclusion, Paradigms, Power and Participation. In *Towards Inclusive Schools?* Routledge.

Battiste, M. (2019). *Decolonizing education: Nourishing the learning spirit*. UBC press.

Baylor University. (2020, December 10). How to Provide a Multicultural Education. *BAY-UMT*. https://onlinegrad.baylor.edu/resources/multicultural-educat ion-strategies/

Beattie, I. R., & Thiele, M. (2016). Connecting in Class? College Class Size and Inequality in Academic Social Capital. *The Journal of Higher Education*, *87*(3), 332–362. doi:10.1080/00221546.2016.11777405

Bell, C. (2020). "Maybe if they let us tell the story I wouldn't have gotten suspended": Understanding Black students' and parents' perceptions of school discipline. *Children and Youth Services Review*, *110*, 104757. doi:10.1016/j. childyouth.2020.104757

Berchini, C. N. (2017). Critiquing Un/Critical Pedagogies to Move Toward a Pedagogy of Responsibility in Teacher Education. *Journal of Teacher Education*, *68*(5), 463–475. doi:10.1177/0022487117702572

Brock, C., Wallace, J., Herschbach, M., Johnson, C., Raikes, B., Warren, K., Nikoli, M., & Poulsen, H. (2006). Negotiating displacement spaces: Exploring teachers' stories about learning and diversity. *Curriculum Inquiry*, *36*(1), 35–62. doi:10.1111/j.1467-873X.2005.00345.x

Brown, M. C., & Ratcliff, J. L. (1998). Multiculturalism and Multicultural Curricula in the United States. *Higher Education in Europe*, *23*(1), 11–21. doi:10.1080/0379772980230102

Burstein, N., Sears, S., Wilcoxen, A., Cabello, B., & Spagna, M. (2004). Moving Toward Inclusive Practices. *Remedial and Special Education*, *25*(2), 104–116. doi:10.1177/07419325040250020501

CAST. (2018). *Universal Design for Learning Guidelines version 2.2*. CAST. http://udlguidelines.cast.org

Communication on College Composition and Communication (CCCC) (1974). *Students' right to their own language position statement*. CCCC.

Crenshaw, K. W. (1988). Race, Reform, and Retrenchment: Transformation and Legitimation in Antidiscrimination Law. *Harvard Law Review*, *101*(7), 1331–1387. doi:10.2307/1341398

De los Ríos, C. V., López, J., & Morrell, E. (2015). Toward a Critical Pedagogy of Race: Ethnic Studies and Literacies of Power in High School Classrooms. *Race and Social Problems*, *7*(1), 84–96. doi:10.100712552-014-9142-1

Dei, G. (2016). Decolonizing the university: The challenges and possibilities of inclusive education. *Socialist Studies/Études Socialistes, 11*(1), 23–23.

Dewsbury, B., & Brame, C. J. (2019). *Evidence Based Teaching Guide: Inclusive Teaching*. CBE Life Science Education. https://lse.ascb.org/evidence-based-teaching-guides/inclusive-teaching/network-leverage/

Dewsbury, B., & Brame, C. J. (2019). Inclusive Teaching. *CBE Life Sciences Education, 18*(2), fe2. doi:10.1187/cbe.19-01-0021 PMID:31025917

Eakins, A., & Eakins, S. L. (2017). African American Students at Predominantly White Institutions: A Collaborative Style Cohort Recruitment & Retention Model. *The Journal of Learning in Higher Education, 13*(2), 51–57.

Elabor-Idemudia, P. (2012). Gender and Identity in a Globalized World. In *The Age of Knowledge* (pp. 109–124). Brill. doi:10.1163/9789004211032_008

Ermine, W., Battiste, M., & Barman, J. (1995). Aboriginal epistemology. *First Nations Education in Canada: The Circle Unfolds*, 101–112.

Fanon, F., & Philcox, R. (2008). Black Skin, White Masks (Revised). Grove Press.

Fanon, F., Sartre, J. P., Farrington, C., & Grove Press. (1963). *The Wretched of the Earth*. Amsterdam University Press.

Foley, J. A., Morris, D., Gounari, P., & Agostinone-Wilson, F. (2015). *Critical education, critical pedagogies, marxist education in the United States. 13*, 110–144. Department of Education.

Freire, P. (2014). *Pedagogy of the Oppressed: 30th Anniversary Edition*. Bloomsberry Academic. https://www.amazon.com/Pedagogy-Oppressed-Anniversary-Paulo-Freire-ebook/dp/B00M0FQHQO

Gillis, A., & Krull, L. M. (2020). COVID-19 remote learning transition in spring 2020: Class structures, student perceptions, and inequality in college courses. *Teaching Sociology, 48*(4), 283–299. doi:10.1177/0092055X20954263

Glass, C. R., & Westmont, C. M. (2014). Comparative effects of belongingness on the academic success and cross-cultural interactions of domestic and international students. *International Journal of Intercultural Relations, 38*, 106–119. doi:10.1016/j.ijintrel.2013.04.004

Glazer, N. (1998). *We are all multiculturalists now*. Harvard University Press.

Goldstein, T., & Selby, D. (2000). *Weaving Connections: Educating for Peace, Social and Environmental Justice* (1st ed.). Sumach Press.

Gottlieb, M., & Ernst-Slavit, G. (2014). *Academic language in diverse classrooms: Definitions and contexts*. Corwin Press.

Haegele, J. A., & Hodge, S. (2016). Disability discourse: Overview and critiques of the medical and social models. *Quest, 68*(2), 193–206. doi:10.1080/003362 97.2016.1143849

Hall, S., Evans, J., & Nixon, S. (2013). *Representation: Cultural Representations and Signifying Practices (Culture, Media and Identities series)* (2nd ed.). SAGE Publications Ltd.

Holbert, R. M. G. (2015). Beginning with Bingo – An Icebreaker to Initiate Classroom Community. *College Teaching, 63*(4), 181–182. doi:10.1080/8756 7555.2015.1052723

Hollinger, D. A. (2006). Postethnic America: Beyond multiculturalism. Hachette UK.

Hundley, S. P., Kahn, S., & Banta, T. W. (2019). *Trends in Assessment: Ideas, Opportunities, and Issues for Higher Education*. Stylus Publishing.

Hurtado, S., & Carter, D. F. (1997). Effects of College Transition and Perceptions of the Campus Racial Climate on Latino College Students' Sense of Belonging. *Sociology of Education, 70*(4), 324. doi:10.2307/2673270

Hussain, M., & Jones, J. M. (2021). Discrimination, diversity, and sense of belonging: Experiences of students of color. *Journal of Diversity in Higher Education, 14*(1), 63–71. doi:10.1037/dhe0000117

Ives, J., & Castillo-Montoya, M. (2020). First-Generation College Students as Academic Learners: A Systematic Review. *Review of Educational Research, 90*(2), 139–178. doi:10.3102/0034654319899707

Jiles, E. (2020, March 19). *PWI (predominately white institution) "was the hardest year of my life."* The Hechinger Report. https://hechingerreport.org/student-voices-black-student-at-a-pwi/

Jiles, E. (2021, April 8). STUDENT VOICE: Having 'the hardest year of my life' at 'a school that's mostly white, conservative and isolated—everything I wasn't.' *The Hechinger Report*. https://hechingerreport.org/student-voices-black-student-at-a-pwi/

Jin, Y. X., & Dewaele, J.-M. (2018). The effect of positive orientation and perceived social support on foreign language classroom anxiety. *System*, *74*, 149–157. doi:10.1016/j.system.2018.01.002

Jivraj, S. (2020). Decolonizing the academy–between a rock and a hard place. *Interventions*, *22*(4), 552–573. doi:10.1080/1369801X.2020.1753559

Johnson, H. E., Molloy Elreda, L., Kibler, A. K., & Futch Ehrlich, V. A. (2020). Creating Classroom Communities in Linguistically Diverse Settings: Teacher-Directed, Classroom-Level Factor Effects on Peer Dynamics. *The Journal of Early Adolescence*, *40*(8), 1087–1120. doi:10.1177/0272431619891238

Kallio, G., & Houtbeckers, E. (2020). Academic Knowledge Production: Framework of Practical Activity in the Context of Transformative Food Studies. *Frontiers in Sustainable Food Systems*, *4*, 577351. https://www.frontiersin.org/articles/10.3389/fsufs.2020.5773 51. doi:10.3389/fsufs.2020.577351

King-Sears, M. E., & Cummings, C. S. (1996). Inclusive Practices of Classroom Teachers. *Remedial and Special Education*, *17*(4), 217–225. doi:10.1177/074193259601700404

Ma, X. (2003). Sense of belonging to school: Can schools make a difference? *The Journal of Educational Research*, *96*(6), 340–349. doi:10.1080/00220670309596617

Margolis, E. (2001). *The hidden curriculum in higher education*. Psychology Press.

McCluney, C. L., Durkee, M. I., Smith, R. E. II, Robotham, K. J., & Lee, S. S.-L. (2021). To be, or not to be… Black: The effects of racial codeswitching on perceived professionalism in the workplace. *Journal of Experimental Social Psychology*, *97*, 104199. doi:10.1016/j.jesp.2021.104199

Mclaren, P. (2020). The future of critical pedagogy. *Educational Philosophy and Theory*, *52*(12), 1243–1248. doi:10.1080/00131857.2019.1686963

McNair, T. B., Albertine, S., Cooper, M. A., McDonald, N., & Jr, M. T. (2017). *Becoming a Student-Ready College: A New Culture of Leadership for Student Success* (2nd ed.). Jossey-Bass.

Meadows, K. (2011). The desegregation of public schools: Ruby Bridges, Millicent E. Brown, and Josephine Boyd Bradley—Black educators by any means necessary. *Vitae Scholasticae*, *28*(2), 23–34.

Merryfield, M. M. (2000). Why aren't teachers being prepared to teach for diversity, equity, and global interconnectedness? A study of lived experiences in the making of multicultural and global educators. *Teaching and Teacher Education*, *16*(4), 429–443. doi:10.1016/S0742-051X(00)00004-4

Mignolo, W. (2003). Globalization and the geopolitics of knowledge: The role of the humanities in the corporate university. *Nepantla*, *4*(1), 97–119.

Mignolo, W. D. (2011). The Darker Side of Western Modernity*: Global Futures, Decolonial Options*. http://syonilan.1sthost.org/file/the-darker-side-of-western-modernity-global-futures-decolonial-options-by-walter-d-mign olo.pdf

Miller, D. (2022). Ungrading Light: 4 Simple Ways to Ease the Spotlight Off Points. *The Chronicles of Higher Education*. https://www.chronicle.com/article/ungrading-light-4-simple-w ays-to-ease-the-spotlight-off-points

Moll, L. C. (1990). Introduction. *Vygotsky and Education*, 1–28. doi:10.1017/CBO9781139173674.002

Molt, L. C., Vélez-lbaðez, C., Greenberg, J., Whitmore, K., Saavedra, E., Dworin, J., & Andrade, F. (1990). *Community knowledge and classroom practice: Combining resources for literacy instruction (OBEMLA Contract No. 300—87-0131)*. Tucson: University of Arizona, College of Education and Bureau of Applied Research in Anthropology.

Montenegro, E., & Jankowski, N. A. (2017). Equity and assessment: Moving towards culturally responsive assessment. *Occasional Paper, 29*.

Morgan, H. (1995). *Historical Perspectives on the Education of Black Children*. ERIC.

Murzi, H. (2022). *Historically Black Colleges and Universities (HBCU) Research Summit- DEI: Culturally Relevant Learning and Teaching Workshop. Presenter*. Virginia Tech Graduate School.

Ndofirepi, A. P., Maringe, F., Vurayai, S., & Erima, G. (2022). Decolonising African University Knowledges, Volume 2: Challenging the Neoliberal Mantra. Taylor & Francis. doi:10.4324/9781003241522

Ng-A-Fook, N. (2013). Fishing for Knowledge Beyond Colonial Disciplines: Curriculum, Social Action Projects, and Indigenous Communities. In Contemporary Studies in Environmental and Indigenous Pedagogies (pp. 285–305). Brill.

Nilholm, C. (2021). Research about inclusive education in 2020 – How can we improve our theories in order to change practice? *European Journal of Special Needs Education, 36*(3), 358–370. doi:10.1080/08856257.2020.1754547

Nortvedt, G. A., Wiese, E., Brown, M., Burns, D., McNamara, G., O'Hara, J., Altrichter, H., Fellner, M., Herzog-Punzenberger, B., Nayir, F., & Taneri, P. O. (2020). Aiding culturally responsive assessment in schools in a globalising world. *Educational Assessment, Evaluation and Accountability, 32*(1), 5–27. doi:10.100711092-020-09316-w

O'Flaherty, J., & Phillips, C. (2015). The use of flipped classrooms in higher education: A scoping review. *The Internet and Higher Education, 25*, 85–95. doi:10.1016/j.iheduc.2015.02.002

O'Keeffe, P. (2013). A Sense of Belonging: Improving Student Retention. *College Student Journal, 47*(4), 605–613.

Ogbu, J. U. (2003). *Black American students in an affluent suburb: A study of academic disengagement.* Routledge. doi:10.4324/9781410607188

Palipane, K., Mateo-Babiano, I., & Hernandez-Santin, C. (2020). Conclusion: Placemaking as Critical Pedagogy of Place. In I. Mateo-Babiano & K. Palipane (Eds.), *Placemaking Sandbox: Emergent Approaches, Techniques and Practices to Create More Thriving Places* (pp. 107–121). Springer. doi:10.1007/978-981-15-2752-4_7

Paseka, A., & Schwab, S. (2020). Parents' attitudes towards inclusive education and their perceptions of inclusive teaching practices and resources. *European Journal of Special Needs Education, 35*(2), 254–272. doi:10.1080/08856257.2019.1665232

Pedler, M. L., Willis, R., & Nieuwoudt, J. E. (2021). A sense of belonging at university: Student retention, motivation and enjoyment. *Journal of Further and Higher Education, 46*(3), 397–408. doi:10.1080/0309877X.2021.1955844

People meeting in a room photo. (2018). photograph, Providencia, Chile. https://unsplash.com/photos/cw-cj_nFa14

Premo, J., Cavagnetto, A., Davis, W. B., & Brickman, P. (2018). Promoting Collaborative Classrooms: The Impacts of Interdependent Cooperative Learning on Undergraduate Interactions and Achievement. *CBE Life Sciences Education*, *17*(2), ar32. doi:10.1187/cbe.17-08-0176 PMID:29799312

Salend, S. J. (2015). *Creating inclusive classrooms: Effective, differentiated and reflective practices*. Pearson.

Sanchez, A. (2018). Canon Fire. *Cambridge Anthropology*, *36*(2), 1–6. doi:10.3167/cja.2018.360202

Schilling, K. M., & Schilling, K. L. (1998). Proclaiming and Sustaining Excellence: Assessment as a Faculty Role (J-B ASHE Higher Education Report Series (AEHE)) (1st ed.). Jossey-Bass.

Schneider, M. L., & Kwan, B. M. (2013). Psychological need satisfaction, intrinsic motivation and affective response to exercise in adolescents. *Psychology of Sport and Exercise*, *14*(5), 776–785. doi:10.1016/j.psychsport.2013.04.005 PMID:24015110

Shahjahan, R. A. (2015). Being 'Lazy' and Slowing Down: Toward decolonizing time, our body, and pedagogy. *Educational Philosophy and Theory*, *47*(5), 488–501. doi:10.1080/00131857.2014.880645

Shahjahan, R. A., Estera, A. L., Surla, K. L., & Edwards, K. T. (2022). "Decolonizing" curriculum and pedagogy: A comparative review across disciplines and global higher education contexts. *Review of Educational Research*, *92*(1), 73–113. doi:10.3102/00346543211042423

Shirley, V. J. (2017). Indigenous Social Justice Pedagogy: Teaching into the Risks and Cultivating the Heart. *Critical Questions in Education*, *8*(2), 163–177.

Skopec, M., Fyfe, M., Issa, H., Ippolito, K., Anderson, M., & Harris, M. (2021). Decolonization in a higher education STEMM institution–is 'epistemic fragility' a barrier? *London Review of Education*, *19*(1), 1–21. doi:10.14324/LRE.19.1.18

Sleeter, C. E. (2000). Creating an Empowering Multicultural Curriculum. *Race, Gender & Class (Towson, Md.)*, *7*(3), 178–196.

Smith, L. T. (2012). *Decolonizing methodologies: Research and Indigenous peoples*. Zed Books.

Spratt, J., & Florian, L. (2015). Inclusive pedagogy: From learning to action. Supporting each individual in the context of 'everybody.'. *Teaching and Teacher Education*, *49*, 89–96. doi:10.1016/j.tate.2015.03.006

Staats, C., Capatosto, K., & Tenney, L. Sarah Mamo S. (2017). State of the Science: Implicit Bias Review. Kirwan Institute for the Study of Race and Ethnicity.

Steinman, E. W. (2016). Decolonization not inclusion: Indigenous resistance to American settler colonialism. *Sociology of Race and Ethnicity (Thousand Oaks, Calif.)*, *2*(2), 219–236. doi:10.1177/2332649215615889

Takacs, D. (2002). Positionality, Epistemology, and Social Justice in the Classroom. *Social Justice (San Francisco, Calif.)*, *29*(4 (90)), 168–181.

Tanaka, G. K. (2003). *The intercultural campus: Transcending culture & power in American higher education* (Vol. 97). Peter Lang.

Taylor, D., & Dorsey-Gaines, C. (1988). Growing Up Literate: Learning from Inner-City Families. Heinemann.

Thiong'O, W. N. (1986). *Decolonising the Mind: The Politics of Language in African Literature*. James Currey Ltd / Heinemann.

Thomazet, S. (2009). From integration to inclusive education: Does changing the terms improve practice? *International Journal of Inclusive Education*, *13*(6), 553–563. doi:10.1080/13603110801923476

Valdez, Z., & Golash-Boza, T. (2020). Master status or intersectional identity? Undocumented students' sense of belonging on a college campus. *Identities (Yverdon)*, *27*(4), 481–499. doi:10.1080/1070289X.2018.1534452

Waldoff, R. A., Wiggins, Y. M., & Washington, H. M. (2011). Black Collegians at a Predominantly White Institution: Toward a Place-Based Understanding of Black Student's Adjustment to College. *Journal of Black Studies*, *42*(7), 1047–1079. doi:10.1177/0021934711400741

Wentling, T. (2015). Trans* Disruptions: Pedagogical Practices and Pronoun Recognition. *Transgender Studies Quarterly*, *2*(3), 469–476. doi:10.1215/23289252-2926437

Woodson, C. G. (1933). *The Mis-Education of the Negro*. http://mrsdaysheffield.weebly.com/uploads/5/5/4/1/5541180/the_miseducation_of_the_negro.pdf

Zidani, S. (2021). Whose pedagogy is it anyway? Decolonizing the syllabus through a critical embrace of difference. *Media Culture & Society*, *43*(5), 970–978. doi:10.1177/0163443720980922

Zion, S., Allen, C. D., & Jean, C. (2015). Enacting a Critical Pedagogy, Influencing Teachers' Sociopolitical Development. *The Urban Review*, *47*(5), 914–933. doi:10.100711256-015-0340-y

ADDITIONAL READINGS

Asher, N. (2017). Engaging Identities and Cultures in a Globalized, Postcolonial India: Implications for Decolonizing Curriculum and Pedagogy. In Springer international handbooks of education (pp. 97–112). Springer Nature (Netherlands). doi:10.1007/978-3-319-40317-5_8

Florian, L., & Linklater, H. (2010). Preparing teachers for inclusive education: Using inclusive pedagogy to enhance teaching and learning for all. *Cambridge Journal of Education*, *40*(4), 369–386. doi:10.1080/0305764X.2010.526588

Kamola, I. (2019). *Making the World Global: U.S. Universities and the Production of the Global Imaginary*. Duke University Press.

Shahjahan, R. A., Estera, A. L., Surla, K. L., & Edwards, K. T. (2021). "Decolonizing" Curriculum and Pedagogy: A Comparative Review Across Disciplines and Global Higher Education Contexts. *Review of Educational Research*, *92*(1), 73–113. doi:10.3102/00346543211042423

Solorzano, D. G., & Yosso, T. J. (2002). Critical Race Methodology: Counter-Storytelling as an Analytical Framework for Education Research. *Qualitative Inquiry*, *8*(1), 23–44. doi:10.1177/107780040200800103

Spratt, J., & Florian, L. (2015). Inclusive pedagogy: From learning to action. Supporting each individual in the context of 'everybody.' *Teaching and Teacher Education*, *49*, 89–96. doi:10.1016/j.tate.2015.03.006

Tomlinson, C. A., Brighton, C. M., Hertberg, H. L., Callahan, C. M., Moon, T. R., Brimijoin, K., Conover, L. A., & Reynolds, T. M. (2003). Differentiating Instruction in Response to Student Readiness, Interest, and Learning Profile in Academically Diverse Classrooms: A Review of Literature. *Journal for the Education of the Gifted*, *27*(2–3), 119–145. doi:10.1177/016235320302700203

KEY TERMS AND DEFINITIONS

Assessment: Variety of methods or tools used by educators to evaluate, measure and document academic readiness, learning progress, skill acquisition or needs of students (Education Glossary).

Decolonization (in Education): The process of undoing colonizing practices by confronting and challenging the colonial practices that influenced education in the past (University of Victoria).

Diversity: The practice of involving people from range of different social and ethnic backgrounds, different genders, and sexual orientation, etc. (Oxford Dictionary)

Historically Black Colleges and Universities (HBCUs): Defined as colleges and universities founded to educate students of African American descent (Oxford dictionary).

Inclusive Pedagogy: Refers to the ways that courses, classroom activities, curricula and assessments consider issues of diversity in an effort to engage all students in learning that is meaningful, relevant and accessible (Uchicago.edu).

Predominately White Institutions (PWIs): A university that has 50% or more students that identifies as white (U.S. Department of Education).

Sense of Belonging: A feeling of security and support when there is a sense of acceptance, inclusion, and diversity for members of a certain group (Cornell.edu).

Chapter 4
Empowering Underrepresented Students:
Designing Innovator Spaces as Sites of Justice, Peace, and Equity Within University Library Ecosystems

Beth Caruso
University of North Carolina at Charlotte, USA

ABSTRACT

Higher education presents students with many opportunities for educational advancement, but not all encounter these opportunities equally. Academic organizations, rooted in structural racism, perpetuate cycles of perceived failure that can prevent students from receiving the encouragement they need, which can result in inadequate career and societal preparation. Not all students benefit from traditional education in the same ways, and when they must all meet the same criteria, then, it is difficult for some to meet their own learning needs and goals based on their own definitions of success. Innovation spaces, such as makerspaces, within academic libraries, have a particular ability to help level the playing field and add equity value to both the classroom and lifelong learning. This chapter delineates current equity issues and provides managers of innovation spaces, especially those in academic libraries, with methods for recognizing opportunities for developing and marketing spaces and services to promote success for every student, both within the classroom and outside of it.

DOI: 10.4018/978-1-6684-7379-5.ch004

FACING THE NEED TO DESIGN LIBRARY ECOSYSTEMS OF INCLUSION, INSPIRATION, AND AGENCY

In the quest for equity in higher education, we like to think that our classrooms have arrived at some sort of destination because of the many opportunities available to such a wide range of students. In addition to the typical funding issues at play, there is also a complex issue in the classroom that tends to get overlooked by even the most well-intentioned instructors and administrators. This is, quite simply, the discrepancy between how we expect students to navigate typical higher education systems versus what we expect them to learn and understand in order to engage with the world post-graduation. However, innovation spaces, specifically those housed within higher education campuses and in academic libraries, are strategically positioned to help counteract this disconnect and develop an ecosystem of inclusion, inspiration, and agency.

This chapter will pose solutions that managers of innovation spaces,[1] can employ to design welcoming, emancipatory spaces that students will want to make use of to take charge of and support their education and their lifelong learning. This chapter focuses especially on innovation spaces within the academic library, highlighting makerspaces most prominently, as well as spaces for digital creation and spaces for gaming, showing how we can transform these spaces to promote practices surrounding Diversity, Equity, Inclusion, and Accessibility (DEIA)[2] to dismantle structural racism in the institution by both supporting students outside of the classroom and partnering with instructors to begin that same process within the classroom. Though this chapter will focus primarily on solutions that can be implemented within higher education and academic libraries, many of the concepts can also be applied within K-12 schools, public library spaces, as well as community spaces for making, which will be addressed toward the end of the chapter.

HIGHER EDUCATION MAKERSPACES, LIBRARIES, AND DEIA

In recent years, there has been a surge in the development of makerspaces and other innovation spaces on higher education campuses. These spaces facilitate various levels and types of hands-on creation and nontraditional work in the realms of making (crafting, prototyping, and more), digital scholarship, video and audio, data visualization, gaming, collaboration, and more. Along with these spaces comes a concept often termed a "maker mindset," coined by Dale Dougherty (2015) of *Make Magazine,* which is commonly acknowledged as a mode of thinking in which a person feels comfortable taking risks that may fail, taking agency in exploring possible creative solutions to problems, and thinking critically about nontraditional tasks, projects, and ideas. Though the term comes from the work associated with makerspaces, it can be applied to all types of innovation spaces, due to the similar nature of work that occurs throughout. This definition will be applied throughout this chapter.

However, much of the time, people assume that a maker mindset is innate or easy to learn, but that is not the case for everyone, particularly for those with past experiences in failure, disappointment, embarrassment, or trauma. There are many students who have simply moved through their academic careers in ways far from an ideal trajectory. Some have arrived at their higher education institution without much encouragement. Some have come from schools with less funding and therefore potentially fewer opportunities than their current counterparts. Some have been bullied and feel uncomfortable deviating from anything straightforward, while others may have a disability and cannot use much of what is available. Some cannot understand how to apply their skills and abilities to what is available. Some have been told that they are underperforming or they are concerned about their grades. These students are often ignored by their educational institutions. Alternatively, there are students who enter and are deterred from using the spaces for reasons that will be covered later in this chapter.

It is important to note that it is not just students of one identity population that are being underserved. This chapter will cover a variety of populations. The term *students from historically exploited or excluded communities* (one term currently used in place of "marginalized populations")[3] can refer to students of color, students who identify as members of the LGBTQ+ community, students with disabilities, students who are members of some religious groups, and anyone else who has had rights withheld or has been the subject of oppressive discourse. Consider too, students who may or may not be included in the above, but have simply been overlooked in the educational system and have not been encouraged to take advantage of opportunities set in front of them. Certainly, it is not a fault that lies with the student, but rather a barrier imposed by rigid academic systems. As educators, we must ensure that every student, regardless of their previous educational experience, gets the tools they need to tear down the inequities posed by these systems.

Libraries are already at the center of intellectual discourse on campus as they are places sought out for research assistance and instruction, research materials, study rooms and space, and even present programming designed to further research, thinking, networking, and more. For years, libraries have also been celebrated as a place for celebrating diversity through book displays and events, and also often through the types of assistance given to patrons. Innovation spaces, particularly those housed in academic libraries, are prime sites for DEIA work, as they can level the playing field by giving students access to tools and opportunities they would not have had otherwise. However, in order to make this a success, much work needs to be done, as not all who would benefit from these opportunities feel welcome or at home in such spaces.

One such place engaging in this work is at Olin College. Their shops and library work together to "focus on student growth, development, and access as an inherent part of the design of these spaces" (Bignoli & Fass, 2022, p. 1). Bignoli and Fass (2022) state,

we are inspired by political sociologist Danielle Allen's idea of participatory readiness, a way of understanding 'citizenship [as] the activity of co-creating a way of life, or world-building...co-creation can occur at many social levels: in a neighborhood or school; in a networked community or association; in a city, state, or nation; at a global scale.' We believe our makerspaces on campus are a site of this type of co-created world building. Because fabrication and making is an integral part of engineering education at Olin College, we have many chances to give students the opportunity to be leaders and instructors in our makerspaces and shops (p. 2).

Participatory readiness. World-building. Co-creation. When innovation spaces are designed around the emancipating concepts of participatory readiness, world-building, and co-creation– concepts that students can engage with to construct their own outcomes, they highlight the potential for students to take agency in their work. It is left up to those who design those spaces, activities, and opportunities where students can engage, to apply a DEIA framework in the design so that they are approachable by any student.

Though many institutions have incorporated a DEIA framework, or rather, initiatives that serve and respond to users' cultures, customs, and identities, many are still at the beginning of this journey and many others are leading the charge at institutions that have not yet made this commitment. This chapter will put forth a number of best practices for managers of innovation spaces to implement in their journeys toward justice and equity for students in higher education. Many of these conversations happen both in practice and in the literature in K-12 levels, but for higher education, while it may happen in practice, it is seldom being discussed in the literature, especially as it relates to maker and innovation spaces. Therefore, much of the background information given here is based on this author's lived experience as an instructor, administrator, and librarian, and discussions this author has had with colleagues and peers over the past fifteen years in a combination of these roles. The lack of preparedness and the difficulties discussed are an assemblage of the issues at play in the academic landscape as gathered from instructors of all levels, administrators, and even students themselves from casual conversations at work and conferences, instructor and employer complaints about lack of student preparedness, and even constructive comments from students wondering about the usefulness of what they are learning in the classroom. Conversations about DEIA are often happening at the classroom level, but they are seldom happening on a broader platform for innovation spaces, making it difficult for professionals to share knowledge and determine best practices to create such spaces that may promote justice and equity.

In order to understand how library innovation spaces can help on this journey, we must first understand the landscape of higher education and what students have been working with in the recent past. While the issues that follow are not the norm in every program at every institution, they are pervasive issues that need to be addressed.

THE STATE OF THE HIGHER EDUCATION CLASSROOM

Traditional modes of academia exist to prepare students for the workforce, but the modern workforce is a dynamic terrain that is no longer easily confined to a single desk, workspace, or knowledge subset. Many positions that used to be relatively solitary now require some level of collaboration or other social skill. However, too many classrooms in higher education are still either lecture-based or fail to incorporate knowledge and skills beyond those needed for discipline-specific knowledge. In many instances, students are leaving their academic careers uncertain of how to apply knowledge from their courses in the real world, but are being asked to combine that course knowledge with soft skills when they exit these programs. Forbes (2022) listed the "15 Skills Employers Seek in 2022." Skills such as "Empathetic Listening," "Agility, Flexibility, and Adaptability," "Emotional Intelligence," "Creative Thinking," "Networking Skills," "Vulnerability and Authenticity," and "DEI Experience" are included in this list – a list which, in its entirety, is similar in comparison to those on other sites in the top Google search results for "top skills employers seek in 2022." Students are used to conducting these types of searches, and as they prepare to enter the workforce, seeing these types of lists from big names such as Forbes, as well as job-related sites, just reinforces the importance of these skills in the workplace. A number of these skills, however, are not being addressed directly in academic programs that are designed to prepare students for their careers, though when applied to their careers, will make the student more versatile and a more attractive candidate for the position.

Many of these skills are not just applicable in the workplace, but also in the social sphere. These skills are helpful for living a rewarding life and navigating the community, whether one is engaging with community groups or simply having one-on-one interactions. Learning these soft skills, however, takes quite some time. Although students are taught soft skills before getting to a higher education setting, a number of soft skills still revolve around politeness and obedience, falling into the category of "character education," – a concept that has often been criticized for teaching values and character traits considered to be dominant to students of all backgrounds, when those values are, in fact, valued by the people in power, often not allowing for views held by a variety of cultures or accounting for differences in lifestyles or ways of being. While we see skills that are valued in current society, such as integrity, inner strength, and some of the Forbes skills being incorporated into classrooms, this is not yet the norm at all institutions and in all courses of study. In fact, Kye (2020), in discussing makerspaces and cultural responsiveness, invoke Atwater, Russel, and Butler's (2014) findings that are still relevant today – that "Many educators continue to assume science and engineering are neutral, objective fields of study and therefore [Culturally Responsive Pedagogy] has no place in science and engineering" (p. 3). Though they discuss pre-college education, and specifically a diversity and equity-related component, this author would argue that this is no less true for college level instruction and other soft skills.

Therefore, once students get to higher education and instructors assume that soft skills instruction is no longer needed, there is a disconnect, as many students have not experienced soft skills instruction, especially as applied to their future careers. Instructors expect students to have certain skills before entering the classroom, some of which they would have had no opportunity to learn, depending on the type of classrooms they had previously experienced. Often, these higher ed instructors assume that they will teach the content of the class, or the "knowledge," and either send students to an alternate resource for remediation or assume that they will learn additional necessary skills on the job or in an internship. The content knowledge and soft skills are seldom interwoven.

There are two underlying problems, both resting within the nature of academia itself and its standards-based and grades-based system. The first is that standards and grades require instructors to "get through" material, putting pressure on them to move away from anything that doesn't directly relate to the goals of the course. Soft skills instruction and DEIA-based issues or content often take a backseat or are not present at all, simply because of how time and course requirements work against one another.

The second is that a grades-based system forces assimilation. When two students get the same grade, they have been indoctrinated into thinking that it should mean that they are both equal and that they have learned the same thing. A grades-based system, as we have established it, does not allow for variation in knowledge or ability, but rather sets a standard for achievement. However, we know that in the most dynamic workplaces, where ideas are shared and innovation of any kind takes place, that difference in skill, knowledge, and ideas is valued because difference contributes to what makes the whole exceptional.

WHY ARE WE AT THIS POINT? OVERLOOKING INTERSECTIONALITY

Why aren't we teaching skills that are valuable in both the workplace and society? Outside of the obvious – that we've been indoctrinated into doing it this way – students do need the content knowledge. They build on what they learn at a young age, then gather more content knowledge to use later on in life, whether in the workplace or in their lives outside of work. We do not need to scrap the concept altogether. We simply need to shift. We need to acknowledge that students' identities have been overlooked in favor of assimilation into structures and ecosystems developed by people often entirely unlike them.

In her landmark article in 1989, Kimberlé Crenshaw discussed the term "intersectionality" which brings realization to the fact that we cannot "treat [different aspects of our identities] as mutually exclusive categories of experience" (139). While this concept certainly deserves a lengthy discourse, it is a baseline concept that needs to be understood and accepted if we are to create effective spaces in which students feel comfortable working as themselves. Students are both students *and* members of other identity and social groups, and these intersections do not dissipate just because they step into a classroom.

However, students are generally asked to engage with ideas using the same methods as every other student as activities and assignments typically do not account for differentiation in intersectionality. There is typically a single way to complete an assignment, and often, these activities and assignments ask students to tap into the same worldviews and background knowledge. Because academia is rooted in white standards, that knowledge they are asked to pull from is often from a white perspective, often mislabeled as the "norm." However, this only fosters the systems of white supremacy embedded in academic structures. Recognizing the identities of students from historically excluded or exploited communities is of the utmost importance in the classroom, not just because embracing difference is the way we move toward innovation and change, but also because if we recognize and embrace students' experiences and backgrounds, they will learn to be adaptable as they engage their ideas instead of learning that there are single routes to success. If they do learn to engage their ideas in more robust ways, then they will not only be able to develop their own definitions of success, but they will also be able to help shape how individuals, industries, and their communities work toward DEIA frameworks to change how they and others move within the world.

WHAT ATTEMPTS HAVE BEEN MADE SO FAR?

Thus far, this author has covered the outmoded, yet still too often instituted structures we see at play in academia. However, instructors who are engaged with current education-focused discourse, such as the importance of DEIA, the benefits of active learning, and teaching for different learning styles, are certainly making attempts to change how we approach learning. Although there are countless approaches, three overarching approaches will be discussed here, as they are presently valued throughout academia.

Lifelong Learning

The first approach is to show students the value of lifelong learning and help them become lifelong learners themselves. While "lifelong learning" can mean something different to each person and at each stage of their life, the basic idea here is that one never stops learning, whether it is extending their own learning outside of the classroom while being a student, going back to school for additional degrees, taking a class in the community, learning a new skill or hobby, or just always being open to new ideas. Having the worldview of a lifelong learner sets one up for success because of the opportunities it can present.

This is certainly an idealized concept, and while many people feel that they are lifelong learners, it can be easy for others to shy away. A lifelong learning mentality has to be encouraged, and if the mindset has not been encouraged by parents, guardians, teachers, other authority figures, or even friends, then it is likely that the person would not value it themselves. Additionally, with the pressure of grades, it is unlikely that a lifelong learning mentality is at the forefront for someone who is struggling with grades. Suggesting that someone should keep learning forever when they are having trouble in school could sound overwhelming. So, when instructors introduce the concept of lifelong learning without considering intersectionality, the best of intentions could backfire.

Engaging With Nontraditional Projects

The second approach that has been popular is to have students engage with nontraditional projects. These are referred to differently in different disciplines, but a nontraditional project is essentially any project in which a student is not writing a paper and is usually making decisions on their own for how to convey the idea using any means necessary. For example, instead of writing a paper to explain a concept, the student could create something like a sculpture, structure, painting, song, board game, or video game to demonstrate that same concept, often for a non-academic audience. Before becoming more widely popular, this approach had been seen in classes attached to professional degrees, such as engineering, where students would build various items to get hands-on experience. Now, however, the approach has moved into classes for academic degrees as well, since there are numerous ways of demonstrating a point, and not just those for scholarly audiences. Nontraditional projects often give students more authentic experiences, as many would not be developing works for scholarly audiences later on in life. Instead, students determine the audience and what type of project would be most effective in catering to that audience.

However, when instructors give students the opportunity to take on nontraditional projects or encourage students to take agency in projects, they often fail to consider intersectionality. These instructors want so desperately for students to get to that "aha moment" that comes from conceptual discovery and play. However, some instructors who are enthusiastic believe that the instructor's enthusiasm is enough to push students to unlock this skill, and they don't teach students how to take agency, how to be comfortably critical of their own work in order to improve, or how to move within the discomfort of uncertainty of a new project with infinite possibilities. This author has certainly been guilty of relying on enthusiasm in the past, and has experienced that this practice is quite ineffective.

We might think that students would want the freedom to implement their own ideas instead of completing a project that is prescribed from on high. However, this author has observed these responses during her time as an instructor introducing projects in her own class and during her time as a librarian introducing nontraditional projects for other instructors' classes, and has had constant conversations with colleagues on these matters. Students have split responses that are rooted in the inequity of past educational support they have received. Some students see this as an opportunity to truly engage with the ideas or show what they can do; these students are typically the ones who have been encouraged throughout their academic careers and whose grades will still be high, even with a bit of fluctuation.

Some students, though, are wildly uncomfortable, and there could be a great many reasons for this discomfort. Some may have been told all their lives that they are underperforming, or they may have had negative classroom experiences, so they have not learned the benefits of positive struggle – a healthy give-and-take of conceptual discovery, since their past educational experiences have taught them to simply keep their heads down and simply get through the work. Instead, they learn a negative struggle – that they aren't like the others and that they can't measure up. For a student who has been consistently told they are underperforming, giving them the "opportunity" to take agency, when in fact, it is a requirement, could present itself as a paralyzing obstacle. Heather Lister (2020) presents a clear explanation of this within the context of making and the Maker Movement.[4]

Making is about trying new things and taking risks, and with risks comes the potential for failure. The Maker Movement celebrates failure as a part of the creative process, as it gets us one step closer to the intended result. Making is an iterative process and success on the first attempt is rarely expected. So, while the maker culture champions failure, it is important for educators to recognize the impact of failure on students who have experienced high levels of trauma. Situations that may seem like nothing more than a creative struggle can be an emotional and physical trigger for some students (p. 115).

No matter the circumstance, whether it is a traditional classroom or an alternative assignment, students who do not get the chance to practice adaptability or critical thinking as much as others are at a disadvantage for future endeavors.

Koh, Ge, Lee, Lewis, Simmons, and Nelson (2020) describe a typical instance of students' hesitance with creative projects. In an instance of working with projects centered on making[5], when given the chance to choose, "some students tended to select a type of maker project that they were already familiar with rather than trying something they had not done before that could be more innovative or challenging. This tendency to make a "safe choice" was due to students' concerns about their grade" (p. 139-140). Although it could be easy to assume that the discomfort stemmed from engaging with making, unfortunately, instructors see this all the time, even when students choose something such as a paper topic. Students tend to choose something they already know about because they feel it is safe and easy. While a student may see this as helpful to relieve grade-based anxiety, they remain underserved, since they do not get the experience of taking that agency. Those in power, in this case, instructors, have a responsibility to help students understand the constraints of the situation and how, exactly, to take agency within it.

Innovation and Making

The third approach, which has seen a surge in recent years, is the push for innovative thinking and work. While this can happen in a classroom, the emergence of campus innovation spaces, such as makerspaces[6], digital production labs[7], and other spaces for nontraditional work[8] has encouraged some instructors to take advantage of such spaces to enhance what they would be able to do in a typical classroom. Innovation, previously seen as a STEM[9] concept, has morphed into something that is able to be harnessed by everyone, no matter what experience the person has had with science, creativity, or critical thinking. Instead of simply having science labs or engineering machine shops available to students in those majors, there are makerspaces that contain crafting materials like clays and paints and versatile machines such as 3D printers, laser cutters, and sewing machines[10]. They allow all students (unless the space resides within and is funded by a specific department) and typically welcome work outside of that being completed for a class. These spaces exist with the academic argument that classroom concepts are reinforced with hands-on learning outside of the classroom, but with the added bonus that the lifelong learning mentality is encouraged.

It is no secret that STEM disciplines typically have ample funding, but often, the spaces STEM departments own do not allow use by students from other departments or undeclared majors and may even restrict use to students in their own major until a specific milestone is hit. It is in this way that campus innovation spaces can promote innovation, creative thinking, and lifelong learning to all students, counteracting what Patton (2016) terms "'intellectual real estate' in the academy[...] This elitism is rooted in racist ideologies, particularly given the historical trajectory of scientific racism and the continued absence of people of color in STEM fields" (p. 327-328). Patton also references a number of instances in which "Scholars describe isolated STEM environments that exude a culture of Whiteness and are unwelcoming to people of color, [...] yet the climate remains unchanged. Faculty are not challenged to rethink their curriculum, relinquish their biases, or connect with students of various racial groups" (p. 328). It is in this way – exposing students of all backgrounds and interests to innovative and creative thinking both inside and outside of the classroom – that we can not only change how they enter into these fields, but also change how those fields operate in the future.

However, simply bringing students to innovation spaces or giving them access is not enough to automatically instill the will for lifelong learning or the agency for engaging unique projects. Academia's grades-based system was not designed to champion independent thinking, however, with a more innovative approach it can be pushed in the direction of creativity that is inclusive. In order to do this, we need a way to shift the narrative and give students the assurance that their ideas, risks, and engagement with challenges are both valued and fostered.

HIGHER ED INNOVATION SPACES

So, what do we do to help students in higher education when we are stuck in a grades-based system and one in which innovation and creativity are being valued, but not fostered for traditionally excluded groups? Understanding the grades-based system and the difficulty that many students have with the freedom to take agency in their work, it would seem that both students and instructors are locked into a system that allows for little to no flexibility. For too many students, the grade will always loom overhead, and even the best of intentions to consider intersectionality could backfire because of it.

Innovation spaces that are open to the full campus community, particularly those housed outside of departments, can be of particular value here. Innovation spaces, within the campus library especially, can offer both co-curricular and extra-curricular opportunities and solutions. Whether or not there is a complete overhaul to the current academic system at the larger level, library innovation spaces present a viable complement to both the traditional and the contemporary classroom and can foster a more positive environment within the classroom and within the institution as a whole. This can happen in a multitude of ways, as will be addressed in later sections, but without intentionally creating and fostering these spaces for students who have been underserved, these spaces can quickly recreate the same dividing problem that classrooms have faced. It is the responsibility of the managers of these spaces to ensure that innovation spaces can serve as a solution.

The Basics of Higher Ed Innovation Spaces

Innovation spaces can vary greatly based on the type of space and the setting within which they are placed. These spaces can range from makerspaces to video and audio studios, to gaming spaces, to data spaces, to any other space for creation, exploration, collaboration, or other creative, critical, or innovative work. However, one makerspace, for example, can look and operate drastically differently from makerspaces at other institutions, or even within the same institution. They can have different purposes, technology, materials, and user populations., and more. One makerspace may contain mostly low- or mid-level maker tech such as sewing machines, 3D printers, and laser cutters. Another may have mostly crafting materials, and yet another may resemble a woodshop or metal shop or may be set up for specialized forms of making. Many are a combination of these.

At the most basic level, institutional innovation spaces give students access to technology, skills training, and services they otherwise may not be able to access, depending on their major or even outside of the university. Using tools in the spaces, rather than having to purchase them, opens up a world of possibility for all students. Some will not or cannot spend money on even the cheaper tools and supplies, such as a paper, paints, or a hammer, but other tools and machines can cost thousands of dollars and would be cost prohibitive to a project from the start no matter a student's financial background. These could include items such as $30 die cutters, $2000 3D printers, $20,000 laser cutters, and larger machines that could be in wood shops or metal shops. Additionally, bringing tools and expertise together into specific spaces ensures that students do not have to learn on their own, but can, instead, learn from others, whether through trainings, observation, casual discussion, or individual or collaborative creation.

Innovation spaces also act as an extension of the classroom and as places to encourage and facilitate lifelong learning. They allow students the space to grapple with concepts, experiment with technology and making, and to think freely without the threat of a grade. Often, since these spaces are also open for personal work (work not associated with academics), these spaces are the ultimate lifelong learning facilitation areas, as students not only extend the learning from their classes, but also work on their personal projects, which develop skills outside of the classroom. These skills could then be applied in the classroom, in their future careers, or even in their general lives. These students are usually the ones who see the value of lifelong learning. Overall, campus innovation spaces are seen as positive spaces that give students the room for creative exploration and development.

Incorporating innovation spaces into higher education spaces effectively re-envisions how we approach learning at academic institutions. Rather than encouraging all learning to take place in the classroom, we open up the view of how, where, and when education can take place. When learning is connected with a space outside the classroom and with actions associated with something other than solely classwork, we can begin to create an equity-based educational ecosystem. This ecosystem is one in which students receive academic support in the classroom and from other academic support services, but can also ensure customized success based on their own individual needs outside of the classroom. These needs are based on their own definitions of success and their own personal goals, rather than those set forth for them by the institution.

Preparing for Intentional DEIA Work

Innovation spaces can facilitate skill development and lifelong learning outside of and alongside the classroom, but these spaces still have a great deal of work to do, particularly those that serve students who are already interested in innovation or making or are confident in those areas. These spaces must also ensure that they are serving students who have not had the opportunity to develop these interests by providing programming that specifically fits the needs of beginners, such as introductory workshops and trainings, as well as information sessions and open houses introducing newcomers to these spaces. Those who don't already have a penchant for this type of work or interaction or those who haven't had access to such spaces before college, typically assume that the spaces are only for faculty or research assistants or for students who already have specific knowledge sets or skills.

There may also be other deterrents that space managers can easily identify and alter. For example, some may see the setup or personnel of the space as the deterrent. Spaces that suggest they are welcoming to all, but have a staff without a single person of color, might deter a person who is interested in a racially inclusive space. Similarly, a male-dominated space might deter people of other genders, suggesting that only activities historically associated with masculine identities are valued there. For others, a makerspace that only displays high-tech projects, such as robotics projects, might unintentionally discourage someone with an interest in low-tech making, such as sewing or painting, even if all of these types of making are welcome. In all three of these examples there is a lack of representation – a lack of seeing one's own identity represented in the space.

Managers of these spaces have the particular responsibility of creating welcoming spaces, though spaces such as these are not general-use spaces. Instead, they are incredibly specific, with specific functions, specific populations that naturally frequent the space based on how it is constructed, and specific populations who are typically "othered" from the space. Creating a space generally welcoming to "all" will not work, since to truly create a space for all means to create a space that welcomes, encourages, and supports underserved populations with intention.[11]

In order to do this work well, we must first acknowledge that we will not always get it right the first time, since no one is a member of every identity group, and since every member of a single identity group does not think or exist in the same ways. It means being open to having the hard conversations and responding in respectful and constructive ways when someone calls you out. It means being anti-racist – an active, and not passive, engagement in conversations and centered on racial equity and standing up for visible and specific change. It means admitting to and changing practices that you have been implementing that *others* people from one or more identity groups. It means advocating for the change of practices in your institution and elsewhere, even when it goes against tradition, because you know that these practices should be changed. It means acknowledging your privilege without making excuses. It means admitting when you are wrong and helping others realize the same. Sanjeet Mann (2020), in reimagining the culture of makerspaces, says, "We must approach our work with humility, particularly when seeking to enter into relationships of solidarity. [...] Collaboration through dialogue is an ongoing process that requires patience, endurance, and the courage to embrace setbacks as part of the process of learning" (p. 237). As we do the work of developing or reimagining inclusive spaces, we must not approach it alone, but instead, gather the insight of many and set aside what we assume has to be done. There is a reason that each innovation space looks different, and listening to the people who will be a part of that space and being open to changing spaces, services, and policies as needed is essential to running a space that will meet the dynamic needs of a diverse student population.

Doing the work of coming to terms with your privilege can look different for each person, and the context you are working within can certainly come into play. For example, white privilege assumptions need to be challenged before creating a space for a racially-inclusive group, but someone with academic faculty status, creating a space may also want to challenge their economic privilege before creating a space for a group spanning a range of socioeconomic backgrounds to understand how someone who is from a different background may approach using a space. For this author, the commitment of coming to terms with privilege was easy, but actually working through it was a struggle. Perhaps this journal entry will explain[12].

"I am a white, cisgender female who grew up in a middle-class suburban household. I went to predominantly white private schools until college, and because my first career was teaching college writing and my current career is as an academic librarian, I have never left school. I have never left academia. After looking at the many advantages I've had, just because of my background and upbringing, and after scrutinizing the racist underpinnings of the US education system, I've been struggling to determine why I keep supporting it. I chose this as my livelihood because my experiences idealized it for me, but knowing what I know now, I feel uncomfortable contributing to a system that oppresses so many people because it ignores their very being. And I've come to a realization. I'm still here because I've committed to doing the work of helping students feel comfortable with unconventional ways of thinking. I have something to give. I help students think differently. The best work that I can do with my talents and my interests is exactly what I'm doing. My guilt is not helpful. I am here to help others learn and succeed in whatever way that looks like for them. I am here to work with intention, to change the things within my power to change, and to help change the things that aren't mine. If I didn't have my job, who would? Would they be committed to the work? My discomfort says that I'm not doing perfect DEIA work, but my commitment says that perfection isn't the concern anyway."

As the journal entry above demonstrates, this author has struggled even with her choice of career because of discomfort with her privilege. While this author has certainly made many DEIA-related mistakes in the past and will make many mistakes in the future, this author has also made a commitment to being anti-racist and being a DEIA advocate. Though some elements of discomfort certainly remain, this journal entry serves as a reminder of the importance of this author doing the work and revisiting it helps this author push forward when the work is difficult.

Working with intention in this way requires introspection and continually-renewed commitment to the cause. Simply deciding that you have a commitment is not enough. Knowing the reasons for your commitment is vital to its sustainability.

Before initiating DEIA work in your space, determine the privileges you bring to the table and understand why you are doing this work. However, while determining your privilege in a larger community context is certainly important, for the purposes of the work discussed in this chapter, it is especially important to figure out your privilege within the context of your work. This includes incorporating the realities of your job into the mix. In discussing the development of library makerspaces, Mann (2020) suggests that

librarians collaborating on a makerspace first examine the mindset with which we approach our work. We need to recognize how we are privileged as information professionals (particularly if we live and work in the Global North), as well as the ways in which our varying institutional situations can marginalize us with respect to likely partners [...] Intersectionality helps us achieve a clearer view of our relationships to the various groups affected by a collaboration, such as students, other library colleagues, IT collaborators, or administrators (p. 237).

In this case, this author would need to examine her status as a female academic librarian, since an overwhelming majority of librarians and educators are female. This author would also need to consider the power that comes with managing people and managing spaces. Since the library's innovation spaces are those in which students come to use tools they don't have, test out ideas they aren't familiar with, or invest themselves in new ideas, students could easily see this author as holding the power in the space, especially if job hierarchies are perceived.

Overall, as a manager of innovation spaces that serve the entire campus community – ones that intend to serve as proponents of DEIA work, how does someone with a number of privileges ensure that equitable spaces are created and sustained that are in alignment with what a diverse population would need and want? No matter your background, the students coming into these spaces will always be different from you in some way, so it is necessary to do this work in order to determine how to best help the students that will come into these spaces, and to figure out the changes to make to ensure that non-users feel welcomed.

REFRAMING THE NARRATIVE: STRATEGIES FOR MANAGERS OF INNOVATION SPACES

Innovation spaces call the norm into question by providing spaces for students to develop nontraditional projects, experiment with new forms of interaction, and generally interact with ideas in ways that they would not see in typical classes. Though these spaces do encourage different mindsets and worldviews, spaces within academia can often have skewed power dynamics that we overlook in our efforts to simply get the spaces up and running. Spaces funded by the institution[13] are often subject to institutional constraints, particularly the vision of those allocating the money to the initiative. For example, small academic makerspaces often have to do more with less, understanding that a number of multi-purpose items will need to be purchased, rather than more specialty items. This encourages creativity and flexibility in the maker, but can be difficult for beginner makers as they realize they need to consistently determine an alternate method when another method of making is more natural. As with most funded initiatives, those providing the funding are not those working in the spaces who either know firsthand what is needed of the spaces or have conducted or produced research on such topics. This makes it more difficult for those working in and using the spaces.

Upper administrators generally see such spaces as benefitting STEM fields and the potential for lifelong learning, but not all make the connection between innovation spaces and DEIA. The Obama administration called for a number of investments, collaborations, and initiatives in the pursuit of a maker mindset for all students (Office of the Press Secretary, 2016). From investing time, money, and energy in both a National Week of Making and maker fairs, to highlighting student and teacher stories and projects that are still available in the archives (Nation of Makers), the value put on hands-on education and curiosity was evident. However, even with this surge, "Research on usage of these spaces has shown a skew towards white and male participants, but there is very little data with regards to race, non-binary gender, and other identities" (Bignoli & Faas, 2022, p. 1). Those involved in this work see the benefits and can give qualitative data in the form of stories and anecdotes about transformations occurring in the spaces, but often, it is the quantitative data that is desired for administrators. This is difficult to measure, though, considering that learning acquired from the spaces can be applied in both overt and discreet ways throughout one's academic career and one's life.

The lack of connection between what innovation spaces can offer and a DEIA focus is not just limited to administrators. In fact, this author has attempted DEIA-focused conversations with a number of managers of innovation spaces and workers in tech-based fields. Many are willing to entertain a discussion on the lack of women in technology and technology leadership. However, approaches this author has made to discuss the concepts of the need for diverse representation[14] in leadership, staffing, setup of physical spaces, the choosing of content displayed in spaces and classes with innovation space managers or emerging technology enthusiasts who have not previously considered these concepts, is often met with silence, blank stares, immediate changing of the conversation, and denial that the needs are there. However frustrating, this is understandable, as coming to terms with acknowledging these needs is quite difficult when you are first confronted with the fact that things need to change, and often does not take place during a single conversation with a colleague. It is important to remember here though, that articulating the need to upper administrators who are not familiar with DEIA work and who are also not familiar with the work of innovation spaces would likely respond more favorably to concrete examples based on what has already occurred or is already in the works, rather than to abstract, avant-garde ideas. This will be more effective in demonstrating not only the need for a DEIA focus for innovation spaces, but continued support for it.

What follows are strategies for reframing the narrative surrounding the development, conceptualization, and running of innovation spaces, using a higher-ed library lens. While the ideas discussed will be specifically applicable to library innovation spaces, one could easily adapt these ideas and solutions for other similar spaces. Additional tips specific to these areas will be addressed in a later section.

Evening the Playing Field: Developing Diverse Spaces

Innovation spaces are typically designed for single or for multiple specific, task-based purposes. Ideally, spaces would be designed for equity from the ground-up, but for already-established spaces, managers should reinvent and intentionally market these as emancipatory spaces for students to take charge of their learning in no-stakes ways. If students have not previously been welcomed into innovation spaces, and if spaces are not intentionally designed to include them, they will be less inclined to walk in or participate in activities the spaces are designed to promote. Since many spaces inadvertently market to students who are already interested in and already do use the spaces, designing spaces for those who have been traditionally excluded and those who have struggled with academia and with engaging with ideas allows us to effectively transform the spaces and what they are meant to do. We can change these spaces from being product-driven, task-based spaces, to spaces of discovery and learning. Although tasks would certainly still be completed, the spaces become inspiration-driven, where students themselves can flourish, instead of solely focusing on how well they do what they do. Here, they can use technology as a means to tell their own stories, whether intentionally, through developing something they have planned, or unintentionally, through the ways in which they negatively struggle or positively thrive. The next sections will detail the major components that we must plan for in developing and managing spaces to guarantee that we are not simply creating white spaces to ensure white futures, but rather creating equitable spaces that ensure success in whatever ways students define it for themselves.

Defining the Spaces

The ways in which we describe spaces and the people who use them can quickly dictate the target audience of the spaces. However, careful marketing is needed if the goal is to welcome all types of users and interaction. For example, if we characterize people who use these spaces as inventors, programmers, builders, makers, and other terms we choose, it presents the target audience of the spaces as those who are already encouraged, rather than as those who never had the opportunity or those who may have interest, but think the spaces are for people who are already sure of themselves. The defined groups are also usually more open to positive failure (a willingness to fail a few times in order to learn from those experiences). Many first-generation students and students from historically exploited or excluded communities, though, are often too fearful of true failure (not positive failure) that they don't try. This is changing with makerspaces and STEAM education being more prevalent in schools, but it is still a hardship for many to get involved because of a lack of information or encouragement if they haven't had these experiences before.

Idealized versions of innovation spaces can present privileged perspectives, and managers of these spaces must consider how to still present a favorable space while celebrating all perspectives. While it is helpful to identify the possible people who could use the spaces, in doing so, we leave out others who could use the spaces. For example, in helping someone understand the culture of a makerspace, we often identify what a maker *is*, using terms such as *maker, hobbyist, programmer,* or how the space is used, mentioning that it is a space to build, or create. However, if you identify what a maker *is* or how a space is used, you inadvertently identify what a maker *is not*, and how the space cannot be used – or at least how hesitant potential users will read the indicators. With the aforementioned identifiers in play, the space may allow unstructured work and thinking, but someone who does not consider themselves a maker or wants to use the space to simply tinker with an item or idea may not believe the space can be used for their preferred ways of interaction. This can be overwhelmingly exclusionary, so developing inclusive marketing messages is of absolute importance.

We must also consider cultural implications of determining how spaces are and are not used. In discussing the outward representation of makerspaces, Kye (2020) addresses Gutiérrez, Schwartz, DiGiacomo, and Vossoughi's (2014) assertions of "reminding educators that making and tinkering are indigenous to non-dominant communities. They call on educators to question assumptions about who does and does not engage in making and to counter narrow definitions of 'making' and 'makers'" (p. 4). It is important to recognize that there are opportunities to emphasize and celebrate aspects of the traditions of making that have been an inherent part of many cultures. A space that highlights cultural maker practices and projects can act as a sign to makers that more personal and nuanced making is valued in a space as well, instead of simply something like prototyping and manufacturing. This also presents the possibility for other users to discover ideas that are new to them by learning from others.

The Design of the Space

Though designing the physical spaces may seem as simple as determining what items fit where, the process should actually be given much more consideration, as the design of the space can directly influence the ways in which the space is used and the people who are interested in using the space. The sections below will show how groups have been excluded from these types of spaces in the past and what we can do to develop inclusionary spaces. It is worth noting that:

One powerful antidote to [...] exclusion is representation. When kids see their identities reflected in media it can help to affirm their identity, make them feel less alone, and discover role models who look like them (Werner, 2021). When people see their identities represented and celebrated by their library, they are more likely to see the library as a space for them. (Farkas, 2020, p. 46)

This is certainly the case with innovation spaces and higher education, as well. Due to the intimidation factors that these spaces and technologies can pose, it is of great importance that students see at least a version or component of themselves represented. Representation can legitimize a space and can position it as one where individuals who see that self-representation feel comfortable expressing themselves and taking risks.

When at all possible, design a space that can feature student work. When featuring this work, include gallery tags or some other form of short-form prose to highlight the creator's main messages, as well as their background. Though this should happen with all work, it is especially important to do so for work developed by creators from historically excluded or exploited communities, as these groups have often been denied legitimacy.

In addition to these general suggestions, the following sections will detail strategies for representing identity in space design throughout spaces used for particular activities. Though these spaces may look different based on the location, the ideas presented can be adapted to fit the particular space in question, as well as other similar spaces throughout the library and the institution.

Designing Makerspaces

Makerspaces have a unique place in the university ecosystems, since they are often spaces where personal and class projects are completed, friendships are formed, new skills are learned, and students become experts in certain areas. It is an atypical microcosm where participants can simultaneously be leaders, learners, and friends.

However, as easily as makerspaces can create sanctuary and inspiration, they can just as easily create the opposite due to interest convergence.

[B]ecause of the public-facing narrative around makerspaces (that they are open, accessible spaces where anyone can learn to make), [shared] interests converge in subtle ways – they're looking to foster a community of users who think like them and who, perhaps, ignore -isms in the same way they do, so that they don't have to talk about, or think about, those -isms. This leads to marginalized folks walking into spaces and immediately feeling unwelcome – perhaps from the stares they receive or from the lack of support when asking questions or learning new tools (Brown, 2020, p. 16-17).

When spaces are created without intentionally designing for inclusivity, the space could easily cause these interest convergence cliques to form. This is why a particular focus on inclusivity in staff training and also visibly highlighting a variety of student work is an important element of the creation and sustaining of a space.

Too often, engineering functions such as electronics use and part creation, are highlighted as the main work of makerspaces, inadvertently relegating uses more aligned with arts disciplines, personal use, and low-tech or no-tech making to lower, and sometimes hidden ranks. Though engineering functions and concepts, as well as similar endeavors, are certainly a large part of makerspaces, favoring these often creates a "white tech-bro culture [which] infiltrates makerspaces, [and] is counterintuitive to the potential of these spaces to allow for creative expression, being able to make mistakes in a supportive environment, and finding solutions to problems that might be applied on a larger scale beyond the makerspace" (Sanchez, Dolan-Sanchez, & Lázaro, 2020, p. 40). However, facilitating a makerspace that radiates this type of attitude does not have to be the reality.

To obviate this phenomenon, be strategic in determining which examples of making you highlight in display areas. This is not to say that complex-looking projects should be hidden or discarded, but instead, feature a variety of projects; include more complex projects alongside beginner projects and projects using all kinds of technologies and making, rather than highlighting only those using more difficult technologies. For example, in Area 49, this author's spaces, which is the library's collection of innovation spaces at UNC Charlotte, sewing machines, a popular low-tech machine, are positioned at the front of the space alongside 3D printers, and both paper projects and Lego builds are featured on the display shelves in the same area with other complex constructions in order to value low-tech, high-tech, and no-tech making to anyone glancing into the space.

Designing Spaces for Digital Creation

Spaces for digital creation, such as high-powered computer labs, data labs, video and audio development rooms, and more are often left with blank walls in favor of simply housing the equipment. However, when this happens, we let the equipment speak for itself, and it does not say the same thing to every student. To some, it suggests that it's available for access for whatever project that fits the equipment, but to others, because there is no indication otherwise, it suggests that the equipment is available only for projects that are somehow legitimized by others.

To counteract this, include project examples of all levels in the space (including beginner projects), not just to help them understand the different types of work that can happen in the space, but also to bring that legitimacy to any project they may have in mind, no matter how small it may be. To work within a DEIA framework, feature those that highlight excluded groups or projects created by those from these groups, projects that comment on social justice issues, or projects that expose injustices.

Designing Gaming Spaces

Gaming spaces in academic settings, including libraries, are becoming more popular, due to the increased interest in gaming in general, but also due to the increase of game development courses and majors in computer science and art. Gaming spaces can offer students the opportunity to simply play, or they can also be a space where students can test out games they have developed themselves. These spaces typically contain video game consoles, and gaming PCs, and if set up for board games and tabletop games, they also may feature tables designed for these purposes.[15] If virtual reality is offered, a dedicated space may be available.

Designing these spaces can be tricky, as providing only the most high-end consoles and games from AAA companies[16] can bring in predominantly male-presenting gamers, as these games typically feature male protagonists and are often focused on fighting and sports. While these games do attract a great many gamers of non-male genders, when an overwhelming percentage of males dominate a physical gaming space, it can be intimidating to walk in as someone of another gender to play a game of any kind, whether it is a fighting or sports game that might cause the gamer to prove their worth, or something like a cozy game that might create the fear of being labeled as someone who is not a legitimate gamer, which is, unfortunately, common in gaming communities.

Though games from AAA companies are working toward diverse representation in characters, plot lines, and development teams, creating a collection that celebrates this representation cannot be intentional by purchasing AAA games alone. A gaming space that operates within a DEIA framework should house games from other companies that meet these criteria, and therefore allow students to see themselves in games in positive lights. Spaces should also acquire accessible gaming peripherals, as having only standard gaming tools can prevent those who require accommodations from using the space. A tremendous proportion of gamers identify as disabled, about 30% of the US gaming population, in fact; but while companies have "begun prioritizing accessibility in their device designs [....] all that additional equipment comes at a literal cost" (Mulrow, 2021). This means that committing to a gaming space in a DEIA framework is committing to purchasing peripherals for accessibility, as well.

Marketing gaming spaces as being available to "all" may still label them as male and ableist spaces, depending on how the constraints above are met, so it is important to be strategic in how marketing occurs. For example, in this author's gaming space, a Diversity in Gaming collection was developed and specific games highlighting diverse populations and accessible controllers are advertised. Masculine-centric gamer decor has been redesigned to be of interest and more welcoming to a broader gaming population that excludes fewer gamers and celebrates diversity and inclusion, and that decor is included in the background or foreground of social media image posts to show DEIA is valued in the space. Planned initiatives include posting notifications in the space to let students know they can request technology accommodations if they don't see their desired accommodation available, and that they can suggest alternative accommodating purchases. Create the conditions for students to contribute to the space and make it their own.

Plan for the Distribution of Knowledge and Power

One important component of developing spaces based within a DEIA framework is planning for the distribution of knowledge and power. This should be accounted for both when considering who staffs the spaces on a daily basis and when determining how knowledge is distributed throughout the space, as discussed in these next sections.

Consider Who Staffs the Spaces

There are a number of staffing models to work with, considering that some spaces are staff-run, some spaces are student-run (with a faculty or staff supervisor or sponsor), and some are a mixture of the two. However, considering the optics of knowledge and power is important, as this can influence how students will use the spaces, as well as their comfort level with different types of work and their willingness to engage with ideas.

Having non-student, university staff run the spaces can ease workload because there will be significantly less turnover. Institutional knowledge will flow more smoothly, and staff training will not need to occur as frequently. However, this can be off-putting for students coming into spaces, since non-student staff can be seen as another kind of instructor, per se, taking authority over the space as an instructor would over a classroom. While this is certainly not equivalent, as grades are not involved, students often are not clear on administration in academia and can see faculty and staff as gatekeepers if they are uncertain about their own role in the situation.

Alternatively, whether they are solely student-run or run by a combination of student and non-student staff, simply having student staff in the space can often put student users at ease. Talking with a peer about ideas, rather than someone who is perceived as an authority figure, can make users more open to working on personal projects, rather than just projects for classes, and can also open them up to lighter conversations that may pull them in for more. Having student workers can significantly lessen the intimidation for first-time users.

In order to move a step further and staff with a DEIA framework in mind, include your diversity statement in your student worker job call. Though diversity statements are often now included in faculty and full-time staff job calls, they are often left out of student worker calls. Include the statement, as well as other inclusive language throughout the call to ensure that you are targeting potential hires who will contribute to a team working toward DEIA efforts. Then, of course, hire a staff that brings diversity to the table in a number of ways.

Consider Who Creates and Distributes Knowledge.

Just as with staffing, the creation and distribution of knowledge within the space shows who holds the power. If faculty and non-student staff are the ones who are in charge of all instruction, training, workshops, workflow development, suggestions for change, student assistance, and more, then the power resides only with them and agency is taken away from any student workers who may staff the space and students users may perceive limits on what they can do in the spaces.

To account for a more widely distributed knowledge base, first work toward student worker agency, instead of faculty and non-student staff hierarchies. Assure hesitant student workers that they can find solutions and provide them with the tools to do so. Guide student users to student workers for assistance when they ask questions of non-student staff. Assign workflow redesign projects to student workers to involve them in the inner workings of the space. Consider having student workers design and lead workshops that align with their interests.

Second, consider how users and non-users alike can contribute to the knowledge base. Those who do not work in the space either enter, use the space, and leave, or do not enter the space at all. However, there are a number of ways that these groups can contribute to the knowledge base. One simple method could include a user creating something in a space and then donating it for display or demonstration.

Another could be a user giving feedback on something not working properly, giving troubleshooting information about a machine on which they happen to have outside expertise, or even contributing to a suggestion box, which is an easy addition that could be prominent in every space.

A much larger initiative, however, could be the direct request for non-users to get involved in developing programming for the spaces. Meredith Farkas (2020) suggests that "Libraries with a less diverse workforce can develop culturally relevant programming that meets community needs and increases representation by collaborating with organizations that serve immigrants and refugees, racial minorities, people with disabilities, the queer community, and other groups" p. 46). However, academic libraries are an invaluable resource right on campus that can meet these same needs in similar ways. Seeking out students for leading programming not only increases representation, and distributes knowledge, but facilitates student agency in those who may not have felt the pull before, particularly if there is a DEIA focus.

For example, this author is instituting a guest-led programming initiative in which anyone, including students, can submit a request to lead a workshop, event, lecture, or other program to help others learn about the connection between DEIA and creativity, innovation, and emerging technologies. While we expect suggestions such as workshops centered around culturally-specific making, and programs focusing on accessibility in gaming or identity, and representation in innovation and design, any feasible suggestion will be welcomed. The intention is also to stay away from hand picking those we feel would fit well in the placement, and instead, open the opportunity to everyone, ensuring that we don't silence voices before we get a chance to hear them[17]. This gives students the opportunity to speak on what they themselves feel passionate about without the need to constrain it within project requirements. It is a genuine delivery of their ideas in the ways they wish to convey them.

This initiative could not only result in non-users becoming users of the spaces, but would also serve to introduce more culturally-relevant programming that spaces often have trouble facilitating because of the limited viewpoints and cultural identities present in staffing. Similar to the concept of Universal Design for Learning (UDL.org), where incorporating accommodations for accessibility benefits everyone, Meredith Farkas (2020) echoes Gricel Dominguez's (2012) urgings for libraries to take a role in multicultural literacies, reminding us that "Culturally relevant programming is not only valuable for members of a particular culture– it also provides cultural literacy education for people outside that group" (p. 46). So, this kind of programming not only welcomes those into our spaces who need to be encouraged, but also introduces necessary ideas to those who either have not had the opportunity to experience them or who have overlooked them in the past. This is yet another way to create change within a DEIA-based framework.

Supporting the Curriculum

In addition to providing space for students to work and engage with ideas, library innovation spaces sometimes support the curriculum by offering one-shot or multi-session instruction classes. Comparable to the model used by subject librarians for delivering instruction on library databases and academic research, librarians within the innovation spaces pair with the instructor, and often the subject librarian as well, to determine what goals the instructor would like to meet, and a custom session is designed with those goals in mind. Typically, once these collaborators begin working together, they are collaborators for the long term, and instructors continue to bring their classes back semester after semester. This means that innovation spaces, and particularly the collaborations that occur because of them, can serve as opportunities for faculty to transform their curriculum to exist in a global scope or expand the means for harnessing those interests. For example, one such collaboration in Area 49 started out with quick information sessions for the students. However, it soon grew into multiple instruction sessions each semester in which students applied design thinking, visual literacy strategies, cultural consciousness perspectives, and more to their community advocacy projects during activities in the innovation spaces.

Pun, Cardenas-Dow, and Flash (2022), suggest that "it is time for libraries to create space for ethnic studies. Examples include [among others,] committing to proactive, culturally competent outreach and engagement in these areas, [and] expanding ethnic studies collections" (p. 46). Libraries can extend their contribute to initiatives such as ethnic studies by supporting the curriculum in the following ways.

Changing How Achievement is Viewed in Classrooms

Experiencing the ways in which concepts are demonstrated and learned within innovation space activities often opens up instructors to reconsider how they see learning in their own classrooms, making way for a less-static hold on grades in the classroom. In these sessions the instructor sees the value of students learning various components of the same lesson and students teaching one another to learn the whole. Kurti, Kurti, and Fleming (2014) discuss engaging a maker mindset, which is common in innovation spaces, but less common in traditional classrooms. Teaching with this mindset means that "some peripheral concepts may not be learned by all students. Yet students faced with a common challenge to design their own unique solutions will naturally come to some common understanding" (p.8) and that moving through work more naturally, instead of following a required procedure, will "allows students to discover the concepts the teacher intended them to learn all along" (p.9).

Creating the conditions for students to be comfortable with voicing alternate ideas and suggestions is key. For example, during activities in the spaces, students may not engage with the same part of each activity, or even the same activity. Instead, they might choose which activity to interact with from a set of three and share their findings with the group in order to teach others about what they discovered. They also may not interact with activities in the same ways as their peers, which is encouraged, and even celebrated here. Students sometimes need reminding that hearing a variety of opinions and findings is exciting, more interesting than hearing one opinion, and is an example of how we create change.

As instructors who may have been more hesitant to modify their methods observe their students learning in this type of environment in innovation spaces, they often begin to ask questions about how they can modify other activities in their courses to push toward similar results. The engagement they see in the spaces is quite a desired outcome, and instructor-librarian collaborations often become strengthened through this process. As innovation librarians continue to collaborate with faculty for classes delivered in the spaces and serve as collaboration leaders who lead discourses designed to empower students, innovative learning concepts will have a positive impact on learning within the classroom and for the future, and in turn, we will see higher grades, due to more genuine engagement.

While this alternative site for learning is certainly developed to give students access to spaces, services, and ways of thinking, it also creates the opportunity for faculty to engage more deeply with their curriculum and make modifications based on how students interact in the spaces, any innovation- or DEIA-based concepts faculty are introduced to, and the collaborations faculty involve themselves in. As faculty make these changes within their classrooms, they often contribute to the discourse on instruction in their disciplines, whether it be through presentations or publications or simply by word-of-mouth in their own departments, encouraging other faculty to make changes, as well. This becomes the instigator for instructors to make alterations to their courses in the realms of innovation, DEIA, and active learning, and in turn, this begins to change what is ultimately valued with respect to how students work and think within those disciplines.

Creating the Conditions for Success

Although incorporating the concepts of failure and imperfection into the design and management of spaces is important, these concepts require added attention for instruction sessions, as sessions are either self-contained or are focused on assisting students with some concept of a larger project for their course.

For self-contained sessions, meaning that the activities delivered during that class time are designed to be completed during the session, set expectations for activities at the time instructions are given. This author has seen too often that when students are interacting with new tools and technologies or learning new skills, and they either don't complete the intended task within the given time frame or they don't develop something they feel meets expectations, there is an automatic sense of failure, and interest in these new ideas is turned off. Instead, students can be encouraged to think about the reasons they are working on these activities, and that the point might not be to leave the class having developed something in a short 20 to 40-minute time frame, but rather to go through a certain thought process.

For example, if students are working on a maker activity, give them options for how they can engage in the creation process. They can sketch something out, build the item, or even just make notes about their ideas to share them with the class alongside smaller drawings of pieces of the item, instead of the whole. Alternatively, if they are working on a digital project, then working on a quick outline, storyboard, or a single visual component, deciding on a color scheme, learning the basics of a program they will use, or even finding information about something they will need for the project could all be ways to push themselves forward, depending on the particular activity being facilitated. However, creating an entire polished item or visual by the end of a class session is probably not a realistic expectation. Setting these expectations for students is important, especially if they are given examples beforehand that show them what they could accomplish, and they don't produce similar results in the short time frame.

For sessions focused on assisting with a course project, it is important to help students understand realistic goals to complete within the time frame of the given project. Examples such as the 1619 Project from *The New York Times Magazine*, Mapping Inequality: Redlining in New Deal America (Nelson, et. al, n.d.), and Native Land Digital (for digital projects) and large art installations and community maker technology initiatives are all instances this author commonly uses in classes in order to show how historical and cultural consciousness is kept alive. Too often, though, students are introduced to projects such as these throughout their coursework and as examples of innovative work at the corporate or community levels that may have been funded by grants, worked on by large teams of people, or have taken years to develop. However, students are seldom informed of this and sometimes feel that their projects must also be on par with these stellar examples, when they only have a week or two to work on them and fewer resources at their disposal. Talking through realistic expectations for student projects, as well as viewing other student projects, is helpful, especially for first time users, as they discover how to implement old and new skills into nontraditional projects in order to develop something that still excites them and conveys their ideas, but is reasonable in the time frame they are given.

No matter the session type, it is important to help students to understand how they can create their own conditions for success and manage their own expectations. It is equally important in both of these instances to help them understand how and when to experiment with failure within a classroom setting. While positive failure is certainly valued within innovation spaces, it is often less so in classrooms with rigid grading structures. Even in those with more flexible grading systems, there may be times when this kind of experimentation is valued more than others. Helping students recognize the times when experimentation is valued can be the key to them successfully using the strategy in both their academic and future careers. Doing so can be as simple as having a conversation about how the day's class in the innovation spaces is different from their typical class sessions. Further, giving students no-stakes opportunities to engage, or facilitating a session on what positive failure could look like within the classroom serves to expand their understanding of the value of the space. Ultimately, sessions of either type are designed to help students succeed.

Inclusive Content

When developing instruction sessions of any kind, it is easy to simply choose the most readily-available content, examples, and tutorials, especially since finding content on specific and specialized concepts, particularly using the desired emerging technology, is so difficult. Some of these items, such as attractive, yet relevant data visualizations, maker projects that demonstrate a specific aspect of making, and recordings of particular video game content are all items this author has attempted to use as examples in instruction sessions. Though a quick search for a data visualization, for example, would elicit a great many search results, visualizations are often not labeled as such, making them difficult to find. Even more difficult is finding one relevant to the course subject matter or the particular content for the day. When the intention behind using the visualization is also to discuss visual design, there is the added need to find something dynamic enough to capture students' attention. Such an effort takes quite a bit of time, and often, visualizations have not been developed on the subject matter, requiring an adjacent example.

It is even more difficult to find an example that represents DEIA well, though if you have a choice in the content included, choose content that:

- Represents or features historically excluded or exploited communities in positive lights
- Is developed by someone who is a part of the community being portrayed or is developed by individuals or groups from backgrounds typically excluded from emerging technologies or the subject area
- Can help spark conversations about DEIA issues that students may need to focus on in their future careers
- Shows, instead of telling, of injustices, in order to teach students how to question assumptions

- Uses language and visuals to positively reference people of color and other exploited communities, especially when deeper, politicized meanings are accounted for
- Has been made by users of the spaces and is more demonstrative of what could be developed in the spaces

Alternatively, if this type of content is not available for the needed example, choose an example that does not do these things well, ensuring that you use it instead to call out the opportunities that could have been taken or the changes that could be made to account for the above content. In lieu of finding an example that does these things well, help students understand how these examples missed the mark, and how easy it could have been to make changes for inclusivity and how important it is to address injustice in this type of work. Doing so is an alternative method of engaging with Pun, Cardenas-Dow, and Flash's (2022) urge for libraries to "expand ethnic studies collections," (p. 46) as examples students would experience in instruction sessions have similar effects as library holdings, as both are given substance by the institution. Either of these paths will show students that you, and by extension, the innovation spaces, value all identities and perspectives. This small victory not only goes a long way in sustaining students' positive outlooks on their own academic and future careers, but also can encourage students who were previously uninterested in the course to begin to participate, if they were inspired to create change.

Unless faculty have specific interests in DEIA work, non-dominant narratives are typically left out of sessions, unless librarians incorporate them. Weaving DEIA content into librarian-led sessions can encourage instructors who have previously been hesitant about including it in their own courses. Faculty are often receptive to the idea, as someone else is developing and teaching the session, which ultimately acts as a sort of modeling for them and a way to test it out in their course. Doing so also creates the opportunity for faculty to include both innovation and DEIA focal points at the same time, which often leads to additional changes in course content. However, working on innovation and DEIA simultaneously is much easier than attempting to incorporate the latter at a later point in time.

Alternative Applications and Community Collaborations

This chapter has focused on using innovation spaces in higher education and academic libraries with the assumption that institutions have access to such spaces. However, there are a number of institutions that have no such spaces or technology available. For example, Rogoswki, Lee, and Recker (2020) emphasize that rural libraries that do not have full-fledged makerspaces, "libraries can offer access to maker activities rather than offering access to a makerspace" (p. 169). In these cases, simply use what is available.

It is important to note that concepts typically taught in innovation spaces, such as design thinking, critical thinking, making, and more, can still be taught without access to technology. Institutions without spaces and resources available can turn to freely available materials to teach students how to be resourceful. Many examples, such as visualizations and photographs or videos of physical projects can be found online. Many beginner maker projects can be completed with inexpensive crafting items, which is often enough to introduce students to innovative concepts. Brainstorming for project ideas, scrutinizing publicly-available projects online, and showing examples of how people have demonstrated ideas well are all possible to do without physical spaces.

In fact, this author's collection of innovation spaces has turned to these types of materials in multiple stages. Outside virtual projects were shown in the beginning days of the spaces (before student projects were available) and are still used today as aspirational projects for students to turn to and also to criticize. The ideas in the above paragraph were all used during the pandemic as instructors turned to the innovation spaces for virtual innovation instruction for sessions that are typically hands-on. However, little shift was necessary, as activities focused on resourcefulness and alternative methods of completing tasks have always been incorporated into innovation instruction sessions.

Alternatively, directing students to public library innovation spaces and community makerspaces, and other community activity spaces can certainly be an option to explore, though encouraging only some students, and not others, can reinforce the privilege-encouragement model, and students who cannot afford the transit or membership fees[18] or who shy away from entering new and unknown spaces will likely not take advantage of these resources. For institutions without innovation spaces, consider if a membership or transit agreement with a public library innovation space or a community makerspace may be feasible. If not, consider collaborating for field trip days to introduce students to the spaces and the concepts they reinforce. This could occur within classes or as excursions sponsored by the academic library.

Libraries that do have innovation spaces also have a particular opportunity for outreach, such as bringing K-12 groups into the spaces to engage in active learning activities and collaborating with public libraries or community spaces and groups for events or community initiatives. As the library and the innovation spaces are increasingly in the public eye, the value of innovation will soar, which means that incorporating DEIA into these initiatives from the start is of the utmost importance.

CONCLUSION

Innovation spaces can add equity value to the higher education classroom and level the playing field for students who have been underserved. However, much more work needs to be done in order to engage students in such a manner that they attain the objectives they have set for themselves. The suggestions put forth in this chapter can help leaders of innovation spaces recognize how and why to market spaces to traditionally excluded and exploited groups for a more cohesive, yet dynamic community, and these rationales serve as an argument for continued collaboration within higher education.

Ultimately, innovation spaces do not just exist in order to give students a space to complete tasks, but rather safe surroundings to falter, grow and take action on their own paths to success. Though these spaces expand opportunities for all students, they have a particular opportunity to support students from traditionally excluded groups when they are designed with attention to inclusive and celebratory practices. When we design spaces that students feel comfortable in, when we help students to become stronger and more critical thinkers, and when we help them contribute to a culturally responsive framework, we have prepared students to apply their ideas in the real world and create real change.

REFERENCES

Bignoli, C., & Faas, D. (2022). Increasing access to shops, makerspaces and libraries across a hands-on, project-based engineering curriculum. 6th International Symposium on Academic Makerspaces. ISAM. https://isam2022.hemi-makers.org/wp-content/uploads/sites/3/2022/09/046.pdf

Brown, J. (2020). Critical Race Theory and makerspaces: A practical approach. In M. Melo & J. T. Nichols (Eds.), *Remaking the library makerspace: Critical theories, reflections, and practices*. Library Juice Press.

Crenshaw, K. (1989). Demarginalizing the intersection of race and sex: A black feminist critique of antidiscrimination doctrine, feminist theory and antiracist politics. *University of Chicago Legal Forum*, *1*(8), 139–167. https://chicagounbound.uchicago.edu/uclf/vol1989/iss1/8

Diversity Officer Magazine. (2023). Historically excluded group. *Diversity Officer Magazine*. https://diversityofficermagazine.com/cultural-competence/diversitypedia/heg/

Dominguez, G. (2012). *Multiculturalism happens: Targeting multicultural literacy in libraries*. Programming Librarian. https://programminglibrarian.org/articles/multiculturalism-happens-targeting-multicultural-literacy-libraries

Dougherty, D. (2015). The maker mindset. *Paper Static*. https://blog.paperstatic.com/wp-content/uploads/2015/12/maker-mindset.pdf

Farkas, M. (2020, March/April). Representation Beyond Books. *American Libraries*, 46.

Forbes. (2022). 15 skills employers seek in 2022 (and ways to gain them midcareer). *Forbes*. https://www.forbes.com/sites/forbescoachescouncil/2022/08/11/15-skills-employers-seek-in-2022-and-ways-to-gain-them-midcareer/?sh=a974fe8481a8

Koh, K., Ge, X., Lee, L., Lewis, K. R., Simmons, S., & Nelson, L. B. (2020). Peace prescription: Inclusive making in school libraries. In M. Melo & J. T. Nichols (Eds.), *Remaking the library makerspace: Critical theories, reflections, and practices*. Library Juice Press.

Kurti, R. S., Kurti, D. L., & Fleming, L. (2014). The philosophy of educational makerspaces. *Teacher Librarian*, *41*(5). https://www.proquest.com/docview/1548230083?parentSessionId=nwJLVgQAvkWXuIPMFvYBBr9FeRWuZMcGPRw2WHaqDDI%3D

Kye, H. (2020). Who is welcome here? A culturally responsive analysis of makerspace websites. *Journal of Pre-College Engineering Education Research*, *10*(2). https://docs.lib.purdue.edu/jpeer/vol10/iss2/1. doi:10.7771/2157-9288.1190

Lister, H. (2020). Trauma-informed making. In M. Melo & J. T. Nichols (Eds.), *Remaking the library makerspace: Critical theories, reflections, and practices*. Library Juice Press.

Mann, S. (2020). Makerspace dialogue as collaboration and resistance. In M. Melo & J. T. Nichols (Eds.), *Remaking the library makerspace: Critical theories, reflections, and practices*. Library Juice Press.

Marshall, B., & Melo, M. (2020). From needs analysis to power analysis: A framework to examine and broker power in makerspaces. In M. Melo & J. T. Nichols (Eds.), *Remaking the library makerspace: Critical theories, reflections, and practices*. Library Juice Press.

Mulrow, J. (2021). *Gaming is becoming accessible, but we need to keep asking for more*. Refinery29. https://www.refinery29.com/en-us/2021/12/10711964/gamers-with-disabilities-accessible-video-games

Nation of Makers. (n.d.) *The White House: President Barack Obama (Archive)*. Obama White House. https://obamawhitehouse.archives.gov/nation-of-makers

Nelson, R. K., Winling, L., Marciano, R., & Connolly, N. (n.d.). Mapping inequality. In. R. K. Nelson & E. L. Ayers (Eds.), *American Panorama*. Mapping Identity. https://dsl.richmond.edu/panorama/redlining/

Office of the Press Secretary. (2016). Fact sheet: New commitments in support of the President's Nation of Makers Initiative to kick off 2016 National Week of Making. *Week of Making*. http://www.weekofmaking.org/wp-content/uploads/2016/03/2016-National-Week-of-Making-Fact-Sheet.pdf

Patton, L. D. (2016). Disrupting postsecondary prose: Toward a critical race theory of higher education. *Urban Education*, *51*(3), 315–342. doi:10.1177/0042085915602542

Pun, R., Cardenas-Dow, M., & Flash, K. (2022, March/April). Prioritizing Ethnic Studies. *American Libraries*, 46.

Rogowski, A., Lee, V. R., & Recker, M. (2020). Supporting making in libraries rather than makerspaces: Rethinking the (maker)space for rural libraries. In M. Melo & J. T. Nichols (Eds.), *Remaking the library makerspace: Critical theories, reflections, and practices*. Library Juice Press.

Sanchez, A., Dolan-Sanchez, D., & Lázaro, V. (2020). Who belongs in the makerspace? Experiences of women of color in an academic library makerspace. In M. Melo & J. T. Nichols (Eds.), *Remaking the library makerspace: Critical theories, reflections, and practices*. Library Juice Press.

Sokolower, J. (2018). Space for young Black women: An interview with Candice Valenzuela. In D. Watson, J. Hagopian, & W. Au (Eds.), Teaching for Black Lives. Rethinking Schools.

The 1619 Project. (2019). *The New York Times Magazine*. https://www.nytimes.com/interactive/2019/08/14/magazine/1619-america-slavery.html

Universal Design for Learning. (2022). *Guidelines*. UDL. https://udlguidelines.cast.org/

KEY TERMS

DEIA: Refers to Diversity, Equity, Inclusion, and Accessibility, this is a common acronym used when Accessibility, an often-forgotten aspect of inclusivity, is also valued.

Historically, Typically, or Intentionally Excluded or Exploited Communities: Current terminology is used in place of terms such as "minorities" in order to call attention to the oppression and active injustices perpetrated upon these groups, rather than suggesting that their struggles are due to passive states of being.

Innovation Spaces: Spaces that provide tools, technology, services, and expertise for users to engage with ideas, creation, and collaboration.

Intersectionality: A term coined by Kimberlé Crenshaw in 1989 to refer to how a person's many identities converge and is often applied in politicized environments.

Makerspace: Areas that facilitate various levels and types of hands-on creation. They typically feature crafting items and low- to mid-tech machines, such as sewing machines, 3D printers, and laser cutters, but can veer into specialty machine shops, depending on the need and location.

Positive Failure: An appreciation of and willingness to fail first in order to learn from one's mistakes.

Privilege: The advantages one has based on the identity and social groups they belong to.

ENDNOTES

[1] Innovation space managers can range from anyone who manages the daily operations of the space to someone who helps develop the outward-presenting identity of the space through developing the space's design, collections, technology, or marketing, or by facilitating idea development through course instruction, workshops, training, leadership, and more.

[2] Current acronyms used to represent inclusionary practices typically include the same letters, but in a variety of orders, such as DEI and IDE. This author will use DEIA, which is a common acronym order used to include "Accessibility" as a vital component of inclusivity.

[3] Historically (or typically or intentionally) excluded or exploited communities is the current terminology used in place of terms such as "minorities," in order to call attention to the oppression and active injustices perpetrated upon these groups, rather than suggesting that their struggles are due to passive states of being. This is "an alternative label [...] used in an effort to get around the controversy concerning the use of minority to the extent possible and because it is inclusive of other underrepresented groups" (Diversity Officer Magazine2023).

[4] Making, within the context of the Maker Movement, is engaging in some element of hands-on creation. Items can be developed using high-tech, low-tech, or no-tech means.

5   Maker projects are considered to be something that a person has physically made. Though the end result may be a completed and polished item, it could alternatively be a prototype or a representation of an idea.

6   Makerspaces are areas that facilitate various levels and types of hands-on creation.

7   Digital production labs could include spaces for data visualization, video and audio creation, or any other space that allows for the development of digital scholarship, digital humanities projects, or other digital technology-based projects.

8   Other spaces for nontraditional work could include those such as gaming spaces, collaboration spaces, and any other space for alternative work.

9   A clarification on acronym usage. In this chapter, outside of quoted usage, this author will use STEM to refer to what people have traditionally thought of as Science, Technology Engineering, and Math, to suggest that these areas typically receive high levels of funding and attention in academia. STEAM will refer to the STEM with the added "Art," as the addition of this creative mode of thinking is essential for innovation and cross-disciplinary collaboration. STEAM will be used with the connotation of the potential dismantling of an impenetrable system that values only the scientific way of thinking in order to apply all sorts of methods to approach a situation.

10   Makerspaces can vary drastically based on their locations within the institution and their general purposes and can veer into the realm of machine shops as they begin to serve more specialized levels of making.

11   To aid in determining how a space meets the needs of everyone and of specific groups, turn to Brianna Marshall and Maggie Melo's (2020) "From Needs Analysis to Power Analysis: A Framework to Examine and Broker Power in Makerspaces." They present critical questions about all aspects of the space, including questions such as "How do new […] users 'know' how to engage with the space?" (p. 91) and "Who is invited to facilitate or lead events? Who is doing the inviting?" (p. 93).

12   This journal entry shows the struggle this author engaged in along her journey in understanding her privilege and how she put the past behind her in order to do the work that needed to be done. It is included here for a few reasons: (1) so that the author is transparent about her privilege, background, and perspective for the purposes of this chapter and the recommendations in it; (2) so that readers may see one demonstration of a move through coming to terms with an area of privilege, even though it may put the author in a vulnerable state; and (3) to show that this author has a genuine want to be a participant in this conversation and this work. It is not a perfect demonstration of this work, as likely none would be, but it is real, and it is worth noting in order to better

understand how the recommendations given throughout the next sections of this chapter were determined.

13   Unless they are funded by an outside grant with a specific purpose in mind, it is possible that the development of the space could have fewer academic power dynamics at play, but there could be other constraints in the mix, particularly due to ongoing funding or constraints set by the grant itself.

14   "Diverse representation" refers to all identities, such as racial identity, LGBTQ+ identities, and others, as well as physical and intellectual abilities.

15   Some gaming spaces also feature board games and tabletop games, but this chapter will focus on spaces for video games.

16   Games from AAA companies typically feature higher-end graphics, longer gameplay lengths, and are generally more well-known, advertised games, as they are produced by larger companies with larger budgets and less-diverse development teams (which typically result in less in-game inclusivity). Games from Independent, or "Indie" publishers, though often not as dominant in these areas, have gained momentum in recent years, and many of these games are produced by more diverse development teams, providing the player with a more inclusive experience.

17   For a unique take on selecting participants for an initiative, see Jody Sokolower's interview with Candice Valenzuela (2018) in which they discuss how Valenzuela created a group for young Black women. In choosing participants, she did not gravitate only to those who were obviously in the most need, but those who "might benefit from community, who might need to support to develop as leaders or to come into their voices, those who might be able to help guide others, who might benefit from added support and be open to receiving it" (p. 52). Involvement in a guest-led programming initiative can lead to similar benefits.

18   Community makerspaces are often membership-based, which could prevent students from taking advantage of the spaces and services.

Chapter 5

Language and Leadership in the Midst of Social Unrest:
A Critical Analysis of Educational Leaders' Responses to Racial Violence in the Era of the Pandemic

Nicole G. DeRonck
Western Connecticut State University, USA

Samantha Gati-Tisi
Western Connecticut State University, USA

Tricia J. Stewart
Western Connecticut State University, USA

Courtney Fragomeli
Western Connecticut State University, USA

ABSTRACT

The civil unrest following the murder of George Floyd exerted a tremendous burden on educational institutions across the USA during the critical era of the global pandemic. Educational leaders including district leaders and principals were taxed with the responsibility of effectively communicating with their stakeholders and bringing a sense of peace and calm to the school environment. This study engaged in a critical discourse analysis of the methods these leaders used to communicate with their constituents in order to determine the extent to which they effectively utilized antiracist strategies to lead, support and build bridges during this turbulent time. Primary source documents created by these leaders were scrutinized in order to determine how they used language to challenge policies and practices within a school district to ensure a safe and supportive environment for all members of the school community. The authors suggest that additional training and resources are necessary for educational leaders to enhance effective crisis response from an anti-racist stance especially in response to issues of social justice. This chapter

DOI: 10.4018/978-1-6684-7379-5.ch005

highlights the challenges for educational leaders in creating culturally responsive, appropriate, and timely communication with recommendations on how to connect across borders.

INTRODUCTION

On May 25, 2020, George Floyd was killed by White police officers in Minneapolis, MN after being accused of using counterfeit currency to purchase cigarettes in a convenience store. Observer video went viral on social media, allowing the world to see the last breath of a Black man whose neck was pinned under the knee of Officer Derrick Chauvin for over nine minutes while fellow White officers failed to intervene. George Floyd's murder sparked weeks of protests and civil unrest in more than 150 cities across America and reignited the call to end systemic racism with a fervor not seen since the 1960's Civil Rights Movement (The New York Times, 2020).

Sadly, police brutality is nothing new in America. The instance of George Floyd's murder is but one example of the many injustices faced by Black and Brown communities. Police brutality is experienced by all races and ethnicities but is disproportionately so for Black people who were 28% of those killed in 2020 at the hands of the police despite being only 13% of the United States population (MappingPoliceViolence.org, 2021). Additionally, hate crimes have been on the rise since the 2016 Presidential Election and the Presidency of Donald Trump. Sadly, this increase in hate is not limited to derogatory language, racist behaviors, and White Nationalist symbolism as prominent for adults, but they have also appeared more prominently in public schools (Costello, 2016). For example, incidences of racism have interrupted school board meetings across the United States. School board members have reported that local and national political issues have polarized their districts, making fact-based and civil communication around racial and educational issues particularly challenging (Reynolds, Silvernell, & Mercer, 2020). While the increase in these incidents has been tied to political ideology and White nationalism, educational leaders are obligated to support all students by fostering learning environments that promote social justice and that are culturally responsive for marginalized students including students of color, immigrants, and those students who identify as LGBTQTIA+ (National Policy Board for Educational Administration, 2015). This qualitative case study utilizes primary source documents from a range of educational organizations within one Northeast state to critically reflect, through content analysis, on communications written by educational leaders following a critical incident, the murder of George Floyd by Minneapolis Police, and the public outcry that sprang from it.

BACKGROUND

Educational leaders are individuals who are charged with creating and managing positive change through educational policy or processes and often hold school district or school-based administrative positions (Wenner & Campbell, 2017). One essential skill educational leaders must possess is the ability to communicate effectively and efficiently to a diverse audience of stakeholders (from students to community leaders) utilizing a culturally responsive stance. The critical nature of this skill is underscored by the fact that most educational leaders remain predominantly White and male despite an increase in diversity among the K-12 student body across the United States (Modan, 2020; National Center for Educational Statistics, 2020). Conceived by Gloria Ladson-Billings (1995), cultural responsiveness is a perspective that capitalizes on the cultural characteristics (i.e., ethnicity, language, traditions, etc.) and identity of a school community, and uses them as tools of empowerment to improve academic achievement, cultural competence, and socio-political awareness for students. Cultural responsiveness requires educational leaders to examine their own cultural competence and biases to foster student development and respect for the cultural heritages of students and their families (Ladson-Billings, 1995). Educational leaders who adopt a culturally responsive perspective enjoy stronger relationships with members of the school community and better educational and social-emotional outcomes. They are also better equipped to solve systemic inequities within their local communities and beyond (Massachusetts Department of Education, 2021). Additionally, educational leaders should work to adopt an anti-racist approach to leadership which includes all public relations messaging. Anti-racism is an active process that requires individuals to identify, challenge and confront racism; this is an approach that goes beyond cultural responsiveness. Racism is a social construct that defines individual worth and access to opportunity based on skin color alone and has been embedded in the foundational structure of organizations and institutions in this country including our educational systems (National Association for Diversity Officers in Higher Education [NADHOE], 2021).

Educational leaders are in the vanguard to redistribute power and assure equitable outcomes for all members of their school communities through the implementation of anti-racist educational policy, curriculum, and community engagement (NADHOE, 2021). Research on cross-cultural communication indicates that effective communication can counter hegemony by providing those involved in an exchange the opportunity for serious contemplation and revision of long-held beliefs (Zadi, Vyas, Hamed, Dornan, & Monahan, 2016).

Strong communication skills and the ability to be an adaptive leader have also been linked to high degrees of emotional intelligence. This is important because examining and confronting personal biases requires a high degree of emotional intelligence and willingness to change. In his book, *What Makes a Leader*, Daniel Goleman (1996) describes five emotional intelligence skills that enhance communication:

1. Self-awareness- the ability to recognize and understand one's emotions and the impact they have on others. It contributes to the authenticity with which the message is received (Goleman, 1996). In other words, self-awareness assists the reader in determining if the person communicating is genuine.
2. Self-regulation- a person's ability to control or redirect impulses. Self-regulation allows people to stop and think before speaking or hitting send on an emotional email. It is the same skill that allows a leader to calmly listen and distill the intent of a heated conversation before deciding how to respond. Self-regulation is important to communication because it establishes trustworthiness and integrity.
3. Motivation- an emotional intelligence skill that enhances communication because it drives people to reach goals and pursue activities out of passion rather than selfish reasons like financial gains or prestige. Motivation is related to the character traits of commitment, optimism, and perseverance.
4. Empathy- the ability to put ourselves in someone else's shoes to better understand their feelings and communicate our support to them. Empathy is not sympathy. Empathy requires active listening and objectivity so that the reaction to an individual in pain is driven by the emotional impact of the person's circumstance, not the act of suffering itself. The latter is known as sympathy. According to psychologist Brené Brown, "Empathy fuels connection. Sympathy drives disconnection (n.d.)." When a person is suffering, they are not looking for a fix, they are looking for understanding. Providing sympathy elicits pity, creating a power differential that results in the isolation of the person or group seeking understanding (Brown, n.d.). A leader who can communicate empathy builds expertise in creating a positive school climate because stakeholders feel like they are being respected and heard. Communicating with empathy leads to improved cross-cultural sensitivity (Chatman, Johnson, White, & Bell, 2020).
5. Social skills- the range of skills that are competence-based and help facilitate positive interactions with others based on societal norms. For leaders, social skills matter because they are the key to building and managing the teams that get the work done (Dowd & Tierney, 2017). Educational leaders who have honed their social skills are persuasive in their messaging. They seek to build rapport with others by finding common ground and communicating with clear and compelling information to make the case for change.

Taken together, the five emotional intelligence skills (self-awareness, self-regulation, motivation, empathy, and social skills) are the core of what is required to be able to effectively communicate about complex and emotionally intense topics.

The aforementioned skills are relevant to the study in this chapter, as the leaders had the motivation to address their stakeholder communities, but with varying levels of success.

CHALLENGING IMPLICIT BIAS, SYSTEMIC RACISM AND HEGEMONY

A dominant culture is a system where one culture imposes its values, language, and behavior as the blueprint for establishing the norms of the larger society often as a result of an economic or political power differential (Hasforth, 2016). The dominant culture utilizes language to maintain power by reinforcing White norms as the preferred and foundational norms for American society. Language serves as the vehicle that marginalizes society members as "other" and informs our implicit biases, which are held outside our awareness but can positively or negatively impact our attitudes and behaviors towards others (Zaidi et al., 2016). Realizing that the values, beliefs, and attitudes we hold are not automatically true is an important step in combating implicit bias. However, acquiring the ability to critically reflect on and be mindful of implicit bias in our interactions with others is no easy task. Zaidi et al. (2016) indicate that the reason it is so difficult to critically reflect on our interactions with others is that not all people have equal access to material and social resources, including quality public schools. Unaddressed, implicit bias upholds hegemony and systemic racism within social institutions like schools. For example, White people report fear of running into a misunderstanding communicating with Black, Indigenous and People of Color (BIPOC) regarding race or racism and know that engaging in such conversations may challenge White assumptions of others (Ruggs & Avery, 2020; Simmons, 2019). As a result, many White people remain silent (Rattan & Ambady, 2014; Zaidi et al. 2016). Declining to engage with other cultural and racial groups is counter-productive for healing the myriad social injustices experienced by BIPOC every day. Language can also be used to keep any marginalized group in "its place" as is experienced through the variety of slurs used to denigrate members of the LGBTQ+ community. This is explicitly pointed out in our work given the increase in violence against this population in 2022. Furthermore, avoiding these difficult conversations negatively impacts school culture and climate, and the physical and emotional health of the school community (Ruggs & Avery, 2020; Simmons, 2019).

Failing to engage in conversation about systemic racism has academic consequences as well. Black students are 1.4 times more likely to be identified for special education services when looking at aggregate disability rates but are underrepresented when data is adjusted to account for achievement and family income (Gordon, 2017).

Rather than focusing on improving educational outcomes by providing all students with the correct level and types of support, too often, the discussion focuses on how many Black students are identified. This serves as a diversion from the real issue, the role systemic racism plays in the underachievement of Black students, and others, living in poverty. While many White educational leaders may wish to disengage from social justice issues because these topics can become political or uncomfortable, opting for silence sends the problematic signal that the school as an institution does not condemn racism or the ideology of White supremacy. The lack of honest conversations about systemic oppression also prevents communities and schools from providing wrap around services that would work to mitigate the hardships families in poverty experience. Far too often, race is used as a proxy for class thereby creating a conflation of issues.

Fortunately, systemic oppression and racism can be addressed. One way to engage in anti-racist, culturally responsive messaging is to remember to use the acronym and process for VPSA: Value, Problem, Solution, Action (The Opportunity Agenda, 2020). VPSA is a formulaic way to think and craft messages that can counter inequitable and unjust policies. VPSA was developed-by The Opportunity Agenda, a communication lab whose aim is to help social justice leaders build and share compelling messages that can shift public discourse, drive policy, and promote cultural change (The Opportunity Agenda, 2020). Effective messaging begins with shared values, through which people are invited to think about what they have in common. Commonalities serve as a foundational building block, which encourages hope and emphasizes the role the community plays in giving all members equitable access to opportunities.

Next, problems are identified, and solutions to address these challenges are generated, which result in calls to action. Therefore, anti-racist messages should describe how racial bias harms everyone, but also follow-up with a plan that results in action to counter hegemony. Utilizing the VPSA model, all forms of communication should use language that embraces the diversity of the community rather than framing the message from the lens of Whiteness. Leaders should be aware of the variety of cultures and narratives in their school districts and use language to address them in relevant messaging. The Opportunity Agenda (2020) posits that messaging from educational leaders should be forward-thinking, end by providing a goal or plan of action for change, and include resources for those who wish to get involved or need assistance. The five emotional intelligence skills (Golman,1996) dovetail with the use of VPSA by helping the leader draft a message that is genuine, persuasive, free of bias, and shows a commitment to caring. Employing emotional intelligence skills makes it easier for educational leaders to start hard conversations with a vision and facts rather than being afraid to act or worse, inadvertently supporting fearmongering.

Method and Sourcing

Utilizing the case study methodology, the researchers critically analyze educational leaders' methods of communicating with their stakeholders regarding the murder of George Floyd. School districts and educational agencies across one state in the Northeast United States sent letters/emails and posted statements on their websites attempting to help their school communities process the murder, the protests, and social unrest that followed. The data utilized in this study was the communications from educational leaders. Data was not generated by the research team but was already in existence and was collected and analyzed by the team (Yin, 2018). It is important to note that because George Floyd's murder, the critical incident in this study, happened during the global COVID-19 Pandemic, schools in this state were not conducting in-person schooling. Instead, online learning was being utilized throughout the state with educators having little or no training, or previous experience with this form of teaching and learning. Educational leaders had to find alternative ways to communicate with their school communities because quarantines made it challenging to connect in person. Superintendent Law, Oak Hill School District, expressed some of the added difficulty that the closure of schools created, as she shared in her letter "It saddens me that because we are not in session, it is difficult to engage our students in such an opportunity to process the events in a way that can produce positive outcomes, particularly in a virtual setting."

While online learning presented uncharted territory, it was still seen as essential that districts acknowledge what was happening in communities across the United States. The primary source statements (letters, emails, and web postings) were collected from websites and via emails received by the research team from educators across the state within the first two weeks of the statements being issued. This was done virtually as the researchers were also in quarantine.

Data Collection

Primary source documents included in this study had to meet two criteria. First, the document must have been written by an educational leader such as a principal, superintendent, or a leader at another educational organization. Documents must also have addressed the social unrest stemming from the police brutality that caused George Floyd's death. Case study was selected for the methodology because it allows "for in-depth analysis of complex and layered issues and flexible enough to account for highly open-ended research questions, data collection protocols, and analyses" (Butin, 2010, p. 80). Case study also has a focus on addressing naturally occurring events, which are not controlled by the researchers (Yin, 2018) and the nature of exploring a critical incident fits well with this parameter. The research questions that guided this case study included 1.) What were the strengths of the educational leaders' correspondences surrounding the critical incident of social unrest following the murder of George Floyd? 2.) What were the limitations of the educational leaders' correspondences surrounding the critical incident of social unrest following the murder of George Floyd? 3.) What were the characteristics of the educational organizations and educational leaders who decided to address stakeholders? These criteria resulted in a variety of communications from fourteen different leaders from school districts, communities, and educational organizations that responded to the critical racial incident under study, with the case at the level of the author/s of the letter (N=15). Pseudonyms were used for towns and educational leaders to protect confidentiality (Table 1). Critical incident narrative inquiry was used for data collection and analysis, which draws on participant narrative (the leader statements) to identify patterns and to learn from the participant's perceptions about the critical incident (Butterfield, Borgen, Amundson, & Maglio, 2005; Flanagan, 1954). A modification was made to the stages of qualitative content analysis in that letters were used in place of interview data (Bengtsson, 2016; Krippendorff, 2016).

Data Analysis

Qualitative content analysis was utilized by the research team to establish thematic similarities through inductive coding (Finfgeld-Connett, 2014; Saldana, 2013) across each of the educational leaders' correspondences to their stakeholders. Coding of each item was completed by all four members of the research team. In phase one inductive coding was used to pull out key terms and quotes which were used to generate themes. During phase two, a constant comparative approach (Boeije, 2002; Miles, Huberman, & Saldana, 2019; Strauss & Corbin, 1998) consisted of individual researcher-generated analysis for each primary source document in conjunction with the coding and themes that were already presented for discrete documents. Working across all the correspondences researchers created a data matrix that listed themes and important supporting evidence. For example, themes that were highlighted in the data matrix included an emphasis on personal reflection, a desire to help students, challenges with the COVID Pandemic and being online, references to famous people of color, and a call to action for the community to come together. These examples are meant to serve as a sample of what was included topically in the data matrix and is not a summation of everything included in the data matrix. This data matrix was then used for the writing of narrative themes that expanded beyond initial categorization. It was this narrative writing that supported the findings. Each research team member reviewed and edited the narrative findings to substantiate the clarity and consensus regarding the data.

Table 1. Representation of critical incident response letters and authors

Educational Leaders Who Wrote Letters (Pseudonym)	Organization (Pseudonym)	Type of Organization	Author's Race	Author's Gender
Harmony Cox	New Hollow	State Educational Organization	White	Female
Alma Bradley	Round River	State Educational Center	Black	Female
Ralph Massy Christopher McKinney Justin Rosen	Great Valley	Communities Represented (2) School District (1)	White White White	Male Male Male
Aimee Law	Oak Hill	School District	White	Female
Peter Norris	Seacoast	School District	White	Male
Veronica Smith	Ocean View	School District	Hispanic	Female
Adam Casey Kim West	Creek Side	School District	White White	Male Female
Patrick Johnson Wayne Pierce	High Meadow	School District	White White	Male Male
Joe King	Mountain Top	School District	White	Male
Robin D'Eville	Stonewall	School District	White	Female
Steve Reynolds	Stonewall	High School	White	Male

Study Results

Communities often look to schools during times of crisis and turmoil, particularly crises that impact student learning and well-being. Community members expect educational leaders to set the tone for how the community should respond, and to provide resources on how to mitigate any associated trauma for students. Therefore, regular communication between educational leaders and the community is important to foster positive relationships and trust between school and home (Moore, Bagin, & Gallagher, 2016) before a critical incident or crisis occurs. These ongoing communications can prove beneficial in times of crisis, like the critical incident that triggered social justice protests and the subsequent need for educational leaders to correspond with their communities. Eleven communications written by fifteen leaders (some communications included town leaders as co-authors) were included in this study. None of the leaders were fully effective in addressing their communities from an anti-racist lens.

The analysis of the data indicated that most of the educational leaders had the desire to connect with their school communities and be broadly supportive of racial and social justice. However, leaders struggled to express a clear and culturally responsive message, and only one attempted to approach the topic of civil unrest from an anti-racism perspective with limited success. From the data analysis, five themes emerged across the documents sent by the educational leaders:

1. educational leader communications centered on the voices of adults in the community over that of the students within the educational organizations;
2. most leaders lacked personal experience with racial injustice and had limited understanding of how to relay culturally responsive messaging;
3. statements were composed predominantly by White men who demonstrated a limited world view from which to frame their statement and instead drew upon the statements of famous people of color;
4. all statements contained messaging related to support for students and the community; and
5. statements attempted to explore the role of education in dismantling systemic racism with varying levels of success.

Centering Community Voices (Adults) Above Student Voices

Educational leaders felt the need to address the George Floyd murder given the societal outcry that took place immediately following his death. The subsequent societal protests were momentous enough that it appeared imperative to the educational leaders that they acknowledge the levels of civic unrest that were taking place across the United States. While the majority of correspondences was addressed to the larger community, only one was sent to and addressed students directly and that was shared by the principal of the high school, an administrator who works more directly with students than the other administrators in this study. The narrow audience range chosen by leaders to receive their messages suggests that the educational leaders, including those at the highest levels, were disproportionately more comfortable and considered it more important to write to the adults in the community. From the investigation of the content of the communications, the researchers inferred that the educational leaders believed that the sensitive topics of murder, violence and racial oppression would be more appropriately covered by the parents of the students. Furthermore, the assertions by the Black Lives Matter movement added to the politically charged atmosphere. It is also possible that because superintendents and other educational leaders frequently focus on communicating with adults as the norm, it was not in their realm of consideration to address students even though witnessing BLM protests inspired a range of emotions in adolescents ranging from hope and inspiration to fear and anxiety (Hathaway, 2021).

One educational leader from a regional school district even went as far as to co-author a community letter with two different town leaders and address it to the larger community, although the communication was shared through the school district emails to parents. In their letter, these three leaders spoke about the difficulty of having hard conversations with youth and offered resources to support parents who wanted to have discussions with their children. They stated:

We are living in complicated times and it is difficult to have conversations so charged with emotion and confusion, especially when talking with young people. There are resources that can help guide conversations about injustice, hate, and intolerance on the website below. We encourage you to have conversations with those around you, to trust one another and to promote compassion within our communities (McKinney, Massey & Rosen, Great Valley District).

This example showcases that emphasis on parents taking the lead in communicating about the social unrest with their children. It also demonstrates the sharing of educational resources, in this case, a website that community members can draw upon for ideas and support. In this way, these educational leaders were centering adult community voices as the foremost importance, as did the other school district leaders who shared resources. Knowing that the schools were not in session in person, the desire to share resources was mostly a response to the schools being closed because of the COVID-19 Pandemic. During this time, district leaders became much more aware of the importance of providing digital resources that could be easily accessed by stakeholders. The only educational leader who communicated directly with students was a high school principal who issued his statement through student-accessible social media. The decision by Stonewall High School's Principal Reynolds to post on social media showed an appreciation of how teenagers consume information and where high school students were most likely to receive the message.

After this initial outreach, the Superintendent for Stonewall Public Schools reached out to the larger community, but this correspondence was targeted only toward adult community members. For many communities, the police are viewed as trusted professionals whose role is to protect citizens. For many in the Black and Brown communities, the police are viewed as agents of racism and perpetrators of violence, as was demonstrated in the case of George Floyd. Schools engage with police departments to teach children personal safety and employ school resource officers. It is understandable that school leaders decided to engage at the adult level due to this complex dichotomy that may have been challenging for younger children to understand. However, educational leaders passed on an opportunity to engage in a teachable moment that could have been used to foster critical conversations about social justice around a real-life event. This is problematic because educational leaders are in the business of overseeing the education of all students and should seek opportunities to meaningfully engage as appropriate.

Some educational leaders who addressed the adult community spoke broadly about curricular opportunities for students and expressed support for their students. Often these messages reflected mission statements or platitudes. Ms. Smith, Superintendent of Ocean View's school district, shared:

We will also emphasize teaching and learning by encouraging our students to read about social change movements and explore their ideas for solutions and a better future through writing, art, music, and cultural expression. At Ocean View Public Schools, we will respond to injustice in our world by treating every student with dignity, by providing culturally responsive teaching, and by building the positive and personal relationships our students need to feel valued and loved. We will model for our students the healthy and safe educational environment that supports their growth: a community that promotes diversity, inclusion, equity, and justice (Veronica Smith, Ocean View).

The same Ocean View leader also praised her students for their civic engagement and discussed it with a sense of pride and support. While Ocean View's Superintendent stated that the district "stands by its Black students during this time," there was no clarity or specific mention as to how district administrators were making their support known and available to students, and instead generalities were described. These examples showcase attempts to be supportive and recognize that students could have been struggling with many emotions and may be in need of support but lacked a call to action to do anything tangible about it. Another leader, Joe King, Mountain Top's Superintendent, committed to working further with resources as opposed to providing them in the initial letter.

In the coming days, you will be receiving follow-up communication from our principals, in collaboration with our Equity and Diversity Committee, about how we are supporting students and with resources to help you in communicating with your own children about these difficult topics (Joe King, Mountain Top).

This quote highlights the desire that was expressed by several leaders to explicitly work with students while recognizing that this could take time to be implemented into the curriculum.

While ten of the letters sent by leaders attempted to be supportive of students and the school community, leaders in one district decided to de-center students entirely and instead responded punitively to the cry for social justice in their town. High Meadow students had expressed their views by painting George Floyd's last words, "I can't breathe," on the school's spirit rock—a large boulder on school property where students regularly paint their names, graduating class year, and other messages. In this instance the students chose to use the rock as their own form of social protest and civic engagement. Rather than address Mr. Floyd's death, and the resulting conversations about racial violence and racial inequities in America directly, the High Meadow District chose instead to condemn the message of its students. The correspondence stated, "It is important to note that the views expressed by students represent those of individual students and not the full student body, staff, Administration, Board of Education, or community in general" (Superintendent Wayne Pierce and Assistant Superintendent Patrick Johnson). The letter went on to state that "the students involved would be reminded of appropriate ways to have debate and discourse." The overall tone of the letter was cold, and this passage in particular, was punitive in nature. As opposed to other forms of communications that put the murder and racial unrest at the forefront of the communications, this letter was crafted in response to the local "vandalism" event and only mentioned national conversations indirectly. Ironically, the rock is there to be painted and expressly share students' views, so it is surprising that this quote could be considered inappropriate. Furthermore, the letter expressed the stance that the community held a wide range of opinions, which were not reflected by painting George Floyd's final words on the rock. Instead, the leaders' response suggested that the adult community held the opposite view of this group of students. Through this unique interpretation, the superintendent suggested that students' voices are devalued and unwelcome. There was also a sense that the discussion of such things should be held within families and not become a public conversation that the school district should engage in or support. Pierce and Johnson wrote:

It is important to understand that views expressed by students represent those of individual students, and not the full student body, staff, Administration, Board of Education, and the community in general. However, as a community, we are all feeling a combination of sadness, anxiety, stress, and resolve....for different reasons. (Superintendent Wayne Pierce and Assistant Superintendent Patrick Johnson High Meadow District)

Without meaning to, the High Meadow school leaders sent the message that student concerns and social justice are perfunctory at best. It is not just the researchers' interpretation that the High Meadow District mis-stepped their reaction. There was community backlash following this communication that prompted the immediate hiring of a consultant to work with the school district on issues of diversity, equity, and inclusion. This example highlights the importance of tone and message when communicating with stakeholders. In this instance, the privileging of adult perspectives over that of students had ongoing consequences that cost the school district. Bringing in a consultant to address issues of diversity, equity, and inclusion was a necessary and important step to ease community concerns.

Experience and Understanding

While addressing race and experiences with racial violence, some letters meandered through a range of topics related to race and the institution of school without addressing the current events unfolding in real-time across the nation. Some educational leaders were uncomfortable addressing the complex societal issues raised by the murder of George Floyd and noted the difficulty in crafting their letters. Letters sent by two school districts directly addressed leaders' personal challenges with communicating with their community. One statement was not only about personal challenges but was also awkward in expression, "We are living in complicated times and it's difficult to have a conversation so charged with emotion and confusion, especially when talking with young people (Ralph Massey, Christopher McKinney, & Justin Rosen, Great Valley Educational Leaders)." The previous example makes assumptions that everyone is confused and unsure of how to communicate with young people. This is an unusual stance to coming from an educational perspective when the very nature of education is to meaningfully engage with students. Another superintendent commented, "I wrote too many versions of this message to count, and yet I could not reconcile how to communicate 'a message' to you, to communicate a singular message, whether it was one of hope or condemnation" (Aimee Law, Oakhill). With this quote, Ms. Law describes her own confliction over what is the "right" message to convey.

In such cases, leaders opted to send messages of comfort or put the onus of the conversation on the families. While other educational leaders opted to disengage from the opportunity to discuss the systemic racism that led to George Floyd's murder itself and instead refocused on the graphic images displayed in the news. Leaders also acknowledged the inconvenience of the pandemic that limited the opportunity for everyone to gather together, which they believed would have made things easier. On that point, Seacoast's Superintendent wrote:

As we consider the possible exposure to these images or events, we know your children will likely seek out answers and support. If we were in school, we would have the opportunity to come together…students or parents can call or send an email to schedule an appointment for such connections (Peter Norris, Seacoast).

Perhaps, an unintended consequence of needing to address an unexpected societal crisis in a time of a global pandemic that was already impacting schools highlighted the reliance the schools had on face-to-face communication and that digital and written communication were areas of growth for most educational institutions. In a few letters, educational leaders attempted to outline the past good work their organizations had done to promote equity and inclusion in their schools. For example, Robin D'Eville, Stonewall Superintendent noted that in the past two years the district had "examined discipline practices, revised curriculum to reflect the background of all our learners…and adapted district policies to support an inclusive environment." This is an important statement because it indirectly acknowledges the ways that policies around discipline and attendance have disproportionately and negatively impacted BIPOC students, who are more likely to be expelled and suspended in comparison to their White counterparts (Morgan, 2021). While only one leader specifically addressed discipline, other educational leaders appeared to suggest that their organizations are welcoming places that take racial and other societal issues seriously. This was the case when the Ocean View Superintendent, Veronica Smith wrote:

These recent events call on us to uphold one of the major priorities of our District Model for Excellence: to ensure all students feel safe, valued, respected, and connected. To make good on that promise to our students, we will listen to their experiences, honor their feelings, and support their social-emotional needs (Veronica Smith).

Unfortunately, other leaders had fewer tangible examples of diversity, equity, and inclusion (DEI) work within their districts from which to draw upon. The lack of examples created a situation where more general comments were shared that failed to illicit confidence in what the schools were doing to incorporate a DEI focus in the school community. The majority of educational leaders who wrote the letters were White, with only one leader acknowledging his Whiteness. The overall lack of personal context for situating the letters indicated a missed opportunity for leaders to address their own positionality and privilege in society. This suggests a lack of understanding about racial issues at large and a lack of understanding that the White lived experience is not truly a universal experience. Rather, White experiences are instead part of the framework from the dominant culture. The limited perspective presented in the communications is misaligned with The National Policy Board for Educational Administration (2015) which indicates in Standard 2 Ethics and Norms, that educational leaders should "Lead with interpersonal and communication skill, social-emotional insight, and understanding of all students' and staff members' backgrounds and cultures" (p. 10).

Similarly, many letters included broad calls to action, with the Stonewall School District leader proclaiming:

We need to continue to engage in a community conversation which recognizes the role of unconscious bias in our culture, reflect on ways our schools might be reinforcing systemic racism and work to empathize and understand others' feelings and experience so we can invoke change (Robin D'Eville, Stonewall).

While this letter mentions several key tenets of anti-racist work, the district did not provide a framework or plan to engage with this work. The district also neglected to define key terms such as "unconscious bias," and "systemic racism" to ground the call to action for community members who may be unfamiliar with these terms. Defining and naming the key issues the school hopes to address would help eliminate some of the ambiguity as is evidenced in the line "continue to engage in community conversation which recognizes the role of unconscious bias in our culture." It is unclear from the quote whether the "unconscious bias" the district hopes to address is at the school/district level or the broader societal level.

Limited Worldview to Discuss Racial Incidents

When it came to naming the critical incident—social unrest from the police murdering of George Floyd, a Black man, some district leaders neglected to mention George Floyd's name at all, opting instead to talk around the subject in platitudes and quotes from famous leaders of color. Specifically, multiple White educational leaders, quoted Dr. Martin Luther King Jr., while others referenced former United States President Obama and former South African President Nelson Mandela in their letters utilizing well-known quotes about racial justice and equality. One letter stated, "We stand with our Black students. They know our society has not yet realized Dr. Martin Luther King, Jr.'s dream of a world in which they are judged by the content of their characters and not the color of their skin." This quote acknowledges the inequities and racism facing Black students, but did not address other BIPOC, who also live within the context of White supremacy and systemic racism. This quote was included in a letter that was written by the Superintendent of Ocean View who identifies as Hispanic. Ocean View is a district that serves a plurality of students from a range of ethnic and racial backgrounds suggesting the need for language that expresses a broader worldview, even from BIPOC educational leaders. Specifically acknowledging powerful men of color aligns with the great man leadership philosophy, where the known talents or traits of great men serve as the role model for what leadership should look like (Brown, 2011). Undoubtedly, the spectrum of leaders who are seen as role models should become more expansive. Educational leaders who can draw upon a range of leaders and express a variety of worldviews will be increasing the diversity that they expose community members and students to as role models. An increase in diversity in role models increases the likelihood of a larger and more inclusive worldview over time.

Other school district based educational leaders used familiar language such as "let's move forward promoting unity, peace, and positive actions to shape our present and our future (Oak Hill)," and "we will model for our students the healthy and safe educational environment that supports their growth: a community that promotes diversity, inclusion, equity, and justice (Seacoast)." Unfortunately, neither of these letters provided specific guidance on how to achieve such idealistic school environments, nor directly mentioned programs currently in place related to the stated goals.

Support for Community Members and Students

Active Support

Some educational leaders expressed a desire to actively support community members and students. Active support is understood to be a declaration from an educational organization that they will be working for change and to support stakeholders. For instance, Mountain Top School District told community members that more correspondence would be sent "in the coming days," and that the district's Equity and Diversity Committee would be convening to discuss how to support students, as well as provide resources parents could use to support their students at home. Other letters (Great Valley, Ocean View, Seacrest, and Stonewall) noted that support staff such as counselors and social workers were available for students, but only on request. The ability to provide emotional support through counselors and other school staff was likely an additional challenge given that school districts were meeting virtually. Providing virtual appointments and arranging support would need to be scheduled and staffed while also providing digital classes, which is a more complex process than staffing a drop-in center at a school, which could be easily accessed without students having to do a great deal of self-advocacy. While the offer of support was positive, the cumbersome process makes it less likely that students would elect to access the services.

Passive Support

In contrast to active support, passive support provided by districts placed ownership and outreach on the individual students and community members to address and understand the issues associated with societal unrest. That responsibility for change was placed on the individual stakeholder may have had the unintended consequence of lessening the responsibility of the educational organizations. School districts provided passive support through the sharing of links to websites and articles as well as offering to make support staff available, but individuals had to arrange for this support. Some specific resources that were shared included: links to the Anti-Defamation League website, a Sesame Street Town Hall for speaking to young children (whose air date had already passed after the date of the letter), and various National Public Radio broadcasts that all addressed the topic of discussing race with children. These resources provided parents the opportunity to decide how and what to discuss with their children, without the school district taking a clear stance or fostering their own culture of anti-racist work within the school community. Districts informed parents that support staff was available to students and community members who wanted to speak privately. In this way, students and community members experiencing trauma were responsible for seeking out their own avenues for support, which may have been difficult given the leader's challenges with anti-racist communications.

Role of Education in Dismantling Systemic Racism

Bigger Than Schools and Calls to Action

Overall, the critical racial incident letters stemming from the social unrest suggested that police violence against BIPOC and systemic racism are both larger than what educational organizations can address. However, there was also repeated hope that "our strength lies in our ability to support each other" (Steve Reynolds, Principal). Put another way, the Oak Hill Superintendent, Aimee Law, stated a declaration that was also a call to action for this time of unrest to be a learning opportunity.

But let us not miss this teachable moment and be the people that all of our students need us to be-- the people who listen, the people who hear, the people who teach, and the people who care. We are all struggling to make sense of it all, in one way or another; we can't let that stop us from being the leaders in society that we are. We all work in schools, so we all shape the future. Let's use this time to recommit to making it a future that advances towards equity, justice, kindness, and safety for all of those we serve. Let's move forward promoting unity, peace, and positive actions to shape our present and our future. (Aimee Law)

Similarly, Joe King, Mountain Top's Superintendent, shared a call to action to be anti-racist: "Anti-racism in our thoughts, our actions, and our professional development, which for the past couple of years has been focused on cultural competence and our own understanding." The tangible action of providing professional development related to cultural competence was present in half of the letters. The idea of training faculty and staff on this topic aligns with the National Policy Board for Educational Administration (2015), uses Standard 3: Equity and Cultural

Responsiveness to call on educational leaders to "Confront and alter institutional biases of student marginalization, deficit-based schooling, and low expectations associated with race, class, culture and language, gender and sexual orientation, and disability or special status" (PSEL, p. 17), thus compelling educational leaders to support all students by actively addressing social justice issues.

While leaders like Joe King indicated that professional development had been provided on cultural competence, all of the communications examined for this study highlighted a lack of comfort in the role of social justice advocate, and limited awareness of how to talk to their communities about experiences of police violence and racial protests that were occurring nationally. Communicating about racial violence was challenging because conversations about race are some of the most difficult to engage in for most people (Appiah, Eveland, Bullock, & Coduto, 2022). Standard 3 is also challenging to address while in a leadership training program, because take-aways learned about social justice advocacy in a controlled classroom setting are different from the real-life understanding that is gained by participating authentically on the job.

SOLUTIONS AND RECOMMENDATIONS

This research revealed the need for educational leaders to receive training in methods of communication that specifically address social unrest and police violence against people of color. Although all the educational organizations attempted to reach out to their school communities none of the educational leaders' communications were entirely effective in structuring an anti-racist message that addressed shared values, clearly stated the problem, offered a solution, and had a call to action. Therefore, it is recommended that educational leaders consider The Opportunity Agenda's VPSA model when crafting messages, particularly when addressing issues of social justice including for BIPOC students, LGBTQ+ students, and other marginalized groups. Communications should use a lens that embraces the diversity of the community rather than framing the message from the lens of Whiteness. For leaders to situate the voices of their community they must be familiar with the lived experiences of those members. Therefore, educational leaders should be aware of narratives that run counter to the dominant White cultural experience to shape their messages (The Opportunity Agenda, 2020).

Community communications are meant to be an opportunity to inform and build support, often around change. Messages from educational leaders should be forward-thinking and provide a goal or plan of action for change that can help their stakeholders understand how to move forward. One of the strengths of the communications was that resources were provided in many instances. Unfortunately, some of these resources were not shared in a timely fashion and others required self-advocacy on behalf of individuals. We recommend that attention be given to the resources that are shared regarding the time in which they are still valid and available, the ease of use for the resources, and the likelihood that these will be of use to a majority of community members. In this way, community members will have additional information, opportunities to be meaningfully involved, or obtain needed assistance.

The content of several letters, including the one from High Meadow's Superintendent Wayne Pierce, revealed that the senders were unable to move beyond their own lived White experience and failed to remove Whiteness as a focal point. This suggests that educational leaders would benefit from additional diversity training to enhance the journey to their own self-awareness around implicit bias, antiracism, and culturally responsive/relevant practices for them to effectively communicate and lead an increasingly diverse community. This is particularly important given that the most appropriate communications came from educational organizations that were led by BIPOC or had specializations that extend beyond district-level leadership training. This speaks to the need to increase the diversity that exists within educational organizations and in leadership positions. There should also be an increase in the number of teachers and staff of color that are found within all educational organizations so that students benefit from adults who represent students' cultures, ethnicity, and race. The lack of BIPOC in education is a national phenomenon in the United States. One way to address this is to make sure that students' experiences and background are valued and they are included as members of their school communities. Research indicates that students who are BIPOC who have exposure to qualified educators who are BIP experience increases in academic success, improvement in social-emotional skills, and positive impacts on college and career readiness (Egalite, Kisida, & Winters, 2015). More must be done to encourage diverse populations to enter educational training programs so that they can be in a variety of educational settings. Furthermore, educational organizations should focus on programming that addresses culturally responsive educational practices and policies to teachers, staff, and students as noted by Alma Bradley, Director of Round River State Educational Center, in her letter to teachers. In this study, there was a desire by educational leaders to do the right thing, but they were limited in their ability to do so effectively through written communication.

Lack of training in how to craft anti-racist and inclusive messages may have limited the effectiveness of the communications. Given that national standards exist for the preparation of educational leaders that require the ability to address social justice and the needs and concerns of diverse and underrepresented students, preparation programs are duty bound to include curriculum that teaches anti-racist communication. While there has been a movement to include social justice into the leadership curriculum, actual conversations around race during training occur less frequently due to the level of discomfort of being labeled a racist or being labeled a complainer (Diem, Carpenter & Lewis-Durham, 2019). Preparation programs and materials for educational leaders emphasize communication from a systems approach focusing on logistics (Hoy & Miskel, 2013). However, preparation programs must also provide opportunities for aspiring leaders to become politically savvy advocates for social justice. Alma Bradley alluded to the lack of training in her letter to teachers when she wrote that her organization needed to continue "building the capacity of our staff to support educators in their own work on race as well as navigate a personal and often agonizing journey of self-discovery" (Alma Bradley, Director Round River State Educational Center).

In order to make meaningful changes to support social justice, additional resource allocation should also be considered. The provisioning of resources can improve communication about and understanding of social justice in educational organizations. While two different educational organizations' sources spoke specifically about the ways that they were addressing equity across their schooling systems before the critical racial incident, most did not. Schools can improve the ability to support the needs of all students by providing relevant programming and dedicating staff to address issues of diversity, equity, and inclusion. Allocating such resources can help support the school community and advise leaders on their responses when racial violence or other critical incidents arise. While some educational organizations offered varying levels of resources to help the community cope with the aftermath of racial violence in the wake of George Floyd's murder, few resources provided additional information that addressed police violence and the distrust that comes from systemic racism.

Across all the correspondence, there was also an emphasis on individuals from the community seeking help on their own rather than schools providing it from a concerted, organizational standpoint. First and foremost, leaders should check the accuracy and timeliness of the information that they share, assure any web-based digital links provided are functioning, and be sure that the voices of BIPOC are included as authors and experts in the material provided. Furthermore, gauging the needs of the community and the level of access to the offered resources is an important step in helping any community heal. For instance, the majority of communications examined in this study were sent to adults (Step 1), next the adult was put in the role of needing to communicate the availability of support to their student (Step 2), and finally, a student would have to reach out directly for support or ask their parent to do it for them (Step 3). Depending on the level of communication within a family, the age, and the self-advocacy skills of individual students, indirect methods of providing student support may be less helpful than educational leaders have realized. A more practical approach would be to have offered push-in support from social workers and counselors in classrooms for facilitating discussions and providing outreach. This would have been challenging during remote learning, because of the COVID-19 Pandemic, when schools were already struggling to provide instruction, however, it was possible and would have been beneficial. This would have placed the responsibility of providing support for students directly on the organization.

Educational leaders should be specific in their plan for how and when members of the school community can access direct services such as school counselors and social workers. In instances, where schools had only been meeting remotely, links to digital counselor office hours could have been provided within the distance learning platforms and embedded inside the communications that were emailed. In educational organizations where electronic resources were offered, educational leaders should have provided information on where people could access free Wi-Fi including locations that provide access to devices for use, such as the public library.

FUTURE RESEARCH DIRECTIONS

Further research regarding the communication practices of educational leaders who are tasked with addressing sensitive topics should focus on the ways that school leader preparation programs include social and racial justice as part of the curriculum, which may take the forms of Diversity, Equity, and Inclusion (DEI). The current research exemplified the challenges individuals employed as educational leaders faced in crafting an appropriate anti-racist message to their communities. The National Policy Board for Educational Administration (2015) compels educational leaders to communicate with emotional intelligence and with understanding of the diversity present in the school community in Standard 2 Ethics and Norms. Given the disconnect between our findings and this national standard, future research should specifically focus on how educational leaders are taught to communicate anti-racist messages, as well as provide additional training on how to advance Standard 3: Equity and Cultural Responsiveness (National Policy Board for Educational Administration, 2015, p. 17) within educational organizations.

CONCLUSION

This case study reveals a series of common challenges that educational leaders faced when trying to craft a message of support for community members in the wake of a critical incident, the murder of George Floyd at the hands of Minneapolis police. Effective leadership requires the leader to be aware of the issues at hand and have the ability to leverage emotional intelligence, planning, and strong communication skills. Educational leaders must find ways to continue to develop as communicators who become more comfortable with their role as social justice leaders for their communities. Hiring more employees who are BIPOC across educational settings is one important action that can be taken to help give voice to the perspective of diverse groups in the school community. It is imperative that schools create a welcoming atmosphere for BIPOC students where they feel valued and included. Such a positive environment will support their agency in working to achieve their goals which could quite possibly include becoming school administrators, counselors and teachers. Further, students benefit from interacting with adult role models who represent their cultures, ethnicity, and race. As organizations become more representative, the more society as a whole will evolve (NADHOE, 2021). It is important to remember that one communication will not end racism. However, a series of well-planned, anti-racist, and consistent messages with a call to action can begin to lay the groundwork for positive social change.

REFERENCES

Appiah, O., Eveland, W. Jr, Bullock, O., & Coduto, K. (2022). Why we can't talk openly about race: The impact of race and partisanship on respondents' perceptions of intergroup conversations. *Group Processes & Intergroup Relations*, *25*(2), 434–452. doi:10.1177/1368430220967978

Bengtsson, M. (2016). How to plan and perform a qualitative study using content analysis. *Nursing Plus One*, *2*, 8–14. doi:10.1016/j.npls.2016.01.001

Boeije, H. R. (2002). A purposeful approach to the constant comparative method in the analysis of qualitative interviews. *Quality & Quantity*, *36*(4), 391–409. doi:10.1023/A:1020909529486

Brown, B. (n.d.). *Empathy vs. sympathy*. [Video]. Twenty-one Toys. https://twentyonetoys.com/blogs/teaching-empathy/brene-brown-empathy- vs- sympathy

Brown, C. (2011). Barack Obama as the great man: Communicative constructions of racial transcendence in White-male elite discourses. *Communication Monographs*, *78*(4), 535–556. doi:10.1080/03637751.2011.618140

Butin, D. W. (2010). *The education dissertation: A guide for practitioner scholars.* Thousand Oaks, CA: Corwin.

Butterfield, L. D., Borgen, W. A., Amundson, N. E., & Maglio, A. T. (2005). Fifty years of the critical incident technique: 1954-2004 and beyond. *Qualitative Research*, *5*(4), 475–497. doi:10.1177/1468794105056924

Chatman, J. E., Johnson, A., White, E., & Bell, R. L. (2020). *The leader as effective communicator.* Research Gate. https://www.researchgate.net/publication /339366410_The_Leader_as_Effective_Communicator

Costello, M. (2016). *After election day: The Trump effect.* Southern Poverty Law Center. https://www.splcenter.org/ sites/default/files/the_trump_effect.pdf

Diem, S., Carpenter, B. W., & Lewis-Durham, T. (2019). Preparing antiracist school leaders in a school choice context. *Urban Education, 54*(5), 706–731. doi:10.1177/0042085918783812

Dowd, T. P., & Tierney, J. (2017). *Teaching Social Skills to Youth: A Step-by-step Guide to 182 Basic to Complex Skills Plus Helpful Teaching Techniques.* Boys Town Press.

Egalite, A. J., Kisida, B., & Winters, M. A. (2015). Representation in the classroom: The effect of own-race teachers on student achievement. *Economics of Education Review, 45*, 44–52. doi:10.1016/j.econedurev.2015.01.007

Finfgeld-Connett, D. (2014). Use of content analysis to conduct knowledge-building and theory-generating qualitative systematic reviews. *Qualitative Research, 14*(3), 341–352. doi:10.1177/1468794113481790

Flanagan, J. C. (1954). The critical incident technique. *Psychological Bulletin, 51*(4), 327–358. doi:10.1037/h0061470 PMID:13177800

Goleman, D. (1995). *What makes a leader?* Bantam Books.

Gordon, N. (2017, September 20). *Race, poverty, and overrepresentation in special education.* Brookings Institute. https://www.brookings.edu/research/race-poverty-and-interpreting- overrepresentation-in-special-education/

Hasforth, J. (2016). Dominant cultural narratives, racism, and resistance in the workplace: A study of the experiences of young Black Canadians. *American Journal of Community Psychology, 57*(1-2), 158–170. doi:10.1002/ajcp.12024 PMID:27217319

Hathaway, R. (2021, October 4). BLM movement engaged youth with both positive and negative effects. *Yale News.* https://news.yale.edu/2021/10/04/blm-movement-engaged-youth-positive-and-negative-effects/

Hoy, W. K., Miskel, C. G., & Tarter, C. J. (2013). *Educational Administration: Theory, Research, and Practice* (6th ed.). McGraw Hill.

Krippendorff, K. (2016). *Content Analysis: An Introduction* (4th ed.). Sage.

Ladson-Billings, G. (1995). Toward a theory of culturally relevant pedagogy. *American Educational Research Journal*, *32*(3), 465–491. doi:10.3102/00028312032003465

Violence, M. P. org (2021). *Police violence map*. https://mappingpoliceviolence.org./

Massachusetts Department of Education. (2021, June 8). *Culturally responsive teaching and leading*. MA DoE. https://www.doe.mass.edu/instruction/culturally-responsive/default.html

Miles, M. B., Huberman, A. M., & Saldana, J. (2019). *Qualitative data analysis: A methods sourcebook* (4th ed.). Sage.

Modan, N. (2020, 13 February). Survey: Superintendents still overwhelmingly White, male. *K-12 Dive*. https://www.k12dive.com/news/survey-superintendents-still-overwhelmingly-White-male/572008/

Moore, E. H., Bagin, D. H., & Gallagher, D. R. (2016). *School and community relations* (11th ed.). Pearson.

Morgan, H. (2021). Restorative justice and the school-to-prison pipeline: A review of existing literature. *Education Sciences*, *11*(4), 159–169. doi:10.3390/educsci11040159

National Association for Diversity Officers in Higher Education (NADHO). (2021). *A framework for advancing anti-racism strategies on campus*. NADHO. https://nadohe.memberclicks.net/assets/2021/Framework/National%20Association%20of%20Diversity%20Officers%20in%20Higher%20Education%20-%20Framework%20for%20Advancing%20Ant-Racism%20on%20Campus%20-%20first%20edition.pdf

National Association for the Advancement of Colored People (NAACP). (n.d.). *Dismantling the school-to-prison pipeline. NAACP Legal Defense and Education Fund*. NAACP. https://www.naacpldf.org/wpcontent/uploads/Dismantling_the_School_to_Prison_Pipeline__Criminal-Justice__.pdf

National Center for Educational Statistics. (2020). *Characteristics of public school. Principals*. NCES. https://nces.ed.gov/programs/coe/indicator_cls.asp#:~:text=In%202017%E2%80%9318%2C%20about%2078,and%209%20percent%20were%20Hispanic

National Policy Board for Educational Administration. (2015). *Professional standards for educational leaders*. National Policy Board for Educational Administration.

Northouse, P. G. (2018). *Leadership: Theory and practice* (8th ed.). Sage.

Rattan, A., & Ambady, N. (2014). How 'it gets better': Effectively communicating supports to targets of prejudice. *Personality and Social Psychology Bulletin*, *40*(5), 555–556. doi:10.1177/0146167213519480 PMID:24443385

Reynolds, H., Silvernell, D., & Mercer, F. (2020). Teaching in an era of political divisiveness: An exploration of strategies for discussing controversial issues. *The Clearing House: A Journal of Educational Strategies, Issues and Ideas*, *93*(4), 205–212. doi:10.1080/00098655.2020.1762063

Ruggs, E. N., & Avery, D. R. (2020). Organizations cannot afford to stay silent on racial injustice. *MIT Sloan Management Review*. https://sloanreview.mit.edu/article/ organizations-cannot-afford-to-stay-silent-on racialinjustice/#:~:text=Your%20 words%20and%20actions%20can,to%20your%20employees%20and%20customers

Saldana, J. (2013). *The coding manual for qualitative researchers* (2nd ed.). Sage.

Simmons, D. (2019). How to be an anti-racist educator. *ASCD Education Update*, *61*(10).

Strauss, A., & Corbin, J. (1998). *Basics of qualitative research. Techniques and procedures for developing grounded theory* (2nd ed.). Sage.

The New York Times. (2021, February 14). What we know about the death of George Floyd in Minneapolis. *The New York Times*. https://www.nytimes.com/ article/george-floyd.html

The Opportunity Agenda. (2020). *Messaging memo: Ten lessons for talking about race, racism, and racial justice*. The Opportunity Agenda. http://www.opportunityagenda. org/sits/default/files/2020.07.27%20-%2010%20Lessons%20Talking%20About%20 Race%20FINAL.pdf

Wenner, J. A., & Campbell, T. (2017). The theoretical and empirical basis of teacher leadership: A review of the literature. *Review of Educational Research*, *87*(1), 134–171. doi:10.3102/0034654316653478

World Health Organization. (n.d.) *What are critical incidents?* WHO. https://www. workpositive.ie/information/whatarecriticalincidents

Yin, R. K. (2018). *Case study research and applications: Design and methods* (6th ed.). Sage.

Zaidi, Z., Verstegen, D., Vyas, R., Hamed, O., Dornan, T., & Morahan, P. (2016). Cultural hegemony? Educators' perspectives on facilitating cross-cultural dialogue. *Medical Education Online*, *21*(1), 33145. doi:10.3402/meo.v21.33145 PMID:27890048

KEY TERMS AND DEFINITIONS

Anti-racism: A way of thinking that strives for racial equity and rejects the idea that one racial group is superior to another.

Anti-racist: A stance that requires white individuals to actively work to change unconscious bias by recognizing and understanding their own privilege and disrupting racism when it is encountered. Being anti-racist requires BIPOC to reflect on how they have been influenced by race and racism through unconscious assimilation, and to discern if racism is being directed at other people of color.

Critical Incident: A sudden event that is overwhelming and not part of a person's normal experience. Critical incidents can include a perception of a life threat or physical or emotional loss.

Cultural Responsiveness: A perspective that capitalizes on the cultural characteristics (i.e., ethnicity, language, traditions, etc.) and identity of a school community, and uses them as tools of empowerment to improve academic achievement, cultural competence, and socio-political awareness

Culturally Responsive Messaging: Communicating in a way that acknowledges and bridges the differences in cultural characteristics of the writer and recipients of the message through the removal of bias.

Dominant Culture: A system where one culture imposes its values, language, and behavior as the blueprint for establishing the norms of the society often as a result of an economic or political power differential.

Educational Leaders: Individuals such as superintendents or principals who are charged with creating and managing positive change in policy or processes in educational organizations including schools.

Hegemony: A system where the cultural dominance of one group over others results in the normalization of oppression and exploitation.

Qualitative Case Study: A research method that looks at how different factors interact with each other to better understand a complex real-world phenomenon.

Racism: A social construct that defines individual worth and access to opportunity based on skin color alone.

Social Justice: Justice in terms of the distribution of wealth, opportunities, and privileges within society.

Social Unrest: Opposition to events or policies that result in people expressing their anger and dissatisfaction through demonstration or rioting.

Standard 3: "Confront and alter institutional biases of student marginalization, deficit-based schooling, and low expectations associated with race, class, culture and language, gender and sexual orientation, and disability or special status." National Policy Board for Educational Administration (2015, p. 17)

Systemic Racism: A form of racism that is built into laws, policies, and regulations of a society or organization that results in discriminatory practices.

The National Policy Board for Educational Administration (NPBEA): A professional organization that focuses on the improvement of the preparation and practice of educational leaders at all levels. NPBEA sets professional standards that educational leaders should know, understand, and be able carry out to be effective and inclusive.

Unconscious Bias: Social stereotypes or factually untrue beliefs that develop outside the realm of conscious awareness and are unfairly attributed to social or identity groups. Everyone has unconscious bias. Unconscious bias is also known as implicit bias.

QUESTIONS FOR DISCUSSION

1. How is communicating with stakeholders a social justice issue?
2. Why is the study of educational leaders' community-focused communications about a critical racial incident important?
3. Why do you think so many White educational leaders drew upon the words of others in their letters? How do you think this was received by community members?
4. Under what obligation are educational leaders to promote social justice? What are your personal thoughts on this? How will you balance this as an educational leader?
5. The National Policy Board for Educational Administration (2015) Standard 3: Equity and Cultural Responsiveness requires educational leaders to "Confront and alter institutional biases of student marginalization, deficit-based schooling, and low expectations associated with race, class, culture and language, gender and sexual orientation, and disability or special status" (PSEL, p. 17). In what ways does the desire to acknowledge the murder of George Floyd and the subsequent protests both address and fail to address this charge based on the information provided within this study?

EXTENSION ACTIVITY

Look through news articles to find a current event on a social justice related issue. Craft a letter to your school community about the current event using Opportunity Agenda's VPSA technique from the vantage point of a School District Superintendent. Share your letter with a partner for feedback.

Chapter 6
The Triumph of Bi-Racial Identity:
Funds of Knowledge as Student Agency

Andrew Kwabena Moss
Independent Researcher, Australia

ABSTRACT

This chapter utilises an autobiographical and creative approach that links cultural history to the education children receive in the classroom. I present a narrative account of my personal story as a child of mixed racial identity as well as mixed cultural identity to explicate the range of emotions, the expanse of experiences evoked by racial hostility and the child's response as he navigates this landscape and journey towards making sense of these experiences in the shaping of his identity. This chapter is grounded in funds of knowledge theory, identity theory and culturally relevant theory. The process of the building and resulting production of my own funds of knowledge challenge the validity of the traditional Eurocentric Western epistemologies that shaped the education I received in the British classrooms of my youth. From this investigation, I have come to the conclusion that bi-racial children have the benefit of a rich, three-dimensional, dual heritage which provides a much-needed emotional foundation that allows them to thrive even within hostile settings. Teachers face the challenge of recognising, acknowledging and tapping into this gourd of cultural capital and effectively using it to heighten students' performance and guide them on the path to academic achievement.

DOI: 10.4018/978-1-6684-7379-5.ch006

INVESTIGATING THE CULTURAL CAPITAL
OF MY FAMILY HISTORY

As an Anglo-Ghanaian, I examine my hybrid historical background with ethnographic attentiveness to education and cultural practices that complicate the simplified (post- and neo) colonial narratives that I was subjected to in school. I acknowledge the effects of such deficit framing (particularly on Black boys), where race and ethnicity are constructed in myopic ways. As a Black male, I highlight the often-ignored importance of the emotional dimensions of learning, and the quest for role models. I investigate how my own funds of knowledge have been developed and shaped by the environment of my home. Furthermore, I interrogate how K-University students should be empowered as curriculum collaborators, validating their own culture and agency. The curriculum is explored as a site that must reflect diverse cultures; positioning students as curators with vital twenty-first century resources.

The chapter emphasises how students and teachers can use creative agency (by looking outside of the Academy to peripheral sites and extending the curriculum, based on students' funds of knowledge) to pursue these aims. Advances in curricula are also considered-as ways to diversify and decolonize teaching and learning to achieve inclusive learning that celebrates and catalogues the Black contribution. There are useful examples to consider including the Black Curriculum, agents of change who succeeded in mandating diverse representation in the new Welsh Curriculum; Hackney's Diverse Curriculum and initiatives such as 'Bangla Stories.' Such curricula build belonging and challenge racism beyond a singular narrative of oppression and destruction. This approach challenges what Gilroy (2004) terms 'postcolonial melancholia,' the denial of colonialism and imperialism in contemporary [political] life; the obstructive melancholic reactions and inability to value ordinary and unruly multiculturism. This multiculturism existed in the author's childhood home and many others globally today, yet continue to be ignored in Eurocentric education systems. Using students own diverse funds of knowledge will allow us to move beyond mere tolerance to the possibility of celebrating multiculturism and attain justice, equity and peace in the global classroom.

I use an autobiographical approach that acknowledges the value of my Anglo-Ghanaian heritage as a fund of knowledge that helped to shape my adolescent identity. While my classroom teachers did not see it fit or perhaps did not have the training to incorporate my cultural heritage as part of the classroom pedagogy, in retrospect, I can readily identify ways in which a teacher may do so in ways that are inclusive. This awareness is now of great value to my work as an educator, teaching and learning in a society still shaped by racism and discrimination. My self-identification is inextricably linked to my role as an educator and how I navigate the world. As McClean (2019) states, "I am deliberate in revealing subjectivities and assert that research is subjective and contextual as well as it may be empirical. People that have suffered are often in a unique position to give voice to the suffering of others" (p.5).

My auto-biographical approach reflects on how, as an educator, I can model and guide students from diverse backgrounds in questioning, challenging and disrupting the accuracy and validity of a Eurocentric curriculum. I provide an example of how I have actively engaged with my cultural heritage to go beyond the hostile parameters of the neo-colonial education I received as a student in Thatcher's Britain . To boost my cultural capital and stand up to the alienation experienced in Eurocentric classrooms, I sought informal avenues to become a critical thinker amidst resurgent xenophobia in 1980s Britain . In the struggle for justice and peace in the global classroom, I seek to share this critical praxis and show how using students' rich autobiographical funds of knowledge can be utilised in classroom instruction and pedagogy. Starting with the cultural environment I grew up in, I analyse its micro-cultural manifestations and link this to the diverse macro-culture of Africa and its diaspora.

I consider the role of expressive culture, music, literature, material culture and societal culture in the shaping of a child's identity. According to identity theorists Gloyn, Crewe, King and Woodham (2018, p. 157), "Four themes illustrate how objects held in family archives, curation practices, and intergenerational narratives reinforce a family's sense of itself: people–object interactions, gender, socialization and identity formation, and the life course."

In linking the micro-cultural with macro-cultural elements (Manning, 2009) and de-centring research from the personal to collective, an alternative vision for decolonisation is provided using the cultural capital of the students themselves. As a teacher, I draw upon my personal narrative and provide it as a model in preparing students as global citizens. As Black boys continue to be side-lined from the curriculum, it is crucial that we engage their critical literacies sensitive to the actual historical, social and cultural conditions that contribute to the forms of knowledge and meaning that children bring to school (Freire & Macedo, 1987) to ensure they participate fully in a globalized world as democratic citizens.

My investigation is directly applicable to promoting the critical awareness of diasporic children moving across the globe, consideration of their needs, socio-cultural background with the type of pedagogies that focus on their cultural heritage and funds of knowledge; a crucial element of curriculum design and pedagogy as teachers disrupt power imbalances resulting from a Eurocentric epistemology and curricula.

HISTORICAL LEGACY IN THE BLACK DIASPORA

Given the failure of Black boys in mainstream education, I seek to provide a model that demonstrates how funds of knowledge may be used in the struggle for justice, peace and equity within the global classroom.

An Institute for Race Relations report, 'How Black Working- Class Youth are Criminalised and Excluded in the English School System' has revealed that exclusion rates for Black Caribbean students in English schools are up to six times higher than those of their white classmates in certain local authorities. In Cambridgeshire, the fixed-term exclusion rate for Black Caribbean pupils was more than six times higher than the rate of their white peers, while in the London boroughs of Brent, (where I taught for ten years), Harrow and Haringey, the rate was over five times higher. Exclusions essentially criminalise children and disproportionately impact the poorest and most vulnerable students. A recent report on the 2018-19 academic year provided the warning of a "PRU (pupil referral unit) to prison" pipeline for working-class Black children. The report notes that 89% of children in detention in 2017-18 reported having been excluded from school, according to the HM Chief Inspector of Prisons for England and Wales (McIntyre, Parveen & Thomas, 2021).

Young Black Caribbean boys are nearly four times more likely to receive a permanent exclusion and twice as likely to receive a fixed-period exclusion than the school population as a whole. This makes them the most excluded group apart from Gypsy and Traveller children (Demie, 2021).

In this period, the state has responded to inner-city youth rebellion, moral panics over serious youth violence and knife crime and political agitation for racial and social justice by depriving working-class communities of education. Consequently, a two-tier education system has developed with those deemed as worthy and aspirational on the one hand in the academy sector and alienated students in PRUs and APs (Alternative Provision) sectors. In London, the proportion of pupils in PRUs and APs is almost double the national rate with young boys of Black Caribbean heritage over-represented in the sector. The Institute of Race Relations report challenges the superficial analysis that stigmatises young Black Londoners for knife crime whilst failing to look at underlying causes. Other factors, austerity, privatisation, and educational enclosure have entrenched racial injustice into society (Perera, 2020).

At GCSE level, Black Caribbean pupils had significantly lower pass rates than the national average. 51.9% of pupils in England attained five or more passes in GCSE English and Maths in the 2020/1 academic year. Only 35.9% of Black Caribbean pupils achieved five or more passes in English and Maths. 42% of Black Caribbean boys attained 9-4 GCSEs in both English and Maths (Roberts & Bolton, 2020).

The overarching research findings confirmed that the mixed White/ Black Caribbean group is consistently the lowest performing mixed race group in England.

The Mixed White/ Black African attainment of five or more GCSE English and Maths passes was under the national average at 50% and the Mixed White/ Black Caribbean performance was well below at 39.1%. Experiences of marginalisation and invisibility in school life; low teacher expectations; lack of knowledge about how to support them at school and exacerbation of these issues by friendship groups have all been highlighted as contributing causes (Lewis & Demie, 2019).

Longitudinal data and research suggest that the mixed-race population is one of the fastest growing ethnic minority groups in Britain, numbering 1.25 million in the 2011 census (Tikly 2007). The Oxford demography group projection suggests this group will be the largest minority group by 2071 (Coleman, 2010). The mixed-race population increased from 168, 900 in 2003 to 388,868 in 2017, an increase of 130%. Of the 388,868 mixed-race pupils, 27% were White and Black Caribbean and 13% White and Black African. There has been a marked growth of both of these mixed populations: a 243% increase in White and Black African groups and a 74% rise in mixed White and Black Caribbean pupils between 2003 and 2017 in schools across England (Demie & Hau, 2018).

I seek to reflect on my autobiographical experiences as a young Black male student who encountered racism in Britain, to my development as an educator who now sees how this may be analysed, interpreted and applied within the context of teaching for justice within the global classroom.

Exploring the Complex Relationship With Name-identity in the Classroom

I had an alternative culture and history that was positive.

Use of student names has been shown to build classroom community, increase student engagement by helping them feel more comfortable, making students feel more accountable to the teacher, ensuring students are secure in seeking help and increasing student satisfaction with a course (Cooper et. al, 2017; Murdoch et. al, 2018; O'Brien et. al, 2014). While teachers may consider learning student names takes valuable time away from class, the benefits to student learning are greater than covering more content. Failure to know or correctly pronounce student names has been tied to implicit bias and feelings of alienation among students, particularly for students with ethnically distinct names (Mitchell, 2016). Research on the use of name tents on desks indicates that students' mere perception that a teacher knows their name can help them feel valued and increases classroom engagement (Cooper et. al, 2017). Knowing and expressing a desire to learn students names can reinforce a teacher's commitment to inclusivity and solicit more focus from students in classrooms (Tanner, 2013).

My name, Andrew Geoffrey Kwabena Moss, reflects the two cultural realms that have been bestowed on me; dual treasures that I have mined more deeply and interrogated over time. I am Anglo-Ghanaian, my father was English, and my mother is Ghanaian. Largely due to my father's influence and love of literature, I was named Andrew after the English poet Andrew Marvell and Geoffrey after Chaucer. In addition to this, I was named Kwabena, the Akan day name for Tuesday born. "In the Akan societies of West Africa, names and the process of naming are essential since everyone and almost every living entity has a place and mission in the world...The name of a person or entity reflects its purpose in life. The *adinto* or *abadinto* (literally to 'throw a name') or naming ceremony takes place usually at the father's house on the eighth day, that is, a week after and on the day the child was born" (Konadu, 2010, p.2).

In my case, a child born on a Tuesday, my naming ceremony took place the following Tuesday. I was aware at an early age that my first name or *kradin* (soul name) was based on the *nnawɔtwe*, eight-day Akan week. Commensurate with Akan naming traditions, in addition to receiving a 'day name', in accordance with the sibling birth order, I was named 'manu' due to being the second born. The cultural traditions of Akan nomenclature and outdooring ceremony provide rich opportunities for students of the African diaspora to connect with extant precolonial practices outside of the Judeo-Christian model, essential to the decolonisation of the curriculum. By considering other cultural practices, part of Manning's (2009) concept of *reflective culture*, a window on Akan philosophy, knowledge and spiritual beliefs outside of the European paradigm is afforded.

Such case studies bring a peripheral site to the fore and co-construct validation of African Diasporan cultural heritage for the historically marginalised. Students can look to their own names as a micro-cultural knowledge funds that connect them to a macro-culture. Teachers can create classroom activities that integrate student knowledge about their historical background and how and why they were named. This can be used as a springboard for the elevation of historical and socio-cultural awareness and promotion of academic achievement if students research their own names and naming systems or those of their cultural heritage.

I was raised in a hostile environment where I was routinely called a host of racist nicknames on the school playground (such as *nig nog, nigger, jungle bunny, coon, chocolate drop, blackie, burnt toast, jungle bunny* and *golliwog*). My Akan names were a source of pride that offered some inoculation of agency and identity against these demeaning labels. I had an alternative culture and history that was positive. I grew up during the late seventies and eighties in Thatcher's Britain, a green and unpleasant land enclosed and xenophobically policed by Tebbit's lilywhite searching cricket tests and tabloid newspapers deriding the 'Argy Bargy' of the Falklands War. It was an insular and insecure culture that denied pluralism, multiple identities or hybrid hyphenation. My Akan names supplied me with an intravenous lifeline to the pulsing heart of my Ghanaian heritage. As early as lower primary school, my parents guided me in an understanding of the meaning of my day name. My very name provided validation and proved to be the buffer between my supportive home environment and the often-barren school environment that denuded any positive African acknowledgement.

I was brought up with a narrative of family history, an *expressive culture* and its intersections with wider *societal expressions* of migration, matrilineality, family patterns and rituals. These rich cultural manifestations provided a rich source of pluralism and fluidity that challenged fixed notions of culture, identity and race. Such immediate funds of knowledge can be capitalised upon to widen and transform national myths of fixed identities and connect students to an appreciation of their heritage, using their own resources to be critical of essentialism.

Seeking my own positive role models and alternatives, I found out about Malcolm X and how he had used an "X" to symbolize his unknown African name, stripped by slavery. I reflected on Malcom's "re-naming" path on a journey to self-identification and greater historical consciousness: from "Detroit Red" hustling Malcolm Little to Malcolm X as a member of the Nation of Islam to Sunnite el-Hajj Malik el-Shabazz (after the completion of his pilgrimage to Mecca). Additionally, I considered Cassius Clay's transformation of his "slave name."

I didn't choose it and I don't want it. I am Muhammad Ali, a free name (Ali, 1964).

Long before I was exposed to Hall's (1990) theorised and grounded arguments that cultural identity is not only a matter, a "being" but of "becoming", "belonging as much to the future as it does to the past" (p, 255); that identities undergo constant transformation, transcending time and space, I started to analyse how I was positioned and "otherised" as Black. Politically and physically, in a market town with very few ethnic minorities and a scarcity of dark-skinned denizens, I was Black or sometimes categorized in "half caste" reductive pseudo-scientific terms (akin to the phoney eugenics based and subhuman connotations of mulatto). On other occasions, I was termed as a milder and less destabilising "coloured" by those more sensitive to liberal naming notions but also in line with the Apartheid system of four-tiered racial classification (native, coloured, Asian, or white) that bombarded us with F. W. de Klerk, tear gas on the 6 o'clock news.

My first visit home to Ghana after leaving there at age two, brought awareness of the colour continuum and pigmentocracy that operate as a construct in different societies. Regarded as Black in the UK, I became painfully aware that I was viewed as *Oborɔnyi. T*he Akan or more specifically, the Fante word for foreigner, literally meaning "those who come from over the horizon (Holsey, 2008)," is often colloquially translated into *white person*. "Oborɔnyi" is not a direct translation of *white*. From this experience, I derived the precarious and shifting nature of race as an arbitrary social and pseudo-scientific construct.

Based on my experience reading and researching literature, I assert that educators can guide students to read books that work to clarify and explicate how various geographical regions take up race as a social construct. In my twenties, during a period of absorbing and synthesizing these experiences, I read Joy Zarembka's (2007) fascinating study, *The Pigment of Your Imagination: Mixed Race in a Global Society*. Through anecdotes of her own travels in various geographical locations (Britain, Kenya, Zimbabwe and Jamaica), historical background and oral histories from mixed-race families, the vastly different interpretations of racial identity in various parts of the world are interrogated. I poured over the pages voraciously, with some personal insight of Hall's (1990) fluid and multiple identities. Such texts provide a powerful tool for teachers to empower Black and Brown student identity by highlighting how throughout the world, people use arbitrary notions of race to define who is *Black* and who is *white*. Myopic racial perceptions are questioned such as where white ends and Black starts; whether society or individuals determine racial classification.

MULTI-LITERACIES – LIVING WITHIN TWO CULTURAL REALMS

Educators may use students' immediate and extended family histories as a vehicle to connect to diverse microculture and wider histories that act as a counterbalance to predatory white supremacist cultural oppression.

Societal Culture

Educators may use students' immediate and extended family histories as a vehicle to connect to diverse microculture and wider histories that act as a counterbalance to predatory white supremacist cultural oppression. Growing up in the UK, my family migration narrative was passed on to me and was a reference point to give me a sense of identity and cultural heritage . In Manning's (2009) micro-cultural terms, "To explore the details of human creativity, we must break down the general term 'culture' into its various micro-cultural aspects. We need to explore the details of how people have represented their outlooks and experiences" (p.21). Unfortunately, my teachers did not do this but, as an educator I now see how effective these strategies can be if effectively applied with the objective of incorporating students' heritage into the classroom pedagogy. I have used these strategies as an educator to empower students. Manning (2009) goes on to classify the creation and modelling of family patterns and rituals as *societal culture*. I had moved from a matrilineal Akan society to a patrilocal one by circumstance rather than design. In 1977. at the age of two and a half years of age, my family moved from Ghana to the UK. My father travelled to West Africa, teaching initially in Nigeria. He then went to Ghana where he met my mother. My father was the first *oborɔnyi* to marry into my mother's family.

Another aspect of societal culture (Manning, 2009) that connected me, through micro-cultural family upbringing (cultural production and representation) to African microculture was the importance of motherhood. "Of the many roles fulfilled in African societies, certain of them have been represented with particular attention: prominent among them are the roles of mother…The role of motherhood, a widely celebrated aspect of societal culture of West Africa and central Africa" (p.22).

Repeatedly told by mum and dad that the Akan was a matrilineal society, we were intrigued and respectful of the opportunities this counterculture provided.

Despite our patrilocal relocation from Ghana to the UK, my upbringing surrounded me with the awareness that in traditional Akan society, children are naturally closer to the mother than their father (Ayim, 2015). My mother and father told me from an early age how each Akan is tied and related to the mother through blood, which determines and defines family. I knew that the word *abusua* or family meant the relatives of the mother alone. To my relief, I would always have a role and place in Ghana through these societal cultural family patterns and associated rituals.

"An Akan would therefore refer to *abusua*, "family," as being the relatives of the mother alone. The father is not considered family. In ancient typology, the father is but putative or, at most, a foster parent. The cohesive bonds that exist between mother and her children are more pronounced in the Akan saying, "family ends with the death of the mother" (Ayim, p.55, 2015).

Finding out about the area from which my mother's family originated, has given me a stronger sense of belonging. For those students who are not lucky enough to have the opportunity to visit their ancestral country other resources may be used. Videos of ancestral homes and/ or establishing video conferences with those from ancestral homes are alternative virtual experiences which can act as a springboard for students to research the societal cultures that they share.

The strength of a student's family heritage can be utilized as a source to embrace that child's background into the classroom space and bolster his identity.

I was aware that my mother, as the eldest of six siblings grounded in a matriarchal society, had in the past operated in a different landscape to the patriarchal system that many of my friends never questioned. By moving to the UK, we assumed a patrilocal position (as mentioned before, more accidental than by design). My brother and I were aware that although dad taught and was a 'breadwinner', mum was to be respected as a strategic financial and domestic manager, a 'homemaker' and 'home defender' from the same warrior class as Yaa Asantewaa. Queen Mother, Yaa Asantewaa (1830-1921), is renowned and respected within African culture and recognized within global scholarship as a warrior against colonialization and the disruption of African culture, systems and spirituality.

Repeatedly told by mum and dad that the Akan was a matrilineal society, we were intrigued and respectful of the opportunities this counterculture provided. Amidst a prevailing Western culture that discriminated against us as 'Black', 'other', abnormal and deficient, we were excited and proud that we could claim allegiance to Mum's family line; an alternative birth right. Dislocated miles away from Ghana in deepest, darkest Bedfordshire in the monocultural conservative enclave of market town Leighton Buzzard, we could find solace in our undisputed connection to *abusua* in Ghana. Despite our lighter skin tone and two English first names and surname, our succession and property inheritance would be governed by matrilineal mother-right rules. This helped me to feel a greater sense of belonging and balance. In England, we assumed our father's surname but remained connected to my mother's line irrespective of geographical distance. Thus, we were stuck fast to mum's sisters and uncles by blood.

The strength of a student's family heritage can be utilized as a source to embrace that child's background into the classroom space and bolster his identity. In Britain, I was raised in the precarious position of racially tense times, including the rippling tides of Enoch Powell's inflammatory 1968 "rivers of blood" speech which appealed to racial hatred as a means to argue for stricter immigration policy, (Savage, 2018). Within Thatcherite xenophobia and casual terrace and tabloid racism, micro- and macro-aggressions, this link mattered. Partially disenfranchised by environment, we were connected to a wider African macro-culture. This *societal culture* (Manning, 2009) immersed us and bolstered our funds of knowledge to resist the formal curriculum of simplified colonial narratives, where Black History was reduced to passive recipients of slavery and civilising missions, begging for enlightened liberal abolitionism. We were granted some insulation against the deficit framing as labourers, victims, criminals, maids etc. projected in British situational 'comedies' on TV in the black and white judgements of Alf Garnett and 'Please Sir'.

This societal culture immersed us and bolstered our funds of knowledge to resist the formal curriculum of simplified colonial narratives.

Teachers have a central role in eliciting and stimulating such autobiographical reflection. Students require models to explore how their own societal culture has been resilient despite the global effects of colonisation and imperialism. Educators may start this process by modelling their own personal life journeys. Storytelling, including autobiographical, memoir, other life writing and auto-ethnography, allow students to engage through an emotional and visual discourse. These pedagogical tools invite students back into history and their cultural heritage. Our ancestors are a vital part of our societal culture and raise our historical and cultural consciousness. This knowledge enables future generations to confront social inequities across the globe.

I knew that I had a richer, three-dimensional dual heritage and this provided a much-needed emotional foundation.

At home we were furnished with some mobility against the debilitating impact of classrooms where race and ethnicity were constructed in a simplistic, one-dimensional terms; the binary oppositions of superiority and inferiority; cultured and backward; free and enslaved in black and white terms. I knew that I had a richer, three-dimensional dual heritage and this provided a much-needed emotional foundation. Our lived existence lay proof to our suspicion of the lie we were fed by the mainstream (i.e., Tebbit's essentialising cricket test used as a way of criticizing one's opponent in many kinds of argument). We were painfully aware of how, 'Nations, social classes, tribes and castes have all been "deconstructed" in the sense of being described as false entities. As the first educators of children, parents and guardians need to be aware of their accountability in promoting awareness of their heritage. In turn, teachers need to connect with parents and guardians and collaborate with them to furnish the curriculum with the cultural resources and diverse funds of knowledge that students from diverse backgrounds bring with them into classrooms.

The organic combining of cultures, which occurred within my home, is referred to by Gilroy (2004) as 'spontaneous convivial culture.' Gilroy has written about this phenomenon in relation to predominantly urban areas in postcolonial cities worldwide. In 1980s Bedfordshire, my family were regarded as mavericks from the outside viewed with English hegemonic suspicion at those who inhabited a household of visibly different ethnicity. In a foreboding monocultural milieu, we were the poster family for multiculturalism.

Thankfully, we felt connected to another family and culture. We were proud that mum belonged to the Asona clan. According to Akan tradition, although most people use the words interchangeably, there is a distinction between clan and family. The eminent anthropologist Rattray (1923), noted the Ashanti word for clan is *abusua*, and this word is synonymous with *mogya* (blood). Due to their patrilineal structures,

Eurocentric cultures define clan as 'family'. However, in the Akan matrilineal concept *abusua* equates with family and *nton,* or *ntoro* refers to the patrilineal entity of clan.

THE LEGACY OF AFRICAN MATERIAL CULTURE

Adinkra and kente have great potential in educational settings, as a vehicle to teach students about aspects of Ghanaian culture.

African people brought with them to this hemisphere, a wide variety of objects which represented very important aspects of their cultural heritage including spirituality, philosophy and political beliefs. With the guidance of teachers, students may be given motivating autobiographical models to investigate manifestations of expressive cultural forms such as textiles and their symbolism and meaning to people of the African Diaspora. Such immersion will act as a rich stimulus for students' own cultural production of their funds of knowledge. Below, I share some specific examples of material culture from my Akan heritage. Through this explication, I hope to convey the deep meaning these objects brought to my family including the sense of connection to the ancient wisdom of the Ashante people.

Kente: A source of pride and symbol of resilience throughout the African Diaspora

In addition to the *adinkra* cloth, *kente*, the Akan textile, is a source of pride and symbol of resilience throughout the African Diaspora. The faric is woven into my formative childhood memories. *Kente*, hand woven fabric on looms, is indubitably the most expensive and elegant traditional and ceremonial cloth in Ghana. I was aware of the folkloric creation story, that *kente* weaving began after some farmers observed a spider, Anansi, weave a mighty web.

Growing up within a racist society, *Kente* provided bright relief. Yellow together with green represented fertility to recalibrate images of a parched cradle of civilization. Bright blue reflected pure spirit and harmony that was enervated by media images, red bled its passion and black stood proudly to represent a union with ancestors and spiritual awareness that made me proud in an era of National Front far right politics, a neo-Nazi renaissance to 'Keep Britain White' as Gilroy (1987) quipped, 'There Ain't No Black in the Union Jack'.

The weaving tools of *kente* are treated and preserved as sacred. I saw varieties of *kente* in our house without understanding their exact meanings at first. I did understand from an early age that together with adinkra, this fabric carried rich linguistic meaning to match its visual vibrance. I knew that each colour had a specific meaning. The main colours of kente cloth are red, gold, yellow, green, blue and white, with occasional pink and brown. Black represents the people of African descent; red stands for the shared blood (kinship) of Black people and the blood that continues to be shed in the struggle for survival; green represents Africa's fertility and abundance; and yellow refers to Africa's wealth. Woven on a horizontal loom in strips of about four inches wide, the ceremonial cloth comes in different textures depending on the technique or mode (single, double or triple) of weave. For males, twenty-four strips of *kente* (measuring twelve feet long and eight feet wide) are standard whereas women usually utilize between six and twelve strips

I watched eagerly as 1988 rap trio Salt-N-Pepa worked its way into the African fashion movement by performing wearing kufis with kente patterns on them (Hamilton, 2010). African American rapper Queen Latifah wore a kente sash in her 1989 video "ladies first', featuring Monie Love. Together, with a recently formed De La Soul, African heritage clothing made its way onto my technicolour television screen, together with flat tops and designs shaved meticulously into the hair (Ashinger, 1990). Suitably inspired, as a thirteen-year-old, I went on a trip completely out of my comfort zone from my monocultural hometown with my dad to the Black cultural Mecca of Brixton Market. Bamboozled by the burgeoning Black consciousness movement that had come through US Hip hop culture, I eagerly pored over 'dope ropes', (correctly termed as African leather medallions) and bought one, before purchasing a *kente* and faux leather kufi cap.

The African leather medallion was introduced in the late 80s and early 90s, a time in which artists like Afrika Bambaataa of the Universal Zulu Nation, A Tribe Called Quest, De La Soul, and Brand Nubians, were building a movement out of the creativity of a new generation of outcast youths with an authentic, liberating worldview. Hip hop around this time was educational, empowering, and fun with a focus of knowledge of self. Knowledge of self meant understanding that all Black people originated from Africa and as such, we were to embrace our culture and history with pride and dignity. The African leather medallion was a badge of honour. The necklace was made of leather, with the shape of Africa carved out of it and typically painted red, yellow, green and black. It replaced fat diamond chains and gold rope chains as a statement to dismiss the glorification of meaningless materialism in hip hop. The necklace had a great impact and reached not only hip-hop groups, but also inmates who wanted to turn their life around, religious groups like the Nation of Islam and everyday individuals.

Utilizing *kente* cloth in my newly acquired kufi cap, *kente* provided the thread that connected me to my Akan heritage and was a way of avoiding complete assimilation into Britain, acknowledging a culture that I was estranged from. Kente has similarly been used as an educational tool to bolster funds of knowledge and cultural pride. Adinkra and kente have great potential in educational settings, as a vehicle to teach students about aspects of Ghanaian culture. In addition, the history and production of the cloth itself can be used to teach students how to design, draft and produce cloth through technology as well as through traditional methods (Badoe & Opoku-Asare, 2014).

The Social and Emotional Value of Literature

Purposefully selected literature can help students experience validation and pride in living in the realm of diverse and underrepresented cultures.

Literature was another powerful and culturally expressive form that supplied me with tools to bolster my funds of knowledge within the realm of Anglo- Ghanaian and wider African Diaspora cultures. The significance of the emotional dimensions of this literature in boosting well-being and psychological health cannot be over-erestimated. Purposefully selected literature can help students experience validation sand pride in living in the realm of diverse and underrepresented cultures. Belittling tropes prevalent in the media and playground were counteracted by 'Comfort Herself', a junior novel by Geraldine Kaye (1987). I vividly remember the day when my mum rushed home from the Lower School she taught at, and I had been a student. We were giddy with excitement that the protagonist shared my mother's name and my Anglo-Ghanaian heritage. Looking at the front cover was the rarest of experiences. For the first time in my life, at around the age of ten or eleven, I looked into a mirror. Finally, having read most Roald Dahl books and a swathe of other literature, I was represented in literature. I voraciously read about a girl who looked like me and came from a similar background. I no longer felt like a freakish oddity for other people's surprised and bewildered gaze. Suddenly, I felt an unfamiliar life affirming validation, a sense of belonging, a calming sensation of being seen and heard.

The initial complication which galvanises the plot is when her mother dies, Comfort, aged eleven, is faced with an impossible dilemma. She could stay in England with her old-fashioned grandparents, or she could travel to Ghana to find her father. Deciding on the latter course of action, Comfort adjusts to Ghanaian village life and returns to England a year later. Comfort's problem to a large extent echoed mine. She was unsure of where she fitted in. At first, Comfort feels stifled in England but what does she know of Ghana? She might find herself to be even more of an outcast there. All that Comfort really knows is there is one way to find out. And so, she decides to travel to Ghana.

Oral and written stories are central to the core of African literature and can be used as tools to teach literature with a global edge. Anansi stories originate the Akan folktale character and the god of stories, wisdom, knowledge, and trickery, most commonly depicted as a spider. This oral and written literature grounds students' pride in connecting to a rich West African storytelling tradition which survived the Middle Passage and provides an entertaining model of power, resistance and adaptability despite Eurocentric attempts to eradicate cultural heritage– tools much needed in the global classroom of the twenty-first century. Anansi presides over a web of tales that stretch across the Atlantic connecting the African Diaspora as a symbolic characterization of resilience and agency in surviving enslavement. An enduring treasure from my childhood, is a lime green Anansi picture book given to me by my parents. As an adult today, Anansi represents a cultural fusion- a hybrid postcolonial Caribbean and its migration. Anansi was the vehicle through which the Eurocentric narratives with their fixed views and traumatic legacies of colonialism surrounding me were challenged. The stories were a celebration of African cultural retentions, hybrid resilience and resistance in hostile environments.

Far from being an evolutionary precursor to the colonially power-driven epistemological privilege given to fairy tales, folklore in Anansi stories have their own cultural leverage equal to and an alternative to those of North American or European origin. Anansi stories are not a myth. From the 17th century to the early 20th century Anansi was part of the Asante political, religious and social life. Although not divine, he was a mediator between men and women, humankind and Nyame. As an Asante folk hero, Anansi tests the boundaries of acceptable behaviour; he acts as a mediator between humankind and Nyame, at the figurative crossroads of two cultures. Instinctively I recognised the power of this dual heritage. Thus, Anansi stories provided me with an effective expressive cultural tool, part of an oral tradition then made material in book form, a portal into the reflective culture of philosophy, knowledge and beliefs rooted in my African heritage.

Anansi stories are the cultural expression of reflective culture (Manning, 2009), tools used to, explain, scrutinise and question the world around us. Anansi stories were, "also celebrations of the intricacies and beauty of language and the Asante delight in Anansi's use of tricky word play and double-entendres to get the better of his adversaries" (Yanka, 1983, p. 11). For this reason, a spider design decorates the staffs of Asante royal spokesman, otherwise known as court linguists (Yanka, 1983).

Texts such as the 'Autobiography of Malcolm X' (Haley & X, 1965) provide teachers with a blueprint for helping students to acquire resilience in spaces where their cultural heritage is undervalued, underrepresented, and misrepresented. Malcolm's formative years firmly put mine in perspective. I learned of how his house in a white neighbourhood had been burned to the ground. His father was killed by what police termed 'a streetcar accident' but Malcolm believed it was the Ku Klux Klan. His mother was diagnosed as mentally ill and consequently, Malcolm was placed, with his siblings in foster families. Teachers may utilise Malcolm's background as a stimulus for comparing struggles for justice and peace.

Students struggling with social anxiety and other issues may learn from the story of Malcolm's life. They may discern lessons in struggle and survival from stories about Malcom's challenges including being kicked out of school in the seventh grade and sent to a juvenile home in the nearly all- white community of Mason, Michigan. Although he did well at school earning straight A's and being elected president of his eighth-grade class, his teacher discouraged him from pursuing his goal of becoming a lawyer. Malcolm faced this and other challenges to educate himself and become a renowned cultural icon and socio-political figure. Reading the literature about Malcolm's life helped to strengthen my journey within the hostile sites of my public life. Furthermore, students who are estranged from other members of diverse communities will feel a sense of solidarity and validation when Malcolm reflects on his 1940 summer visit (age 15) to Roxbury in Boston where he was entranced, "I couldn't have feigned indifference if I had tried to... I didn't know the world contained as many Negroes as I saw thronging downtown Roxbury at night" (Haley, A. & X, Malcolm, 1965). Teachers can utilise these connections to acknowledge the complexities of growing up in hostile cultural environments.

The text can be used to raise students' awareness of how systemic racism may lead to internalisation of negative stereotyping. Malcolm's reflections on self-hatred and brain washing which led him to 'conk' his hair so it would be whiter. "This was my first really big step towards self-degradation: on when I enjoyed all of that pain, literally burning my flesh to have it look like a white man's hair. I had joined that multitude of Negro men and women in America who are brainwashed into believing that black people are inferior- and white people superior but they will even violate and mutilate their God- created bodies to try to look pretty by white standards" (Haley & X, 1965, p.91). Malcolm finally gets rid of his conk when he becomes a member of the Nation of Islam. According to Malcolm, straightening nappy hair with a host of caustic chemicals stands as an emblem of black self-denial. Malcolm X's cutting off his chemically processed hair was a symbol of change in his mentality. The extensive literature on Malcolm X may be used to analyse the importance of hairstyles as symbolic cultural representations in pride and heritage by teachers and extended to a discussion of Black political self-determinism.

The narratives and biographies of role models were especially important in my identity formation. Students who are bullied as I was, can be directed to ancestral writing and images as blueprints to guide their path and connect to stories of historical empowerment within the African Diaspora. I keenly sought out these images and texts; tools of an expressive culture that took me on peripheral paths beyond the confines of Eurocentric epistemologies present in the formal classroom. These life stories, discovered outside of the formal monocultural UK classrooms of the eighties and nineties, provided a validation of my cultural life as an underrepresented member of the African Diaspora. These were guides and counterpoints to historical narratives and national myths of passive Black slaves that I learned about in my middle school and upper school classroom 'History Lessons.'

Teachers can incorporate worldwide music as a pedagogical tool in the struggle for justice, equity and peace in the global classroom. Music such as that of Bob Marley can help teens to embrace their mixed heritage whilst respecting a diverse range of cultures. Such resources can be used by teachers as rich text models that reflect and amplify diverse students' identities through providing role models who raise their historical and cultural consciousness. In my teenage years, I eagerly learned about Bob Marley's challenges, the discrimination he faced in Trench Town from both black Jamaicans and white people due to his mixed heritage (Grant, 2011). I could identify with the liminal landscape in which he grew up, stereotyped as lighter-skinned in a predominantly darker skinned milieu. I was inspired by Bob Marley's contribution to fighting racism. His songs are a legacy of peace and love. Marley wanted Jamaica to unite beyond the colonial hangover of its pigmentocracy. He sought to integrate Black and white worlds. Having a white father and Black mother he was often ridiculed by terms such as half-caste and this obviously resonated with me. At times he was reduced to not being whole, not being white enough or Black enough. Like me, Marley wanted to be seen for himself. One of his most iconic songs, 'Get Up Stand Up (1973) was written to galvanise people in Jamaica to stand up against racism. In 1975, the year I was born, Bob Marley made a clear statement regarding his beliefs about race during a television interview: "My father was white and my mother Black, you know. Them call me half-caste, or whatever. Well, me don't dip on nobody's side. Me don't dip on the black man's side nor the white man's side. Me dip on God's side, the one who create me and cause me to come from black and white, who give me this talent." He believed love was the answer. I empathised with Marley's life story. I appreciated the complexities of growing up othered, from a visibly different ethnic group, in a predominantly different ethnic area.

Trench Town was diametrically opposite to Leighton Buzzard in terms of its ethnic makeup, but the concept was the same. Marley's father left at a young age and being born from an interracial marriage was something people were not used to during that time, as was the case where I grew up. Marley's resentment of his father leaving, and poor treatment of his mother created an alienation that I felt due to my ties being cut from Ghana. I felt a deep resonance with the sense of belonging Bob Marley felt through Rastafarianism . His biography connected my identity with pride in an estranged African heritage and is therefore a potent resource for teachers to use for students to connect with their African Diasporic culture.

The critical reading of (neo) colonial texts and the established Eurocentric literary canon is vital in the search for culturally appropriate change and development for people of colour. I have continued to expand my awareness of literary figures who have skilfully expressed the resilience of African Diaspora identity in hostile environments. In my twenties in London, I sought to widen my historical consciousness and one afternoon in the Willesden Green bookshop next to the Library, I came across 'A New World Order - Selected Essays by Caryl Phillips' (2002). In the book Phillips argues that there is a new world order of cultural plurality, one which is being promoted by the increasingly central role of the migrant and the refugee in the modern world. Phillips proceeds to reflect on the work of such seminal figures as the African American writers Richard Wright, James Baldwin and South African writer, Nadine Gordimer. He investigates others, including Coetzee and Soyinka in Africa; Walcott, CLR James, Glisson, Naipaul, Chamoiseau, Lamming and Selvon in the Caribbean and in Britain's tradition from Ignatius Sancho to Linton Kwesi Johnson and Zadie Smith. Rather fittingly, I bought this book in the multicultural streets that had been immortalised in Smith's zeitgeist defining 'White Teeth. '

Talking of Drums

Drums are another rich resource for teachers to use to stimulate students' curiosity about their rich heritage. Drums are another example of material cultural capital which combines expressive culture, music, communication and literature to develop students' pride in and awareness of their African Diaspora identity. Talking drums are used as a form of communication between tribes. Due to their dexterity in mimicking the spoken word effectively, they have been employed to relay long distance messages of coronations, deaths, celebration and war. *Odondo* have been used for entertainment, praise singing, fun, folklore and leisure. They harbour mystical connotations and are linked to deities and gods. Talking drums are used for prayer and as a means of blessing the community and individuals.

The communicative use of talking drums was noted by Europeans in the first half of the 19th century in admiration that messages could be sent from one village to another faster than a person on horseback. The missionary R.T Clarke (1934, p.34) zealously reflected upon how, "… the signals represent the tones of the syllables of conventional phrases of a traditional and highly poetic character," capturing the male and female tones of the Niger-Congo language group. Drums communicate through phrases and pauses which can travel over five miles. Although these messages may take eight times longer than communicating a normal sentence, they were a highly effective tool in telling neighbouring villages of possible attacks and ceremonies. For each short word beaten on drums, an extra pause is added that is redundant in speech but provides a context for the core drum signal.

Finnegan (1970) in her chapter 'Drum Language and Literature in Africa' analyses 'drum' messages are not just utilitarian but include diverse literary forms: proverbs, panegyrics, historical poems, dirges; in fact, any kind of poetry. The ritualised forms and drum names constitute a type of oral literature and are highly developed among the Ashanti and Yoruba. Drum language and literature involves specialised and often hereditary learning by expert drummers who have a mastery of the accepted vocabulary. Master drummers were historically attached to a king's courts.

My African diasporic heritage continues to be a source of my fascination and inspiration with the language of identity. Given my formative feelings of disenfranchisement and alienation from my African heritage, it is no wonder that I feel a deep (visceral) connection with the events of the Middle Passage and its genetic memories (recent research postulates Post Traumatic Slave Syndrome as a lived experience) passed down through generations of Afro-Caribbean and African American peoples. The Akan Drum, the oldest surviving African American object, is a powerful symbol of the language of identity, resilience and survival. It was originally used as a 'talking drum' that skilled drummers would use to replicate the tones, punctuation and accents of the Akan language in order to send messages from village to village. In this way, Akan people could be called to a celebration or to war. It is believed that the Akan Drum was taken to Virginia on a slave ship, but not by an enslaved African, as slaves were not allowed to carry possessions with them. The drum may have been gifted to a ship's captain or, since we know that the sons of Asante chiefs sometimes accompanied the voyages as part of their education, perhaps it was taken to America by one of them. It is highly likely that the Akan Drum and others like it, were used to exercise the captives or dance the slaves' body and mind as economic commodities like horses or cars, preserving them for slave labour (The British Museum, 2022).

Drumming and other African musical traditions continued in the colonies (at first permitted and then in some states covertly due to plantation owners' fears that it could incite revolt) and gave rise to different kinds of music including shouts, hollers, spirituals, fife and drum and work songs. In this way, the Akan Drum continued to be used to spread an evolving language of African identity. Drums are a material manifestation of the creative energy of musical expression that is a potent vehicle for transmitting the reflective culture of philosophy, knowledge and belief systems. Resounding throughout the societal culture of the African Diaspora and beyond, drumming is a means of sustaining, adapting and syncretic re-synthesizing and remixing family patterns, political culture and rituals. Therefore, drums are repositories that reverberate with expressive, material, reflective and societal culture with macro-cultural African traditions.

Drums hold a great personal relevance within wider historic-cultural and socio-political developments. Inspired by these strengthening connections, I have written several poems about how drums have helped me to develop my funds of knowledge in the struggle for justice, peace and equity within and beyond the global classroom.

Some Final Thoughts on the Triumph of Bi-Racial Identity

Diaspora, Stuart Hall (1990) advises, must be treated metaphorically.

Diaspora does not refer to those scattered tribes whose identity can only be secured in relation to some sacred homeland to which they must at all costs return…not by essence or purity, but recognition of a necessary heterogeneity and diversity: by conception of 'identity' that lives with and through as process, the idea of difference by hybridity (p.235).

Growing up, I tried to piece together the brickwork of two cultures, seeing where there were boundaries, where I might fit and where there was an overlap.

My 'otherness' changed according to the context that I was in. Had we stayed in Ghana it would have been likely that I would have felt disenfranchised and alienated from an exotic and faraway Merrie England. Cultural identity is not fixed or predetermined. Rather, it is "an articulation fostered in a complex structure of diverse and contradictory yet connected relations." Hall (1990) continues his analysis, "Cultural identity is not a fixed essence at all, lying unchanged outside history and culture. It is not a once-and-for-all and it is not a fixed origin to which we can make some final and absolute Return" (p.226). In fact, my 'Return' to the loving bosom of Mother Ghana was a challenging experience, brought 'home' in the cries of '*Oborɔnyi!*' and the successive culture shock. I abruptly came face to face with the reality of how English my cultural identity was. I experienced what it was to "… belong to the marginal…the periphery, the 'Other'" (Hall, 1990 p.228).

'In Britain I am black
In Ghana I am white
The realisation of the Middle way is born,
Shades of grey unhinge my door.' (Moss, 2021,p.193).

Cultural identities are the points of identification or suture, the unstable points of identification or suture, which are made, within the discourses of history and culture. Not an essence but a positioning. Hence, there is always a politics of identity, a politics of position, which has no absolute guarantee in an unproblematic, transcendental "law of origin" (Hall, 1990, p.226).

My positioning changed depending on the country I was in and how others regarded me. I was on a continuum of colour, closer to a black 'other' or stranger in the overwhelmingly white UK and closer to a white 'other' or outsider in predominantly black Ghana.

As Michael McMillan (2008) recognises in 'The West Indian Front Room: Reflections on a Diasporic Phenomenon', "The front room was a contradictory space" (p.44) between cultures in one way. Carved Asante stools held up the Yellow Pages and Phone Directory, a drinks cabinet housed medium dry sherry and Stone's Ginger Wine with kente and adinkra curtains in the background. The Ghanaian artefacts that I wrote about earlier were sensorial stimuli that triggered bittersweet feelings of alienation, loss, longing, and pride. As I have become older, I have revisited these materials in the light of a return visit to Ghana and growing consciousness, through studying of Akan history and culture. The process of sharing my ideas has led to my realisation of my emotional responses and memories in a performative context. As a child I felt a deep desire to connect with my Ghanaian heritage. However, a watershed moment occurred when I revisited Ghana and discovered the extent of my English acculturation. The reality clashed with the 'imagined geography' (Said, 1978) of Ghana that I had conjured up to fill the lacunae of memories. Outside of the family home, I inhabited a very English milieu. I had, however, underestimated the significance of Ghanaian culture within the four walls and conifer lined garden boundaries that I grew up in. I am still influenced by these experiences and continue to synthesise them to this day.

Closer inspection of my Anglo-Ghanaian house shows how reductive concepts of assimilation can be. In angry teenage mode, I accused my mum of 'selling out' to the prevailing British culture. Yet, I failed to appreciate the agency and determination that my parents exerted in amalgamating what they valued from both English and Ghanaian culture. To use the term coined by the Cuban sociolinguist Fernando Ortiz, our home was a 'contact zone.'

Our house, garden and the objects within them reflected my parents' union. Our microcosm, with its expressive, material, societal and reflective microcultural elements (Manning, 2009) were inextricably linked to contacts and power relations between the British Empire and Ghana, processes of colonisation, independence and post-independence. My father moved to West Africa to contribute to post-independence efforts to establish and sustain a state free from colonialism. He taught the first generation of leaders in the three government branches and public service representatives. My mother was the first of her family to marry outside of her tribe and to move abroad. This was a cultural exchange initiated by the bonds of love.

The various precolonial Akan artefacts in my home maintained a flow to the motherland. These objects were curated to create memory and pride in autochthonous culture, which served to address mis(sed)representations of colonial prejudices and epistemologies. Our artefacts were juxtaposed with the surrounding British culture in a largely symbolic and organic way, keeping pace with my parents intertwining their lives romantically and building a family together. They were the active participants in a dynamic cultural exchange, negotiation and compromise. At times there were practical compromises such as the use of marbles to replace bonduc seeds in *oware*. Dad identified strongly with Ghanaian culture and learned eagerly about it whilst mum studied British culture; by living it and by being situated in it.

The Ghanaian artefacts were vectors of "similarity" or "continuity" with the Ghana of my birth, the shift to an England in the throes of Thatcherism presented a "vector of difference and rupture" (Hall, 1990, p. 226). Hall, in fact coined the phrase whilst working at the Centre for Contemporary Cultural Studies, "Thatcherism is simply a way of talking about the programmes of the new right, or the radical right, or the monetarist right which has made fitful appearances elsewhere in the world, but which is fully established in Britain since the 1979 election at which the Conservative Party led by Mrs Thatcher came to power" (Hall, 1990). We lived in a casually racist and xenophobic milieu that heightened our fear as outsiders inhabiting a precarious position in mainstream society. Inner city macroagressions and tensions reached boiling points in the riots of '81 and '85. Rather than overt and physical hostilities, in the market town where I grew up, although there were less sizeable ethnic populations to target, we were subjected to microaggressions.

Somewhat in common with the Caribbean identities that Hall analyses, my identity could be "thought of in terms of the dialogic relationship between these two axes. The one gives us some grounding in, some continuity with the past. The second reminds us that what we share is precisely the experience of a profound discontinuity…peoples dragged into…colonisation" (Hall, 1990, p. 226-227). Not the traumatic rupture of transatlantic slavery, but the experience of moving from Ghana to a hostile UK, contributing to what DuBois termed "double consciousness." In Hall's words, "the shock of the 'doubleness' of similarity and difference" (Hall, p.227). When "othered" by the false lens of essentialism, I am treated as neither Ghanaian nor English. Cultural identity is misrepresented as "shared culture" with a false sense of fixed identity.

"For too many of us, this is a matter not of too little but too much…Europe belongs irrevocably to the play of power, to the lines of force and consent, to the role of dominant…(positioning) the black subject within its dominant regimes of representation: the colonial discourse…" (Hall, 1990, p. 233).

Fanon (1967) prompts us in *Black Skin, White Masks* to recognise this power has become part of our identities. The "otherising" gaze has become internalized and this has led to our alienation from ourselves, in Homi Bhaba's (1986) words, "the ambivalent identifications of the racist world…the 'otherness' of the self-inscribed in the perverse palimpsest of cultural identity" (p. 109). I often felt an erasure, a splitting of the doubling of my heritage and sense of disappointment that my Ghanaian heritage, or symbiosis between Ghanaian and British culture was not valued in the British dominated environment I was raised in.

The architecture and artefacts of my childhood home provided stimuli for me to develop these funds of knowledge to bridge two cultural realms and in the struggle for justice, peace and equity within and beyond the global classroom. Such microcultural manifestations of expressive, material, societal and reflective culture (Manning, 2009) are powerful tools to connect students with diverse heritages beyond Eurocentric choke holds. I still hold a residual wistfulness that I lacked exposure to Ghanaian culture in my formative years. However, in the process of writing this chapter, I feel an empowerment, gratitude and raised consciousness of how much Ghanaian culture was present within my immediate environment. This reflective process enables me to model how traditional Eurocentric epistemologies may be challenged with our own funds of knowledge.

STRATEGIES TO CREATE CULTURALLY APPROPRIATE CHANGE & DEVELOPMENT INITIATIVES FOR BIPOC YOUTH IN GLOBAL CLASSROOMS

A classroom based on social justice, equity and peace should model, share, guide and allow for independent inquiry into multi-modal expressions of culture. Using the autobiographical details of our own lives, as educators we can create a classroom curriculum which will encourage students to anchor their identity, experience world culture, navigate complex emotions, acknowledge, and strengthen their own funds of knowledge. This is a global classroom that explores name identity and capitalises on multi-literacies within diverse cultural realms. Cultural tools such as fabric, literature, visual arts, creative and practical arts and food are resources at our grasp.

Black and Indigenous People of Colour (BIPOC) should be furnished with strategies to empower them to act as critical cultural curators and producers. Micro-cultural representations, such as those I have written about, offer them an empowering history of connections and 'history through culture' to inoculate themselves against predatory white supremacist cultural oppression.

Students should be provided with autobiographical and auto-ethnographic models, such as my own. I have reflected on my experiences as a young Black male student who experienced racism in Britain, to an educator who now sees how these experiences may be analysed, interpreted and applied within the context of teaching for justice within the global classroom. These are templates to investigate societal, expressive, material and reflective culture in their own immediate environments. These micro-cultural productions are authentic manifestations of actual practices of human creativity, representations of our outlooks and experiences. Empowering connections can then be made to a wider macro-cultural history and communities.

Starting with their own family names and nomenclature, BIPOC youths can investigate their societal cultural connections. They can explore the patrilineal, matrilineal and kinship systems that operated from precolonial times and analyse change, continuity and resilience since the disruption and dislocation of (neo) colonialism.

As I have shown, there are myriad manifestations of expressive, material, societal and reflective culture within our immediate environments that may be utilised as part of a strategy against (neo)colonial oppression to bolster positive identity for marginalised children in schools across the globe. Educators must direct students to resources such as Anansi storytelling and role models such as Yaa Asantewaa as figures with the power to inspire resistance to colonial oppression. These categories of material, expressive, reflective and societal culture indicate a range of human creative multi-literacies and often overlap. Drums, for example are an example of material culture that expresses societal and reflective culture.

Exemplars of these microcultural forms are a powerful model and stimulus for students to create their own multi-modal and interdisciplinary literacies that move beyond narrow Eurocentric pedagogies and epistemologies. As a first step, BIPOC youths need to be given opportunities to act as critical investigators receiving and curating culture as an inspiration to creating their own.

As a bi-racial adult now living in Australia raising tri-racial children, I am determined that they are connected to the significant African Diaspora contribution to British and Australian culture. Drawing upon my experiences as a bi-racial child growing up in Britain, I am offering the following strategies to teachers across the globe to counter racism and enrich classroom pedagogy with the rich history and culture of Black people:

1. Unpacking Critical Race Theory (CRT): We must facilitate student agency in joining the '(CRT) movement…a collection of activists and scholars engaged in studying and transforming the relationship among race, racism, and power (Delgado and Stefanic, 2017, p.3).
2. Explore Adolescent Identity and connect to the angst of being regarded as an outsider.
3. Classroom activities such as writing narratives, autobiographies, journal writing, poetry and creative non-fiction etc. that will allow psychic distancing from trauma, allowing the control over experience as part of a healing process. "Telling stories about ourselves also implies choice: we can modify the story, tell it slightly differently to last week, put a different slant on it, and perhaps think differently about ourselves. This gives us a sense of control over our lives. Importantly, it also gives us distance from our own experience: we can

analyse the story, interpret, even critique it, as if it belongs to someone else" (Bullock, 2021, p.12).

4.   The study of global literature must be central to the curriculum. Teachers should incorporate literature from different sections of the globe into the study of literature and guide students to understand how writers utilize this knowledge to create particular texts and shape readers' perspectives about race, culture and ethnicity. A rich body of literature by writers of African ancestry should be included with space for students to interrogate why and how people respond to texts based on their background, including nationality, ethnicity and racial identity.

REFERENCES

Ashinger, P. (1990). Dress and adornment of African American entertainers. In B. M. Starke, L. O. Holoman, & B.K. Nordquist (Eds.) African American Dress and Adornment: A Cultural Perspective (179-187). Dubuque, Iowa: Kendall/Hunt Publishing Company.

Bhaba, H. (1986). *Foreword. In F. Fanon (Ed.), Black Skin White Masks.* Paladin.

Bullock, O. (2021). Poetry and Trauma: Exercises for Creating Metaphors and Using Sensory Detail. *The International Journal for the Practice and Theory of Creative Writing.*

Butler, J. (2015). *Senses of the subject.* Fordham University Press.

Clarke, R. T. (1934). The Drum Language of the Tumba People. *American Journal of Sociology, 40*(1), 34–48. doi:10.1086/216650

Cooper, K., Haney, B., Krieg, A., & Brownell, S. (2017). What's in a Name? That Importance of Students Perceiving That an Instructor Knows Their Names in a High-Enrolment Biology Classroom. *CBE Life Sciences Education, 16*(1), 1-13.

Dark, P. (1973). *An Introduction to Benin Art and Technology.* Clarendon Press.

Delgado, R., & Stefanic, J. (2017). *Critical Race Theory – An Introduction.* New York University Press.

Demie, F. (2021). The experience of Black Caribbean pupils in school exclusion in England. *Educational Review, 73*(1), 55–70. doi:10.1080/00131911.2019.1590316

Demie, F., & Hau, A. (2018). *Mixed race Pupils' Educational Achievement in England: An Empirical Analysis*. Academic Press.

Essel, O. Q. (2017). *Searchlight on Ghanaian iconic creative hands in the world of dress fashion design culture* [Unpublished doctoral dissertation]. University of Education, Winneba.

Fanon, F. (1986). *Black Skin White Masks*. Paladin.

Finnegan, R. (1970). *Oral Literature in Africa*. Clarendon Press.

Freire, P., & Macedo, D. (1987). *Literacies: Reading the word and the world*. Bergin & Harvey.

Gilroy, P. (2004). *After Empire, Melancholia or Convivial Culture?* Routledge. doi:10.4324/9780203482810

Gloyn, L., Crewe, V., King, L., & Woodham, A. (2018). The Ties That Bind: Materiality, Identity, and the Life Course in the "Things" Families Keep. *Journal of Family History, 43*(2), 157–176. https://doi.org/10.1177/0363199017746451

Grant, C. (2011). *I & I: The Natural Mystics: Marley, Tosh and Wailer*. Jonathan Cape.

Green, T. (2019). *A Fistful of Shells – West Africa from the Rise of the Slave Trade to the Age of Revolution*. Penguin.

Haley, A. & X, M. (1965). *The Autobiography of Malcolm X*. Grove Press.

Hall, S. (1983). Thatcherism — Rolling Back the Welfare State. *Thesis Eleven, 7*(1), 6–19. doi:10.1177/072551368300700102

Hall, S. (1990). Cultural Identity and Diaspora. In J. Rutherford (Ed.), Identity, Community, Culture, Difference (pp. 222-237). Lawrence & Wishart.

Hall, S. (1998). Aspiration and Attitude...Reflections on Black Britain in the Nineties. *New Formations: Frontlines/Backyards, 33*, 38.

Hosley, B. (2008). *Routes of Remembrance: Refashioning the Slave Trade in Ghana*. University of Chicago Press.

Kaye, G. (1987). *Comfort Herself*. Heinemann Educational.

Konadu, K. (2010). *Adinto: Akan Naming and Outdooring Ceremony*. http://www.afropedea.org/adinto-akan-naming-and-outdooring-ceremony

Lewis, K., & Demie, F. (2019). The School Experiences of Mixed Race White and Black Caribbean children in England. Department of Educational Studies, Goldsmiths (University of London) and School of Education, University of Durham. doi:10.1 080/01419870.2018.1519586

WorldM. (2002). https://mancala.fandom.com/wiki/Oware

Manning, P. (2009). *The African Diaspora: History Through Culture*. Columbia University Press.

McClean, M. (2019). *From the Middle Passage to Black Lives Matter: Ancestral Writing as a Pedagogy of Hope*. Peter Lang.

McIntyre, N., Parveen, N., & Thomas, T. (2021). Exclusion rates five times higher for black Caribbean pupils in parts of England. *The Guardian*. /education/2021/mar/24/exclusion-rates-black-caribbean-pupils-england#:~:text=Wokingham%20 reported%20the%20largest%20disparity,than%20the%20white%20British%20rate

McMillan, M. (2008). The 'West Indian' front room: Reflections on a diasporic phenomenon. *Kunapipi*, *30*(2).

Miller, K. (2014). *The Cartographer Tries to Map a Way to Zion*. Carcanet Press.

Moss, A. G. K. (2021a). *This is the Drum*. The Decolonial Passage.

Moss, A. G. K. (2021c). MLE. In R. Acharya (Ed.), An anthology by Wingless Dreamer, BIPOC Issue. Academic Press.

Moss, A. G. K. (2022). *Nicked Names*. RoseyRavelston Books.

Murdoch, Y., Hyejung, L., & Kang, A. (2018). Learning Students' Given Names Benefits EMI Classes. *English in Education, 52*(3), 225-247.

des Civilisations de Côte d'IvoireM. (2022) Musée des Civilisations de Côte d'Ivoire

National Museums Scotland. (2022). https://www.nms.ac.uk/explore-our-collections/stories/global-arts-cultures-and-design/gold-weights-from-ghana/

O'Brien, M., Leiman, T., & Duffy, J. (2014). The Power of Naming: The Multifaceted Value of Learning Students' Names. *QUT Law Review, 14*(1), 114-128.

Pelton, R. D. (1989). *Trickster in West Africa: A Study of Mythic Irony and Sacred Delight*. University of California Press.

Perera, J. (2020). *How Black Working-Class Youth are Criminalised and Excluded in the English School System*. Academic Press.

Phillips, C. (2002). A New World Order, selected essays. Vintage.

Pratt, M. L. (1999). Arts of the Contact Zone. In D. Bartholomae & A. Petrosky (Eds.), Ways of Reading (5th ed.) St. Martins.

Rattray, R. S. (1923). *Ashanti*. Clarendon Press.

Rattray, R. S. (1927). *Religion and Art in Ashanti*. Oxford University Press.

Riello, G. (2011). The object of fashion: Methodological approaches to the history. *Journal of Aesthetics & Culture*, *3*(1), 456–463. doi:10.3402/jac.v3i0.8865

Roberts, N & Bolton, P. (2020 October 8). *Education outcomes of Black pupils and students.* House of Commons Library Briefing Paper, Number 09023.

The British Museum. (2022). http://teachinghistory100.org/objects/about_the_object/akan_drum

Savage. (2018). Fifty years on, what is the legacy of Enoch Powell's 'rivers of blood' speech? *The Guardian*.

Yanka, K. (1983). *The Akan Trickster Cycle: Myth or Folk Tale?* Indian University: African Studies Program.

Zack-Williams, A. B., & Uduku, O. (2004). African Diaspora – African development concerns: An Introduction. In O. Uduku & A. B. Zack-Williams (Eds.), *Africa Beyond the Post-colonial: Political and Social Identities* (pp. 1–19). Ashgate Publishing Limited.

Zarembka, J. (2007). *The Pigment of Your Imagination: 'Mixed Race' in a Global Society*. Madera Press.

Zobel Marshall, E. (2012). *Anansi's Journey: A Story of Jamaican Cultural Resistance*. University Press of the West Indies.

Chapter 7
Everyone Wins:
The Mentoring of Black Students Into Science, Technology, Engineering, and Math (STEM) Programs

Christine Todd
Miami-Dade County Public Schools, USA

ABSTRACT

Countries, including the USA, are examining ways in which they can bring a high-quality program of Science, Technology, Engineering, and Math (STEM) to their youth in preparation for the role they must play in economic development. Black and Brown students are traditionally reported as lagging behind in academic performance, and there is concern that this status may lead to their exclusion from STEM programs and thus limit their ability to participate in a program that leads them to higher academic achievement with an inroad to higher education and higher financial rewards in a profession that is high yielding not only in the USA, but the across the globe. The chapter highlights how three mentoring programs support Black high school students to do STEM, including collaborations between STEM professionals and students, a summer camp, and an after-school program. It includes curricula to influence students' interest in STEM. Recommendations for program revisions include e-mentoring, hosting workshops in central locations, and incorporating reflections after workshops to improve session quality.

DOI: 10.4018/978-1-6684-7379-5.ch007

DEFINITIONS

Under-resourced is defined as not provided with as much money or as many staff, materials, etc. as are needed. Macmillan Dictionary defines under-resourced as without enough money or equipment to operate effectively. Under-resourced is described in context as schools that lack staff, materials, and money to engage in extra-curricular activities in Science, Technology, Engineering, and Math (STEM). STEM Professionals are individuals that have or are in pursuit of a doctorate or graduate degree in STEM or hold a STEM job.

PROBLEM

The statistics reporting on educational outcomes in the USA continue to reveal the disparity between the performance of Black, White, and Latino students. Researchers including Gloria Ladson Billings (2021), have noted that students under-perform or fail in school because they are not effectively taught or embraced into the learning environment with high expectations of their abilities to do well. Secondary students in under-resourced schools in Southeastern Florida have historically less participation in STEM enrichment activities that will lead them to STEM majors and careers in comparison to students in schools with established STEM programs.

BACKGROUND TO THE PROBLEM

As a STEM educator teaching in the public school system for almost thirty years, I have witnessed students identified as failing by standardized tests, rise up and achieve highly when the curriculum is organized and delivered in such a manner where their funds of knowledge are acknowledged and brought center into the curriculum (Sleeter, 2008). Where their special needs, circumstances, and characteristics are taken into consideration and especially when the time is taken to mentor them and guide them through the different stages right through into academic success, they rise up and achieve. This study focuses on Black students in under-resourced schools and communities (also identified as low socio-economic schools) who participated in three different STEM programs where they were mentored and monitored towards the attainment of academic success. It is particularly important for Black, Indigenous, and all students of color (BIPOC) to be given the opportunity to receive an education that exposes them to the field of STEM as it is the fastest growing area of education and one that has high demands for graduates in this field and one that pays high incomes for these professionals.

Industries in Science, Technology, Engineering, and Mathematics (STEM) have enriched the economy of the United States because the country's economic wellbeing depends on STEM industries. The U.S. Department of Commerce, STEM Jobs, 2017 Update reported that skills attained through STEM, such as critical thinking, creative problem-solving, and technological processes are highly prized skills in very high-level jobs. These high-level jobs tend to be reward employees with advanced salaries that may be the gateway to a financially secure standard of living and thus, upward mobility.

This researcher asserts that students who attend under-resourced schools are at risk of being excluded from STEM based programs as these schools, typically located in low socio- economic status (SES) neighborhoods, often do not provide the required curricula. In keeping with the demand for social justice and equity in schools, this chapter puts forth research that demonstrates ways in which teachers may respond to this inequity and provide STEM programs and activities in under-resourced schools and engage students in such a manner that sustains their participation and high academic achievement in STEM.

As the research demonstrates, students who enter STEM programs at an early age, are quite likely to continue their participation right through to graduation, especially if they are nurtured and mentored throughout the grades. This may direct them to choose these fields as their majors in college and their careers (U.S. Department of Commerce, STEM Jobs, 2017 Update).

Reports by the U.S. Department of Commerce, (2017) showed that STEM jobs had increased to 6.6% of all jobs since 2015 and that growth of STEM jobs will increase more than 2.5% than non-STEM jobs between 2014 to 2024. STEM workers will demand 29% higher salaries and have more degreed people than non-STEM workers. STEM jobs were critical in the battle against COVID -19. U.S. Bureau of Labor Statistics projects that there will be more than 1,000,000 STEM jobs added throughout the 2020's according to the 2021 STEM Job Growth Index. (Logan, et.al, 2021). These data points indicate that youth in under-resourced schools need to acquire continuous knowledge and skills in STEM in order to meet the growing demands of the workplace and to affect the nation's economy positively. In particular, mentoring by STEM professionals to support under-resourced high school students to do quality research and compete in national and international STEM competitions is key.

Policy makers and researchers have addressed the need to maintain the flow of K-12 students into STEM related majors in order that they may pursue careers in these highly regarded areas. The government of the USA has indicated the importance of preparing the nation's students for careers in STEM programs especially as this field is one of high competition across the globe (U.S. Department of Education). In keeping with the national call for social justice and equity in education, it is extremely important that Black students are not deprived of the opportunity to participate simply because the schools they attend are under-resourced and do not provide these programs at their sites (Smedley, 2001).

In support of the need to increase Black students' interests in STEM are international statistics which indicate that today's U.S. students are not prepared today nor are they ready to meet future demands, (TIMSS, 2019; PISA, 2018). For instance, Trends in International Mathematics and Science Study has shown that United States 8th grade students have not made any significant difference in knowing and reasoning in science and declined in mathematics in 2011- 2019. Additionally, PISA scores have shown that there was no significant difference in scientific and mathematical literacy in 2013- 2018. The implication is that the U.S.'s global leadership is in danger. To change the direction, the United States must put more effort on K-12 students to enter STEM fields (Sahin, 2013). Within the school district being researched, there is 13% Black students, 49% White students, 30% Hispanic students, and 8% other students. Of the Black secondary students, less than 5% submit projects to the regional science and engineering fair.

RESEARCH REVIEW

Educational theorist, Gloria Ladson Billings, claims that the answer to why African American are not successful in the classroom is that they are culturally deprived. Billings asserts that teachers share a set of beliefs that drive their teaching and represents the foundation of culturally relevant pedagogy. Teachers' beliefs about themselves and others, about how to structure social relations, and the nature of knowledge help them to improve student learning and cultivate cultural competence. To attain cultural responsiveness, there must be a relationship between home/community culture and school culture (Ladson-Billings, 1995).

Successful examples of cultural congruence within small -scale communities include Native Americans and Native Hawaiians. However, there has been a mismatch between language patterns of African Americans, the school, and history of African American educational success. To promote academic success and maximize learning for African American students, it is necessary to have cultural synchronization between teachers and African American students. Analysis of teacher-student interpersonal contexts, teacher and student expectations, institutional contexts, and societal contexts is used to develop educational interventions. The next step is to develop effective pedagogical practices that address student achievement and help students to accept their cultural identity, hence the term culturally relevant pedagogy (Ladson-Billings, 1995).

Factors Influencing Interest in STEM

Based on the Social Cognitive Career Theory (SCCT), four crucial factors that affect STEM careers are environmental factors, STEM self-efficacy, perception of STEM careers and interest in STEM careers. Environmental factors include activities in the classroom, activities outside the classroom, social influences, and media influences. STEM activities will be supported in the classroom where teaching and learning strategies develop skills needed in STEM fields. Such curricula include hands on activities, problem solving strategies, science content associated with everyday life applications, cooperative learning, investigative activities, and groupwork (Halim et al., 2018).

Activities outside the classroom include "science field work, science camps, learning in science centers, museums, zoos, robotics competitions, clubs related to STEM activities, and interviews with scientists." Informal STEM education can prove very beneficial to students. Mentoring by STEM professionals is one such example. When activities are infused with fun and engaging strategies, students tend to respond, often applying mathematics and science process, and building strong confidence to continue participation in STEM programs. Parents, teachers, friends, counselors, and other role models will have a tremendous influence on students' participation in these programs when they work to motivate students and guide them not only to participate but to achieve highly in these endeavors. This form of guidance plays an important role in building students' self-efficacy or the belief in their own abilities. In my research process, it became clear that self-efficacy increased when parents and teachers stressed the importance of STEM. Parental attitudes directly affect students career choices. Teacher quality and expectations also affect their perceptions of students to engage in STEM subject areas. Most counselors are not from a STEM background and do not have expertise in STEM, therefore may not steer students into STEM (Halim et al., 2018). All doorkeepers of STEM research and programs should all be versed in guidelines for entry into such programs.

Media sources also influence students' interest in STEM and STEM careers. Such media may include the internet, newspapers, popular scientific magazines, books, movies, and science-related programs on television. These are quick ways to disseminate the benefits of STEM, by providing fun activities and exploration. In addition, interviews with STEM professionals about STEM jobs affected students' interest in STEM (Halim et al., 2018).

The perception of STEM careers and interest in STEM careers will also affect a person's desire to pursue activities, majors in college and careers in STEM. Perceptions of careers refers to what people think about related to job prospects and skills needed for STEM fields. "Job prospects in STEM fields include the working environment in terms of safety, job satisfaction, perception of STEM as a prestigious career, high employment opportunities, higher income, and contribution to society. Basic skills to be mastered in careers related to STEM fields are higher order thinking skills, creative problem-solving skills, teamwork, as well as constructing, designing and repairing things" (Halim et al., 2018). STEM careers involve concepts of science, technology, engineering, and mathematics. Skills necessary to perform STEM are research, application of concepts, producing new ideas, and contributing to innovation and economic development (Halim et al., 2018).

There is a reciprocal relationship between STEM professionals and youth gained through mentoring. In a study by Nelson et al., (2017), undergraduate STEM mentors reflected about their experiences. The reflections were used to inform the design of mentoring programs to ensure academic benefit for mentors and mentees. "In this way, prompts for reflection after teaching will promote active monitoring, evaluating and modifying (of) one's thinking to help undergraduate mentors make sense of the experience, problem solve, and adapt to different teaching (and learning) environments" (pg.2). Additionally, promoting self-evaluation after mentoring can encourage the undergraduate student to consider both their own content knowledge and how to best support younger students in life science lessons (Nelson et al., 2017).

Students, especially those in under-resourced school require mentors to increase their skills to do STEM. Tenenbaum, S. et al. (2014) described a similar study to Nelson et al. (2017) involving a near-peer mentor, an undergraduate or post-baccalaureate student who mentors middle and high school students in a mathematics and science program. The mentors introduce inquiry-based STEM modules to the students, offer educational and career guidance, build supportive relationships with their mentees, and encourage students to pursue their goals. This study uses strategies described by Tenenbaum, S. et al. (2014) to equip students attend schools that are under-resourced.

According to Tenenbaum et al. (2014), mentoring youth ignited personal growth and development of participants. Even mentees are benefited from mentoring by growing and maturing as professionals, teachers, and scientists. Participants increased maturation in professional expectations, the importance of learning to be adaptable, subject area knowledge, oral and written language skills that all contributed to career development. (Tenenbaum et al., 2014). Table 1 lists various activities and experiences that children at all stages can indulge in to establish interests in STEM.

Funk (2022) reported from government analysis that Black people continue to be underrepresented in STEM jobs and there has been minimal change in college graduates getting into STEM training programs in over a decade. When asked what would help attract Black students to STEM fields, a majority of Black people said it would be to see more examples of higher achievers in those areas. "Compared to other professions, fewer Black adults see people of their race at highest levels of success in science, engineering." In addition, Black Americans rated scientists and engineers low as professional groups that are welcoming of Blacks (Funk, 2022).

Table 1. What parents and their children can do to establish interests in STEM

Developmental Stage	Activities
Parents	• Be a positive role model! • Focus on the fun of learning new adventures or investigations! • Encourage curiosity and problem solving!
Early childhood	• Get outside and explore the natural setting • Observe the stars, insects, the weather, backyard birds, and changing colors of leaves • Learn through science centers • Grow vegetables and flowering plants • Visit museums and zoos • Read books about nature
Middle childhood	• Participate in Citizen Science Projects, such as beach clean up • Participate in youth, afterschool, and out of school time programs • Take care of a pet • Participate in STEM clubs and activities at school - science fairs, SECME, robotics club, Math Challenge Team
Older adolescence	• Tinker with computer apps • Create podcasts and videos • Speak with STEM professionals about their careers • Research world problem and develop solutions through engineering and science field work • Participate in science camps and robotics competitions • Be mentored by a STEM professional • Conduct research under the supervision of STEM professionals at a university

According to Funk (2022), Black high school graduates recalled positive experience in STEM classes, but also recall mistreatment. The report indicated that 39% of high school graduates experienced negative treatment, such as being treated as if they couldn't understand, made to feel like they don't belong, and receiving negative comments about their race. Deliberate efforts are needed to repair the shoddy pipeline of minority students in STEM. "Change begins by recognizing the fields of influence in a situation and identifying the points at which there are "gatekeepers" that impede the flow of change in a system" (Estrada et al., 2016). Black students must be fostered into learning and applying STEM concepts through research and experimentation. Once interested, Black students will benefit from the increasing career opportunities and salaries in STEM.

Studies by Sahin (2013) and Sahini and Onder (2014) described the direct relationship between students' STEM after school clubs and science fair participation and their college STEM major choice. The impact that science fairs and exhibits had on elementary through high school students was great. Schools outperformed the national average in terms of post-secondary admissions and STEM majors' selections when students participated in annual science fairs, including underrepresented groups such as African American, females, and economically disadvantaged students. In turn, students who attended STEM after school clubs had a higher percentage of post-secondary matriculation in STEM majors than the national average implicating that engaging students with STEM-related clubs from earlier years of their education cultivates STEM interest in students to pursue STEM careers.

Mentoring students increases self-confidence and interest for student participation in science fairs. Sahini and Onder (2014) conducted a study to determine the impacts of the science exhibition on secondary school student researchers in charge in Turkey. Students participated in science fairs in which the experimental design, results and procedures of projects in biology, chemistry and physics were presented to the public. In the study, teachers were responsible to organize the science fair but only interacted with students, to help with experiments discussion if necessary (Sahini and Onder, 2014).

The impact of the science exhibition on secondary school student researchers was determined by responses to interviews. Interviews from students revealed major positive emotions that were categorized as communication, experience, awareness, and knowledge. Students reported that communication was positive, especially with friends and that they enjoyed communication next with other visitors of the science fair, and then with teachers and family. Other experiences that contributed to positive emotions/skills were due to having a good time, being curious, controlling the excitement, feeling himself/herself be important, being aware of the responsibilities and being aware of his/her own deficiencies/faults. Obtaining new information, applying the new information, and remembering the old information also generated positive emotions for students (Sahini and Onder, 2014). Similarly, the Society for Science and the Public, governing bodies of International Science and Engineering Fair, recommend that students learn, grow, and connect at STEM competitions to gain their greatest benefits from the experiences (Society for Science and the Public, 2019).

The interviews with students in the study by Sahini and Onder (2014) also revealed the major negative emotions that were related to deficiencies from teachers including lack of coordination, losing students' passions, obligations, and giving difficult topics to students. The audience impacted students negatively due to negative reactions of the guests, and unreactive reactions of the guests. Negative emotions were also related to environmental conditions and students' lack of interest to each other (Sahini and Onder, 2014). Having conversations with science fair coordinators and teachers about stimuli to affect students' emotions can impact students' overall experiences at science fairs.

RESEARCH DESIGN

The chapter describes three mentoring programs developed and initiated by STEM professionals and launched through STEM professionals mentoring program, summer STEM program, and an after-school STEM program. The research will show that when students have STEM mentors and opportunities to explicitly practice with STEM activities, they become interested in the STEM fields.

I utilized a qualitative research design to gain perceptions of how mentoring programs through STEM professionals affect Black students. Students at under-resourced schools are disadvantaged by not having mentors to assist them in developing research that will benefit them in competing in national and international science fairs, winning scholarships to universities and programs, and strengthening their confidence and passion for STEM fields.

Three STEM mentoring programs were developed in Waterside for the secondary students ranging from grades six through twelve. A program to connect under-resourced secondary students with STEM professionals was specifically developed for students in the central region of Waterside School District that had the majority of under-resourced schools and lowest participation of all Waterside regions. STEM professionals engaged students through TED Talks about their research and then collaborated with students to develop their individual research ideas into projects that would be submitted to the regional science and engineering fair. Additionally, a summer STEM camp was developed for secondary students in a Waterside neighborhood that is populated largely with Black and Hispanic students. Mentors engaged students through robotics and other STEM hands on activities. Last, students in secondary science courses were trained to do science research while in virtual classrooms. The students received structured lessons to develop a science and engineering project that were later submitted to the regional science and engineering fair competition.

OBSERVATIONS

Scientific Research Saturdays Program (SRS)

High school students from the Central region of Waterside School District lack skills, developed through guidance and mentoring, necessary to conduct research and present research competitively at local, state, and international science fairs because of their limited opportunities to collaborate with STEM professionals. This was evidenced by the central region historically submitting significantly less projects to the regional science and engineering fair. As a result of the problem with the high school students, the Scientific Research Saturdays (SRS) program was developed and implemented for students in the Central region of the Waterside School district. The intent of the program was to connect the students at the under-resourced schools to STEM professionals from local higher education institutions to collaborate about students' research ideas and to develop competitive research projects. The goal for students was to complete projects for submission to compete at local schools, District, State and International science and engineering fairs.

The process to develop the SRS program began with planning meetings between community enthusiasts interested in equity for students to do research and the members of the science department at the school district. Members of the committee planned outreach to high school students, marketing schedules, program logistics, STEM professional selection process and expectations, and program deliverables. Deliberate effort was taken to ensure students' safety therefore students met with STEM professionals exclusively at the events sponsored by the school District rather than with STEM professional at their work locations.

Outreach and Marketing Schedule: Outreach to high school students were made through invitations to teachers for professional development. Invitations were formally sent through a District weekly briefing to secondary schools sent directly to principals, assistant principals, and teachers and was followed up through monthly emails to science fair coordinators. Science fair coordinators were asked to inform secondary students interested in conducting research in STEM areas of the SRS program. The emails were attached with a flyer intended for students and teachers, registration links for students and teachers to attend, and directions for teachers to receive master plan points for participation in the workshops. Invitations to participate in SRS were later extended to high school students across all regions and then middle school students across all regions based on low numbers of registrants for the first SRS session.

Logistics: Three SRS workshops were held in two locations of the district, one in the north region of the county at a local community college and the other in the central region of the county at a major university. SRS workshops were held twice at the north location and once at the central location. Sessions were held once monthly from 9AM to 12PM every second Saturday for 3 consecutive months. The SRS workshops coincided with the schedule of student research being done at local schools to compete at the Regional Science and Engineering Fair.

STEM Professional Selection Process and Expectations: STEM professionals were invited by the community liaison and District Science department to the program. The members were affiliated to various local and national universities and organizations. STEM professionals were mainly PhDs and graduate students and consisted of few professors and community leaders. STEM professionals were selected based on peer associations and invitations by professors to graduate students at host universities. STEM professionals' research represented science fair categories and they were open to present to students based on their own styles. Expectations of the mentors were to engage students with 3-minute TED talks of their research, offer research ideas based on their topics, and hold individual or small group collaborations with students to assist with the development of students' research projects.

Program Deliverables: Specific deliverables were set for each workshop and escalated to students' finished research projects.

Session 1: Students will identify research topics, questions, and experimental designs.
Session 2: Students will refine experimental designs and data collection processes.
Session 3: Students will discuss data collected, results, ways to showcase data, and practice presentation skills.

Results and Findings of SRS Program Implementation

The outcome of the program was successful in supporting 10% of the focus students in the Central region, however, it was anticipated that a greater number of students would participate. The targeted high school students from the Central region represented only 10 percent of the students that participated in the SRS program overall. The majority participation was from non-targeted high school students (44%) and middle school students (46%).

The targeted high school students only attended the session which was in the Central region of the Waterside school district. This may be because the location was closer to their homes or that they were attracted to the major university. SRS attendance was highest at the session in the central location at a major university. One student travelled from the opposite end of the county to participate in the last session held in the north of the county. Parents of the students expressed gratitude, however, were dismayed by the long commute to the north location and requested more sessions in central and south areas.

The ratio of STEM professionals to students was adequate for all sessions, 1 : 2 on average. STEM professionals were more numerous and shared research representing more science fair categories in the central location at a major university. Six STEM professionals from the host university in the central location presented their work in chemistry. This may have been due to the convenience of being affiliated to the host university. Additional STEM professionals traveled from out of state to participate at the major university. Table 2 shows numbers of participants at the Scientific Research Saturday program. The number of focus students who participated in the program from the central region was significantly less.

Table 2. Numbers of participants at the scientific research saturday program

SRS Session	# of Students	# of Students From Central Region	# of HS Students	# of MS Students	# of STEM Professionals	# of Teachers
1. North	15	0	10	5	6	8
2. Central	73	9	37	36	13	8
3. North	1	0	1	0	6	5
Total	89	9	48	41	25	21

The content presented by STEM professionals was current and addressed community needs. Both students and teachers asked several questions after the presentations. Students connected with STEM professionals that their project ideas aligned with or that were most interesting to them during the workshops. During the second round of collaborations, students met with other STEM professionals to gain insight on how to further improve their experimental designs, data collection, and analysis processes. Both teachers and students expressed satisfaction for the help that they had received during the sessions.

Student responses to the STEM professionals TED Talks were also consistent. When STEM professionals discussed their research starting with the needs and problems that they tried to address and held interactive presentations involving students, students seemed more focused and asked more questions. When presentations surpassed 3 minutes, did not present the need or applications that were understood by the audience, were not interactive, students lost focus, which was evidenced by them using phones, looking around, and paying attention to the timekeeper. Inconsistencies with the format of presentations by STEM professionals affected the expected program outcome and responses by students. STEM professionals were initially directed to give 3-minute TED talks, however, could surpass the time sometimes by 2 minutes. Presentations mostly encompassed topics in biology and chemistry instead of the intended variety of categories represented at the local, national, and international science fairs. The level of interactivity with the audience varied greatly with STEM professionals. The program did not include reflective feedback by STEM professionals that would have been necessary to address subsequent SRS sessions or to develop themselves professionally.

STEM professionals must lead students to act in the world by solving real problems. As such, resources such as local international newspapers and journal are used to identify the problem needing to be addressed. Tables 3- 5 identify guidelines to leading students to do competitive research. Tables 6-9 provide components of science and engineering research projects and steps to organizing a school science

Table 3. Guidelines to leading students to do competitive research

Make OBSERVATIONS Passions	Identify your absolute interest and passion! Topics must be of significant value, address real-world problems, fill in gaps in science or engineering research or brings something new to the field, and be of solid science, sound methodology, and have significant applications. • What are your recreational, social, personal, educational, and vocational passions?
Make OBSERVATIONS World problems	Make an observation of the current world problems of interest through reading newspapers and magazines • What are current world problems of interest? o Education, environment, food security and agriculture, health, shelter, water, and sanitation o Climate change / destruction of nature- deforestation, ozone layer, depletion, water pollution, air pollution, loss of biodiversity o Hunger, mental health, energy consumption
Develop the BIG QUESTION!	• What is the problem in the field? • What has motivated the field to discuss the problem? • What is evidence of the problem? • What are you trying to solve? • Why are you trying to solve this problem?
Research - BIG QUESTION	Research the work being done in the field to answer the BIG QUESTION 1. What do experts in the field say? 2. Identify limitations of the work done 3. Identify work needing to be done, according to field 4. Be concise 5. Include 5 or more sources in reference list, using APA format
RESEARCH QUESTION	Develop a specific research question. What are you trying to answer with your experiment?
Hypothesis	Research answers to the research question and form hypothesis. Explain what is known or has already been done about the research question. • Identify the hypotheses, including null hypothesis, if appropriate • Hypothesis-proposed explanation made based on limited evidence as a starting point for further investigation. • Null Hypothesis- (in a statistical test) the hypothesis that there is no significant difference between specified populations • Is your hypothesis TESTABLE? • Is it experimental? • Do you have enough time? • Can you access the appropriate facility to conduct your experiment? • Do you have access to the necessary materials and equipment? • Include your variables within the hypothesis- independent and dependent • For example: Sleep-deprived people will perform worse on a test than individuals who are not sleep-deprived.
Methodology- Your Approach	Indicate the following: • Quantitative/ qualitative approach • Sample size (10 or 10,000?) • Control group and variables tested • Repeated trials • Materials with specific quantities, time • What data will you collect and how will you collect that data? • Tables, graphs, figures, photos, logbook Draw a diagram for the experiment- Is it replicable?
Variables	Identify Variables • Independent • Dependent • Control • Constants
Data Analysis/ Results and Interpretations	Data Analysis/ Results • Write one or more paragraphs to summarize your data • Include figures and tables which illustrate your data • Do the results answer the problem statement? • Include relevant statistical analysis of the data. Interpretation of Results • How do your results compare with theories, published data, and expected results? • Use words "significant" and "non-significant" as necessary • Discuss possible errors. • Did any questions or problems arise that you were not expecting? • How did the data vary between repeated observations of similar events? • How were results affected by uncontrolled events?

continued on following page

Table 3. continued

Conclusions	• What do you think the results mean in the context of the literature review and other work being done in your research area? • How do the results address your research question? • Do your results support your hypothesis? • What are weaknesses in the experiment? • Did you miss anything in doing the experiment? • What are next steps to the study? • What application(s) do you see for your work?

Table 4. Example #1 of a developed big question

Source: Meszaros, J. 2021., Tampa Bay Algae Blooms Could Be Fed By Piney Point Wastewater, The Florida Roundup WUSF Public Media - WUSF 89.7, https://wusfnews.wusf.usf.edu/environment/2021-06-11/tampa-bay-algae-blooms-could-be-fed-by-piney-point-wastewater

1. What is the problem in the field?
• Tampa Bay is experiencing multiple algae blooms
• More than 200 million gallons of nutrient-rich wastewater was dumped near where algae blooms are found.
2. What has motivated the field to discuss the problem?
• Scientists think nutrients, such as nitrogen, from the spill are feeding the algae blooms.
3. What is evidence of the problem?
• There are red tide and other algae blooms floating in Joe Bay, Anna Maria Sound, and just north of Port Manatee
• Algae blooms are in the vicinity of the place where more than 200 tons of nitrogen were discharged over the period of 10 days.
• Excessive rain causes increased nutrients in the Bay
• Fish kills
4. What are you trying to solve?
• Reducing the amount of nitrogen fertilizer being used in the rainy season
5. Why are you trying to solve this problem?
• Nitrogen fertilizer will feed the algae blooms when they run off into bay.
6. Sample BIG QUESTIONS:
• How do we use less nitrogen rich fertilizers?
• How do we prevent nitrogen run off to maintain the bay using buffer crops?
• How does the presence of nitrogen affect the growth of microorganisms?
• How does nutrient pollution cause optimal conditions for algae blooms?
7. Sample research questions
• How do buffer crops affect runoff of nitrogen fertilizer?
• How does the presence of nitrogen/ salt affect the growth of microorganisms?

and engineering fair. Students become effective problem solvers when these steps are taken.

Summer Science, Technology, Engineering, Art, and Mathematics (STEAM) Camp

A free summer STEAM camp was developed in the Miami Gardens, Florida to attract Black students to participate. The camp location was on a church ground but had no connection to the camp. The location was deliberately chosen because it was within proximity to communities with majority of African American residents. The

Table 5. Example #2 of a developed big question

Source: Visser, N. 2021. Surgeon General Portends Return Of Mask Mandates Amid COVID-19 Surges, https://www.huffpost.com/entry/surgeon-general-masks-los-ang
eles_n_60f4f57be4b0b2a04a254f8f
1. What is the problem in the field?
• Public health officials have warned that unvaccinated Americans are particularly vulnerable.
• Surgeon General reported that tech companies fail to rein in anti-vaccination posts from social media giants that have "enabled misinformation" about being unvaccinated
2. What has motivated the field to discuss the problem?
• The delta variant is highly transmissible and already accounts for a majority of the new cases in the U.S.
3. What is evidence of the problem?
• There is a surge of case linked to more transmissible variants of the coronavirus.
• According to The New York Times, new coronavirus cases have soared 140% in the past two weeks. And less than half of the country is fully vaccinated.
• Almost all of the nation's current coronavirus deaths are among people who were not vaccinated.
4. What are you trying to solve?
• Increase the numbers of students to become vaccinated
5. Why are you trying to solve this problem?
• With more people vaccinated, there will be less transmission of the COVID virus and less death and illnesses
6. Sample BIG QUESTION
• How does the information on social media affect human behavior?
7. Sample research question:
• How can a system identify a post as factual or not, needing censorship, or concerning?

organizers expected 50 students, however, received 16 throughout the three-week program. Seven students were in the elementary level and nine students were in the secondary school level. Workign with the secondary students were five high school counselors. Camp counselors assisted campers STEM and recreational activities. Two of the counselors were proficient in robotics. Twelve students were Black and four were Hispanic. Both camp supervisors were experienced Science, Technology, Engineering, Art, and Mathematics (STEAM)educators.

The curriculum was centered around robotics (technology), and included science, engineering, art, and mathematics. Each week was preplanned to include various STEAM activities.

Sample STEAM Curriculum for Summer Stem Camp

- **Science Activities:** Seeds for Hunger (planting vegetable seeds), Lava lamps, Rainfall in a Bottle, yeast test
- **Technology Activities:** Vex activities
- **Engineering Activities:** Build Your Dream Home, research engineering careers, Marshmallow Tower, Parachute Challenge-softest landing, Egg Drop Challenge, Aviation engineering, Aeronautical engineering rockets
- **Art Activities:** T-shirt design
- **Mathematics Activities:** Measure to scale, data collection and graphing data

Table 6. Project presentation template: Science project

INTRODUCTION What is your research question?	Explain what is known or has already been done in your research area. Include a brief review of relevant literature. If this is a continuation project, a summary of your prior research is appropriate here. Be sure to distinguish your previous work from this year's project. What were you trying to find out? Include a description of your purpose, your research question, and/or your hypothesis.
METHODS Explain your methodology and procedures for carrying out your project in detail.	What did you do? What data did you collect and how did you collect that data? Discuss your control group and the variables you tested. DO NOT include a list of materials.
RESULTS What were the result(s) of your project?	Include tables and figures which illustrate your data. Include relevant statistical analysis of the data.
DISCUSSION What is your interpretation of these results?	What do these results mean? Compare your results with theories, published data, commonly held beliefs, and expected results. Discuss possible errors. Did any questions or problems arise that you were not expecting? How did the data vary between repeated observations of similar events? How were results affected by uncontrolled events?
CONCLUSIONS What conclusions did you reach?	What do these results mean in the context of the literature review and other work being done in your research area? How do the results address your research question? Do your results support your hypothesis? What application(s) do you see for your work?
REFERENCES	This section should not exceed one page. Limit your list to the most important references. List the references/documentation used which were not of your own creation (i.e., books, journal articles).

The camp environment fostered friendship and mutual respect through morning ice breakers, sports and outdoor games, and local field trips. Campers' enthusiasm grew over the three weeks. None of the Black campers had experienced robotics before arriving, however, could explain the process of building and operating the robots to parents at the Parent Showcase. Parents were also impressed by the degree of knowledge that their children attained and articulated. They were delighted that students looked forward to attending each day.

AFTER-SCHOOL STEM CAMP

An after-school STEM program is facilitated at a Waterside Dade middle School. The population of the school is racially, ethnically, and linguistically diverse. The STEM program is held on one day, Monday immediately after school each week,

Table 7. Project presentation template: Engineering project

INTRODUCTION What is your engineering problem and goal?	What problem were you trying to solve? Include a description of your engineering goal. Explain what is known or has already been done to solve this problem, including work on which you may build. You may include a brief review of relevant literature. If this is a continuation project, a summary of your prior work is appropriate here. Be sure to distinguish your previous work from this year's project.
METHODS Explain your methods and procedures for building your design.	What did you do? How did you design and produce your prototype? If there is a physical prototype, you may want to include pictures or designs of the prototype. If you tested the prototype, what were your testing procedures? What data did you collect and how did you collect that data? DO NOT include a separate list of materials.
RESULTS What were the result(s) of your project?	How did your prototype meet your engineering goal? If you tested the prototype, provide a summary of testing data tables and figures that illustrate your results. Include relevant statistical analysis of the data.
DISCUSSION What is your interpretation of these results?	What do these results mean? You may compare your results with theories, published data, commonly held beliefs, and/or expected results. Did any questions or problems arise that you were not expecting? Were these problems caused by uncontrolled events? How did you address these? How is your prototype an improvement or advancement over what is currently available?
CONCLUSIONS What conclusions did you reach?	Did your project turn out as you expected? What application(s) do you see for your work?
REFERENCES	This section should not exceed one page. Limit your list to the most important references. List the references/documentation used which were not of your own creation (i.e., books, journal articles).

and is attended by 27- 30 students who attend the middle school. There is one White-Hispanic participant and the remaining are African Americans.

The curriculum is centered around STEM activities and resembles the summer curriculum previously discussed. There is a point system to manage behaviors and allow healthy competition. Interactions with students indicate that they look forward to Mondays when they engage with STEM through the after-school program. Each session is centered around key science concept(s) that is applied through hands on activities. Students rush into the cafetorium to greet the facilitators, ask what they will be doing, and offer to help setting up stations. Further evidence of students' desire to learn STEM concepts are seen by their attempts to ask questions and answer questions, to volunteer to do new things, and by their overall enthusiasm.

Table 8. Project presentation template: Mathematics/computer science

INTRODUCTION What is your research question?	Explain what is known or has already been done in your research area. Include a brief review of relevant literature. Explain what is known or has already been done in your research area. Include a brief review of relevant literature. If this is a continuation project, a summary of your prior work is appropriate here. Be sure to distinguish your previous work from this year's project.
FRAMEWORK Notation and framework.	Introduce the concepts and notation needed to specify your research question, methods, and results precisely. Define relevant terms and explain prior/background results. (Novel concepts developed as part of your project can be presented here or in Conclusions, as appropriate.)
FINDINGS Present your findings and supporting arguments	What did you discover and/or prove? Describe your result(s) in detail. If possible, provide both formal and intuitive/verbal explanations of each major finding. Describe your methods in general terms. Present rigorous proofs of the theory results – or, if the arguments are long, give sketches of the proofs that explain the main ideas. For numerical/statistical results, include tables and figures that illustrate your data. Include relevant statistical analysis. Were any of your results statistically significant? How do you know this?
CONCLUSIONS What is your assessment of your findings?	How do the results address your research question? And how have you advanced our understanding relative to what was already known? Discuss possible limitations. Did any questions or problems arise that you were not expecting? What challenges do you foresee in extending your results further? • What application(s), if any, do you see for your work?
REFERENCES	This section should not exceed one page. Limit your list to the most important references. List the references/documentation used which were not of your own creation (i.e., books, journal articles).

Sample Session for After-School STEM Camp

- Announcement of current team points, accumulated through group victories and participation
- Engaging hook to explain key science concept(s)
- Unscrambling of key words related to the concept of the day
- **Activity:** Each team will build a glider using a kit that is provided within 10 minutes. Teams will test the glider, then compete to see which glider will go the furthest distance. Distance will be measured using a tape measure.
- Teams will revise prototypes, share revisions with whole group, and repeat competition of furthest distance travelled.

Table 9. Guidelines to organizing a school science and engineering fair

Student preparation	Prepare students to develop experimental research Orient students to complete safety forms prior to experimentation Present rules for all projects, including ethics, scientific and fraud misconduct, eligibility and limitations, research categories, approval and documentation, and continuation and team projects Provide research presentation styles and templates Provide time after school for mentoring
Teacher preparation	Establish Science Fair Coordinator Orient teachers to complete safety forms prior to experimentation Present guidelines for ethical experimental research Train teachers on the scientific method, including how to develop competitive topics Establish timeline for research and date for school science fair
Establish Safety Committees	Scientific Review Committee (SRC)/ Institutional Review Board (IRB) composed of a minimum of three persons, including at least: 1) a biomedical scientist (PhD, MD, DDS, DO, or DVM), 2) a science teacher, and 3) one other member. One of the members must be familiar with animal care procedures, when animal experimentation is involved. One member must be named Chairman; the SRC must be formed prior to the school's science and engineering fair.
Regional Competition	Register Science Fair Coordinator with regional science and engineering fair Register students in regional science and engineering fair (RSEF) Submit payments to RSEF
Grants	
Judging	Solicit judges for school science and engineering fair Develop a judge's handbook and train judges Provide judges their assignments and schedule Have 2 rounds of judging for participants
Awards	Purchase trophies for top research projects
School Science and Engineering Fair	Create program for event

FINDINGS

Deliberate efforts to connect students in under-resourced schools to STEM professionals will increase Black students' skills to do participate in STEM programs, to conduct research, and to select majors and careers in STEM. Estrada et al. (2016) strategy to evaluate, diagnose, plan action, take action, and re-evaluate should be employed to cause change to ensure that minorities do not slip through holes of the STEM pipeline to enjoy and benefit from STEM degrees and careers. Gatekeepers of the plan including STEM educators in K-12 and higher education should be knowledgeable of how to support under-resourced students into STEM worlds. Collaborations with STEM professionals will provide students guidance and mentoring needed to develop competitive science fair projects and confidence to pursue unthinkable objectives related to STEM.

The onus to establish equity in education continues to be on parents and educators. Parents need to search for opportunities to get their children interested in STEM. Educators need to work with professionals in STEM to build their own knowledge to help students more directly to develop skills to conduct research. Research skills are essential to success in college and support readiness for careers in STEM. Working directly with under-resourced students will increase their chance to engage in STEM opportunities and to be included as contributors of world problem solvers and forces that positively affect the nation's economy.

Strategies to Improve STEM Mentoring Programs

Mentoring for students at under-resourced schools is effective when geographic and time barriers are not of concern. During the Covid-19 pandemic, students were unable to attend brick and mortar schools and could not access live mentors. It became necessary to institute virtual mentors. The study by Ensher et al, (2003) identified electronic mentoring (e-mentoring) as a key strategy for supporting the retention, persistence, and graduation of underrepresented postsecondary students with disabilities in STEM majors. To have effective mentoring, multiple factors must be in place, including the purpose, the relationship between the mentor and the mentee, the consistency in the mentoring relationships and the mentoring objectives. The resulting advantages associated with e-mentoring include access to mentors and reduced cost, challenges to e-mentoring are difficulty communicating nonverbally, slower development of relationships, wide-range of written communications skills and technology barriers. The findings of the study were that mentors greatly affected the personal and academic lives of mentees. Mentees recognized strongest gains during the mentoring, including the development of trusting and supportive relationships, self -determination, and self -advocacy.

RECOMMENDATIONS

Plan for Revision of the Scientific Research Program (SRS)

A reevaluation of the SRS intervention program will be done to address the problem of low submissions of science and engineering fair projects by under resourced high school students as suggested Estrada et al. (2016) to cause change. The SRS program was successful in meeting the needs of students to develop science fair projects and to teach the process of research. However, the targeted group, high school students in the Central region of the district, had the lowest participation in comparison to students in the north and south regions. Another aspect that will be studied is ensuring that the potential gatekeepers of students into STEM get trained on how to make the process seamless.

Students will use e-mentoring processes if they have transportation problems to pursue mentoring. Such processes will include ZOOM, WhatsApp, Google meeting, and Facetime. These processes will ensure that students are independent to view presentations by STEM professionals and participate in workshops. For live sessions, the location for students will be within their community, for convenience to travel to the workshops.

Feedback sessions are essential for continuous improvement of the program. Feedback will be asked from all stakeholders, organizers, STEM professionals, and students. STEM professionals would internalize their experiences with participants to refine the later sessions efficiently and to develop themselves as researchers and community members. It would help to inform the group's knowledge of gaps in the teaching and learning in K-12 STEM research to address the gaps for undergraduate learners. Additional benefits of feedback sessions are to help STEM professionals and organizers adhere to implementation guidelines more consistently and to improve preparedness of STEM professionals.

REFERENCES

Estrada, M., Burnett, M., Campbell, A. G., Campbell, P. B., Denetclaw, W. F., Gutiérrez, C. G., ... Zavala, M. E. (2016). Improving underrepresented minority student persistence in stem. *CBE Life Sciences Education, 15*(3). doi:10.1187/cbe.16-01-0038

Gregg, N., Wolfe, G., Jones, S., Todd, R., Moon, N., & Langston, C. (2017). STEM E-Mentoring and Community College Students with Disabilities. *Career Development and Transition for Exceptional Individuals SAGE, 40*(4), 47–63.

Halim, L., Rahman, N., Wahab, N., & Mohtar, L. (2018). Factors influencing interest in STEM careers: An exploratory factor analysis. *Asia-Pacific Forum on Science Learning and Teaching, 19*(2). https://www.eduhk.hk/apfslt/v19_issue2/rahman/page3.htm#:~:text=Based%20on%20career%20trajectory%20theories,and%20interest%20in%20STEM%20careers

Ladson-Billings, G. (1995, Autumn). Toward a Theory of Culturally Relevant Pedagogy. *American Educational Research Journal, 32*(3), 465–491. doi:10.3102/00028312032003465

Logan, G., Pischke, K., & Guerdan, R. (2021). *2021 STEM Job Growth Index.* https://www.rclco.com/publication/2021-stem-job-growth-index/

MacMillan Dictionary. (n.d.). https://www.macmillandictionary.com/dictionary/british/underresourced

Meszaros, J. (2021). *Tampa Bay Algae Blooms Could Be Fed By Piney Point Wastewater.* The Florida Roundup WUSF Public Media - WUSF 89.7, https://wusfnews.wusf.usf.edu/environment/2021-06-11/tampa-bay-algae-blooms-could-be-fed-by-piney-point-wastewater

Nelson, K., Sabel, J., Forbes, C., Grandgenett, N., Tapprich, W., & Cutucache, C. (2017). How do undergraduate STEM mentors reflect upon their mentoring experiences in an outreach program engaging K-8 youth? *International Journal of STEM Education*, *4*(1), 3. doi:10.118640594-017-0057-4 PMID:30931241

Oxford Learner's Dictionary. (n.d.). https://www.oxfordlearnersdictionaries.com/definition/english/under-resourced

Programme for International Student Assessment PISA. (2018). *International student assessment (PISA) - Science performance.* PISA.

Sahin, A. (2013). STEM Clubs and Science Fair Competitions: Effects on Post-Secondary Matriculation. *Journal of STEM Education: Innovations and Research*, *14*, 1, 5–11.

Şahin, E., Önder Çelikkanli, N., & Onsekiz, C. (2014). The Impacts of a Secondary School Science Exhibition on The Students in Charge. *NFE-EJMSE*, *8*, 2.

Sleeter, C. (2008). An Invitation To Support Diverse Students Through Teacher Education. *Journal of Teacher Education*, *59*(3), 212–219. doi:10.1177/0022487108317019

Smedley, B. D., Stith, A. Y., Colburn, L., & the Institute of Medicine (US). (2001). *The Right Thing to Do, The Smart Thing to Do: Enhancing Diversity in the Health Professions: Summary of the Symposium on Diversity in Health Professions in Honor of Herbert W. Nickens, M.D.* National Academies Press. Available from: https://www.ncbi.nlm.nih.gov/books/NBK223640/

Tenenbaum, L. S., Anderson, M. K., Jett, M., & Yourick, D. L. (2014). An innovative near-peer mentoring model for undergraduate and secondary students: STEM focus. *Innovative Higher Education*, *39*(5), 375–385. doi:10.100710755-014-9286-3

Trends in International Mathematics and Science Study (TIMSS). (2019). *Welcome to TIMSS and TIMSS Advanced Results from 2019.* TIMSS.

U.S. Department of Commerce. (2017). *STEM Jobs, 2017 Update.* https://www.commerce.gov/news/reports/2017/03/stem-jobs-2017-update

Compilation of References

Abdulkadir, A. (2020). Do parents value school effectiveness? *The American Economic Review, 110*(5), 1502–1539. doi:10.1257/aer.20172040

Adam, H., & Harper, L. (2016). Assessing and selecting culturally diverse literature for the classroom. *Practical Literacy: The Early and Primary Years, 21*(2), 10–13. doi:10.3316/aeipt.212531

Addison, R., & Brundrett, M. (2008). Motivation and demotivation of teachers in primary schools: The challenge of change. *Education 3-13, 36*(1), 79–94. https://doi.org/doi:10.1080/03004270701733254

Akena, F. A. (2012). Critical Analysis of the Production of Western Knowledge and Its Implications for Indigenous Knowledge and Decolonization. *Journal of Black Studies, 43*(6), 599–619. doi:10.1177/0021934712440448

Alford, L., & Muller, C. (1984). *Breakdancing: Let Colin & Venol Show You How*. Willowisp Press.

Alim, H. S., & Smitherman, G. (2012). *Articulate while Black: Barack Obama, language, and race in the US*. Oxford University Press.

Almethhib, M. (2009). The Impact of Ice Breaking Exercises on Trainees' Interactions and Skill Acquisition: An Experimental Study. *Journal of King Abdulaziz University-Economics and Administration, 23*(1), 3–20. doi:10.4197/Eco.23-1.1

Almond, M. R.Monica R. Almond. (2012). The Black charter school effect: Black students in American charter schools. *The Journal of Negro Education, 81*(4), 354–365. doi:10.7709/jnegroeducation.81.4.0354

Alvares, C., & Faruqi, S. S. (2014). *Decolonising the University: The Emerging Quest for Non-Eurocentric Paradigms (Penerbit USM)*. Penerbit USM.

Ambrose, S. A., Bridges, M. W., DiPietro, M., Lovett, M. C., & Norman, M. K. (2010). *How learning works: Seven research-based principles for smart teaching*. John Wiley & Sons.

Anderson, J. (1988). *The education of Blacks in the South: 1860-1935*. University of North Carolina. doi:10.5149/uncp/9780807842218

Andreotti, V. (2007). An ethical engagement with the other: Spivak's ideas on education. *Critical Literacy: Theories and Practices*, *1*(1), 69–79.

Anila, S. (2017). Inclusion Requires Fracturing. *Journal of Museum Education*, *42*(2), 108–119. doi:10.1080/10598650.2017.1306996

Appiah, K. (1992). *In my Father's House: Africa in the Philosophy of Culture*. Oxford University Press.

Appiah, O., Eveland, W. Jr, Bullock, O., & Coduto, K. (2022). Why we can't talk openly about race: The impact of race and partisanship on respondents' perceptions of intergroup conversations. *Group Processes & Intergroup Relations*, *25*(2), 434–452. doi:10.1177/1368430220967978

Arday, J., Zoe Belluigi, D., & Thomas, D. (2021). Attempting to break the chain: Reimaging inclusive pedagogy and decolonising the curriculum within the academy. *Educational Philosophy and Theory*, *53*(3), 298–313. doi:10.1080/00131857.2020.1773257

Ayim, K. (2015). *The Akan of Ghana, Aspects of Past and Present Practices*. Createspace Independent Publishing Platform.

Badoe, W., & Opoku-Asare, N. A. (2014). Structural patterns in Asante kente: An indigenous instructional resource for design education in textiles. *Journal of Education and Practice*, *5*(25), 52–62.

Ballard, K. (1995). Inclusion, Paradigms, Power and Participation. In *Towards Inclusive Schools?* Routledge.

Barcia, M. (2006, October). The usage of the colonial legal framework by 19th century Cuban slaves. [Taylor & Francis, Routledge.]. *Atlantic Studies*, *3*(2). doi:10.1080/14788810600875307

Battiste, M. (2019). *Decolonizing education: Nourishing the learning spirit*. UBC press.

Baylor University. (2020, December 10). How to Provide a Multicultural Education. *BAY-UMT*. https://onlinegrad.baylor.edu/resources/multicultural-education-strategies/

Beachum, L. P. (1984). Effective urban schools: Building student pride. *American Secondary Education*, *13*(2), 30–31.

Beattie, I. R., & Thiele, M. (2016). Connecting in Class? College Class Size and Inequality in Academic Social Capital. *The Journal of Higher Education*, *87*(3), 332–362. doi:10.1080/00221546.2016.11777405

Bell, D.A. (2004). *Silent covenants: Brown v Board of Education: And the unfulfilled hopes of racial reform*. New York, Oxford University Press.

Bell, C. (2020). "Maybe if they let us tell the story I wouldn't have gotten suspended": Understanding Black students' and parents' perceptions of school discipline. *Children and Youth Services Review*, *110*, 104757. doi:10.1016/j.childyouth.2020.104757

Bell, D. A. (1975). Waiting on the promise of "Brown.". *Law and Contemporary Problems*, *39*(2), 341–373. doi:10.2307/1191105

Bengtsson, M. (2016). How to plan and perform a qualitative study using content analysis. *Nursing Plus One*, *2*, 8–14. doi:10.1016/j.npls.2016.01.001

Berchini, C. N. (2017). Critiquing Un/Critical Pedagogies to Move Toward a Pedagogy of Responsibility in Teacher Education. *Journal of Teacher Education*, *68*(5), 463–475. doi:10.1177/0022487117702572

Bhaba, H. (1986). *Foreword. In F. Fanon (Ed.), Black Skin White Masks*. Paladin.

Bhabha, H. K. (1994). *The location of culture*. Routledge.

Bignoli, C., & Faas, D. (2022). Increasing access to shops, makerspaces and libraries across a hands-on, project-based engineering curriculum. 6th International Symposium on Academic Makerspaces. ISAM. https://isam2022.hemi-makers.org/wp-content/uploads/sites/3/2022/09/046.pdf

Blassingame, J. (1972). *The slave community*. Oxford University Press.

BLY. (2008). "Pretends he can read": Runaways and literacy in colonial America, 1730—1776. *Early American Studies*, *6*(2), 261–294. doi:10.1353/eam.0.0004

Boeije, H. R. (2002). A purposeful approach to the constant comparative method in the analysis of qualitative interviews. *Quality & Quantity*, *36*(4), 391–409. doi:10.1023/A:1020909529486

Boylorn, R. M., & Orbe, M. (2014). *Critical Auto-ethnography: Intersecting cultural identities in everyday lives*. Left Coast Press.

Brock, C., Wallace, J., Herschbach, M., Johnson, C., Raikes, B., Warren, K., Nikoli, M., & Poulsen, H. (2006). Negotiating displacement spaces: Exploring teachers' stories about learning and diversity. *Curriculum Inquiry*, *36*(1), 35–62. doi:10.1111/j.1467-873X.2005.00345.x

Broward County Schools. (n.d.). *Home*. Broward County Schools. https://www.browardschools.com/site/default.aspx?PageType=3&DomainID=14019&ModuleInstanceID=60855&ViewID=6446EE88-D30C-497E-9316-3F8874B3E108&RenderLoc=0&FlexDataID=292587&PageID=39081

Brown, B. (n.d.). *Empathy vs. sympathy*. [Video]. Twenty-one Toys. https://twentyonetoys.com/blogs/teaching-empathy/brene-brown-empathy- vs- sympathy

Brown, C. (2011). Barack Obama as the great man: Communicative constructions of racial transcendence in White-male elite discourses. *Communication Monographs*, *78*(4), 535–556. doi:10.1080/03637751.2011.618140

Compilation of References

Brown, J. (2020). Critical Race Theory and makerspaces: A practical approach. In M. Melo & J. T. Nichols (Eds.), *Remaking the library makerspace: Critical theories, reflections, and practices*. Library Juice Press.

Brown, M. C., & Ratcliff, J. L. (1998). Multiculturalism and Multicultural Curricula in the United States. *Higher Education in Europe*, *23*(1), 11–21. doi:10.1080/0379772980230102

Bullock, O. (2021). Poetry and Trauma: Exercises for Creating Metaphors and Using Sensory Detail. *The International Journal for the Practice and Theory of Creative Writing*.

Burstein, N., Sears, S., Wilcoxen, A., Cabello, B., & Spagna, M. (2004). Moving Toward Inclusive Practices. *Remedial and Special Education*, *25*(2), 104–116. doi:10.1177/07419325040250020501

Bush, L. (2004). Access, school choice, and independent Black institutions: A historical perspective. *Journal of Black Studies*, *34*(3), 386–401. doi:10.1177/0021934703258761

Butin, D. W. (2010). *The education dissertation: A guide for practitioner scholars*. Thousand Oaks, CA: Corwin.

Butler, J. (2015). *Senses of the subject*. Fordham University Press.

Butterfield, L. D., Borgen, W. A., Amundson, N. E., & Maglio, A. T. (2005). Fifty years of the critical incident technique: 1954-2004 and beyond. *Qualitative Research*, *5*(4), 475–497. doi:10.1177/1468794105056924

Byrd, C. D., & Mason, R. S. (2021). *Precollegiate ptograms in academic pipeline programs: diversifying pathways from the bachelor's to the professoriate*. Lever Press.

CAST. (2018). *Universal Design for Learning Guidelines version 2.2*. CAST. http://udlguidelines.cast.org

Chatman, J. E., Johnson, A., White, E., & Bell, R. L. (2020). *The leader as effective communicator*. Research Gate. https://www.researchgate.net/publication/339366410_The_Leader_as_Effective_Communicator

Clarke, R. T. (1934). The Drum Language of the Tumba People. *American Journal of Sociology*, *40*(1), 34–48. doi:10.1086/216650

Cohodes, S. (2018). Policy Issue: Charter schools and the achievement gap. *The Future of Children*, *1000*(1), 1–16. doi:10.1353/foc.2018.0008

Communication on College Composition and Communication (CCCC) (1974). *Students' right to their own language position statement*. CCCC.

Cooper, K., Haney, B., Krieg, A., & Brownell, S. (2017). What's in a Name? That Importance of Students Perceiving That an Instructor Knows Their Names in a High-Enrolment Biology Classroom. *CBE Life Sciences Education, 16*(1), 1-13.

Cornelius, J. (1983). "We slipped and learned to read:" Slave accounts of the literacy process, 1830-1865. *Phylon (1960-), 44*(3), 171–186

Costello, M. (2016). *After election day: The Trump effect.* Southern Poverty Law Center. https://www.splcenter.org/ sites/default/files/the_trump_eff ect.pdf

Crenshaw, K. (1989). Demarginalizing the intersection of race and sex: A black feminist critique of antidiscrimination doctrine, feminist theory and antiracist politics. *University of Chicago Legal Forum, 1*(8), 139–167. https://chicagounbound.uchicago.edu/uclf/vol1989/iss1/8

Crenshaw, K. W. (1988). Race, Reform, and Retrenchment: Transformation and Legitimation in Antidiscrimination Law. *Harvard Law Review, 101*(7), 1331–1387. doi:10.2307/1341398

Crooke, Fraser, & Davidson. (2023). *Building Intercultural Engagement Through Music.* University of Melbourne

Dark, P. (1973). *An Introduction to Benin Art and Technology.* Clarendon Press.

De los Ríos, C. V., López, J., & Morrell, E. (2015). Toward a Critical Pedagogy of Race: Ethnic Studies and Literacies of Power in High School Classrooms. *Race and Social Problems, 7*(1), 84–96. doi:10.100712552-014-9142-1

Dei, G. (2016). Decolonizing the university: The challenges and possibilities of inclusive education. *Socialist Studies/Études Socialistes, 11*(1), 23–23.

Delgado, R., & Stefanic, J. (2017). *Critical Race Theory – An Introduction.* New York University Press.

Delpit, L. (2006). *Other people's children: Cultural conflict in the classroom.* New Press.

Delpit, L., & Dowdy, K. J. (2008). *The skin that we speak: Thoughts on language and culture in the classroom.* New Press.

Demie, F., & Hau, A. (2018). *Mixed race Pupils' Educational Achievement in England: An Empirical Analysis.* Academic Press.

Demie, F. (2021). The experience of Black Caribbean pupils in school exclusion in England. *Educational Review, 73*(1), 55–70. doi:10.1080/00131911.2019.1590316

des Civilisations de Côte d'IvoireM. (2022). http://civ. abidjan.net/index.php/visiter/musees/81-musee-des -civilisations-de-cote-d-ivoire

Dewsbury, B., & Brame, C. J. (2019). *Evidence Based Teaching Guide: Inclusive Teaching.* CBE Life Science Education. https://lse.ascb.org/evidence-based-teaching-guides/inclusiv e-teaching/network-leverage/

Dewsbury, B., & Brame, C. J. (2019). Inclusive Teaching. *CBE Life Sciences Education, 18*(2), fe2. doi:10.1187/cbe.19-01-0021 PMID:31025917

Diem, S., Carpenter, B. W., & Lewis-Durham, T. (2019). Preparing antiracist school leaders in a school choice context. *Urban Education, 54*(5), 706–731. doi:10.1177/0042085918783812

Diversity Officer Magazine. (2023). Historically excluded group. *Diversity Officer Magazine*. https://diversityofficermagazine.com/cultural-competence/diversitypedia/heg/

Dominguez, G. (2012). *Multiculturalism happens: Targeting multicultural literacy in libraries*. Programming Librarian. https://programminglibrarian.org/articles/multiculturalism-happens-targeting-multicultural-literacy-libraries

Dougherty, D. (2015). The maker mindset. *Paper Static*. https://blog.paperstatic.com/wp-content/uploads/2015/12/maker-mindset.pdf

Dowd, T. P., & Tierney, J. (2017). *Teaching Social Skills to Youth: A Step-by-step Guide to 182 Basic to Complex Skills Plus Helpful Teaching Techniques*. Boys Town Press.

Dreeben, R. (2002). *On what is learned in school*. University of Illinois Press.

Eakins, A., & Eakins, S. L. (2017). African American Students at Predominantly White Institutions: A Collaborative Style Cohort Recruitment & Retention Model. *The Journal of Learning in Higher Education*, *13*(2), 51–57.

Edmonds, R. R. (1981). A report on the research project "Search for effective schools ···" and certain of the designs for school improvement that are associated with the project. [Unpublished report prepared for NIE, Institute for Research on Teaching, Michigan State University].

Egalite, A. J., Kisida, B., & Winters, M. A. (2015). Representation in the classroom: The effect of own-race teachers on student achievement. *Economics of Education Review*, *45*, 44–52. doi:10.1016/j.econedurev.2015.01.007

Elabor-Idemudia, P. (2012). Gender and Identity in a Globalized World. In *The Age of Knowledge* (pp. 109–124). Brill. doi:10.1163/9789004211032_008

Ermine, W., Battiste, M., & Barman, J. (1995). Aboriginal epistemology. *First Nations Education in Canada: The Circle Unfolds*, 101–112.

Essel, O. Q. (2017). *Searchlight on Ghanaian iconic creative hands in the world of dress fashion design culture* [Unpublished doctoral dissertation]. University of Education, Winneba.

Estrada, M., Burnett, M., Campbell, A. G., Campbell, P. B., Denetclaw, W. F., Gutiérrez, C. G., ... Zavala, M. E. (2016). Improving underrepresented minority student persistence in stem. *CBE Life Sciences Education, 15*(3). doi:10.1187/cbe.16-01-0038

Fanon, F., & Philcox, R. (2008). Black Skin, White Masks (Revised). Grove Press.

Fanon, F., Sartre, J. P., Farrington, C., & Grove Press. (1963). *The Wretched of the Earth*. Amsterdam University Press.

Fanon, F. (1986). *Black Skin White Masks*. Paladin.

Farkas, M. (2020, March/April). Representation Beyond Books. *American Libraries*, 46.

Finfgeld-Connett, D. (2014). Use of content analysis to conduct knowledge-building and theory-generating qualitative systematic reviews. *Qualitative Research*, *14*(3), 341–352. doi:10.1177/1468794113481790

Finnegan, R. (1970). *Oral Literature in Africa*. Clarendon Press.

Flanagan, J. C. (1954). The critical incident technique. *Psychological Bulletin*, *51*(4), 327–358. doi:10.1037/h0061470 PMID:13177800

Flores-Gonzales, N. (2003). *School kids/street kids: Identity development in Latino students*. Teachers College Press.

Foley, J. A., Morris, D., Gounari, P., & Agostinone-Wilson, F. (2015). *Critical education, critical pedagogies, marxist education in the United States*. *13*, 110–144. Department of Education.

Forbes. (2022). 15 skills employers seek in 2022 (and ways to gain them midcareer). *Forbes*. https://www.forbes.com/sites/forbescoachescouncil/2022/08/11 /15-skills-employers-seek-in-2022-and-ways-to-gain-them-midc areer/?sh=a974fe8481a8

Fountain, D. L. (1995). Historians and historical archaeology: Slave sites. *The Journal of Interdisciplinary History*, *26*(1), 67–77. doi:10.2307/205550

Freire, P. (2005). *Teachers as cultural workers: Letters to those who dare to teach*. Westview Press.

Freire, P. (2014). *Pedagogy of the Oppressed: 30th Anniversary Edition*. Bloomsberry Academic. https://www.amazon.com/Pedagogy-Oppressed-Anniversary-Paulo-Freire-ebook/ dp/B00M0FQHQO

Freire, P. (1970). *Pedagogy of the oppressed*. Seabury Press.

Freire, P. (1993). *Pedagogy of the City*. Continuum.

Freire, P., & Macedo, D. (1987). *Literacies: Reading the word and the world*. Bergin & Harvey.

Gay, G. (2000). *Culturally responsive teaching: Theory, research and practice*. Teachers College Press.

Gillis, A., & Krull, L. M. (2020). COVID-19 remote learning transition in spring 2020: Class structures, student perceptions, and inequality in college courses. *Teaching Sociology*, *48*(4), 283–299. doi:10.1177/0092055X20954263

Gilroy, P. (2004). *After Empire, Melancholia or Convivial Culture?* Routledge. doi:10.4324/9780203482810

Glass, C. R., & Westmont, C. M. (2014). Comparative effects of belongingness on the academic success and cross-cultural interactions of domestic and international students. *International Journal of Intercultural Relations*, *38*, 106–119. doi:10.1016/j.ijintrel.2013.04.004

Glazer, N. (1998). *We are all multiculturalists now*. Harvard University Press.

Gloyn, L., Crewe, V., King, L., & Woodham, A. (2018). The Ties That Bind: Materiality, Identity, and the Life Course in the "Things" Families Keep. *Journal of Family History, 43*(2), 157–176. https://doi.org/10.1177/0363199017746451

Goldstein, T., & Selby, D. (2000). *Weaving Connections: Educating for Peace, Social and Environmental Justice* (1st ed.). Sumach Press.

Goleman, D. (1995). *What makes a leader?* Bantam Books.

Gonzalez, N. Moll, L. & Amanti, C. (Eds.). (2005). Funds of knowledge: Theorizing practices in households, communities, and classrooms. Mahwah, NJ: Lawrence Erlbaum.

Gordon, N. (2017, September 20). *Race, poverty, and overrepresentation in special education.* Brookings Institute. https://www.brookings.edu/research/race-poverty-and-interpre ting- overrepresentation-in-special-education/

Gottlieb, M., & Ernst-Slavit, G. (2014). *Academic language in diverse classrooms: Definitions and contexts.* Corwin Press.

Grant, C. (2011). *I & I: The Natural Mystics: Marley, Tosh and Wailer.* Jonathan Cape.

Green, T. (2019). *A Fistful of Shells – West Africa from the Rise of the Slave Trade to the Age of Revolution.* Penguin.

Gregg, N., Wolfe, G., Jones, S., Todd, R., Moon, N., & Langston, C. (2017). STEM E-Mentoring and Community College Students with Disabilities. *Career Development and Transition for Exceptional Individuals SAGE, 40*(4), 47–63.

Haegele, J. A., & Hodge, S. (2016). Disability discourse: Overview and critiques of the medical and social models. *Quest, 68*(2), 193–206. doi:10.1080/00336297.2016.1143849

Haley, A. & X, M. (1965). *The Autobiography of Malcolm X.* Grove Press.

Halim, L., Rahman, N., Wahab, N., & Mohtar, L. (2018). Factors influencing interest in STEM careers: An exploratory factor analysis. *Asia-Pacific Forum on Science Learning and Teaching, 19*(2). https://www.eduhk.hk/apfslt/v19_issue2/rahman/page3.htm#:~:t ext=Based%20on%20career%20trajectory%20theories,and%20intere st%20in%20STEM%20careers

Hall, S. (1983). Thatcherism — Rolling Back the Welfare State. *Thesis Eleven, 7*(1), 6–19. doi:10.1177/072551368300700102

Hall, S. (1990). Cultural Identity and Diaspora. In J. Rutherford (Ed.), Identity, Community, Culture, Difference (pp. 222-237). Lawrence & Wishart.

Hall, S. (1998). Aspiration and Attitude...Reflections on Black Britain in the Nineties. *New Formations: Frontlines/Backyards, 33*, 38.

Hall, S., Evans, J., & Nixon, S. (2013). *Representation: Cultural Representations and Signifying Practices (Culture, Media and Identities series)* (2nd ed.). SAGE Publications Ltd.

Harrison, L. (1949). Thomas Roderick Dew: Philosopher of the Old South. *The Virginia Magazine of History and Biography*, *57*(4), 390–404.

Hasforth, J. (2016). Dominant cultural narratives, racism, and resistance in the workplace: A study of the experiences of young Black Canadians. *American Journal of Community Psychology*, *57*(1-2), 158–170. doi:10.1002/ajcp.12024 PMID:27217319

Hathaway, R. (2021, October 4). BLM movement engaged youth with both positive and negative effects. *Yale News*. https://news.yale.edu/2021/10/04/blm-movement-engaged-youth-positive-and-negative-effects/

Holbert, R. M. G. (2015). Beginning with Bingo – An Icebreaker to Initiate Classroom Community. *College Teaching*, *63*(4), 181–182. doi:10.1080/87567555.2015.1052723

Hollinger, D. A. (2006). Postethnic America: Beyond multiculturalism. Hachette UK.

Hollins, E. R., & Spencer, K. (1990). Restructuring schools for cultural inclusion: Changing the schooling process for African-American children. *Journal of Education*, *172*(2), 89–100. doi:10.1177/002205749017200208

Hooks, B. (1994). *Teaching to transgress: Education as the practice of freedom.* New York: Routledge.

Horsford, S. D. (2009). From Negro student to Black superintendent: Counternarratives on segregation and desegregation. *The Journal of Negro Education*, *78*(2), 172–187.

Hosley, B. (2008). *Routes of Remembrance: Refashioning the Slave Trade in Ghana.* University of Chicago Press.

Hoyles, M. (1999). *Remember Me: Achievements of Mixed-Race People, Past and Present.* Turnaround Books.

Hoyles, M. (2013). *William Cuffay – The Life & Times of a Chartist Leader.* Hansib Publications.

Hoy, W. K., Miskel, C. G., & Tarter, C. J. (2013). *Educational Administration: Theory, Research, and Practice* (6th ed.). McGraw Hill.

Hughes, L. (1994). *The Dream keeper and other poems.* Alfred A. Knopf.

Hundley, S. P., Kahn, S., & Banta, T. W. (2019). *Trends in Assessment: Ideas, Opportunities, and Issues for Higher Education.* Stylus Publishing.

Hunt-Hurst, P. (2013, September). *Out of Africa: Elements of design inspiration in the twentieth century.* Paper presented at FASH5: Fashion Critical Issues, Oxford, UK.

Hurtado, S., & Carter, D. F. (1997). Effects of College Transition and Perceptions of the Campus Racial Climate on Latino College Students' Sense of Belonging. *Sociology of Education*, *70*(4), 324. doi:10.2307/2673270

Hussain, M., & Jones, J. M. (2021). Discrimination, diversity, and sense of belonging: Experiences of students of color. *Journal of Diversity in Higher Education*, *14*(1), 63–71. doi:10.1037/dhe0000117

Irvine, J. J. (1988). Urban schools that work: A summary of relevant factors. [JSTOR]. *The Journal of Negro Education*, *57*(3), 236–242. doi:10.2307/2295422

Ives, J., & Castillo-Montoya, M. (2020). First-Generation College Students as Academic Learners: A Systematic Review. *Review of Educational Research*, *90*(2), 139–178. doi:10.3102/0034654319899707

Jeynes, W. H. (2016). A meta-analysis: The relationship between parental involvement and African American school outcomes. *Journal of Black Studies*, *47*(3), 195–216. doi:10.1177/0021934715623522

Jiles, E. (2020, March 19). *PWI (predominately white institution) "was the hardest year of my life."* The Hechinger Report. https://hechingerreport.org/student-voices-black-student-at-a-pwi/

Jiles, E. (2021, April 8). STUDENT VOICE: Having 'the hardest year of my life' at 'a school that's mostly white, conservative and isolated — everything I wasn't.' *The Hechinger Report.* https://hechingerreport.org/student-voices-black-student-at-a-pwi/

Jin, Y. X., & Dewaele, J.-M. (2018). The effect of positive orientation and perceived social support on foreign language classroom anxiety. *System*, *74*, 149–157. doi:10.1016/j.system.2018.01.002

Jivraj, S. (2020). Decolonizing the academy–between a rock and a hard place. *Interventions*, *22*(4), 552–573. doi:10.1080/1369801X.2020.1753559

Johnson, A. M. (2019). *A walk in their kicks: Literacy, identity & the schooling of young Black males.* Teachers College Press.

Johnson, H. E., Molloy Elreda, L., Kibler, A. K., & Futch Ehrlich, V. A. (2020). Creating Classroom Communities in Linguistically Diverse Settings: Teacher-Directed, Classroom-Level Factor Effects on Peer Dynamics. *The Journal of Early Adolescence*, *40*(8), 1087–1120. doi:10.1177/0272431619891238

Kaisary, P. (2023). *The Haitian revolution in literary imagination: Radical horizons Conservative constraints.* University of Virginia Press.

Kallio, G., & Houtbeckers, E. (2020). Academic Knowledge Production: Framework of Practical Activity in the Context of Transformative Food Studies. *Frontiers in Sustainable Food Systems*, *4*, 577351. https://www.frontiersin.org/articles/10.3389/fsufs.2020.577351. doi:10.3389/fsufs.2020.577351

Kanu, Y. (2006). *Curriculum as cultural practice.* University of Toronto Press. doi:10.3138/9781442686267

Karl, A. (2016). Is It Family or School? Getting the Question Right. *The Russell Sage Foundation Journal of the Social Sciences : RSF*, *2*(5), 18–33. doi:10.7758/RSF.2016.2.5.02

Kaye, G. (1987). *Comfort Herself*. Heinemann Educational.

Kelly, S. (2023). *Slavers: Merchants, mariners and the Transatlantic commerce in captives 1644-1865*. Yale University Press.

Kincheloe & Steinberg. (1997). *Changing multiculturalism*. Open University Press.

King-Sears, M. E., & Cummings, C. S. (1996). Inclusive Practices of Classroom Teachers. *Remedial and Special Education*, *17*(4), 217–225. doi:10.1177/074193259601700404

Koh, K., Ge, X., Lee, L., Lewis, K. R., Simmons, S., & Nelson, L. B. (2020). Peace prescription: Inclusive making in school libraries. In M. Melo & J. T. Nichols (Eds.), *Remaking the library makerspace: Critical theories, reflections, and practices*. Library Juice Press.

Konadu, K. (2010). *Adinto: Akan Naming and Outdooring Ceremony*. http://www.afropedea.org/adinto-akan-naming-and-outdooring-c eremony

Krippendorff, K. (2016). *Content Analysis: An Introduction* (4th ed.). Sage.

Kurti, R. S., Kurti, D. L., & Fleming, L. (2014). The philosophy of educational makerspaces. *Teacher Librarian*, *41*(5). https://www.proquest.com/docview/1548230083?parentSessionId=nwJLVgQAvkWXuIPMFvYBBr9FeRWuZMcGPRw2WHaqDDI%3D

Kye, H. (2020). Who is welcome here? A culturally responsive analysis of makerspace websites. *Journal of Pre-College Engineering Education Research*, *10*(2). https://docs.lib.purdue.edu/jpeer/vol10/iss2/1. doi:10.7771/2157-9288.1190

Ladson-Billings, G. (1995). Toward a theory of Cclturally relevant pedagogy. *American Educational Research Journal*, *32*(3), 465–491. doi:10.3102/00028312032003465

Ladson-Billings, G. (2009). *The dream- keepers: Successful teachers of African American children*. Jossey Bass.

Ladson-Billings, G. (2009). *The dreamkeepers: Successful teachers of African American children*. Jossey Bass.

Lauer, P., Akiba, M., Wilkerson, S. B., Apthorp, H. S., Snow, D., & Martin-Glenn, M. L. (2006). Out-of-School-Time Programs: A meta-analysis of effects for t-risk students. *Review of Educational Research*, *76*(2), 275–313. doi:10.3102/00346543076002275

Levine, D. U. (1990). Update on effective schools: Findings and implications from research and practice. *The Journal of Negro Education*, *59*(4), 577–584. doi:10.2307/2295314

Levine, D. U., Cooper, E. J., & Hilliard, A. (2000). National Urban Alliance Professional Development Model for improving achievement in the context of effective schools research. *The Journal of Negro Education*, *69*(4), 305–322. doi:10.2307/2696247

Lewis, K., & Demie, F. (2019). The School Experiences of Mixed Race White and Black Caribbean children in England. Department of Educational Studies, Goldsmiths (University of London) and School of Education, University of Durham. doi:10.1080/01419870.2018.1519586

Lister, H. (2020). Trauma-informed making. In M. Melo & J. T. Nichols (Eds.), *Remaking the library makerspace: Critical theories, reflections, and practices*. Library Juice Press.

Litwack, L. L. (1979). *Been in the storm so long: The aftermath of slavery, The*. Athlone Press.

Logan, G., Pischke, K., & Guerdan, R. (2021). *2021 STEM Job Growth Index*. https://www.rclco.com/publication/2021-stem-job-growth-index /

MacMillan Dictionary. (n.d.). https://www.macmillandictionary.com/dictionary/british/ underresourced

Manning, P. (2009). *The African Diaspora: History Through Culture*. Columbia University Press.

Mann, S. (2020). Makerspace dialogue as collaboration and resistance. In M. Melo & J. T. Nichols (Eds.), *Remaking the library makerspace: Critical theories, reflections, and practices*. Library Juice Press.

Mansfield, S. (1967). Thomas Roderick Dew at William and Mary: A main prop of that venerable institution.. *The Virginia Magazine of History and Biography*, *75*(4), 429–442.

Margolis, E. (2001). *The hidden curriculum in higher education*. Psychology Press.

Marshall, B., & Melo, M. (2020). From needs analysis to power analysis: A framework to examine and broker power in makerspaces. In M. Melo & J. T. Nichols (Eds.), *Remaking the library makerspace: Critical theories, reflections, and practices*. Library Juice Press.

Massachusetts Department of Education. (2021, June 8). *Culturally responsive teaching and leading*. MA DoE. https://www.doe.mass.edu/instruction/culturally-responsive/default.html

Ma, X. (2003). Sense of belonging to school: Can schools make a difference? *The Journal of Educational Research*, *96*(6), 340–349. doi:10.1080/00220670309596617

McClean, M. (2019). *From the middle passage to Black lives matter: Ancestral writing as a pedagogy of hope*. New York: Peter lang.

McClean, M. (2019). *From the Middle Passage to Black lives matter: Ancestral writing as a pedagogy of hope*. Peter Lang.

McClean, M. (2019). *From the Middle Passage to Black Lives Matter: Ancestral Writing as a Pedagogy of Hope*. Peter Lang.

McClean, M., & Waters, M. (2020). *Indigenous Epistemology: Descent into the womb of decolonized research methodologies*. Peter Lang.

McCluney, C. L., Durkee, M. I., Smith, R. E. II, Robotham, K. J., & Lee, S. S.-L. (2021). To be, or not to be… Black: The effects of racial codeswitching on perceived professionalism in the workplace. *Journal of Experimental Social Psychology*, *97*, 104199. doi:10.1016/j.jesp.2021.104199

McIntyre, N., Parveen, N., & Thomas, T. (2021). Exclusion rates five times higher for black Caribbean pupils in parts of England. *The Guardian*. /education/2021/mar/24/exclusion-rates-black-caribbean-pupils-england#:~:text=Wokingham%20reported%20the%20largest%20disparity,than%20the%20white%20British%20rate

McLaren, P. (1995). *Critical Pedagogy & Predatory Culture: Oppositional Politics in a Postmodern Era*. Routledge.

Mclaren, P. (2020). The future of critical pedagogy. *Educational Philosophy and Theory*, *52*(12), 1243–1248. doi:10.1080/00131857.2019.1686963

McMillan, M. (2008). The 'West Indian' front room: Reflections on a diasporic phenomenon. *Kunapipi*, *30*(2).

McNair, T. B., Albertine, S., Cooper, M. A., McDonald, N., & Jr, M. T. (2017). *Becoming a Student-Ready College: A New Culture of Leadership for Student Success* (2nd ed.). Jossey-Bass.

Meadows, K. (2011). The desegregation of public schools: Ruby Bridges, Millicent E. Brown, and Josephine Boyd Bradley—Black educators by any means necessary. *Vitae Scholasticae*, *28*(2), 23–34.

Merryfield, M. M. (2000). Why aren't teachers being prepared to teach for diversity, equity, and global interconnectedness? A study of lived experiences in the making of multicultural and global educators. *Teaching and Teacher Education*, *16*(4), 429–443. doi:10.1016/S0742-051X(00)00004-4

Merseth, K. K., Sommer, J., & Dickstein, S. (2008). Bridging worlds: Changes in personal and professional identities of pre-service urban teachers. *Teacher Education Quarterly*, *35*(3), 89–108.

Meszaros, J. (2021). *Tampa Bay Algae Blooms Could Be Fed By Piney Point Wastewater*. The Florida Roundup WUSF Public Media - WUSF 89.7, https://wusfnews.wusf.usf.edu/environment/2021-06-11/tampa-bay-algae-blooms-could-be-fed-by-piney-point-wastewater

Miami-Dade Public Schools National Center for Education Statistics. (NCES). (2022). *Public High School Graduation Rates*. NCES. https://nces.ed.gov/programs/coe/indicator/coi/high-school-graduation-rates

Middleton, E. J. (1978). The Louisiana Education Association, 1901-1970. *The Journal of Negro Education*, *47*(4), 363–378. doi:10.2307/2295001

Mignolo, W. D. (2011). The Darker Side of Western Modernity: *Global Futures, Decolonial Options*. http://syonilan.1sthost.org/file/the-darker-side-of-western-modernity-global-futures-decolonial-options-by-walter-d-mignolo.pdf

Mignolo, W. (2003). Globalization and the geopolitics of knowledge: The role of the humanities in the corporate university. *Nepantla*, *4*(1), 97–119.

Miles, M. B., Huberman, A. M., & Saldana, J. (2019). *Qualitative data analysis: A methods sourcebook* (4th ed.). Sage.

Miller, D. (2022). Ungrading Light: 4 Simple Ways to Ease the Spotlight Off Points. *The Chronicles of Higher Education.* https://www.chronicle.com/article/ungrading-light-4-simple-ways-to-ease-the-spotlight-off-points

Miller, K. (2014). *The Cartographer Tries to Map a Way to Zion*. Carcanet Press.

Modan, N. (2020, 13 February). Survey: Superintendents still overwhelmingly White, male. *K-12 Dive.* https://www.k12dive.com/news/survey-superintendents-still-overwhelmingly-White-male/572008/

Moll, L. C. (1990). Introduction. *Vygotsky and Education*, 1–28. doi:10.1017/CBO9781139173674.002

Molt, L. C., Vélez-lbafiez, C., Greenberg, J., Whitmore, K., Saavedra, E., Dworin, J., & Andrade, F. (1990). *Community knowledge and classroom practice: Combining resources for literacy instruction (OBEMLA Contract No. 300—87-0131)*. Tucson: University of Arizona, College of Education and Bureau of Applied Research in Anthropology.

Montenegro, E., & Jankowski, N. A. (2017). Equity and assessment: Moving towards culturally responsive assessment. *Occasional Paper, 29*.

Moore, E. H., Bagin, D. H., & Gallagher, D. R. (2016). *School and community relations* (11th ed.). Pearson.

Morgan, H. (1995). *Historical Perspectives on the Education of Black Children*. ERIC.

Morgan, H. (2021). Restorative justice and the school-to-prison pipeline: A review of existing literature. *Education Sciences*, *11*(4), 159–169. doi:10.3390/educsci11040159

Moss, A. G. K. (2021c). MLE. In R. Acharya (Ed.), An anthology by Wingless Dreamer, BIPOC Issue. Academic Press.

Moss, A. G. K. (2021a). *This is the Drum*. The Decolonial Passage.

Moss, A. G. K. (2021b). *Twi Phone-ology*. The Good Life Review.

Moss, A. G. K. (2021d). My Golden Coast. *The Best New British and Irish Poets Anthology*, *2019-2021*, 191–193.

Moss, A. G. K. (2022). *Nicked Names*. RoseyRavelston Books.

Moss, A. G. K. (in press). *Childish Recollections. Academic Press.*

Mulrow, J. (2021). *Gaming is becoming accessible, but we need to keep asking for more.* Refinery29. https://www.refinery29.com/en-us/2021/12/10711964/gamers-with-disabilities-accessible-video-games

Murdoch, Y., Hyejung, L., & Kang, A. (2018). Learning Students' Given Names Benefits EMI Classes. *English in Education, 52*(3), 225-247.

Murzi, H. (2022). *Historically Black Colleges and Universities (HBCU) Research Summit- DEI: Culturally Relevant Learning and Teaching Workshop. Presenter.* Virginia Tech Graduate School.

Nash, H. D. (1989). Blacks in Arkansas during Reconstruction: The ex-slave narratives. *The Arkansas Historical Quarterly, 48*(3), 243–259.

Nash, H. D. (1989). Blacks in Arkansas during Reconstruction: The x-slave Narratives. *The Arkansas Historical Quarterly, 48*(3), 243–259.

Nation of Makers. (n.d.) *The White House: President Barack Obama (Archive).* Obama White House. https://obamawhitehouse.archives.gov/nation-of-makers

National Association for Diversity Officers in Higher Education (NADHO). (2021). *A framework for advancing anti-racism strategies on campus.* NADHO. https://nadohe.memberclicks.net/assets/2021/Framework/National%20Association%20of%20Diversity%20Officers%20in%20Higher%20Education%20-%20Framework%20for%20Advancing%20Ant-Racism%20on%20Campus%20-%20first%20edition.pdf

National Association for the Advancement of Colored People (NAACP). (n.d.). *Dismantling the school-to-prison pipeline. NAACP Legal Defense and Education Fund.* NAACP. https://www.naacpldf.org/wpcontent/uploads/Dismantling_the_School_to_Prison_Pipeline__Criminal-Justice__.pdf

National Center for Educational Statistics. (2020). *Characteristics of public school. Principals.* NCES. https://nces.ed.gov/programs/coe/indicator_cls.asp#:~:text=In%202017%E2%80%9318%2C%20about%2078,and%209%20percent%20were%20Hispanic

National Museums Scotland. (2022). https://www.nms.ac.uk/explore-our-collections/stories/global-arts-cultures-and-design/gold-weights-from-ghana/

National Policy Board for Educational Administration. (2015). *Professional standards for educational leaders.* National Policy Board for Educational Administration.

Ndofirepi, A. P., Maringe, F., Vurayai, S., & Erima, G. (2022). Decolonising African University Knowledges, Volume 2: Challenging the Neoliberal Mantra. Taylor & Francis. doi:10.4324/9781003241522

Nelson, R. K., Winling, L., Marciano, R., & Connolly, N. (n.d.). Mapping inequality. In. R.K. Nelson & E.L. Ayers (Eds.), *American Panorama.* Mapping Identity. https://dsl.richmond.edu/panorama/redlining/

Nelson, K., Sabel, J., Forbes, C., Grandgenett, N., Tapprich, W., & Cutucache, C. (2017). How do undergraduate STEM mentors reflect upon their mentoring experiences in an outreach program engaging K-8 youth? *International Journal of STEM Education, 4*(1), 3. doi:10.118640594-017-0057-4 PMID:30931241

Ng-A-Fook, N. (2013). Fishing for Knowledge Beyond Colonial Disciplines: Curriculum, Social Action Projects, and Indigenous Communities. In Contemporary Studies in Environmental and Indigenous Pedagogies (pp. 285–305). Brill.

Nilholm, C. (2021). Research about inclusive education in 2020 – How can we improve our theories in order to change practice? *European Journal of Special Needs Education, 36*(3), 358–370. doi:10.1080/08856257.2020.1754547

Northouse, P. G. (2018). *Leadership: Theory and practice* (8th ed.). Sage.

Nortvedt, G. A., Wiese, E., Brown, M., Burns, D., McNamara, G., O'Hara, J., Altrichter, H., Fellner, M., Herzog-Punzenberger, B., Nayir, F., & Taneri, P. O. (2020). Aiding culturally responsive assessment in schools in a globalising world. *Educational Assessment, Evaluation and Accountability, 32*(1), 5–27. doi:10.100711092-020-09316-w

O'Brien, M., Leiman, T., & Duffy, J. (2014). The Power of Naming: The Multifaceted Value of Learning Students' Names. *QUT Law Review, 14*(1), 114-128.

O'Flaherty, J., & Phillips, C. (2015). The use of flipped classrooms in higher education: A scoping review. *The Internet and Higher Education, 25*, 85–95. doi:10.1016/j.iheduc.2015.02.002

O'Keeffe, P. (2013). A Sense of Belonging: Improving Student Retention. *College Student Journal, 47*(4), 605–613.

O'Neil, S. (2015). *Young People on the Drop Out Crisis.* Raise Up Project. www.raiseupproject.org.

Oakes, J., Maier, A., & Daniel, J. (2017). *Community schools: an evidence-based strategy for equitable school improvement.* National Education Policy Center.

Oakes, J. (1986). Keeping Track, Part 2: Curriculum Inequality and School Reform. *Phi Delta Kappan, 68*(2), 148–154.

Office of the Press Secretary. (2016). Fact sheet: New commitments in support of the President's Nation of Makers Initiative to kick off 2016 National Week of Making. *Week of Making.* http://www.weekofmaking.org/wp-content/uploads/2016/03/2016-National-Week-of-Making-Fact-Sheet.pdf

Ogbu, J. U. (2003). *Black American students in an affluent suburb: A study of academic disengagement.* Routledge. doi:10.4324/9781410607188

Olsavsky, J. (2019). Runaway slaves, Vigilance Committees, and the pedagogy of revolutionary abolitionism, 1835–1863. In M. Rediker, T. Chakraborty, & M. van Rossum (Eds.), *A Global History of Runaways: Workers, Mobility, and Capitalism, 1600–1850* (1st ed., pp. 216–234). University of California Press.

Olsavsky, J. (2022). *The most absolute abolition: runaways, Vigilance Committees, and the rise of revolutionary abolitionism, 1835-1861*. Louisiana State University Press.

Oxby, C., & Avery, C. (2013). The missing "One-Offs": The hidden supply of high-achieving, low-income students. *Brookings Papers on Economic Activity*, 1–50.

Oxford Learner's Dictionary. (n.d.). https://www.oxfordlearnersdictionaries.com/definition/english/under-resourced

Palipane, K., Mateo-Babiano, I., & Hernandez-Santin, C. (2020). Conclusion: Placemaking as Critical Pedagogy of Place. In I. Mateo-Babiano & K. Palipane (Eds.), *Placemaking Sandbox: Emergent Approaches, Techniques and Practices to Create More Thriving Places* (pp. 107–121). Springer. doi:10.1007/978-981-15-2752-4_7

Paseka, A., & Schwab, S. (2020). Parents' attitudes towards inclusive education and their perceptions of inclusive teaching practices and resources. *European Journal of Special Needs Education*, *35*(2), 254–272. doi:10.1080/08856257.2019.1665232

Patton, L. D. (2016). Disrupting postsecondary prose: Toward a critical race theory of higher education. *Urban Education*, *51*(3), 315–342. doi:10.1177/0042085915602542

Pedler, M. L., Willis, R., & Nieuwoudt, J. E. (2021). A sense of belonging at university: Student retention, motivation and enjoyment. *Journal of Further and Higher Education*, *46*(3), 397–408. doi:10.1080/0309877X.2021.1955844

Pelton, R. D. (1989). *Trickster in West Africa: A Study of Mythic Irony and Sacred Delight*. University of California Press.

People meeting in a room photo. (2018). photograph, Providencia, Chile. https://unsplash.com/photos/cw-cj_nFa14

Perera, J. (2020). *How Black Working-Class Youth are Criminalised and Excluded in the English School System*. Academic Press.

Phillips, C. (2002). A New World Order, selected essays. Vintage.

Phillips, P. P. (2001). A wider field in a new country: Chartism in Colonial Australia. In M. Sawyer (Ed.), Elections: Full, Free and Fair (pp. 28-32). Federation Press.

Porter, D. B. (1936). The organized educational activities of Negro literary societies, 1828-1846. *The Journal of Negro Education*, *5*(4), 555–576. doi:10.2307/2292029

Porter, D. B. (1960). The anti-slavery movement in North Hampton. *Negro History Bulletin*, *24*(2), 33–41.

Pratt, M. L. (1999). Arts of the Contact Zone. In D. Bartholomae & A. Petrosky (Eds.), Ways of Reading (5th ed.) St. Martins.

Compilation of References

Premo, J., Cavagnetto, A., Davis, W. B., & Brickman, P. (2018). Promoting Collaborative Classrooms: The Impacts of Interdependent Cooperative Learning on Undergraduate Interactions and Achievement. *CBE Life Sciences Education*, *17*(2), ar32. doi:10.1187/cbe.17-08-0176 PMID:29799312

Programme for International Student Assessment PISA. (2018). *International student assessment (PISA) - Science performance*. PISA.

Pun, R., Cardenas-Dow, M., & Flash, K. (2022, March/April). Prioritizing Ethnic Studies. *American Libraries*, 46.

Pybus, C. (2006a). *Black Founders*. UNSW Press.

Pybus, C. (2006b). *Epic Journeys of Freedom: Runaway Slaves of the American Revolution and Their Global Quest for Liberty*. Beacon Press Books.

Rattan, A., & Ambady, N. (2014). How 'it gets better": Effectively communicating supports to targets of prejudice. *Personality and Social Psychology Bulletin*, *40*(5), 555–556. doi:10.1177/0146167213519480 PMID:24443385

Ratteray, J. D. (1992). Independent neighborhood schools: A Framework for the education of African Americans. *The Journal of Negro Education*, *61*(2), 138–147. doi:10.2307/2295411

Rattray, R. S. (1923). *Ashanti*. Clarendon Press.

Rattray, R. S. (1927). *Religion and Art in Ashanti*. Oxford University Press.

Ravitch, D. (2000). A different kind of education for Black children. *The Journal Of Blacks In Higher Education, 30*, 98–106.

Reynolds, H., Silvernell, D., & Mercer, F. (2020). Teaching in an era of political divisiveness: An exploration of strategies for discussing controversial issues. *The Clearing House: A Journal of Educational Strategies, Issues and Ideas*, *93*(4), 205–212. doi:10.1080/00098655.2020.1762063

Riello, G. (2011). The object of fashion: Methodological approaches to the history. *Journal of Aesthetics & Culture*, *3*(1), 456–463. doi:10.3402/jac.v3i0.8865

Roberts, N & Bolton, P. (2020 October 8). *Education outcomes of Black pupils and students*. House of Commons Library Briefing Paper, Number 09023.

Rogowski, A., Lee, V. R., & Recker, M. (2020). Supporting making in libraries rather than makerspaces: Rethinking the (maker)space for rural libraries. In M. Melo & J. T. Nichols (Eds.), *Remaking the library makerspace: Critical theories, reflections, and practices*. Library Juice Press.

Ruggs, E. N., & Avery, D. R. (2020). Organizations cannot afford to stay silent on racial injustice. *MIT Sloan Management Review*. https://sloanreview.mit.edu/article/organizations-cannot-afford-to-stay-silent-on racialinjustice/#:~:text=Your%20words% 20and%20actions%20can,to%20your%20employees%20and%20customer s

Sahin, A. (2013). STEM Clubs and Science Fair Competitions: Effects on Post-Secondary Matriculation. *Journal of STEM Education: Innovations and Research, 14*, 1, 5–11.

Şahin, E., Önder Çelikkanli, N., & Onsekiz, C. (2014). The Impacts of a Secondary School Science Exhibition on The Students in Charge. *NFE-EJMSE, 8*, 2.

Said, E. (1978). *Orientalism*. Pantheon Books.

Saldana, J. (2013). *The coding manual for qualitative researchers* (2nd ed.). Sage.

Salend, S. J. (2015). *Creating inclusive classrooms: Effective, differentiated and reflective practices*. Pearson.

Sanchez, A. (2018). Canon Fire. *Cambridge Anthropology, 36*(2), 1–6. doi:10.3167/cja.2018.360202

Sanchez, A., Dolan-Sanchez, D., & Lázaro, V. (2020). Who belongs in the makerspace? Experiences of women of color in an academic library makerspace. In M. Melo & J. T. Nichols (Eds.), *Remaking the library makerspace: Critical theories, reflections, and practices*. Library Juice Press.

Savage. (2018). Fifty years on, what is the legacy of Enoch Powell's 'rivers of blood' speech? *The Guardian*.

Schilling, K. M., & Schilling, K. L. (1998). Proclaiming and Sustaining Excellence: Assessment as a Faculty Role (J-B ASHE Higher Education Report Series (AEHE)) (1st ed.). Jossey-Bass.

Schneider, M. L., & Kwan, B. M. (2013). Psychological need satisfaction, intrinsic motivation and affective response to exercise in adolescents. *Psychology of Sport and Exercise, 14*(5), 776–785. doi:10.1016/j.psychsport.2013.04.005 PMID:24015110

Schon, D. (1983). *The reflective practitioner*. Basic Books.

Scott, J. C. (1985). *The Weapons of the Weak. Everyday Forms of Peasant Resistance*. Yale University Press.

Scott, J. C. (1992). *Domination ad the arts of resistance: hidden transcripts*. Yale University Press.

Semali, L. M., & Kincheloe, J. (Eds.). (2002). *What is Indigenous Knowledge? Voices from the Academy*. Routledge. doi:10.4324/9780203906804

Shahjahan, R. A. (2015). Being 'Lazy' and Slowing Down: Toward decolonizing time, our body, and pedagogy. *Educational Philosophy and Theory, 47*(5), 488–501. doi:10.1080/00131857.2014.880645

Shahjahan, R. A., Estera, A. L., Surla, K. L., & Edwards, K. T. (2022). "Decolonizing" curriculum and pedagogy: A comparative review across disciplines and global higher education contexts. *Review of Educational Research, 92*(1), 73–113. doi:10.3102/00346543211042423

Shirley, V. J. (2017). Indigenous Social Justice Pedagogy: Teaching into the Risks and Cultivating the Heart. *Critical Questions in Education, 8*(2), 163–177.

Compilation of References

Sibal, V. (2018). *Food: Identity of Culture and Religion.* Academic Press.

Simmons, D. (2019). How to be an anti-racist educator. *ASCD Education Update, 61*(10).

Simms & Queen. (2021, March 21). *Strong in the Broken Places: Poetics of the African Diaspora.* Facebook.

Skopec, M., Fyfe, M., Issa, H., Ippolito, K., Anderson, M., & Harris, M. (2021). Decolonization in a higher education STEMM institution–is 'epistemic fragility' a barrier? *London Review of Education, 19*(1), 1–21. doi:10.14324/LRE.19.1.18

Sleeter, C. (2008). An Invitation To Support Diverse Students Through Teacher Education. *Journal of Teacher Education, 59*(3), 212–219. doi:10.1177/0022487108317019

Sleeter, C. E. (2000). Creating an Empowering Multicultural Curriculum. *Race, Gender & Class (Towson, Md.), 7*(3), 178–196.

Sloley, P. (2021, June 8). *Jollof Wars: Who does West Africa's iconic rice dish best?* https://www.bbc.com/travel/article/20210607-jollof-wars-who-does-west-africas-iconic-rice-dish-best

Smedley, B. D., Stith, A. Y., Colburn, L., & the Institute of Medicine (US). (2001). *The Right Thing to Do, The Smart Thing to Do: Enhancing Diversity in the Health Professions: Summary of the Symposium on Diversity in Health Professions in Honor of Herbert W. Nickens, M.D.* National Academies Press. Available from: https://www.ncbi.nlm.nih.gov/books/NBK223640/

Smith, L. T. (2012). *Decolonizing methodologies: Research and Indigenous peoples.* Zed Books.

Sokolower, J. (2018). Space for young Black women: An interview with Candice Valenzuela. In D. Watson, J. Hagopian, & W. Au (Eds.), Teaching for Black Lives. Rethinking Schools.

Span, C. M. (2005). Learning in spite of opposition: African Americans and their history of educational exclusion in antebellum America. Counterpoints, 2005. Peter Lang, New York

Spratt, J., & Florian, L. (2015). Inclusive pedagogy: From learning to action. Supporting each individual in the context of 'everybody.'. *Teaching and Teacher Education, 49*, 89–96. doi:10.1016/j.tate.2015.03.006

Staats, C., Capatosto, K., & Tenney, L. Sarah Mamo S. (2017). State of the Science: Implicit Bias Review. Kirwan Institute for the Study of Race and Ethnicity.

Stampp, K. M. (1942). An analysis of T. R. Dew's review of the debates in the Virginia Legislature. *The Journal of Negro History, 27*(4), 380–387. doi:10.2307/2715183

Stanton, S. (2001). *The Virginia Magazine of History and Biography, 109*(3), 331–332.

Steinman, E. W. (2016). Decolonization not inclusion: Indigenous resistance to American settler colonialism. *Sociology of Race and Ethnicity (Thousand Oaks, Calif.), 2*(2), 219–236. doi:10.1177/2332649215615889

Stevenson, B. (2015). *What is slavery?* Polity Press.

Strauss, A., & Corbin, J. (1998). *Basics of qualitative research. Techniques and procedures for developing grounded theory* (2nd ed.). Sage.

Strayhorn, T. L. (2010). The role of schools, families, and psychological variables on math achievement of Black high school students. *High School Journal*, *93*(4), 177–194. doi:10.1353/hsj.2010.0003

Stringfield, S., Teddlie, C., & Suarez, S. (2017). Classroom interaction in effective and ineffective schools: Preliminary results from Phase III of the Louisiana School Effectiveness Study. *Journal of Classroom Interaction*, *52*(1), 4–14.

Stuckey, P. S. (2013). *Slave culture: nationalist theory and the foundations of Black America*. Oxford Press. doi:10.1093/acprof:oso/9780199931675.001.0001

Takacs, D. (2002). Positionality, Epistemology, and Social Justice in the Classroom. *Social Justice (San Francisco, Calif.)*, *29*(4 (90)), 168–181.

Tanaka, G. K. (2003). *The intercultural campus: Transcending culture & power in American higher education* (Vol. 97). Peter Lang.

Tanner, K. (2013). Structure Matters: Twenty-One Teaching Strategies to Promote Student Engagement and Cultivate Classroom Equity. *CBE Life Sciences Education, 12*(3), (22-331.

Taylor, D., & Dorsey-Gaines, C. (1988). Growing Up Literate: Learning from Inner-City Families. Heinemann.

Taylor, E. R. (2006). If we must die, Baton Rouge. Louisiana State University Press.

Tenenbaum, L. S., Anderson, M. K., Jett, M., & Yourick, D. L. (2014). An innovative near-peer mentoring model for undergraduate and secondary students: STEM focus. *Innovative Higher Education*, *39*(5), 375–385. doi:10.100710755-014-9286-3

The 1619 Project. (2019). *The New York Times Magazine*. https://www.nytimes.com/interactive/2019/08/14/magazine/1619 -america-slavery.html

The British Museum. (2022). http://teachinghistory100.org/objects/about_the_object/akan_drum

The Met Museum New York. (2022). https://www.metmuseum.org/art/collection/search/317678

The New York Times. (2021, February 14). What we know about the death of George Floyd in Minneapolis. *The New York Times*. https://www.nytimes.com/article/george-floyd.html

The Opportunity Agenda. (2020). *Messaging memo: Ten lessons for talking about race, racism, and racial justice*. The Opportunity Agenda. http://www.opportunityagenda.org/sits/default/files/2020.07.27%20- %2010%20Lessons%20Talking%20About%20Race%20FINAL.pdf

Compilation of References

Thiong'O, W. N. (1986). *Decolonising the Mind: The Politics of Language in African Literature.* James Currey Ltd / Heinemann.

Thomazet, S. (2009). From integration to inclusive education: Does changing the terms improve practice? *International Journal of Inclusive Education*, *13*(6), 553–563. doi:10.1080/13603110801923476

Time Magazine. (1963, June 14). *Games: Pits and Pebbles.* https://content.time.com/time/subscriber/article/0,33009,874841-1,00.html

Trends in International Mathematics and Science Study (TIMSS). (2019). *Welcome to TIMSS and TIMSS Advanced Results from 2019.* TIMSS.

Tuhiwai-Smith, L. (2012). *Decolonizing methodologies: Research and Indigenous peoples.* London & New York: Zed Books. https://uis.unesco.org/en/topic/out-school-children-and-youth

U.S. Department of Commerce. (2017). *STEM Jobs, 2017 Update.* https://www.commerce.gov/news/reports/2017/03/stem-jobs-2017-update

Universal Design for Learning. (2022). *Guidelines.* UDL. https://udlguidelines.cast.org/

Valdez, Z., & Golash-Boza, T. (2020). Master status or intersectional identity? Undocumented students' sense of belonging on a college campus. *Identities (Yverdon)*, *27*(4), 481–499. doi:10.1080/1070289X.2018.1534452

Vecchio, G. (2009). *Central Markets Excursion.* SACE Board of South Australia.

Violence, M. P. org (2021). *Police violence map.* Mapping Police Violence. https://mappingpoliceviolence.org./

Waldoff, R. A., Wiggins, Y. M., & Washington, H. M. (2011). Black Collegians at a Predominantly White Institution: Toward a Place-Based Understanding of Black Student's Adjustment to College. *Journal of Black Studies*, *42*(7), 1047–1079. doi:10.1177/0021934711400741

Wenner, J. A., & Campbell, T. (2017). The theoretical and empirical basis of teacher leadership: A review of the literature. *Review of Educational Research*, *87*(1), 134–171. doi:10.3102/0034654316653478

Wentling, T. (2015). Trans* Disruptions: Pedagogical Practices and Pronoun Recognition. *Transgender Studies Quarterly*, *2*(3), 469–476. doi:10.1215/23289252-2926437

White, L. R. (1973). Effective teachers for inner city schools. *The Journal of Negro Education*, *42*(3), 308–314. doi:10.2307/2966666

Williams, H. A. (2005). *Self-taught: African-American education in slavery and freedom.* University of North Carolina.

Woodson, C. G. (1933). *The Mis-Education of the Negro.* http://mrsdaysheffield.weebly.com/uploads/5/5/4/1/5541180/th e_miseducation_of_the_negro.pdf

World Health Organization. (n.d.) *What are critical incidents?* WHO. https://www.workpositive. ie/information/whatarecriticalincidents

WorldM. (2002). https://mancala.fandom.com/wiki/Oware

Yanka, K. (1983). *The Akan Trickster Cycle: Myth or Folk Tale?* Indian University: African Studies Program.

Yin, R. K. (2018). *Case study research and applications: Design and methods* (6th ed.). Sage.

Young, J. R. (2007). *Rituals of resistance: African Atlantic religion in Kongo and the Lowcountry South in the era of slavery.* Louisiana State University Press.

Zack-Williams, A. B., & Uduku, O. (2004). African Diaspora – African development concerns: An Introduction. In O. Uduku & A. B. Zack-Williams (Eds.), *Africa Beyond the Post-colonial: Political and Social Identities* (pp. 1–19). Ashgate Publishing Limited.

Zaidi, Z., Verstegen, D., Vyas, R., Hamed, O., Dornan, T., & Morahan, P. (2016). Cultural hegemony? Educators' perspectives on facilitating cross-cultural dialogue. *Medical Education Online, 21*(1), 33145. doi:10.3402/meo.v21.33145 PMID:27890048

Zarembka, J. (2007). *The Pigment of Your Imagination: 'Mixed Race' in a Global Society.* Madera Press.

Zidani, S. (2021). Whose pedagogy is it anyway? Decolonizing the syllabus through a critical embrace of difference. *Media Culture & Society, 43*(5), 970–978. doi:10.1177/0163443720980922

Zion, S., Allen, C. D., & Jean, C. (2015). Enacting a Critical Pedagogy, Influencing Teachers' Sociopolitical Development. *The Urban Review, 47*(5), 914–933. doi:10.100711256-015-0340-y

Zobel Marshall, E. (2012). *Anansi's Journey: A Story of Jamaican Cultural Resistance.* University Press of the West Indies.

Related References

To continue our tradition of advancing academic research, we have compiled a list of recommended IGI Global readings. These references will provide additional information and guidance to further enrich your knowledge and assist you with your own research and future publications.

Aburezeq, I. M., & Dweikat, F. F. (2017). Cloud Applications in Language Teaching: Examining Pre-Service Teachers' Expertise, Perceptions and Integration. *International Journal of Distance Education Technologies*, *15*(4), 39–60. doi:10.4018/IJDET.2017100103

Acharjya, B., & Das, S. (2022). Adoption of E-Learning During the COVID-19 Pandemic: The Moderating Role of Age and Gender. *International Journal of Web-Based Learning and Teaching Technologies*, *17*(2), 1–14. https://doi.org/10.4018/IJWLTT.20220301.oa4

Adams, J. L., & Thomas, S. K. (2022). Non-Linear Curriculum Experiences for Student Learning and Work Design: What Is the Maximum Potential of a Chat Bot? In S. Ramlall, T. Cross, & M. Love (Eds.), *Handbook of Research on Future of Work and Education: Implications for Curriculum Delivery and Work Design* (pp. 299–306). IGI Global. https://doi.org/10.4018/978-1-7998-8275-6.ch018

Adera, B. (2017). Supporting Language and Literacy Development for English Language Learners. In J. Keengwe (Ed.), *Handbook of Research on Promoting Cross-Cultural Competence and Social Justice in Teacher Education* (pp. 339–354). Hershey, PA: IGI Global. doi:10.4018/978-1-5225-0897-7.ch018

Ahamer, G. (2017). Quality Assurance for a Developmental "Global Studies" (GS) Curriculum. In I. Management Association (Ed.), Educational Leadership and Administration: Concepts, Methodologies, Tools, and Applications (pp. 438-477). Hershey, PA: IGI Global. https://doi.org/ doi:10.4018/978-1-5225-1624-8.ch023

Akayoğlu, S., & Seferoğlu, G. (2019). An Analysis of Negotiation of Meaning Functions of Advanced EFL Learners in Second Life: Negotiation of Meaning in Second Life. In M. Kruk (Ed.), *Assessing the Effectiveness of Virtual Technologies in Foreign and Second Language Instruction* (pp. 61–85). IGI Global. https://doi.org/10.4018/978-1-5225-7286-2.ch003

Akella, N. R. (2022). Unravelling the Web of Qualitative Dissertation Writing!: A Student Reflects. In A. Zimmerman (Ed.), *Methodological Innovations in Research and Academic Writing* (pp. 260–282). IGI Global. https://doi.org/10.4018/978-1-7998-8283-1.ch014

Alegre de la Rosa, O. M., & Angulo, L. M. (2017). Social Inclusion and Intercultural Values in a School of Education. In S. Mukerji & P. Tripathi (Eds.), *Handbook of Research on Administration, Policy, and Leadership in Higher Education* (pp. 518–531). Hershey, PA: IGI Global. doi:10.4018/978-1-5225-0672-0.ch020

Alexander, C. (2019). Using Gamification Strategies to Cultivate and Measure Professional Educator Dispositions. *International Journal of Game-Based Learning*, *9*(1), 15–29. https://doi.org/10.4018/IJGBL.2019010102

Anderson, K. M. (2017). Preparing Teachers in the Age of Equity and Inclusion. In I. Management Association (Ed.), Medical Education and Ethics: Concepts, Methodologies, Tools, and Applications (pp. 1532-1554). Hershey, PA: IGI Global. doi:10.4018/978-1-5225-0978-3.ch069

Awdziej, M. (2017). Case Study as a Teaching Method in Marketing. In D. Latusek (Ed.), *Case Studies as a Teaching Tool in Management Education* (pp. 244–263). Hershey, PA: IGI Global. doi:10.4018/978-1-5225-0770-3.ch013

Bakos, J. (2019). Sociolinguistic Factors Influencing English Language Learning. In N. Erdogan & M. Wei (Eds.), *Applied Linguistics for Teachers of Culturally and Linguistically Diverse Learners* (pp. 403–424). IGI Global. https://doi.org/10.4018/978-1-5225-8467-4.ch017

Banas, J. R., & York, C. S. (2017). Pre-Service Teachers' Motivation to Use Technology and the Impact of Authentic Learning Exercises. In L. Tomei (Ed.), *Exploring the New Era of Technology-Infused Education* (pp. 121–140). Hershey, PA: IGI Global. doi:10.4018/978-1-5225-1709-2.ch008

Related References

Barton, T. P. (2021). Empowering Educator Allyship by Exploring Racial Trauma and the Disengagement of Black Students. In C. Reneau & M. Villarreal (Eds.), *Handbook of Research on Leading Higher Education Transformation With Social Justice, Equity, and Inclusion* (pp. 186–197). IGI Global. https://doi.org/10.4018/978-1-7998-7152-1.ch013

Benhima, M. (2021). Moroccan English Department Student Attitudes Towards the Use of Distance Education During COVID-19: Moulay Ismail University as a Case Study. *International Journal of Information and Communication Technology Education*, *17*(3), 105–122. https://doi.org/10.4018/IJICTE.20210701.oa7

Beycioglu, K., & Wildy, H. (2017). Principal Preparation: The Case of Novice Principals in Turkey. In I. Management Association (Ed.), Educational Leadership and Administration: Concepts, Methodologies, Tools, and Applications (pp. 1152-1169). Hershey, PA: IGI Global. https://doi.org/ doi:10.4018/978-1-5225-1624-8.ch054

Bharwani, S., & Musunuri, D. (2018). Reflection as a Process From Theory to Practice. In M. Khosrow-Pour, D.B.A. (Ed.), Encyclopedia of Information Science and Technology, Fourth Edition (pp. 1529-1539). Hershey, PA: IGI Global. doi:10.4018/978-1-5225-2255-3.ch132

Bhushan, A., Garza, K. B., Perumal, O., Das, S. K., Feola, D. J., Farrell, D., & Birnbaum, A. (2022). Lessons Learned From the COVID-19 Pandemic and the Implications for Pharmaceutical Graduate Education and Research. In C. Ford & K. Garza (Eds.), *Handbook of Research on Updating and Innovating Health Professions Education: Post-Pandemic Perspectives* (pp. 324–345). IGI Global. https://doi.org/10.4018/978-1-7998-7623-6.ch014

Bintz, W., Ciecierski, L. M., & Royan, E. (2021). Using Picture Books With Instructional Strategies to Address New Challenges and Teach Literacy Skills in a Digital World. In L. Haas & J. Tussey (Eds.), *Connecting Disciplinary Literacy and Digital Storytelling in K-12 Education* (pp. 38–58). IGI Global. https://doi.org/10.4018/978-1-7998-5770-9.ch003

Bohjanen, S. L., Cameron-Standerford, A., & Meidl, T. D. (2018). Capacity Building Pedagogy for Diverse Learners. In J. Keengwe (Ed.), *Handbook of Research on Pedagogical Models for Next-Generation Teaching and Learning* (pp. 195–212). Hershey, PA: IGI Global. doi:10.4018/978-1-5225-3873-8.ch011

Brewer, J. C. (2018). Measuring Text Readability Using Reading Level. In M. Khosrow-Pour, D.B.A. (Ed.), Encyclopedia of Information Science and Technology, Fourth Edition (pp. 1499-1507). Hershey, PA: IGI Global. doi:10.4018/978-1-5225-2255-3.ch129

Brookbanks, B. C. (2022). Student Perspectives on Business Education in the USA: Current Attitudes and Necessary Changes in an Age of Disruption. In A. Zhuplev & R. Koepp (Eds.), *Global Trends, Dynamics, and Imperatives for Strategic Development in Business Education in an Age of Disruption* (pp. 214–231). IGI Global. doi:10.4018/978-1-7998-7548-2.ch011

Brown, L. V., Dari, T., & Spencer, N. (2019). Addressing the Impact of Trauma in High Poverty Elementary Schools: An Ecological Model for School Counseling. In K. Daniels & K. Billingsley (Eds.), *Creating Caring and Supportive Educational Environments for Meaningful Learning* (pp. 135–153). IGI Global. https://doi.org/10.4018/978-1-5225-5748-7.ch008

Brown, S. L. (2017). A Case Study of Strategic Leadership and Research in Practice: Principal Preparation Programs that Work – An Educational Administration Perspective of Best Practices for Master's Degree Programs for Principal Preparation. In V. Wang (Ed.), *Encyclopedia of Strategic Leadership and Management* (pp. 1226–1244). Hershey, PA: IGI Global. doi:10.4018/978-1-5225-1049-9.ch086

Brzozowski, M., & Ferster, I. (2017). Educational Management Leadership: High School Principal's Management Style and Parental Involvement in School Management in Israel. In V. Potocan, M. Üngan, & Z. Nedelko (Eds.), *Handbook of Research on Managerial Solutions in Non-Profit Organizations* (pp. 55–74). Hershey, PA: IGI Global. doi:10.4018/978-1-5225-0731-4.ch003

Cahapay, M. B. (2020). Delphi Technique in the Development of Emerging Contents in High School Science Curriculum. *International Journal of Curriculum Development and Learning Measurement, 1*(2), 1–9. https://doi.org/10.4018/IJCDLM.2020070101

Camacho, L. F., & Leon Guerrero, A. E. (2022). Indigenous Student Experience in Higher Education: Implementation of Culturally Sensitive Support. In P. Pangelinan & T. McVey (Eds.), *Learning and Reconciliation Through Indigenous Education in Oceania* (pp. 254–266). IGI Global. https://doi.org/10.4018/978-1-7998-7736-3.ch016

Cannaday, J. (2017). The Masking Effect: Hidden Gifts and Disabilities of 2e Students. In P. Dickenson, P. Keough, & J. Courduff (Eds.), *Preparing Pre-Service Teachers for the Inclusive Classroom* (pp. 220–231). Hershey, PA: IGI Global. doi:10.4018/978-1-5225-1753-5.ch011

Related References

Cederquist, S., Fishman, B., & Teasley, S. D. (2022). What's Missing From the College Transcript?: How Employers Make Sense of Student Skills. In Y. Huang (Ed.), *Handbook of Research on Credential Innovations for Inclusive Pathways to Professions* (pp. 234–253). IGI Global. https://doi.org/10.4018/978-1-7998-3820-3.ch012

Cockrell, P., & Gibson, T. (2019). The Untold Stories of Black and Brown Student Experiences in Historically White Fraternities and Sororities. In P. Hoffman-Miller, M. James, & D. Hermond (Eds.), *African American Suburbanization and the Consequential Loss of Identity* (pp. 153–171). IGI Global. https://doi.org/10.4018/978-1-5225-7835-2.ch009

Cohen, M. (2022). Leveraging Content Creation to Boost Student Engagement. In T. Driscoll III, (Ed.), *Designing Effective Distance and Blended Learning Environments in K-12* (pp. 223–239). IGI Global. https://doi.org/10.4018/978-1-7998-6829-3.ch013

Contreras, E. C., & Contreras, I. I. (2018). Development of Communication Skills through Auditory Training Software in Special Education. In M. Khosrow-Pour, D.B.A. (Ed.), Encyclopedia of Information Science and Technology, Fourth Edition (pp. 2431-2441). Hershey, PA: IGI Global. doi:10.4018/978-1-5225-2255-3.ch212

Cooke, L., Schugar, J., Schugar, H., Penny, C., & Bruning, H. (2020). Can Everyone Code?: Preparing Teachers to Teach Computer Languages as a Literacy. In J. Mitchell & E. Vaughn (Eds.), *Participatory Literacy Practices for P-12 Classrooms in the Digital Age* (pp. 163–183). IGI Global. https://doi.org/10.4018/978-1-7998-0000-2.ch009

Cooley, D., & Whitten, E. (2017). Special Education Leadership and the Implementation of Response to Intervention. In F. Topor (Ed.), *Handbook of Research on Individualism and Identity in the Globalized Digital Age* (pp. 265–286). Hershey, PA: IGI Global. doi:10.4018/978-1-5225-0522-8.ch012

Cosner, S., Tozer, S., & Zavitkovsky, P. (2017). Enacting a Cycle of Inquiry Capstone Research Project in Doctoral-Level Leadership Preparation. In I. Management Association (Ed.), Educational Leadership and Administration: Concepts, Methodologies, Tools, and Applications (pp. 1460-1481). Hershey, PA: IGI Global. doi:10.4018/978-1-5225-1624-8.ch067

Crawford, C. M. (2018). Instructional Real World Community Engagement. In M. Khosrow-Pour, D.B.A. (Ed.), Encyclopedia of Information Science and Technology, Fourth Edition (pp. 1474-1486). Hershey, PA: IGI Global. doi:10.4018/978-1-5225-2255-3.ch127

Crosby-Cooper, T., & Pacis, D. (2017). Implementing Effective Student Support Teams. In P. Dickenson, P. Keough, & J. Courduff (Eds.), *Preparing Pre-Service Teachers for the Inclusive Classroom* (pp. 248–262). Hershey, PA: IGI Global. doi:10.4018/978-1-5225-1753-5.ch013

Curran, C. M., & Hawbaker, B. W. (2017). Cultivating Communities of Inclusive Practice: Professional Development for Educators – Research and Practice. In C. Curran & A. Petersen (Eds.), *Handbook of Research on Classroom Diversity and Inclusive Education Practice* (pp. 120–153). Hershey, PA: IGI Global. doi:10.4018/978-1-5225-2520-2.ch006

Dass, S., & Dabbagh, N. (2018). Faculty Adoption of 3D Avatar-Based Virtual World Learning Environments: An Exploratory Case Study. In I. Management Association (Ed.), Technology Adoption and Social Issues: Concepts, Methodologies, Tools, and Applications (pp. 1000-1033). Hershey, PA: IGI Global. https://doi.org/ doi:10.4018/978-1-5225-5201-7.ch045

Davison, A. M., & Scholl, K. G. (2017). Inclusive Recreation as Part of the IEP Process. In C. Curran & A. Petersen (Eds.), *Handbook of Research on Classroom Diversity and Inclusive Education Practice* (pp. 311–330). Hershey, PA: IGI Global. doi:10.4018/978-1-5225-2520-2.ch013

DeCoito, I. (2018). Addressing Digital Competencies, Curriculum Development, and Instructional Design in Science Teacher Education. In M. Khosrow-Pour, D.B.A. (Ed.), Encyclopedia of Information Science and Technology, Fourth Edition (pp. 1420-1431). Hershey, PA: IGI Global. https://doi.org/ doi:10.4018/978-1-5225-2255-3.ch122

DeCoito, I., & Richardson, T. (2017). Beyond Angry Birds™: Using Web-Based Tools to Engage Learners and Promote Inquiry in STEM Learning. In I. Levin & D. Tsybulsky (Eds.), *Digital Tools and Solutions for Inquiry-Based STEM Learning* (pp. 166–196). Hershey, PA: IGI Global. doi:10.4018/978-1-5225-2525-7.ch007

Delmas, P. M. (2017). Research-Based Leadership for Next-Generation Leaders. In R. Styron Jr & J. Styron (Eds.), *Comprehensive Problem-Solving and Skill Development for Next-Generation Leaders* (pp. 1–39). Hershey, PA: IGI Global. doi:10.4018/978-1-5225-1968-3.ch001

Demiray, U., & Ekren, G. (2018). Administrative-Related Evaluation for Distance Education Institutions in Turkey. In K. Buyuk, S. Kocdar, & A. Bozkurt (Eds.), *Administrative Leadership in Open and Distance Learning Programs* (pp. 263–288). Hershey, PA: IGI Global. doi:10.4018/978-1-5225-2645-2.ch011

Dickenson, P. (2017). What do we Know and Where Can We Grow?: Teachers Preparation for the Inclusive Classroom. In P. Dickenson, P. Keough, & J. Courduff (Eds.), *Preparing Pre-Service Teachers for the Inclusive Classroom* (pp. 1–22). Hershey, PA: IGI Global. doi:10.4018/978-1-5225-1753-5.ch001

Ding, Q., & Zhu, H. (2021). Flipping the Classroom in STEM Education. In J. Keengwe (Ed.), *Handbook of Research on Innovations in Non-Traditional Educational Practices* (pp. 155–173). IGI Global. https://doi.org/10.4018/978-1-7998-4360-3.ch008

Dixon, T., & Christison, M. (2021). Teaching English Grammar in a Hybrid Academic ESL Course: A Mixed Methods Study. In K. Kelch, P. Byun, S. Safavi, & S. Cervantes (Eds.), *CALL Theory Applications for Online TESOL Education* (pp. 229–251). IGI Global. https://doi.org/10.4018/978-1-7998-6609-1.ch010

Donne, V., & Hansen, M. (2017). Teachers' Use of Assistive Technologies in Education. In L. Tomei (Ed.), *Exploring the New Era of Technology-Infused Education* (pp. 86–101). Hershey, PA: IGI Global. doi:10.4018/978-1-5225-1709-2.ch006

Donne, V., & Hansen, M. A. (2018). Business and Technology Educators: Practices for Inclusion. In I. Management Association (Ed.), Business Education and Ethics: Concepts, Methodologies, Tools, and Applications (pp. 471-484). Hershey, PA: IGI Global. https://doi.org/ doi:10.4018/978-1-5225-3153-1.ch026

Dos Santos, L. M. (2022). Completing Student-Teaching Internships Online: Instructional Changes During the COVID-19 Pandemic. In M. Alaali (Ed.), *Assessing University Governance and Policies in Relation to the COVID-19 Pandemic* (pp. 106–127). IGI Global. https://doi.org/10.4018/978-1-7998-8279-4.ch007

Dreon, O., Shettel, J., & Bower, K. M. (2017). Preparing Next Generation Elementary Teachers for the Tools of Tomorrow. In M. Grassetti & S. Brookby (Eds.), *Advancing Next-Generation Teacher Education through Digital Tools and Applications* (pp. 143–159). Hershey, PA: IGI Global. doi:10.4018/978-1-5225-0965-3.ch008

Durak, H. Y., & Güyer, T. (2018). Design and Development of an Instructional Program for Teaching Programming Processes to Gifted Students Using Scratch. In J. Cannaday (Ed.), *Curriculum Development for Gifted Education Programs* (pp. 61–99). Hershey, PA: IGI Global. doi:10.4018/978-1-5225-3041-1.ch004

Egorkina, E., Ivanov, M., & Valyavskiy, A. Y. (2018). Students' Research Competence Formation of the Quality of Open and Distance Learning. In V. Mkrttchian & L. Belyanina (Eds.), *Handbook of Research on Students' Research Competence in Modern Educational Contexts* (pp. 364–384). Hershey, PA: IGI Global. doi:10.4018/978-1-5225-3485-3.ch019

Ekren, G., Karataş, S., & Demiray, U. (2017). Understanding of Leadership in Distance Education Management. In I. Management Association (Ed.), Educational Leadership and Administration: Concepts, Methodologies, Tools, and Applications (pp. 34-50). Hershey, PA: IGI Global. https://doi.org/ doi:10.4018/978-1-5225-1624-8.ch003

Elmore, W. M., Young, J. K., Harris, S., & Mason, D. (2017). The Relationship between Individual Student Attributes and Online Course Completion. In K. Shelton & K. Pedersen (Eds.), *Handbook of Research on Building, Growing, and Sustaining Quality E-Learning Programs* (pp. 151–173). Hershey, PA: IGI Global. doi:10.4018/978-1-5225-0877-9.ch008

Ercegovac, I. R., Alfirević, N., & Koludrović, M. (2017). School Principals' Communication and Co-Operation Assessment: The Croatian Experience. In I. Management Association (Ed.), Educational Leadership and Administration: Concepts, Methodologies, Tools, and Applications (pp. 1568-1589). Hershey, PA: IGI Global. https://doi.org/ doi:10.4018/978-1-5225-1624-8.ch072

Everhart, D., & Seymour, D. M. (2017). Challenges and Opportunities in the Currency of Higher Education. In K. Rasmussen, P. Northrup, & R. Colson (Eds.), *Handbook of Research on Competency-Based Education in University Settings* (pp. 41–65). Hershey, PA: IGI Global. doi:10.4018/978-1-5225-0932-5.ch003

Farmer, L. S. (2017). Managing Portable Technologies for Special Education. In V. Wang (Ed.), *Encyclopedia of Strategic Leadership and Management* (pp. 977–987). Hershey, PA: IGI Global. doi:10.4018/978-1-5225-1049-9.ch068

Farmer, L. S. (2018). Optimizing OERs for Optimal ICT Literacy in Higher Education. In J. Keengwe (Ed.), *Handbook of Research on Mobile Technology, Constructivism, and Meaningful Learning* (pp. 366–390). Hershey, PA: IGI Global. doi:10.4018/978-1-5225-3949-0.ch020

Ferguson, B. T. (2019). Supporting Affective Development of Children With Disabilities Through Moral Dilemmas. In S. Ikuta (Ed.), *Handmade Teaching Materials for Students With Disabilities* (pp. 253–275). IGI Global. doi:10.4018/978-1-5225-6240-5.ch011

Fındık, L. Y. (2017). Self-Assessment of Principals Based on Leadership in Complexity. In I. Management Association (Ed.), Educational Leadership and Administration: Concepts, Methodologies, Tools, and Applications (pp. 978-991). Hershey, PA: IGI Global. https://doi.org/ doi:10.4018/978-1-5225-1624-8.ch047

Flor, A. G., & Gonzalez-Flor, B. (2018). Dysfunctional Digital Demeanors: Tales From (and Policy Implications of) eLearning's Dark Side. In I. Management Association (Ed.), The Dark Web: Breakthroughs in Research and Practice (pp. 37-50). Hershey, PA: IGI Global. https://doi.org/ doi:10.4018/978-1-5225-3163-0.ch003

Floyd, K. K., & Shambaugh, N. (2017). Instructional Design for Simulations in Special Education Virtual Learning Spaces. In T. Kidd & L. Morris Jr., (Eds.), *Handbook of Research on Instructional Systems and Educational Technology* (pp. 202–215). Hershey, PA: IGI Global. doi:10.4018/978-1-5225-2399-4.ch018

Freeland, S. F. (2020). Community Schools: Improving Academic Achievement Through Meaningful Engagement. In R. Kronick (Ed.), *Emerging Perspectives on Community Schools and the Engaged University* (pp. 132–144). IGI Global. https://doi.org/10.4018/978-1-7998-0280-8.ch008

Ghanbarzadeh, R., & Ghapanchi, A. H. (2019). Applied Areas of Three Dimensional Virtual Worlds in Learning and Teaching: A Review of Higher Education. In I. Management Association (Ed.), *Virtual Reality in Education: Breakthroughs in Research and Practice* (pp. 172-192). IGI Global. https://doi.org/10.4018/978-1-5225-8179-6.ch008

Giovannini, J. M. (2017). Technology Integration in Preservice Teacher Education Programs: Research-based Recommendations. In M. Grassetti & S. Brookby (Eds.), *Advancing Next-Generation Teacher Education through Digital Tools and Applications* (pp. 82–102). Hershey, PA: IGI Global. doi:10.4018/978-1-5225-0965-3.ch005

Good, S., & Clarke, V. B. (2017). An Integral Analysis of One Urban School System's Efforts to Support Student-Centered Teaching. In J. Keengwe & G. Onchwari (Eds.), *Handbook of Research on Learner-Centered Pedagogy in Teacher Education and Professional Development* (pp. 45–68). Hershey, PA: IGI Global. doi:10.4018/978-1-5225-0892-2.ch003

Guetzoian, E. (2022). Gamification Strategies for Higher Education Student Worker Training. In C. Lane (Ed.), *Handbook of Research on Acquiring 21st Century Literacy Skills Through Game-Based Learning* (pp. 164–179). IGI Global. https://doi.org/10.4018/978-1-7998-7271-9.ch009

Hamidi, F., Owuor, P. M., Hynie, M., Baljko, M., & McGrath, S. (2017). Potentials of Digital Assistive Technology and Special Education in Kenya. In C. Ayo & V. Mbarika (Eds.), *Sustainable ICT Adoption and Integration for Socio-Economic Development* (pp. 125–151). Hershey, PA: IGI Global. doi:10.4018/978-1-5225-2565-3.ch006

Hamim, T., Benabbou, F., & Sael, N. (2022). Student Profile Modeling Using Boosting Algorithms. *International Journal of Web-Based Learning and Teaching Technologies*, *17*(5), 1–13. https://doi.org/10.4018/IJWLTT.20220901.oa4

Henderson, L. K. (2017). Meltdown at Fukushima: Global Catastrophic Events, Visual Literacy, and Art Education. In R. Shin (Ed.), *Convergence of Contemporary Art, Visual Culture, and Global Civic Engagement* (pp. 80–99). Hershey, PA: IGI Global. doi:10.4018/978-1-5225-1665-1.ch005

Hudgins, T., & Holland, J. L. (2018). Digital Badges: Tracking Knowledge Acquisition Within an Innovation Framework. In I. Management Association (Ed.), Wearable Technologies: Concepts, Methodologies, Tools, and Applications (pp. 1118-1132). Hershey, PA: IGI Global. https://doi.org/ doi:10.4018/978-1-5225-5484-4.ch051

Hwang, R., Lin, H., Sun, J. C., & Wu, J. (2019). Improving Learning Achievement in Science Education for Elementary School Students via Blended Learning. *International Journal of Online Pedagogy and Course Design*, *9*(2), 44–62. https://doi.org/10.4018/IJOPCD.2019040104

Jančec, L., & Vodopivec, J. L. (2019). The Implicit Pedagogy and the Hidden Curriculum in Postmodern Education. In J. Vodopivec, L. Jančec, & T. Štemberger (Eds.), *Implicit Pedagogy for Optimized Learning in Contemporary Education* (pp. 41–59). IGI Global. https://doi.org/10.4018/978-1-5225-5799-9.ch003

Janus, M., & Siddiqua, A. (2018). Challenges for Children With Special Health Needs at the Time of Transition to School. In I. Management Association (Ed.), Autism Spectrum Disorders: Breakthroughs in Research and Practice (pp. 339-371). Hershey, PA: IGI Global. doi:10.4018/978-1-5225-3827-1.ch018

Jesus, R. A. (2018). Screencasts and Learning Styles. In M. Khosrow-Pour, D.B.A. (Ed.), Encyclopedia of Information Science and Technology, Fourth Edition (pp. 1548-1558). Hershey, PA: IGI Global. doi:10.4018/978-1-5225-2255-3.ch134

John, G., Francis, N., & Santhakumar, A. B. (2022). Student Engagement: Past, Present, and Future. In S. Ramlall, T. Cross, & M. Love (Eds.), *Handbook of Research on Future of Work and Education: Implications for Curriculum Delivery and Work Design* (pp. 329–341). IGI Global. https://doi.org/10.4018/978-1-7998-8275-6.ch020

Karpinski, A. C., D'Agostino, J. V., Williams, A. K., Highland, S. A., & Mellott, J. A. (2018). The Relationship Between Online Formative Assessment and State Test Scores Using Multilevel Modeling. In M. Khosrow-Pour, D.B.A. (Ed.), Encyclopedia of Information Science and Technology, Fourth Edition (pp. 5183-5192). Hershey, PA: IGI Global. doi:10.4018/978-1-5225-2255-3.ch450

Kats, Y. (2017). Educational Leadership and Integrated Support for Students with Autism Spectrum Disorders. In I. Management Association (Ed.), Educational Leadership and Administration: Concepts, Methodologies, Tools, and Applications (pp. 101-114). Hershey, PA: IGI Global. https://doi.org/ doi:10.4018/978-1-5225-1624-8.ch007

Kaya, G., & Altun, A. (2018). Educational Ontology Development. In M. Khosrow-Pour, D.B.A. (Ed.), Encyclopedia of Information Science and Technology, Fourth Edition (pp. 1441-1450). Hershey, PA: IGI Global. doi:10.4018/978-1-5225-2255-3.ch124

Keough, P. D., & Pacis, D. (2017). Best Practices Implementing Special Education Curriculum and Common Core State Standards using UDL. In P. Dickenson, P. Keough, & J. Courduff (Eds.), *Preparing Pre-Service Teachers for the Inclusive Classroom* (pp. 107–123). Hershey, PA: IGI Global. doi:10.4018/978-1-5225-1753-5.ch006

Kilburn, M., Henckell, M., & Starrett, D. (2018). Factors Contributing to the Effectiveness of Online Students and Instructors. In M. Khosrow-Pour, D.B.A. (Ed.), Encyclopedia of Information Science and Technology, Fourth Edition (pp. 1451-1462). Hershey, PA: IGI Global. doi:10.4018/978-1-5225-2255-3.ch125

Koban Koç, D. (2021). Gender and Language: A Sociolinguistic Analysis of Second Language Writing. In E. Hancı-Azizoglu & N. Kavaklı (Eds.), *Futuristic and Linguistic Perspectives on Teaching Writing to Second Language Students* (pp. 161–177). IGI Global. https://doi.org/10.4018/978-1-7998-6508-7.ch010

Konecny, L. T. (2017). Hybrid, Online, and Flipped Classrooms in Health Science: Enhanced Learning Environments. In I. Management Association (Ed.), Flipped Instruction: Breakthroughs in Research and Practice (pp. 355-370). Hershey, PA: IGI Global. https://doi.org/ doi:10.4018/978-1-5225-1803-7.ch020

Kupietz, K. D. (2021). Gaming and Simulation in Public Education: Teaching Others to Help Themselves and Their Neighbors. In N. Drumhiller, T. Wilkin, & K. Srba (Eds.), *Simulation and Game-Based Learning in Emergency and Disaster Management* (pp. 41–62). IGI Global. https://doi.org/10.4018/978-1-7998-4087-9.ch003

Kwee, C. T. (2022). Assessing the International Student Enrolment Strategies in Australian Universities: A Case Study During the COVID-19 Pandemic. In M. Alaali (Ed.), *Assessing University Governance and Policies in Relation to the COVID-19 Pandemic* (pp. 162–188). IGI Global. https://doi.org/10.4018/978-1-7998-8279-4.ch010

Lauricella, S., & McArthur, F. A. (2022). Taking a Student-Centred Approach to Alternative Digital Credentials: Multiple Pathways Toward the Acquisition of Microcredentials. In D. Piedra (Ed.), *Innovations in the Design and Application of Alternative Digital Credentials* (pp. 57–69). IGI Global. https://doi.org/10.4018/978-1-7998-7697-7.ch003

Llamas, M. F. (2019). Intercultural Awareness in Teaching English for Early Childhood: A Film-Based Approach. In E. Domínguez Romero, J. Bobkina, & S. Stefanova (Eds.), *Teaching Literature and Language Through Multimodal Texts* (pp. 54–68). IGI Global. https://doi.org/10.4018/978-1-5225-5796-8.ch004

Lokhtina, I., & Kkese, E. T. (2022). Reflecting and Adapting to an Academic Workplace Before and After the Lockdown in Greek-Speaking Cyprus: Opportunities and Challenges. In A. Zhuplev & R. Koepp (Eds.), *Global Trends, Dynamics, and Imperatives for Strategic Development in Business Education in an Age of Disruption* (pp. 126–148). IGI Global. https://doi.org/10.4018/978-1-7998-7548-2.ch007

Lovell, K. L. (2017). Development and Evaluation of Neuroscience Computer-Based Modules for Medical Students: Instructional Design Principles and Effectiveness. In J. Stefaniak (Ed.), *Advancing Medical Education Through Strategic Instructional Design* (pp. 262–276). Hershey, PA: IGI Global. doi:10.4018/978-1-5225-2098-6.ch013

Maher, D. (2019). The Use of Course Management Systems in Pre-Service Teacher Education. In J. Keengwe (Ed.), *Handbook of Research on Blended Learning Pedagogies and Professional Development in Higher Education* (pp. 196–213). IGI Global. https://doi.org/10.4018/978-1-5225-5557-5.ch011

Makewa, L. N. (2019). Teacher Technology Competence Base. In L. Makewa, B. Ngussa, & J. Kuboja (Eds.), *Technology-Supported Teaching and Research Methods for Educators* (pp. 247–267). IGI Global. https://doi.org/10.4018/978-1-5225-5915-3.ch014

Mallett, C. A. (2022). School Resource (Police) Officers in Schools: Impact on Campus Safety, Student Discipline, and Learning. In G. Crews (Ed.), *Impact of School Shootings on Classroom Culture, Curriculum, and Learning* (pp. 53–70). IGI Global. https://doi.org/10.4018/978-1-7998-5200-1.ch004

Related References

Marinho, J. E., Freitas, I. R., Leão, I. B., Pacheco, L. O., Gonçalves, M. P., Castro, M. J., Silva, P. D., & Moreira, R. J. (2022). Project-Based Learning Application in Higher Education: Student Experiences and Perspectives. In A. Alves & N. van Hattum-Janssen (Eds.), *Training Engineering Students for Modern Technological Advancement* (pp. 146–164). IGI Global. https://doi.org/10.4018/978-1-7998-8816-1.ch007

McCleskey, J. A., & Melton, R. M. (2022). Rolling With the Flow: Online Faculty and Student Presence in a Post-COVID-19 World. In S. Ramlall, T. Cross, & M. Love (Eds.), *Handbook of Research on Future of Work and Education: Implications for Curriculum Delivery and Work Design* (pp. 307–328). IGI Global. https://doi.org/10.4018/978-1-7998-8275-6.ch019

McCormack, V. F., Stauffer, M., Fishley, K., Hohenbrink, J., Mascazine, J. R., & Zigler, T. (2018). Designing a Dual Licensure Path for Middle Childhood and Special Education Teacher Candidates. In D. Polly, M. Putman, T. Petty, & A. Good (Eds.), *Innovative Practices in Teacher Preparation and Graduate-Level Teacher Education Programs* (pp. 21–36). Hershey, PA: IGI Global. doi:10.4018/978-1-5225-3068-8.ch002

McDaniel, R. (2017). Strategic Leadership in Instructional Design: Applying the Principles of Instructional Design through the Lens of Strategic Leadership to Distance Education. In V. Wang (Ed.), *Encyclopedia of Strategic Leadership and Management* (pp. 1570–1584). Hershey, PA: IGI Global. doi:10.4018/978-1-5225-1049-9.ch109

McKinney, R. E., Halli-Tierney, A. D., Gold, A. E., Allen, R. S., & Carroll, D. G. (2022). Interprofessional Education: Using Standardized Cases in Face-to-Face and Remote Learning Settings. In C. Ford & K. Garza (Eds.), *Handbook of Research on Updating and Innovating Health Professions Education: Post-Pandemic Perspectives* (pp. 24–42). IGI Global. https://doi.org/10.4018/978-1-7998-7623-6.ch002

Meintjes, H. H. (2021). Learner Views of a Facebook Page as a Supportive Digital Pedagogical Tool at a Public South African School in a Grade 12 Business Studies Class. *International Journal of Smart Education and Urban Society, 12*(2), 32–45. https://doi.org/10.4018/IJSEUS.2021040104

Melero-García, F. (2022). Training Bilingual Interpreters in Healthcare Settings: Student Perceptions of Online Learning. In J. LeLoup & P. Swanson (Eds.), *Handbook of Research on Effective Online Language Teaching in a Disruptive Environment* (pp. 288–310). IGI Global. https://doi.org/10.4018/978-1-7998-7720-2.ch015

Meletiadou, E. (2022). The Use of Peer Assessment as an Inclusive Learning Strategy in Higher Education Institutions: Enhancing Student Writing Skills and Motivation. In E. Meletiadou (Ed.), *Handbook of Research on Policies and Practices for Assessing Inclusive Teaching and Learning* (pp. 1–26). IGI Global. https://doi.org/10.4018/978-1-7998-8579-5.ch001

Memon, R. N., Ahmad, R., & Salim, S. S. (2018). Critical Issues in Requirements Engineering Education. In I. Management Association (Ed.), Computer Systems and Software Engineering: Concepts, Methodologies, Tools, and Applications (pp. 1953-1976). Hershey, PA: IGI Global. doi:10.4018/978-1-5225-3923-0.ch081

Mendenhall, R. (2017). Western Governors University: CBE Innovator and National Model. In K. Rasmussen, P. Northrup, & R. Colson (Eds.), *Handbook of Research on Competency-Based Education in University Settings* (pp. 379–400). Hershey, PA: IGI Global. doi:10.4018/978-1-5225-0932-5.ch019

Mense, E. G., Griggs, D. M., & Shanks, J. N. (2018). School Leaders in a Time of Accountability and Data Use: Preparing Our Future School Leaders in Leadership Preparation Programs. In E. Mense & M. Crain-Dorough (Eds.), *Data Leadership for K-12 Schools in a Time of Accountability* (pp. 235–259). Hershey, PA: IGI Global. doi:10.4018/978-1-5225-3188-3.ch012

Mense, E. G., Griggs, D. M., & Shanks, J. N. (2018). School Leaders in a Time of Accountability and Data Use: Preparing Our Future School Leaders in Leadership Preparation Programs. In E. Mense & M. Crain-Dorough (Eds.), *Data Leadership for K-12 Schools in a Time of Accountability* (pp. 235–259). Hershey, PA: IGI Global. doi:10.4018/978-1-5225-3188-3.ch012

Mestry, R., & Naicker, S. R. (2017). Exploring Distributive Leadership in South African Public Primary Schools in the Soweto Region. In I. Management Association (Ed.), Educational Leadership and Administration: Concepts, Methodologies, Tools, and Applications (pp. 1041-1064). Hershey, PA: IGI Global. doi:10.4018/978-1-5225-1624-8.ch050

Monaghan, C. H., & Boboc, M. (2017). (Re)Defining Leadership in Higher Education in the U.S. In V. Wang (Ed.), *Encyclopedia of Strategic Leadership and Management* (pp. 567–579). Hershey, PA: IGI Global. doi:10.4018/978-1-5225-1049-9.ch040

Morall, M. B. (2021). Reimagining Mobile Phones: Multiple Literacies and Digital Media Compositions. In C. Moran (Eds.), *Affordances and Constraints of Mobile Phone Use in English Language Arts Classrooms* (pp. 41-53). IGI Global. https://doi.org/10.4018/978-1-7998-5805-8.ch003

Mthethwa, V. (2022). Student Governance and the Academic Minefield During COVID-19 Lockdown in South Africa. In M. Alaali (Ed.), *Assessing University Governance and Policies in Relation to the COVID-19 Pandemic* (pp. 255–276). IGI Global. https://doi.org/10.4018/978-1-7998-8279-4.ch015

Muthee, J. M., & Murungi, C. G. (2018). Relationship Among Intelligence, Achievement Motivation, Type of School, and Academic Performance of Kenyan Urban Primary School Pupils. In M. Khosrow-Pour, D.B.A. (Ed.), Encyclopedia of Information Science and Technology, Fourth Edition (pp. 1540-1547). Hershey, PA: IGI Global. https://doi.org/ doi:10.4018/978-1-5225-2255-3.ch133

Naranjo, J. (2018). Meeting the Need for Inclusive Educators Online: Teacher Education in Inclusive Special Education and Dual-Certification. In D. Polly, M. Putman, T. Petty, & A. Good (Eds.), *Innovative Practices in Teacher Preparation and Graduate-Level Teacher Education Programs* (pp. 106–122). Hershey, PA: IGI Global. doi:10.4018/978-1-5225-3068-8.ch007

Nkabinde, Z. P. (2017). Multiculturalism in Special Education: Perspectives of Minority Children in Urban Schools. In J. Keengwe (Ed.), *Handbook of Research on Promoting Cross-Cultural Competence and Social Justice in Teacher Education* (pp. 382–397). Hershey, PA: IGI Global. doi:10.4018/978-1-5225-0897-7.ch020

Nkabinde, Z. P. (2018). Online Instruction: Is the Quality the Same as Face-to-Face Instruction? In J. Keengwe (Ed.), *Handbook of Research on Digital Content, Mobile Learning, and Technology Integration Models in Teacher Education* (pp. 300–314). Hershey, PA: IGI Global. doi:10.4018/978-1-5225-2953-8.ch016

Nugroho, A., & Albusaidi, S. S. (2022). Internationalization of Higher Education: The Methodological Critiques on the Research Related to Study Overseas and International Experience. In H. Magd & S. Kunjumuhammed (Eds.), *Global Perspectives on Quality Assurance and Accreditation in Higher Education Institutions* (pp. 75–89). IGI Global. https://doi.org/10.4018/978-1-7998-8085-1.ch005

Nulty, Z., & West, S. G. (2022). Student Engagement and Supporting Students With Accommodations. In P. Bull & G. Patterson (Eds.), *Redefining Teacher Education and Teacher Preparation Programs in the Post-COVID-19 Era* (pp. 99–116). IGI Global. https://doi.org/10.4018/978-1-7998-8298-5.ch006

O'Connor, J. R. Jr, & Jackson, K. N. (2017). The Use of iPad® Devices and "Apps" for ASD Students in Special Education and Speech Therapy. In Y. Kats (Ed.), *Supporting the Education of Children with Autism Spectrum Disorders* (pp. 267–283). Hershey, PA: IGI Global. doi:10.4018/978-1-5225-0816-8.ch014

Okolie, U. C., & Yasin, A. M. (2017). TVET in Developing Nations and Human Development. In U. Okolie & A. Yasin (Eds.), *Technical Education and Vocational Training in Developing Nations* (pp. 1–25). Hershey, PA: IGI Global. doi:10.4018/978-1-5225-1811-2.ch001

Pack, A., & Barrett, A. (2021). A Review of Virtual Reality and English for Academic Purposes: Understanding Where to Start. *International Journal of Computer-Assisted Language Learning and Teaching*, *11*(1), 72–80. https://doi.org/10.4018/IJCALLT.2021010105

Pashollari, E. (2019). Building Sustainability Through Environmental Education: Education for Sustainable Development. In L. Wilson, & C. Stevenson (Eds.), *Building Sustainability Through Environmental Education* (pp. 72-88). IGI Global. https://doi.org/10.4018/978-1-5225-7727-0.ch004

Paulson, E. N. (2017). Adapting and Advocating for an Online EdD Program in Changing Times and "Sacred" Cultures. In I. Management Association (Ed.), *Educational Leadership and Administration: Concepts, Methodologies, Tools, and Applications* (pp. 1849-1876). Hershey, PA: IGI Global. https://doi.org/doi:10.4018/978-1-5225-1624-8.ch085

Petersen, A. J., Elser, C. F., Al Nassir, M. N., Stakey, J., & Everson, K. (2017). The Year of Teaching Inclusively: Building an Elementary Classroom for All Students. In C. Curran & A. Petersen (Eds.), *Handbook of Research on Classroom Diversity and Inclusive Education Practice* (pp. 332–348). Hershey, PA: IGI Global. doi:10.4018/978-1-5225-2520-2.ch014

Pfannenstiel, K. H., & Sanders, J. (2017). Characteristics and Instructional Strategies for Students With Mathematical Difficulties: In the Inclusive Classroom. In C. Curran & A. Petersen (Eds.), *Handbook of Research on Classroom Diversity and Inclusive Education Practice* (pp. 250–281). Hershey, PA: IGI Global. doi:10.4018/978-1-5225-2520-2.ch011

Phan, A. N. (2022). Quality Assurance of Higher Education From the Glonacal Agency Heuristic: An Example From Vietnam. In H. Magd & S. Kunjumuhammed (Eds.), *Global Perspectives on Quality Assurance and Accreditation in Higher Education Institutions* (pp. 136–155). IGI Global. https://doi.org/10.4018/978-1-7998-8085-1.ch008

Preast, J. L., Bowman, N., & Rose, C. A. (2017). Creating Inclusive Classroom Communities Through Social and Emotional Learning to Reduce Social Marginalization Among Students. In C. Curran & A. Petersen (Eds.), *Handbook of Research on Classroom Diversity and Inclusive Education Practice* (pp. 183–200). Hershey, PA: IGI Global. doi:10.4018/978-1-5225-2520-2.ch008

Randolph, K. M., & Brady, M. P. (2018). Evolution of Covert Coaching as an Evidence-Based Practice in Professional Development and Preparation of Teachers. In V. Bryan, A. Musgrove, & J. Powers (Eds.), *Handbook of Research on Human Development in the Digital Age* (pp. 281–299). Hershey, PA: IGI Global. doi:10.4018/978-1-5225-2838-8.ch013

Rell, A. B., Puig, R. A., Roll, F., Valles, V., Espinoza, M., & Duque, A. L. (2017). Addressing Cultural Diversity and Global Competence: The Dual Language Framework. In L. Leavitt, S. Wisdom, & K. Leavitt (Eds.), *Cultural Awareness and Competency Development in Higher Education* (pp. 111–131). Hershey, PA: IGI Global. doi:10.4018/978-1-5225-2145-7.ch007

Richards, M., & Guzman, I. R. (2020). Academic Assessment of Critical Thinking in Distance Education Information Technology Programs. In I. Management Association (Ed.), *Learning and Performance Assessment: Concepts, Methodologies, Tools, and Applications* (pp. 1-19). IGI Global. https://doi.org/10.4018/978-1-7998-0420-8.ch001

Riel, J., Lawless, K. A., & Brown, S. W. (2017). Defining and Designing Responsive Online Professional Development (ROPD): A Framework to Support Curriculum Implementation. In T. Kidd & L. Morris Jr., (Eds.), *Handbook of Research on Instructional Systems and Educational Technology* (pp. 104–115). Hershey, PA: IGI Global. doi:10.4018/978-1-5225-2399-4.ch010

Roberts, C. (2017). Advancing Women Leaders in Academe: Creating a Culture of Inclusion. In S. Mukerji & P. Tripathi (Eds.), *Handbook of Research on Administration, Policy, and Leadership in Higher Education* (pp. 256–273). Hershey, PA: IGI Global. doi:10.4018/978-1-5225-0672-0.ch012

Rodgers, W. J., Kennedy, M. J., Alves, K. D., & Romig, J. E. (2017). A Multimedia Tool for Teacher Education and Professional Development. In C. Martin & D. Polly (Eds.), *Handbook of Research on Teacher Education and Professional Development* (pp. 285–296). Hershey, PA: IGI Global. doi:10.4018/978-1-5225-1067-3.ch015

Romanowski, M. H. (2017). Qatar's Educational Reform: Critical Issues Facing Principals. In I. Management Association (Ed.), Educational Leadership and Administration: Concepts, Methodologies, Tools, and Applications (pp. 1758-1773). Hershey, PA: IGI Global. https://doi.org/ doi:10.4018/978-1-5225-1624-8.ch080

Ruffin, T. R., Hawkins, D. P., & Lee, D. I. (2018). Increasing Student Engagement and Participation Through Course Methodology. In M. Khosrow-Pour, D.B.A. (Ed.), Encyclopedia of Information Science and Technology, Fourth Edition (pp. 1463-1473). Hershey, PA: IGI Global. doi:10.4018/978-1-5225-2255-3.ch126

Sabina, L. L., Curry, K. A., Harris, E. L., Krumm, B. L., & Vencill, V. (2017). Assessing the Performance of a Cohort-Based Model Using Domestic and International Practices. In I. Management Association (Ed.), Educational Leadership and Administration: Concepts, Methodologies, Tools, and Applications (pp. 913-929). Hershey, PA: IGI Global. https://doi.org/ doi:10.4018/978-1-5225-1624-8.ch044

Samkian, A., Pascarella, J., & Slayton, J. (2022). Towards an Anti-Racist, Culturally Responsive, and LGBTQ+ Inclusive Education: Developing Critically-Conscious Educational Leaders. In E. Cain-Sanschagrin, R. Filback, & J. Crawford (Eds.), *Cases on Academic Program Redesign for Greater Racial and Social Justice* (pp. 150–175). IGI Global. https://doi.org/10.4018/978-1-7998-8463-7.ch007

Santamaría, A. P., Webber, M., & Santamaría, L. J. (2017). Effective School Leadership for Māori Achievement: Building Capacity through Indigenous, National, and International Cross-Cultural Collaboration. In I. Management Association (Ed.), Educational Leadership and Administration: Concepts, Methodologies, Tools, and Applications (pp. 1547-1567). Hershey, PA: IGI Global. https://doi.org/ doi:10.4018/978-1-5225-1624-8.ch071

Santamaría, L. J. (2017). Culturally Responsive Educational Leadership in Cross-Cultural International Contexts. In I. Management Association (Ed.), Educational Leadership and Administration: Concepts, Methodologies, Tools, and Applications (pp. 1380-1400). Hershey, PA: IGI Global. https://doi.org/ doi:10.4018/978-1-5225-1624-8.ch064

Segredo, M. R., Cistone, P. J., & Reio, T. G. (2017). Relationships Between Emotional Intelligence, Leadership Style, and School Culture. *International Journal of Adult Vocational Education and Technology*, 8(3), 25–43. doi:10.4018/IJAVET.2017070103

Shalev, N. (2017). Empathy and Leadership From the Organizational Perspective. In Z. Nedelko & M. Brzozowski (Eds.), *Exploring the Influence of Personal Values and Cultures in the Workplace* (pp. 348–363). Hershey, PA: IGI Global. doi:10.4018/978-1-5225-2480-9.ch018

Siamak, M., Fathi, S., & Isfandyari-Moghaddam, A. (2018). Assessment and Measurement of Education Programs of Information Literacy. In R. Bhardwaj (Ed.), *Digitizing the Modern Library and the Transition From Print to Electronic* (pp. 164–192). Hershey, PA: IGI Global. doi:10.4018/978-1-5225-2119-8.ch007

Siu, K. W., & García, G. J. (2017). Disruptive Technologies and Education: Is There Any Disruption After All? In I. Management Association (Ed.), Educational Leadership and Administration: Concepts, Methodologies, Tools, and Applications (pp. 757-778). Hershey, PA: IGI Global. https://doi.org/ doi:10.4018/978-1-5225-1624-8.ch037

Slagter van Tryon, P. J. (2017). The Nurse Educator's Role in Designing Instruction and Instructional Strategies for Academic and Clinical Settings. In J. Stefaniak (Ed.), *Advancing Medical Education Through Strategic Instructional Design* (pp. 133–149). Hershey, PA: IGI Global. doi:10.4018/978-1-5225-2098-6.ch006

Slattery, C. A. (2018). Literacy Intervention and the Differentiated Plan of Instruction. In *Developing Effective Literacy Intervention Strategies: Emerging Research and Opportunities* (pp. 41–62). Hershey, PA: IGI Global. doi:10.4018/978-1-5225-5007-5.ch003

Smith, A. R. (2017). Ensuring Quality: The Faculty Role in Online Higher Education. In K. Shelton & K. Pedersen (Eds.), *Handbook of Research on Building, Growing, and Sustaining Quality E-Learning Programs* (pp. 210–231). Hershey, PA: IGI Global. doi:10.4018/978-1-5225-0877-9.ch011

Souders, T. M. (2017). Understanding Your Learner: Conducting a Learner Analysis. In J. Stefaniak (Ed.), *Advancing Medical Education Through Strategic Instructional Design* (pp. 1–29). Hershey, PA: IGI Global. doi:10.4018/978-1-5225-2098-6.ch001

Spring, K. J., Graham, C. R., & Ikahihifo, T. B. (2018). Learner Engagement in Blended Learning. In M. Khosrow-Pour, D.B.A. (Ed.), Encyclopedia of Information Science and Technology, Fourth Edition (pp. 1487-1498). Hershey, PA: IGI Global. doi:10.4018/978-1-5225-2255-3.ch128

Storey, V. A., Anthony, A. K., & Wahid, P. (2017). Gender-Based Leadership Barriers: Advancement of Female Faculty to Leadership Positions in Higher Education. In V. Wang (Ed.), *Encyclopedia of Strategic Leadership and Management* (pp. 244–258). Hershey, PA: IGI Global. doi:10.4018/978-1-5225-1049-9.ch018

Stottlemyer, D. (2018). Develop a Teaching Model Plan for a Differentiated Learning Approach. In *Differentiated Instructional Design for Multicultural Environments: Emerging Research and Opportunities* (pp. 106–130). Hershey, PA: IGI Global. doi:10.4018/978-1-5225-5106-5.ch005

Stottlemyer, D. (2018). Developing a Multicultural Environment. In *Differentiated Instructional Design for Multicultural Environments: Emerging Research and Opportunities* (pp. 1–27). Hershey, PA: IGI Global. doi:10.4018/978-1-5225-5106-5.ch001

Swagerty, T. (2022). Digital Access to Culturally Relevant Curricula: The Impact on the Native and Indigenous Student. In E. Reeves & C. McIntyre (Eds.), *Multidisciplinary Perspectives on Diversity and Equity in a Virtual World* (pp. 99–113). IGI Global. https://doi.org/10.4018/978-1-7998-8028-8.ch006

Swami, B. N., Gobona, T., & Tsimako, J. J. (2017). Academic Leadership: A Case Study of the University of Botswana. In N. Baporikar (Ed.), *Innovation and Shifting Perspectives in Management Education* (pp. 1–32). Hershey, PA: IGI Global. doi:10.4018/978-1-5225-1019-2.ch001

Swanson, K. W., & Collins, G. (2018). Designing Engaging Instruction for the Adult Learners. In M. Khosrow-Pour, D.B.A. (Ed.), Encyclopedia of Information Science and Technology, Fourth Edition (pp. 1432-1440). Hershey, PA: IGI Global. doi:10.4018/978-1-5225-2255-3.ch123

Swartz, B. A., Lynch, J. M., & Lynch, S. D. (2018). Embedding Elementary Teacher Education Coursework in Local Classrooms: Examples in Mathematics and Special Education. In D. Polly, M. Putman, T. Petty, & A. Good (Eds.), *Innovative Practices in Teacher Preparation and Graduate-Level Teacher Education Programs* (pp. 262–292). Hershey, PA: IGI Global. doi:10.4018/978-1-5225-3068-8.ch015

Taliadorou, N., & Pashiardis, P. (2017). Emotional Intelligence and Political Skill Really Matter in Educational Leadership. In I. Management Association (Ed.), Educational Leadership and Administration: Concepts, Methodologies, Tools, and Applications (pp. 1274-1303). Hershey, PA: IGI Global. https://doi.org/doi:10.4018/978-1-5225-1624-8.ch060

Tandoh, K. A., & Ebe-Arthur, J. E. (2018). Effective Educational Leadership in the Digital Age: An Examination of Professional Qualities and Best Practices. In J. Keengwe (Ed.), *Handbook of Research on Digital Content, Mobile Learning, and Technology Integration Models in Teacher Education* (pp. 244–265). Hershey, PA: IGI Global. doi:10.4018/978-1-5225-2953-8.ch013

Tobin, M. T. (2018). Multimodal Literacy. In M. Khosrow-Pour, D.B.A. (Ed.), Encyclopedia of Information Science and Technology, Fourth Edition (pp. 1508-1516). Hershey, PA: IGI Global. doi:10.4018/978-1-5225-2255-3.ch130

Related References

Torres, K. M., Arrastia-Chisholm, M. C., & Tackett, S. (2019). A Phenomenological Study of Pre-Service Teachers' Perceptions of Completing ESOL Field Placements. *International Journal of Teacher Education and Professional Development*, 2(2), 85–101. https://doi.org/10.4018/IJTEPD.2019070106

Torres, M. C., Salamanca, Y. N., Cely, J. P., & Aguilar, J. L. (2020). All We Need is a Boost! Using Multimodal Tools and the Translanguaging Strategy: Strengthening Speaking in the EFL Classroom. *International Journal of Computer-Assisted Language Learning and Teaching*, 10(3), 28–47. doi:10.4018/IJCALLT.2020070103

Torres, M. L., & Ramos, V. J. (2018). Music Therapy: A Pedagogical Alternative for ASD and ID Students in Regular Classrooms. In P. Epler (Ed.), *Instructional Strategies in General Education and Putting the Individuals With Disabilities Act (IDEA) Into Practice* (pp. 222–244). Hershey, PA: IGI Global. doi:10.4018/978-1-5225-3111-1.ch008

Toulassi, B. (2017). Educational Administration and Leadership in Francophone Africa: 5 Dynamics to Change Education. In S. Mukerji & P. Tripathi (Eds.), *Handbook of Research on Administration, Policy, and Leadership in Higher Education* (pp. 20–45). Hershey, PA: IGI Global. doi:10.4018/978-1-5225-0672-0.ch002

Umair, S., & Sharif, M. M. (2018). Predicting Students Grades Using Artificial Neural Networks and Support Vector Machine. In M. Khosrow-Pour, D.B.A. (Ed.), Encyclopedia of Information Science and Technology, Fourth Edition (pp. 5169-5182). Hershey, PA: IGI Global. doi:10.4018/978-1-5225-2255-3.ch449

Vettraino, L., Castello, V., Guspini, M., & Guglielman, E. (2018). Self-Awareness and Motivation Contrasting ESL and NEET Using the SAVE System. In M. Khosrow-Pour, D.B.A. (Ed.), Encyclopedia of Information Science and Technology, Fourth Edition (pp. 1559-1568). Hershey, PA: IGI Global. doi:10.4018/978-1-5225-2255-3.ch135

Wiemelt, J. (2017). Critical Bilingual Leadership for Emergent Bilingual Students. In I. Management Association (Ed.), Educational Leadership and Administration: Concepts, Methodologies, Tools, and Applications (pp. 1606-1631). Hershey, PA: IGI Global. doi:10.4018/978-1-5225-1624-8.ch074

Wolf, F., Seyfarth, F. C., & Pflaum, E. (2018). Scalable Capacity-Building for Geographically Dispersed Learners: Designing the MOOC "Sustainable Energy in Small Island Developing States (SIDS)". In U. Pandey & V. Indrakanti (Eds.), *Open and Distance Learning Initiatives for Sustainable Development* (pp. 58–83). Hershey, PA: IGI Global. doi:10.4018/978-1-5225-2621-6.ch003

Woodley, X. M., Mucundanyi, G., & Lockard, M. (2017). Designing Counter-Narratives: Constructing Culturally Responsive Curriculum Online. *International Journal of Online Pedagogy and Course Design*, *7*(1), 43–56. doi:10.4018/IJOPCD.2017010104

Yell, M. L., & Christle, C. A. (2017). The Foundation of Inclusion in Federal Legislation and Litigation. In C. Curran & A. Petersen (Eds.), *Handbook of Research on Classroom Diversity and Inclusive Education Practice* (pp. 27–52). Hershey, PA: IGI Global. doi:10.4018/978-1-5225-2520-2.ch002

Zinner, L. (2019). Fostering Academic Citizenship With a Shared Leadership Approach. In C. Zhu & M. Zayim-Kurtay (Eds.), *University Governance and Academic Leadership in the EU and China* (pp. 99–117). IGI Global. https://doi.org/10.4018/978-1-5225-7441-5.ch007

About the Contributors

Marva Sylvana McClean is a poet, author and scholar/activist whose research agenda focuses on the African Diaspora and the historical empowerment of people of color across the globe. She has an expertise in curriculum inquiry and strategies to attain student achievement. Dr. McClean is the Gladstone Library, UK, Political Scholar in Residence 2020, author of *From the Middle Passage to Black Lives Matter: Ancestral Writing as a Pedagogy of Hope* (2019), Bridges to Memory: Poems by Marva McClean (2007) and co-author (with Marcus Waters, Griffith University, Australia) of *Indigenous Epistemology: Descent into the Womb of Decolonized Research Methodologies* (2020). Recognized as a Fulbright Specialist 2014-2019, she advocates for conscientization of curriculum and pedagogy to foster students' ability to become agents of change. Her research brings critical considerations to preparing educators to achieve educational justice through innovative experiences such as fieldwork in post- colonial nations and underserved school communities, engaging students as knowledge producers and critics in the classroom through an assertion of decolonized pedagogy. Dr. McClean most recently taught Writing about Literature at the Florida Institute of Technology (2022-2023). She has taught in the department of Educational Leadership & Research Methodology at Florida Atlantic University and Educational Leadership in Charter Schools at Nova Southeastern University. She leads the literary initiative, Strong in the Broken Places: Poetics of the African Diaspora and is editor of the online newsletter, Sound the Abeng: Writing Black, Aboriginal & Indigenous Lives. She has an expressed interest in collaborative inquiry with international scholars, activists, writers, artists and community leaders.

* * *

Isil Anakok is a Ph.D. candidate in Engineering Education at Virginia Tech. She holds M.s in Mechanical Engineering from Virginia Tech, and B.s in Mechatronics Engineering at Kocaeli University, Turkey. Her research interests are engineering ethics, Diversity, Equity, and Inclusion in Engineering Education, engineering faculty members' mental models, and a sense of belonging.

Anne Bouie is an independent historian and visual artist whose research interests center on enslavement and how material culture and vernacular art were used to resist enslavement. Her scholarly presentations include The Lapidus Center, Schomburg Museum, Maroon Conference Charlestown, Jamaica, The International Gullah Geechee And African Diaspora Conference, Coastal Carolina University, the International African Diaspora Conference at Howard University, and the Washington Historical Society. She authored *After School Success*, *Academic Enrichment for Urban Youth* and is currently preparing a manuscript on material culture and resistance. She designed *Ancestors, Guardians and Guides*, included a keynote by Dr. David Driskell and a pilgrimage to Slave Cemetery at Button Farm Living History Center and *The Ante-Bellum Black Church and Resistance in WDC*.

Beth Caruso is the Digital Pedagogy & Emerging Technologies Librarian in Area 49, Atkins Library's collection of innovation spaces at the University of North Carolina at Charlotte. She provides consultation, support, instruction, and training to those using the makerspace, gaming lab, and visualization lab, and develops programs for outreach and engagement. She holds a Bachelor of Arts Master of Arts in English and a Graduate Certificate in Anti-Racism in Urban Education from the University of North Carolina at Charlotte and a Master of Library and Information Science from the University of South Carolina.

Shania Clinedinst is a diversity specialist for graduate education and a second year master's student in Instructional Design Technology. Her research focuses on the application of DEIB (diversity, equity, inclusion, and belonging) based practices within the structure of higher education curricula.

Nicole G. DeRonck is an Associate Professor in the Counselor Education Program at Western Connecticut State University. Dr. DeRonck earned her Ph.D in Counselor Education from the University of Connecticut, and her Ed.D in Educational Leadership from Central Connecticut State University. She has extensive experience working in the counseling field both as a clinician working with adolescents struggling with addiction, and as a school counselor. Her experience as a counselor inspired her to move into an educational leadership role to impact policy and improve access to education and services for kids in her state. She enjoys researching and writing on the topics of college and career readiness, access, and equity in education in underserved populations, and school counseling program development and evaluation.

Courtney Fragomeli received her M.S. in Counselor Education from Western Connecticut State University in 2021, during which she worked as a Graduate Assistant and Researcher under the advisement of Dr. Nicole DeRonck. Ms. Fragomeli earned her B.A. in Psychology from Western Connecticut State University in 2018. Ms. Fragomeli is currently a School Counselor at John Read Middle School in Redding, Connecticut and has experience counseling both middle and high school age students.

Samantha Gati-Tisi is a middle school teacher with over 12 years of experience in the field of education. Her passion for understanding the impact of social media on school districts and fostering positive communication between schools and families has driven her research and writing. Residing in Connecticut with her family, Samantha combines her practical experiences as a teacher with her insightful analysis to shed light on the intricate dynamics between social medial and educational institutions. Her work aims to navigate the challenges and opportunities presented by digital platforms, helping educators and administrators harness the potential of social media while mitigating its potential pitfalls.

Shernita Lee is the Assistant Dean and Director of the Graduate School's Office of Diversity, Inclusion, and Strategic Partnerships at Virginia Tech and is interested in diversity education and its practical applications to enhance the student experience. She has a Bachelor's of Science in Mathematics from Alabama State University and a Doctorate in Genetics, Bioinformatics, and Computational Biology from Virginia Tech.

Andrew Kwabena Moss is a writer and teacher who has lived in the UK, Japan and currently Australia. Of Anglo-Ghanaian heritage, his work seeks to explore liminal landscapes, complex identities and the social constructs of race. Widely published internationally, Andrew's work is featured in 'The Best New British and Irish Poets Anthology 2019-2021', The Black Spring Press Group and the Year's Best African Speculative Fiction 2022. Andrew has received a Best of the Net Award, Pushcart Prize and Rhysling Award nominations. Andrew's debut novella Nicked Names was published by RoseyRavelston in 2022. He released three full length poetry books Japanabandon, Manifest.oh! and Diaspora^3 through RoseyRavelston in 2023. 'Childish Recollections', Andrew's fourth poetry collection will be published by The Black Spring Press Group. Andrew read History/ Politics (Jt Hons) and holds a Postgraduate Certificate in Education. He tutors Creative Writing at the University of Canberra.

Tricia J. Stewart, Ph.D., is a Professor in the Doctor of Education in Instructional Leadership in the Education and Educational Counseling Department at Western Connecticut State University. Her Doctor of Philosophy was earned in Educational Policy and Theory from the University of Rochester in Rochester, NY. She has extensive experience teaching diverse populations in doctoral education programs since 2009. Her research interests include Struggling School Districts: Urban and Rural, Educational Policy Studies: Accountability and Choice, and Social Class and Inequality in Education. Since arriving at WCSU, she has been granted four $10,000 grants through the CSUS-AAUP to study students in rural areas, Teaching During COVID-19, and other leadership topics. Stewart is also part of Connecticut State Department of Education funded grant for $300,000 with colleagues across Connecticut to study Pandemic Effects, including stress and supports, certification and supply/shortages. and educator mobility. She has numerous research articles published in top-tier research journals and she is committed to helping doctoral students gain publishing opportunities and has published three book chapters to this end.

Christine Todd is an experienced educator with an extensive background teaching science curriculum to both teachers and students in the Miami-Dade County Public School system where she has worked as a classroom teacher, assistant principal, and district instructional support specialist during a career spanning more than twenty-five years. She has an extensive background in STEM education and the design and implementation of programs that focus on culturally relevant pedagogy in science. She has served as the regional science and engineering fair director for South Florida for several years. Dr. Todd strives to ensure that secondary students at under-resourced schools are supported to do STEM research. She has implemented a mentoring program connecting students to STEM professionals. Accordingly, students develop research and participate in science and engineering fairs and programs. Dr. Todd holds a Doctor of Philosophy in Curriculum, Culture, and Educational Inquiry from Florida Atlantic University.

Zuleka Randell Woods is a Ph.D. candidate in Planning, Governance, and Globalization at Virginia Tech. Her research centers on race and representation for Africa and the diaspora, Diversity, Equity and Inclusion and cultural evaluation. Zuleka has a master's in public health and is the author of Ba-Ya (Play Cook), an anthology of short stories highlighting gender-based violence in Liberia.

Index

T

U